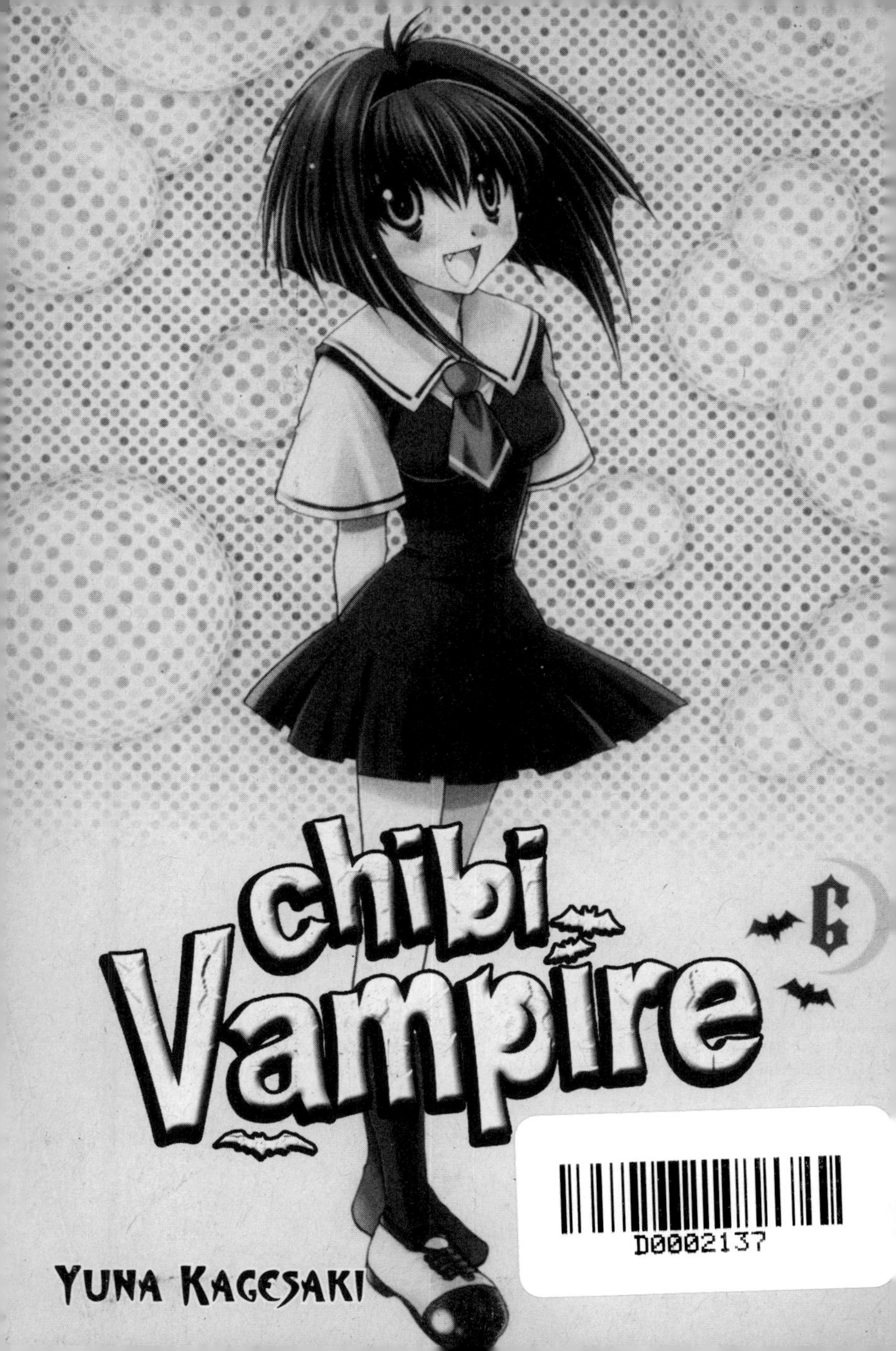

Chibi Vampire 6

Yuna Kagesaki

Chibi Vampire Volume 6
Created by Yuna Kagesaki

Translation - Alexis Kirsch
English Adaptation - Christine Boylan
Copy Editor - Stephanie Duchin
Retouch and Lettering - Star Print Brokers
Production Artist - Rui Kyo
Graphic Designer - Fawn Lau

Editor - Tim Beedle
Digital Imaging Manager - Chris Buford
Pre-Production Supervisor - Erika Terriquez
Production Manager - Elisabeth Brizzi
Managing Editor - Vy Nguyen
Creative Director - Anne Marie Horne
Editor-in-Chief - Rob Tokar
Publisher - Mike Kiley
President and C.O.O. - John Parker
C.E.O. and Chief Creative Officer - Stuart Levy

A  Manga

TOKYOPOP and  are trademarks or registered trademarks of TOKYOPOP Inc.

TOKYOPOP Inc.
5900 Wilshire Blvd. Suite 2000
Los Angeles, CA 90036

E-mail: info@TOKYOPOP.com
Come visit us online at www.TOKYOPOP.com

ISBN: 978-1-59816-880-8

First TOKYOPOP printing: November 2007
10 9 8 7 6 5 4
Printed in the USA

Chibi Vampire

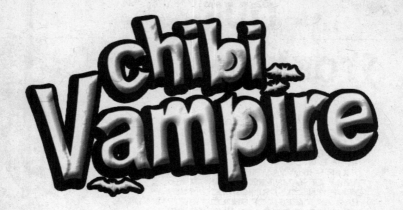

Volume 6

Created by

Yuna Kagesaki

TOKYOPOP®

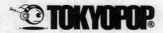

HAMBURG // LONDON // LOS ANGELES // TOKYO

OUR STORY SO FAR...

KARIN MAAKA ISN'T LIKE OTHER GIRLS. ONCE A MONTH, SHE EXPERIENCES PAIN, FATIGUE, HUNGER, IRRITABILITY—AND THEN SHE BLEEDS. FROM HER NOSE. KARIN IS A VAMPIRE, FROM A FAMILY OF VAMPIRES, BUT INSTEAD OF NEEDING TO DRINK BLOOD, SHE HAS AN EXCESS OF BLOOD THAT SHE MUST GIVE TO HER VICTIMS. IF DONE RIGHT, GIVING THIS BLOOD TO HER VICTIM CAN BE AN EXTREMELY POSITIVE THING. THE PROBLEM WITH THIS IS THAT KARIN NEVER SEEMS TO DO THINGS RIGHT...

KARIN IS HAVING A BIT OF BOY TROUBLE. KENTA USUI—THE HANDSOME NEW STUDENT AT HER SCHOOL AND WORK—IS A NICE ENOUGH GUY, BUT HE EXACERBATES KARIN'S PROBLEM. KARIN, YOU SEE, IS DRAWN TO PEOPLE WHO HAVE SUFFERED MISFORTUNE, AND KENTA HAS SUFFERED PLENTY OF IT. KARIN DISCOVERED THIS WHEN SHE BIT KENTA'S MOTHER, AN INCIDENT THAT WAS UNFORTUNATELY WITNESSED BY KENTA. NOW, KARIN'S CONVINCED THAT SHE CAN KEEP HER NOSEBLEEDS UNDER CONTROL AS LONG AS SHE KEEPS KENTA HAPPY, AND KENTA HAS PROMISED KARIN'S PARENTS THAT HE'D HELP HER OUT DURING THE DAYTIME. A SIMPLE ENOUGH PLAN, BUT IT'S ABOUT TO BECOME A LOT MORE COMPLICATED, AS IT'S BECOME CLEAR TO KARIN THAT SHE'S IN LOVE WITH KENTA...SOMETHING THAT CAN ONLY BRING TROUBLE. LOVE BETWEEN HUMANS AND VAMPIRES IS FROWNED UPON IN VAMPIRE SOCIETY, AND CONSIDERING THAT KARIN IS ALREADY SEEN AS AN OUTCAST, CAN SHE REALLY AFFORD THE ADDITIONAL STIGMA?

THE MAAKA FAMILY

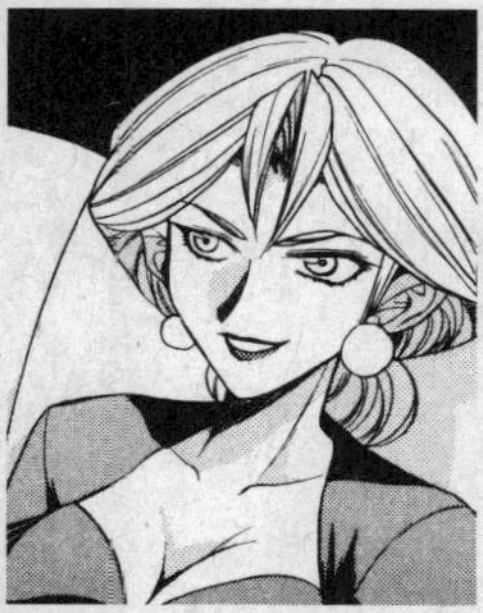

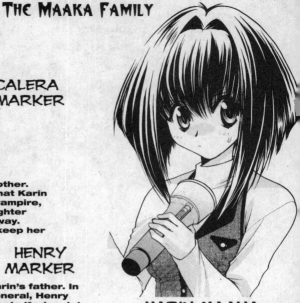

CALERA MARKER

Karin's overbearing mother. While Calera resents that Karin wasn't born a normal vampire, she does love her daughter in her own obnoxious way. Calera has chosen to keep her European last name.

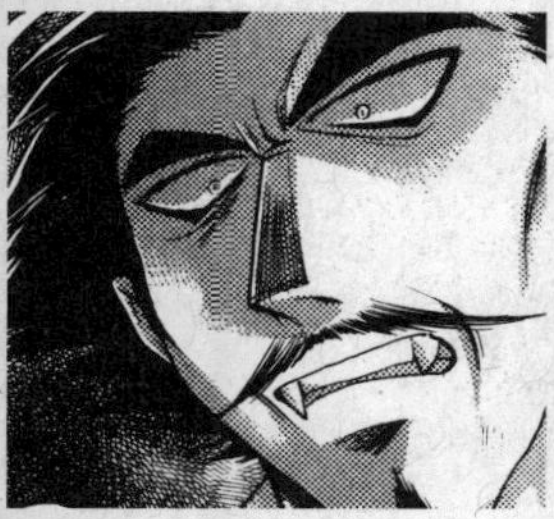

HENRY MARKER

Karin's father. In general, Henry treats Karin a lot better than her mother does, but the pants in this particular family are worn by Calera. Henry has also chosen to keep his European last name.

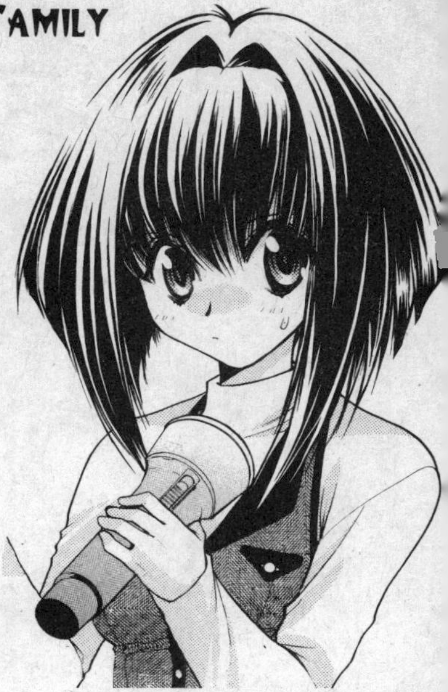

KARIN MAAKA

Our little heroine. Karin is a vampire living in Japan, but instead of sucking blood from her victims, she actually GIVES them some of her blood. She's a vampire in reverse!

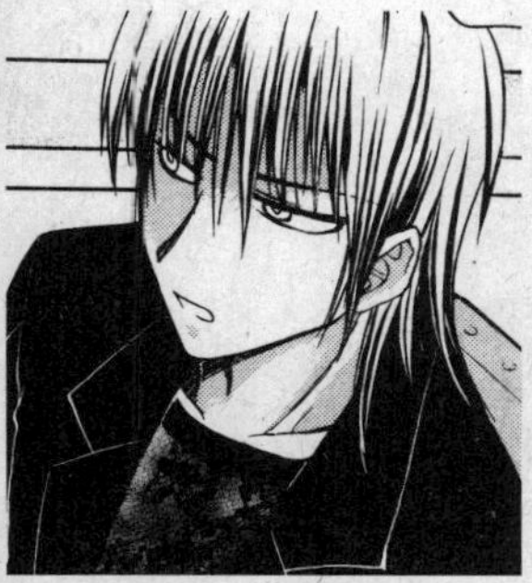

REN MAAKA

Karin's older brother. Ren milks the "sexy creature of the night" thing for all it's worth and spends his nights in the arms (and beds) of attractive young women.

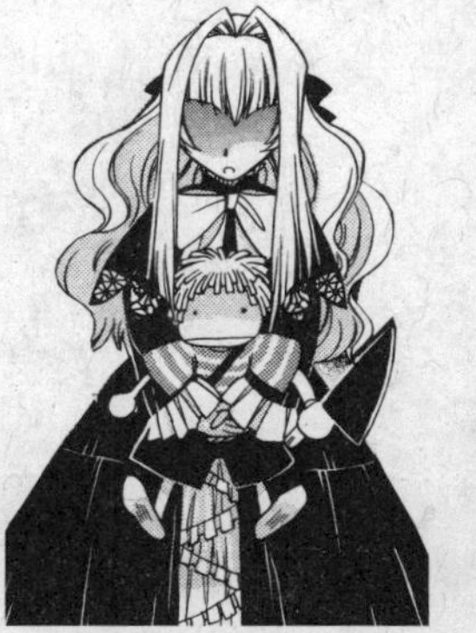

ANJU MAAKA

Karin's little sister. Anju has not yet awoken as a full vampire, but she can control bats and is usually the one who cleans up after Karin's messes. Rarely seen without her "talking" doll, Boogie.

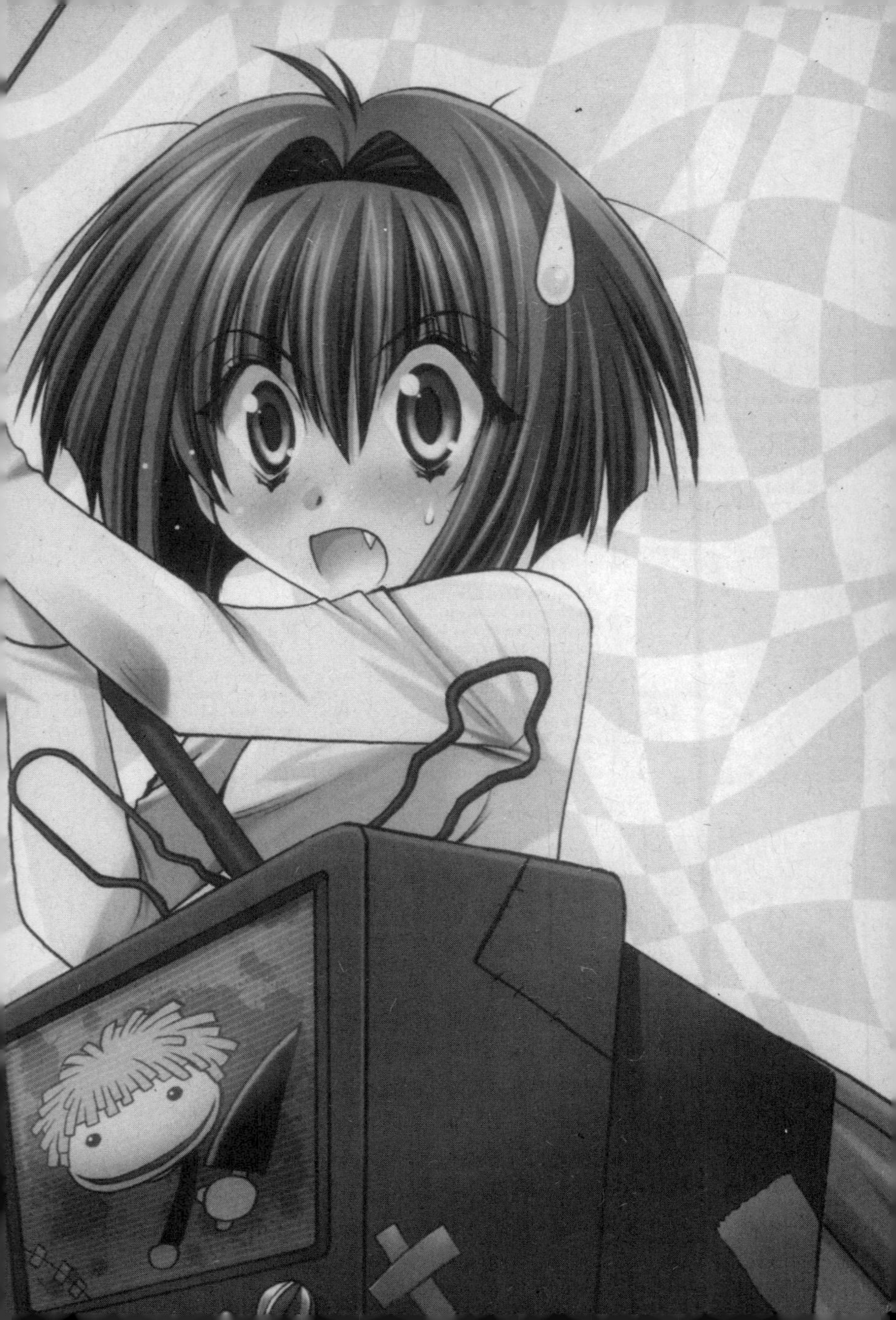

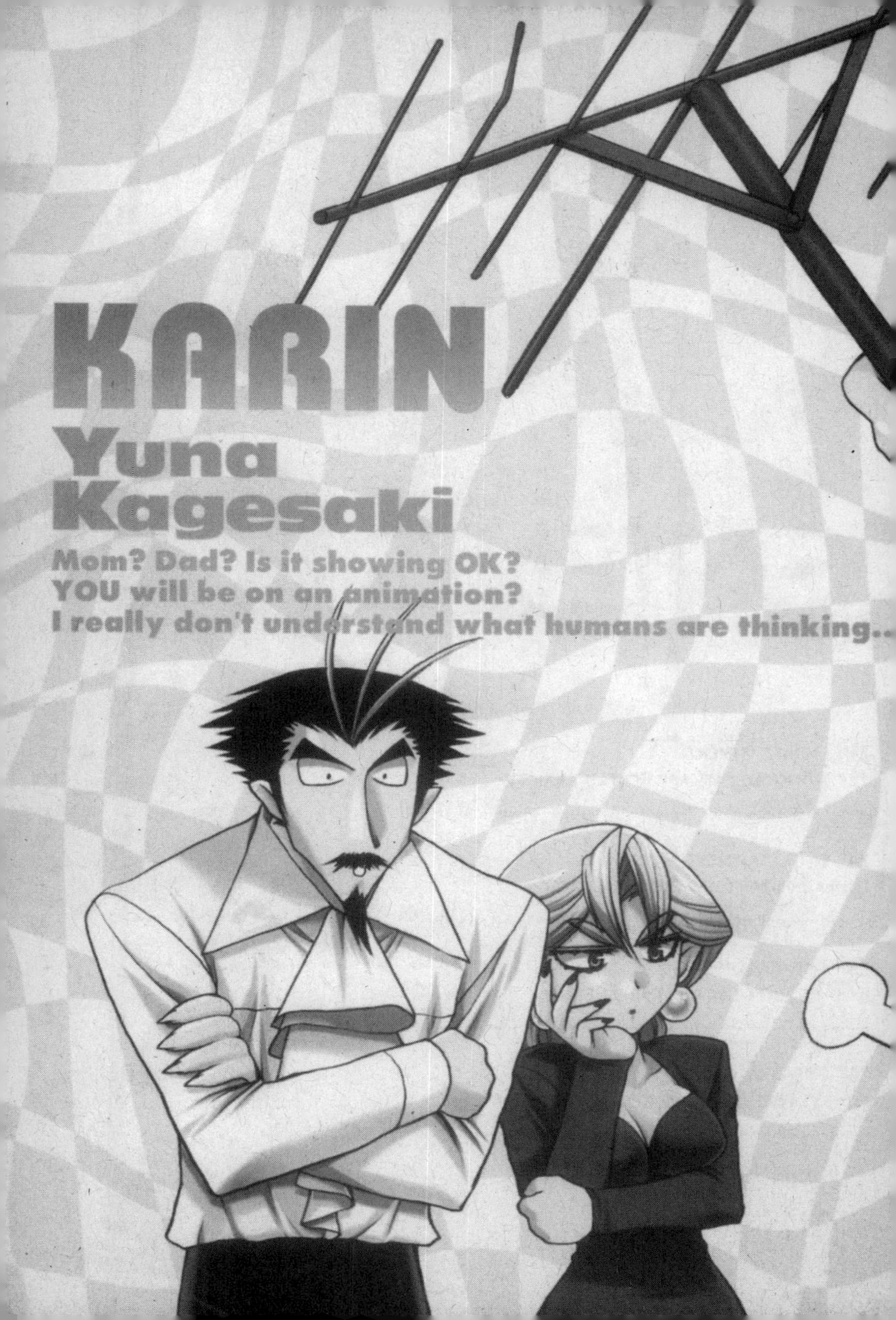
KARIN
Yuna Kagesaki
Mom? Dad? Is it showing OK?
YOU will be on an animation?
I really don't understand what humans are thinking...

VOL.6
CONTENTS

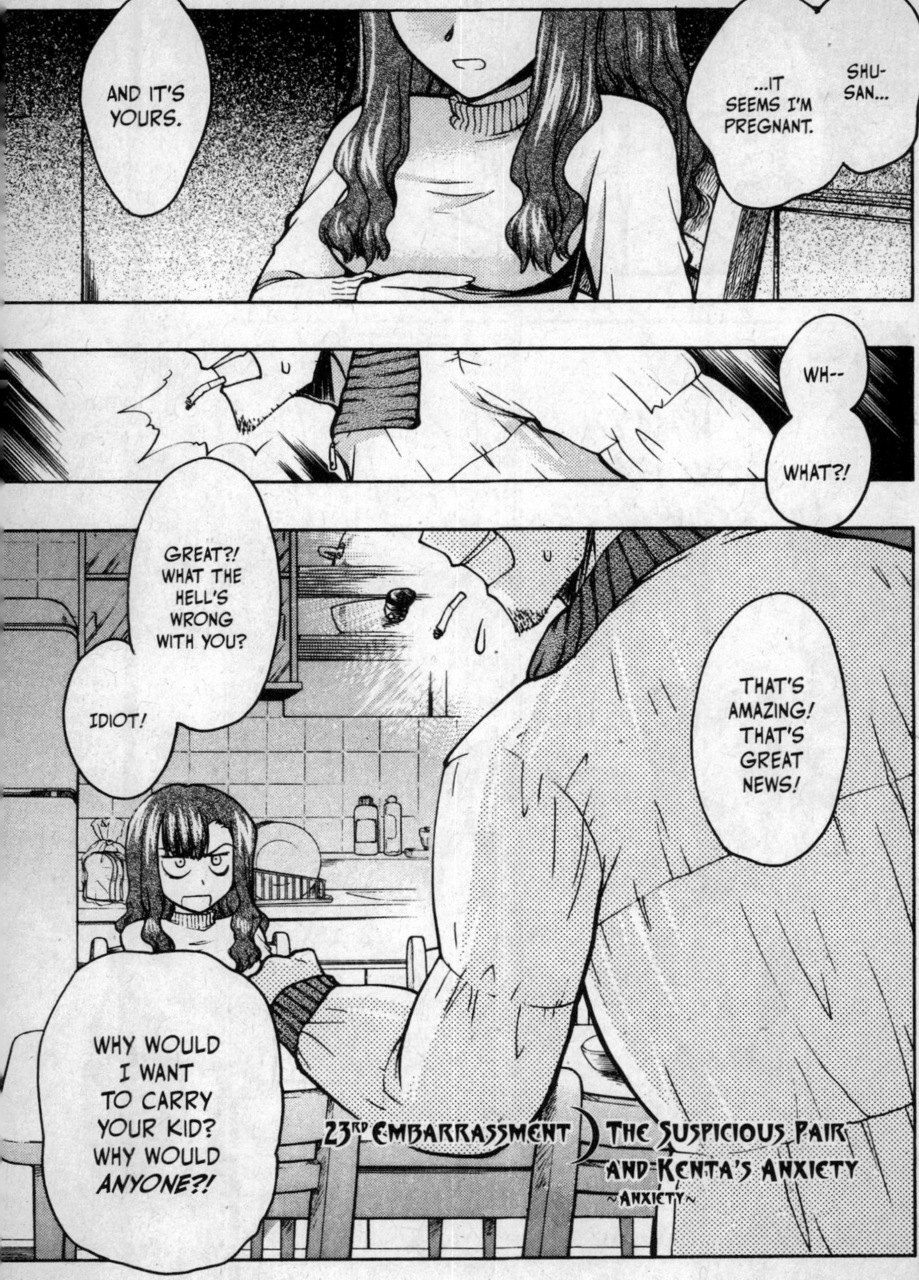
SHU-SAN...
...IT SEEMS I'M PREGNANT.
AND IT'S YOURS.
WH--
WHAT?!
THAT'S AMAZING! THAT'S GREAT NEWS!
GREAT?! WHAT THE HELL'S WRONG WITH YOU?
IDIOT!
WHY WOULD I WANT TO CARRY YOUR KID? WHY WOULD ANYONE?!
23RD EMBARRASSMENT
THE SUSPICIOUS PAIR AND KENTA'S ANXIETY
~ANXIETY~

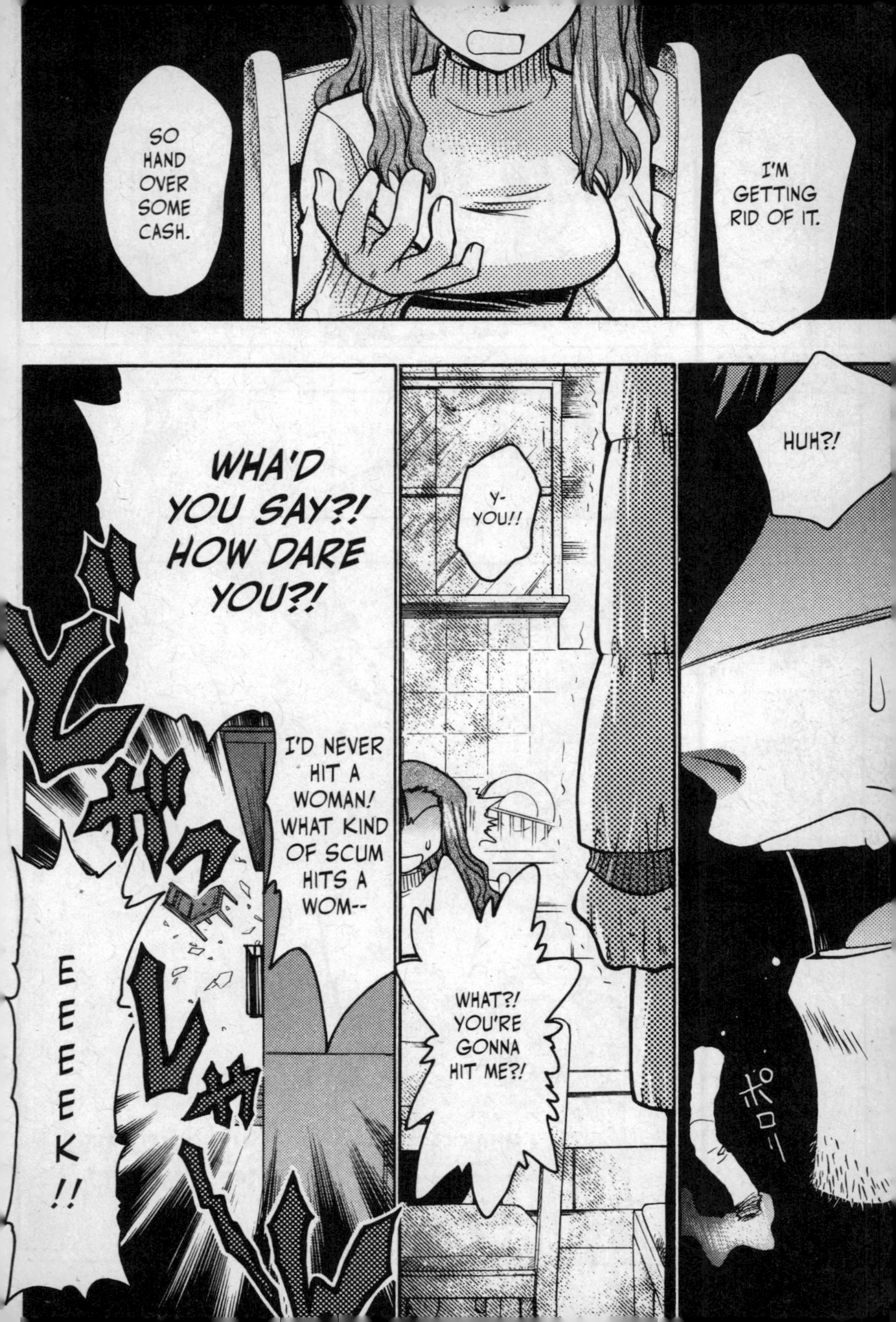
I'M GETTING RID OF IT.
SO HAND OVER SOME CASH.
HUH?!
ポロリ
Y-YOU!!
WHAT?! YOU'RE GONNA HIT ME?!
WHA'D YOU SAY?! HOW DARE YOU?!
I'D NEVER HIT A WOMAN! WHAT KIND OF SCUM HITS A WOM--
EEEEEK!!

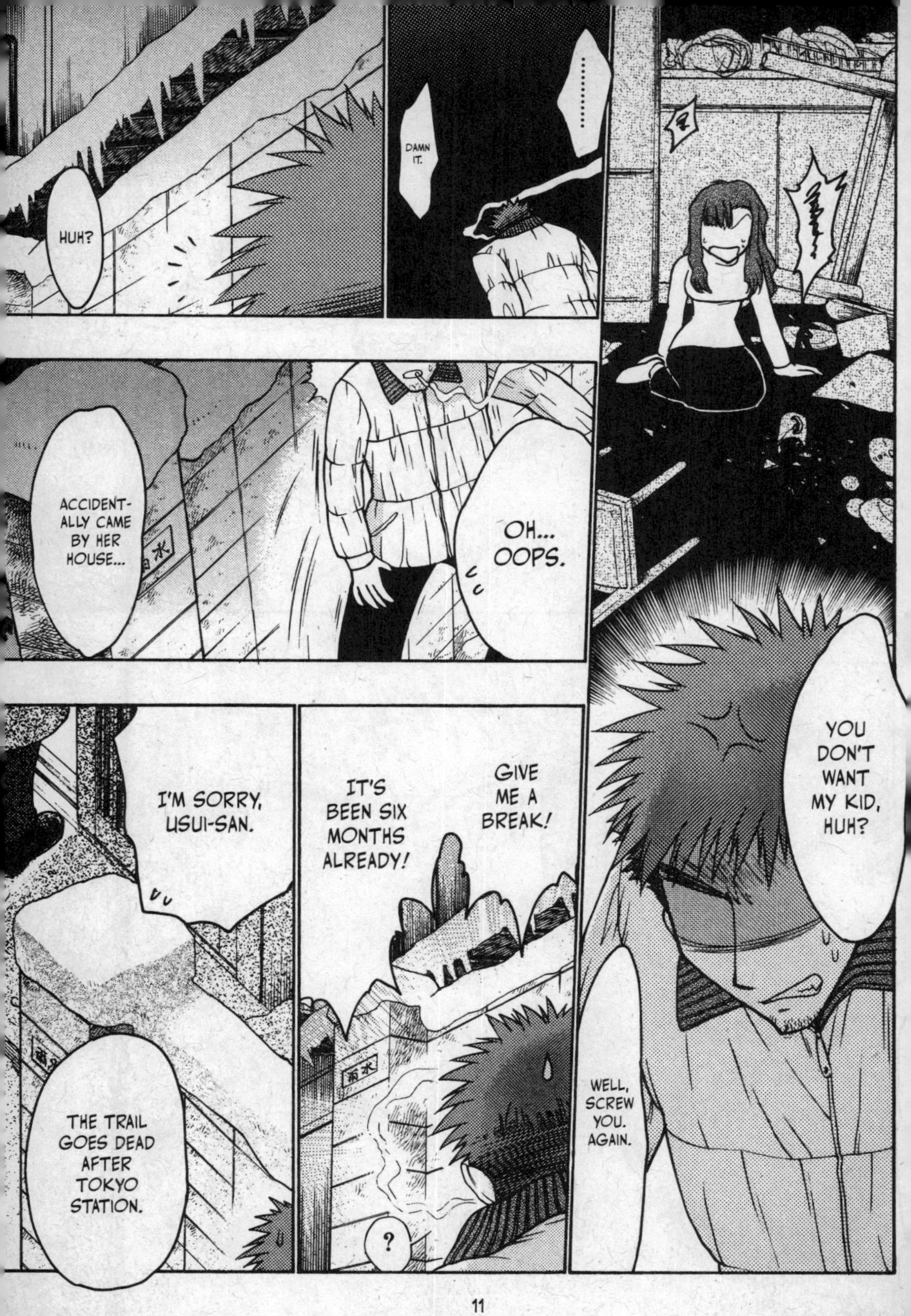
YOU DON'T WANT MY KID, HUH?
WELL, SCREW YOU. AGAIN.
......
DAMN IT.
HUH?
OH... OOPS.
ACCIDENT-ALLY CAME BY HER HOUSE...
GIVE ME A BREAK!
IT'S BEEN SIX MONTHS ALREADY!
?
I'M SORRY, USUI-SAN.
THE TRAIL GOES DEAD AFTER TOKYO STATION.

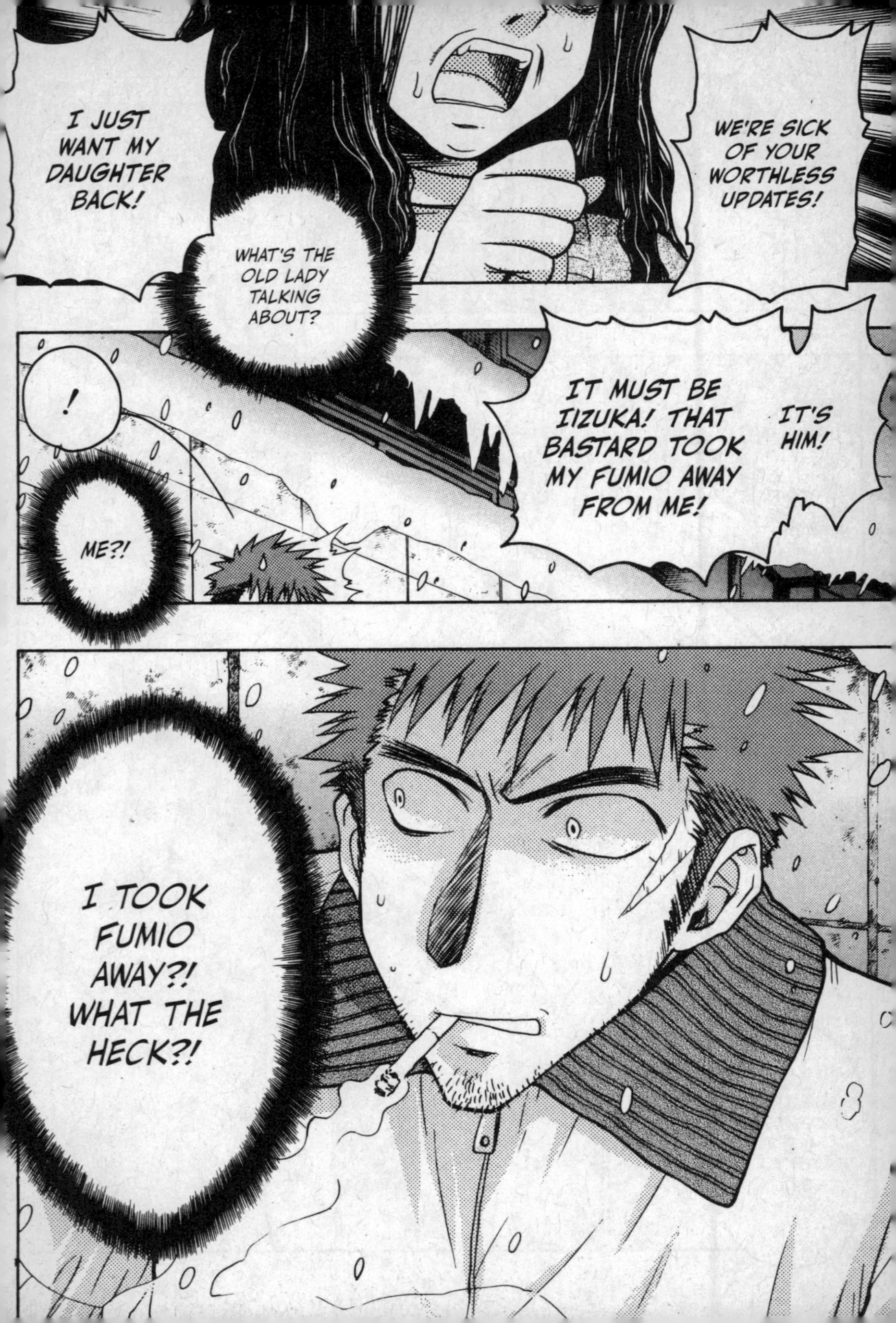
WE'RE SICK OF YOUR WORTHLESS UPDATES!
I JUST WANT MY DAUGHTER BACK!
WHAT'S THE OLD LADY TALKING ABOUT?
IT'S HIM!
IT MUST BE IIZUKA! THAT BASTARD TOOK MY FUMIO AWAY FROM ME!
!
ME?!
I TOOK FUMIO AWAY?! WHAT THE HECK?!

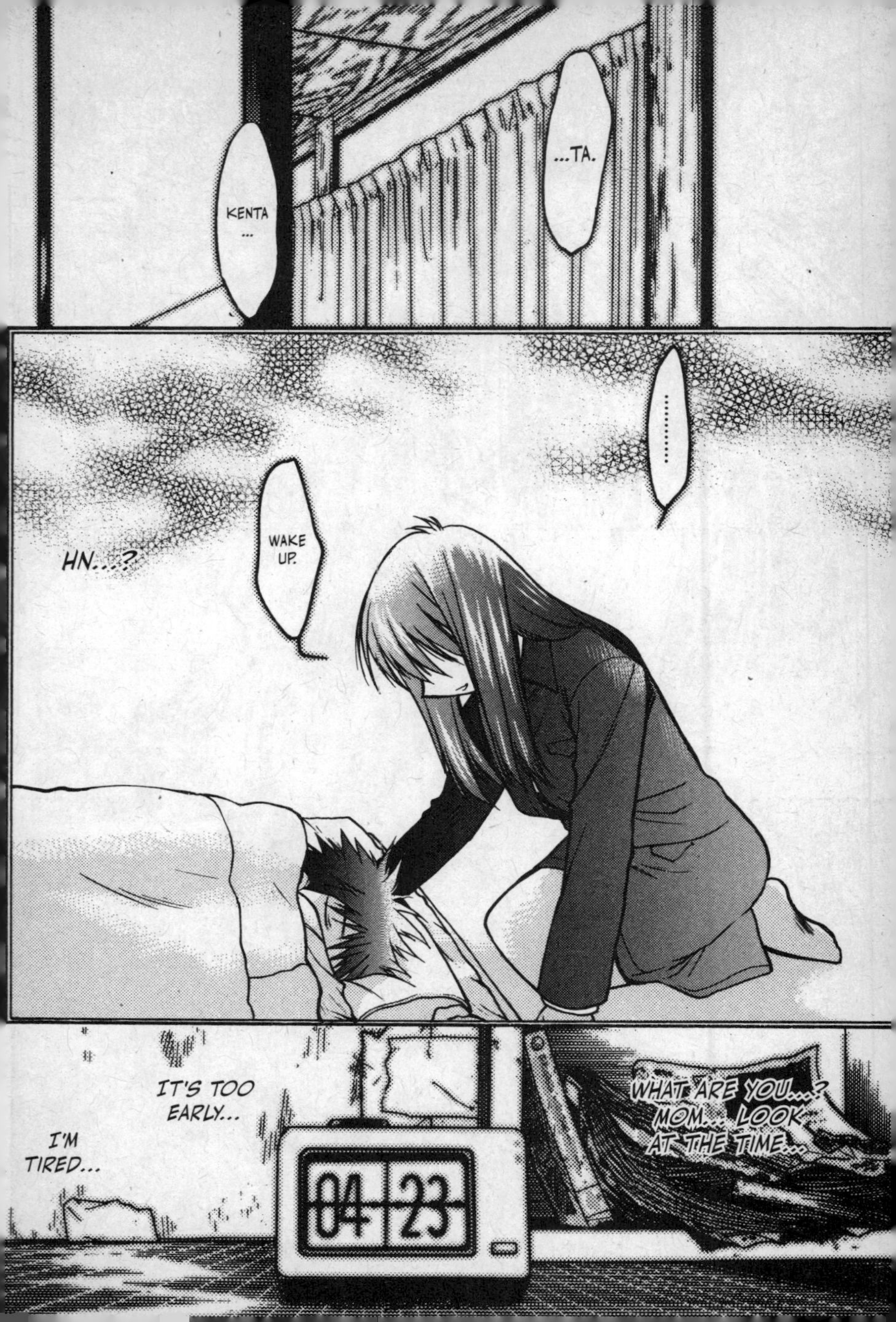

...TA.
KENTA ...
......
WAKE UP.
HN...?
WHAT ARE YOU...? MOM... LOOK AT THE TIME...
04 23
IT'S TOO EARLY...
I'M TIRED...

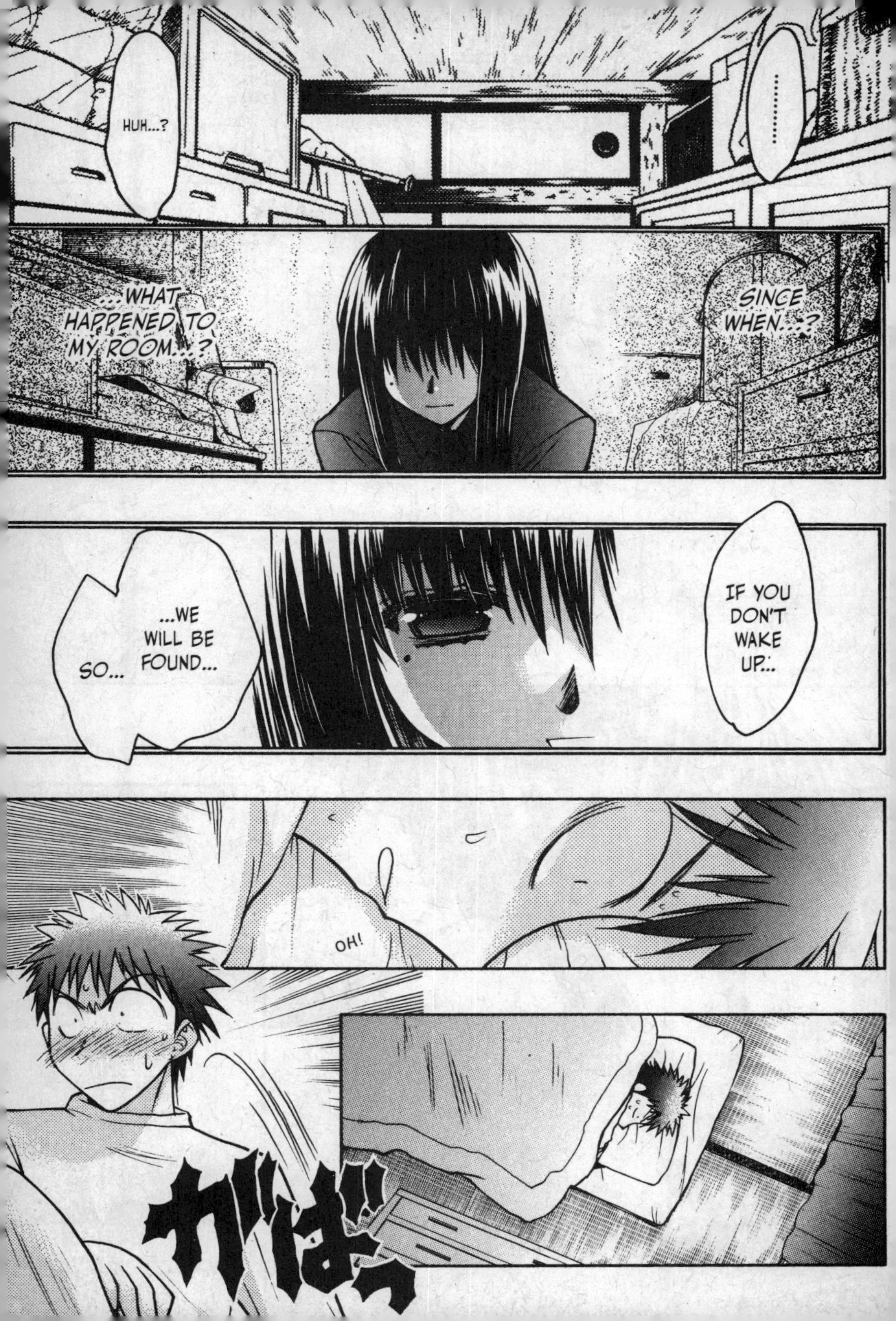

......
HUH...?
SINCE WHEN...?
...WHAT HAPPENED TO MY ROOM...?
IF YOU DON'T WAKE UP...
...WE WILL BE FOUND... SO...
OH!
ガばっ

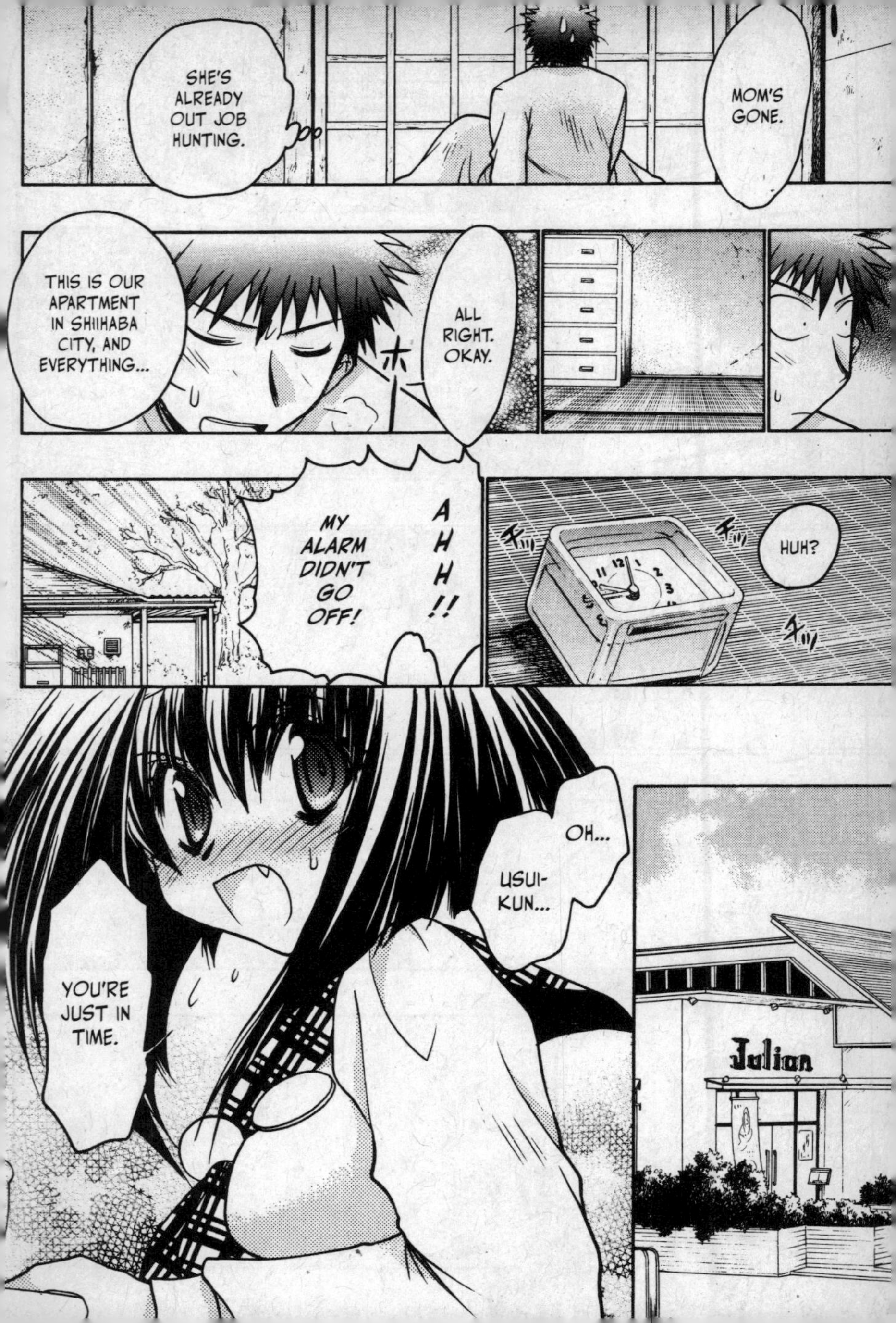

MOM'S GONE.
SHE'S ALREADY OUT JOB HUNTING.
ALL RIGHT. OKAY.
THIS IS OUR APARTMENT IN SHIIHABA CITY, AND EVERYTHING...
HUH?
AHH!!
MY ALARM DIDN'T GO OFF!
Julion
OH...
USUI-KUN...
YOU'RE JUST IN TIME.

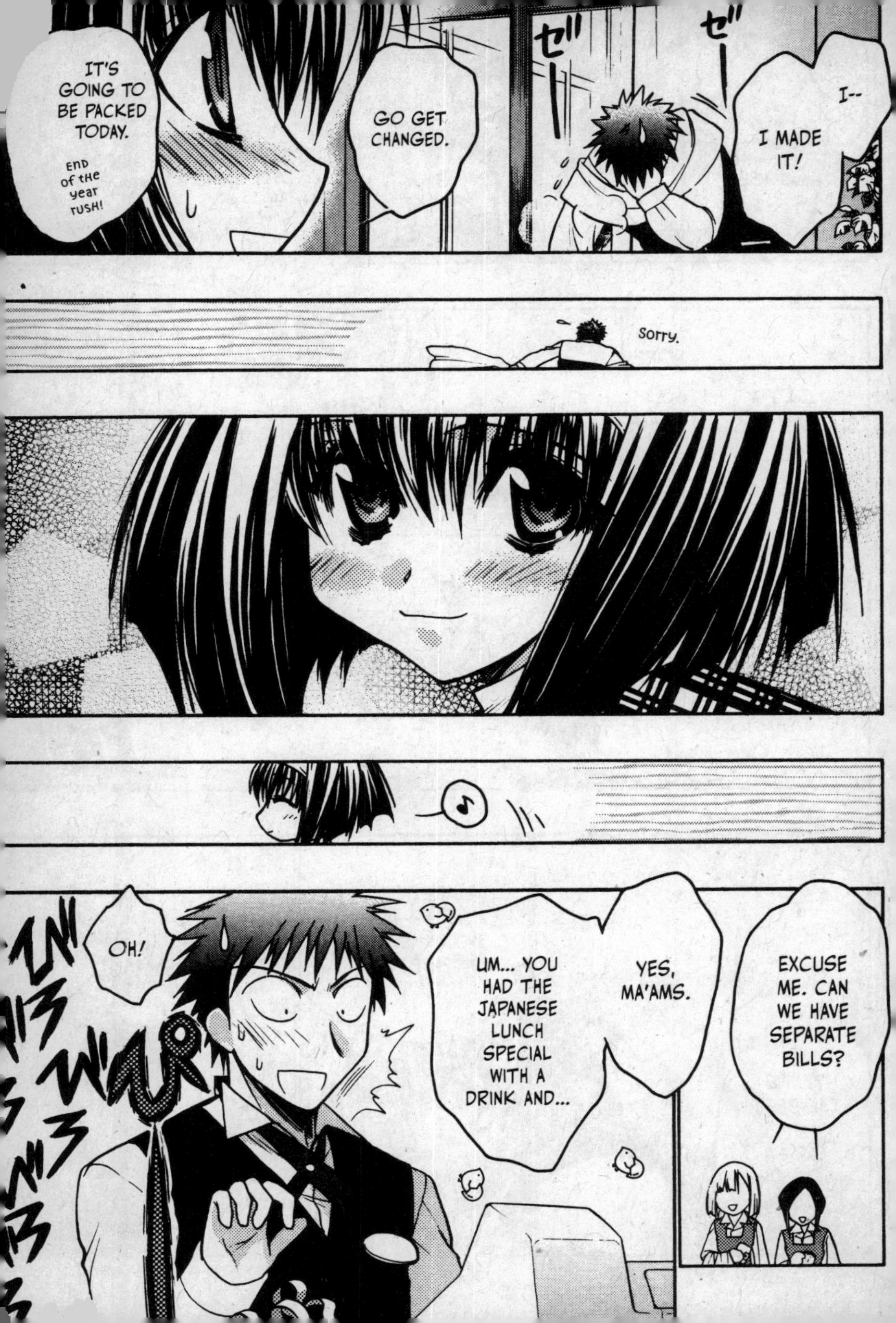
I--
I MADE IT!
GO GET CHANGED.
IT'S GOING TO BE PACKED TODAY.
End of the year rush!
Sorry.
EXCUSE ME. CAN WE HAVE SEPARATE BILLS?
YES, MA'AMS.
UM... YOU HAD THE JAPANESE LUNCH SPECIAL WITH A DRINK AND...
OH!

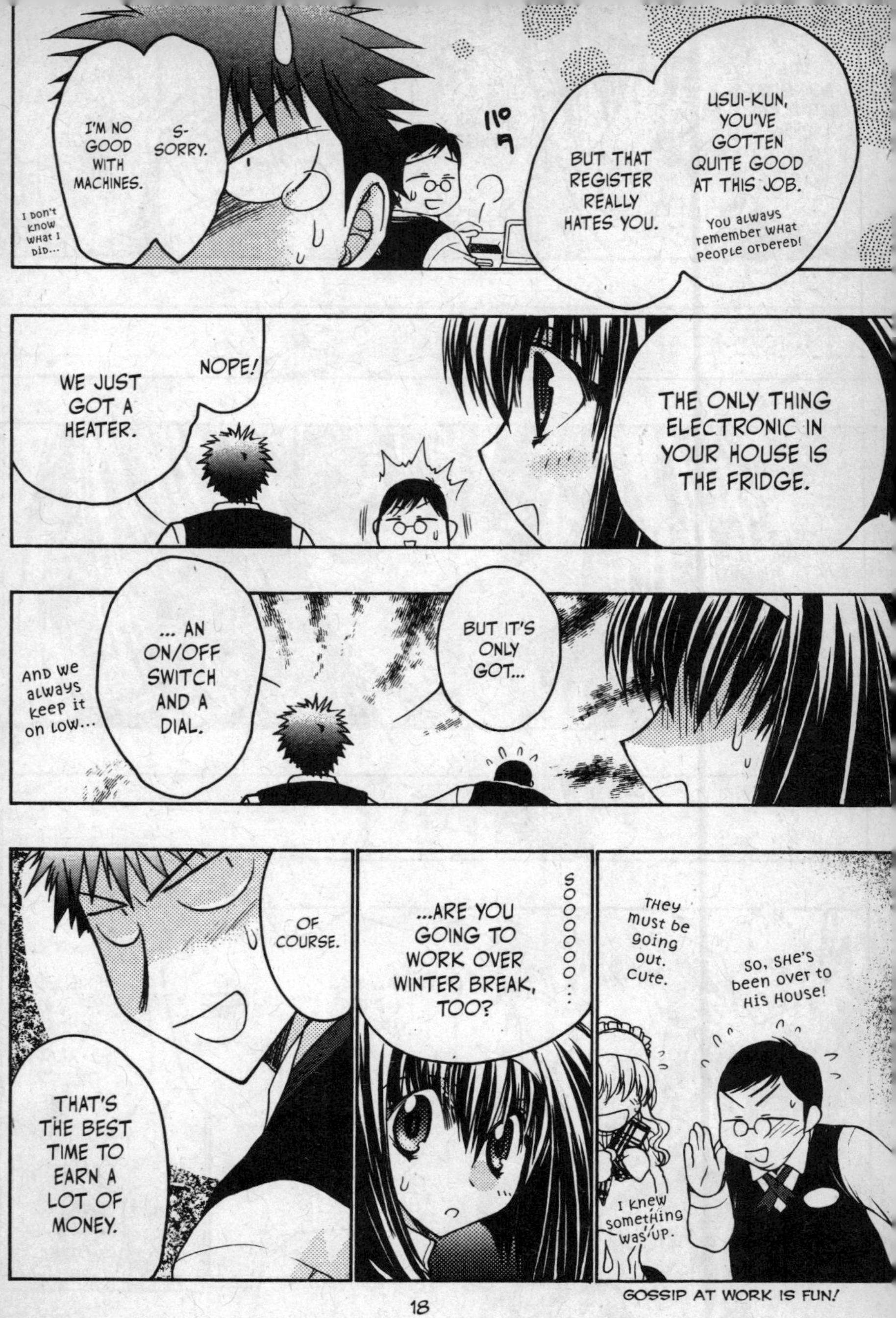
USUI-KUN, YOU'VE GOTTEN QUITE GOOD AT THIS JOB.
You always remember what people ordered!
BUT THAT REGISTER REALLY HATES YOU.
S-SORRY.
I'M NO GOOD WITH MACHINES.
I don't know what I did...
THE ONLY THING ELECTRONIC IN YOUR HOUSE IS THE FRIDGE.
NOPE!
WE JUST GOT A HEATER.
BUT IT'S ONLY GOT...
... AN ON/OFF SWITCH AND A DIAL.
And we always keep it on low...
So, she's been over to his house!
They must be going out. Cute.
I knew something was up.
SOOOOOO...
...ARE YOU GOING TO WORK OVER WINTER BREAK, TOO?
OF COURSE.
THAT'S THE BEST TIME TO EARN A LOT OF MONEY.
GOSSIP AT WORK IS FUN!

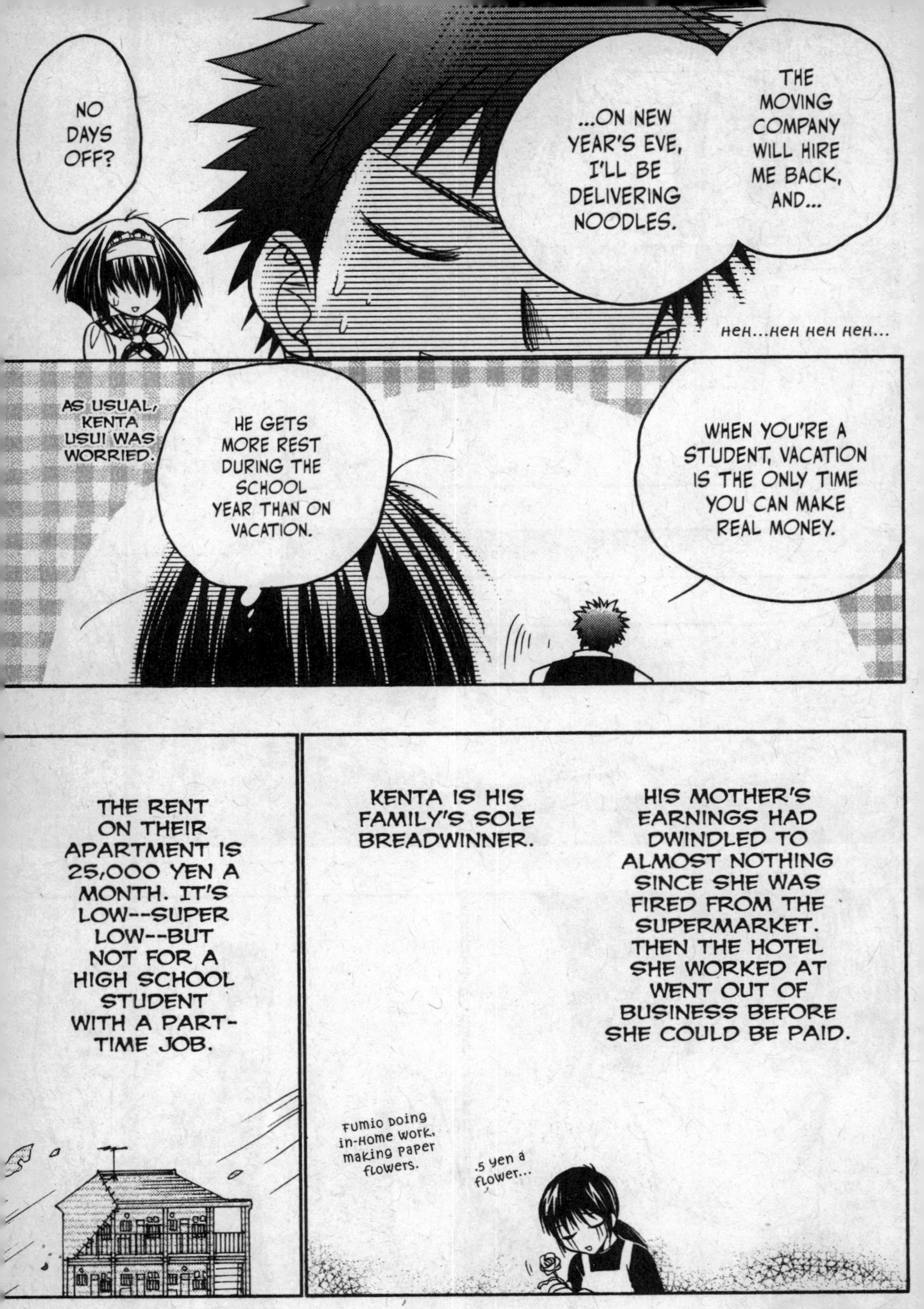
THE MOVING COMPANY WILL HIRE ME BACK, AND...
...ON NEW YEAR'S EVE, I'LL BE DELIVERING NOODLES.
HEH...HEH HEH HEH...
NO DAYS OFF?
WHEN YOU'RE A STUDENT, VACATION IS THE ONLY TIME YOU CAN MAKE REAL MONEY.
HE GETS MORE REST DURING THE SCHOOL YEAR THAN ON VACATION.
AS USUAL, KENTA USUI WAS WORRIED.
HIS MOTHER'S EARNINGS HAD DWINDLED TO ALMOST NOTHING SINCE SHE WAS FIRED FROM THE SUPERMARKET. THEN THE HOTEL SHE WORKED AT WENT OUT OF BUSINESS BEFORE SHE COULD BE PAID.
KENTA IS HIS FAMILY'S SOLE BREADWINNER.
.5 yen a flower...
Fumio doing in-home work, making paper flowers.
THE RENT ON THEIR APARTMENT IS 25,000 YEN A MONTH. IT'S LOW--SUPER LOW--BUT NOT FOR A HIGH SCHOOL STUDENT WITH A PART-TIME JOB.

HUMAN RESOURCES

. . . .

I'M SORRY.

YOU'RE WELCOME TO REAPPLY IN THE FUTURE.

I SEE.

AT THIS RATE...

...I'LL TAKE ANYTHING.

WHAT ARE MY OPTIONS ...?

WHAT CAN I DO...?

WHAT CAN I DO...?

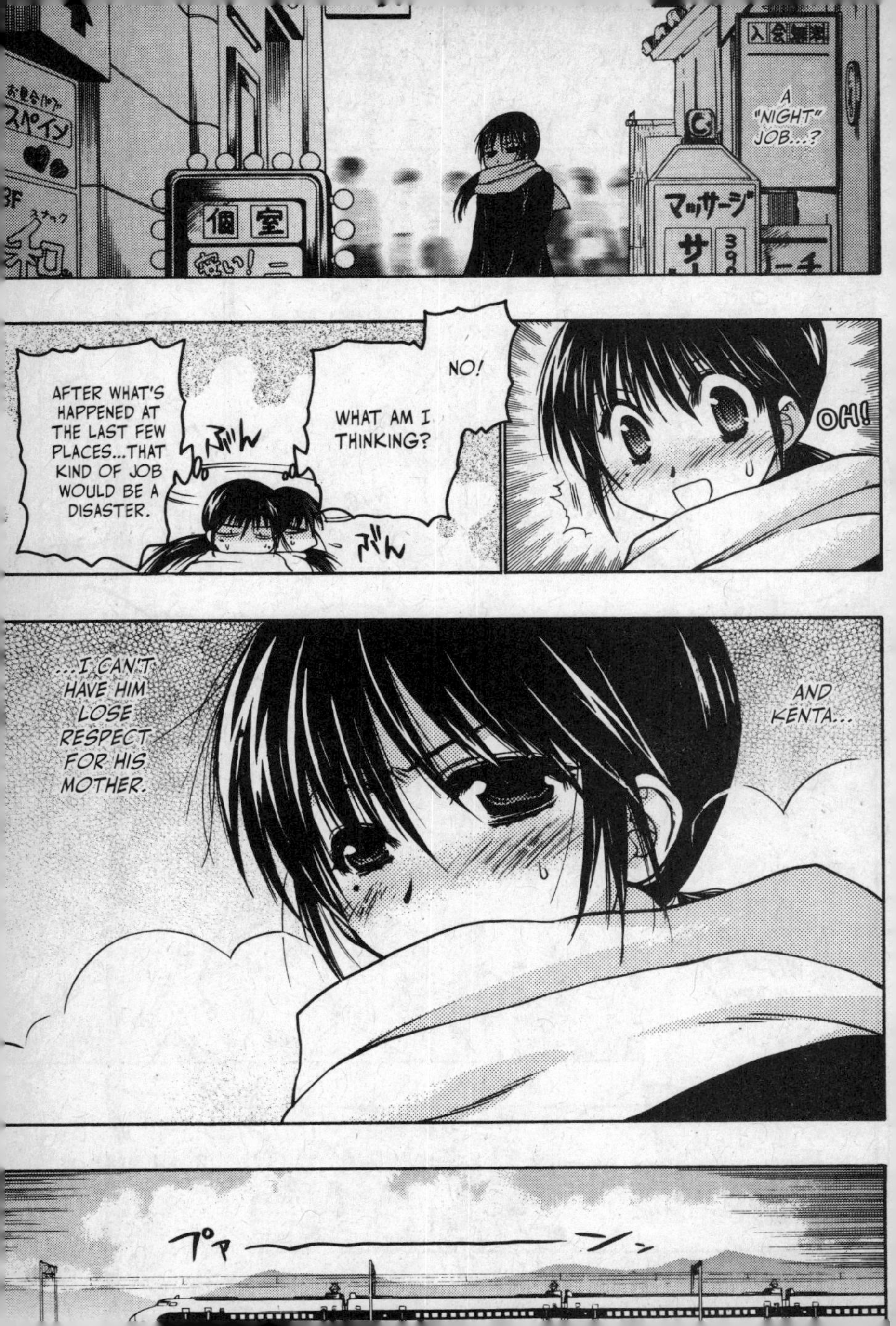
個室
マッサージ
A "NIGHT" JOB...?
OH!
NO!
WHAT AM I THINKING?
ぶん
ぶん
AFTER WHAT'S HAPPENED AT THE LAST FEW PLACES...THAT KIND OF JOB WOULD BE A DISASTER.
AND KENTA...
...I CAN'T HAVE HIM LOSE RESPECT FOR HIS MOTHER.
プァーーーンン

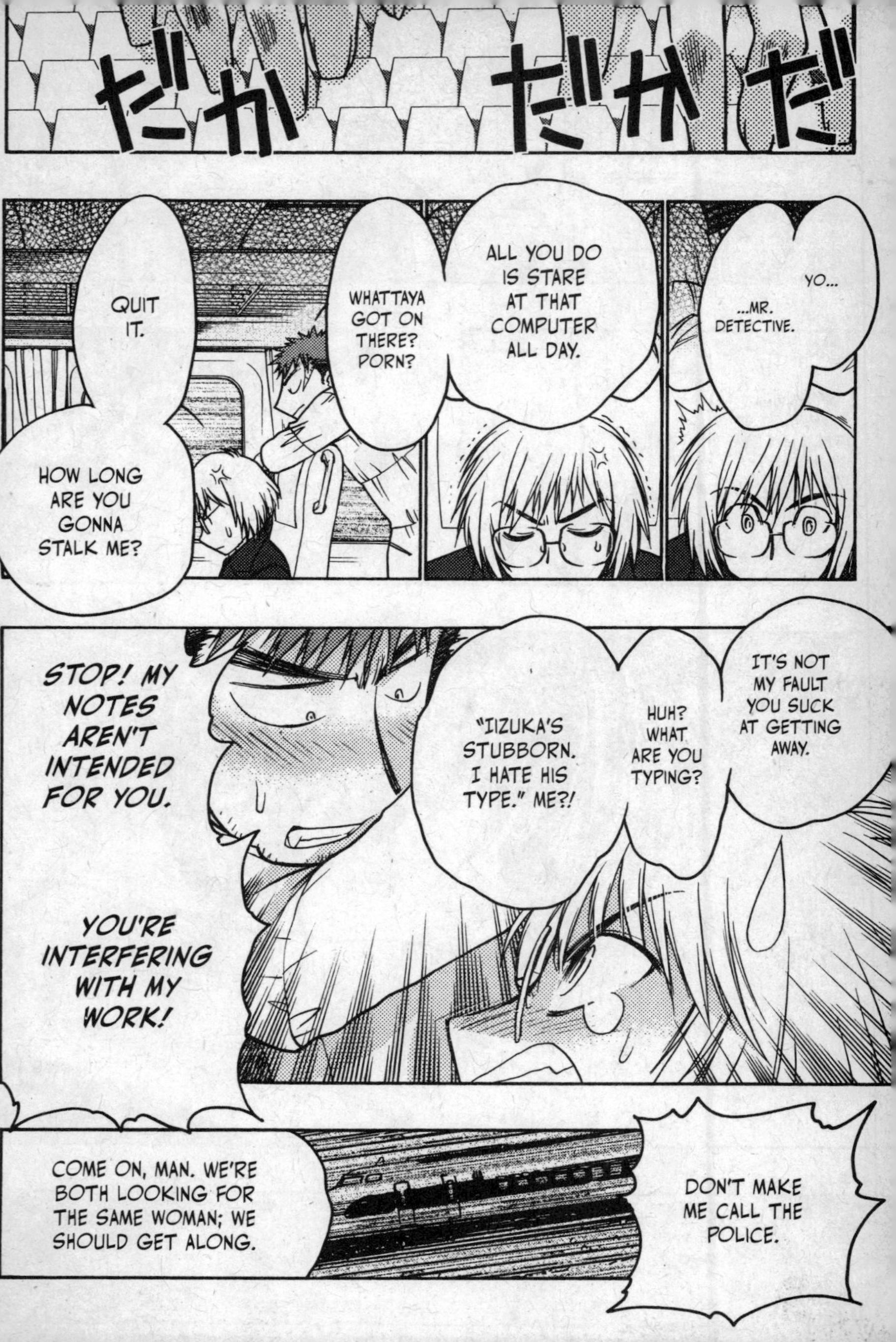
だかだかだ
YO...
...MR. DETECTIVE.
ALL YOU DO IS STARE AT THAT COMPUTER ALL DAY.
WHATTAYA GOT ON THERE? PORN?
QUIT IT.
HOW LONG ARE YOU GONNA STALK ME?
IT'S NOT MY FAULT YOU SUCK AT GETTING AWAY.
HUH? WHAT ARE YOU TYPING?
"IIZUKA'S STUBBORN. I HATE HIS TYPE." ME?!
STOP! MY NOTES AREN'T INTENDED FOR YOU.
YOU'RE INTERFERING WITH MY WORK!
DON'T MAKE ME CALL THE POLICE.
COME ON, MAN. WE'RE BOTH LOOKING FOR THE SAME WOMAN; WE SHOULD GET ALONG.

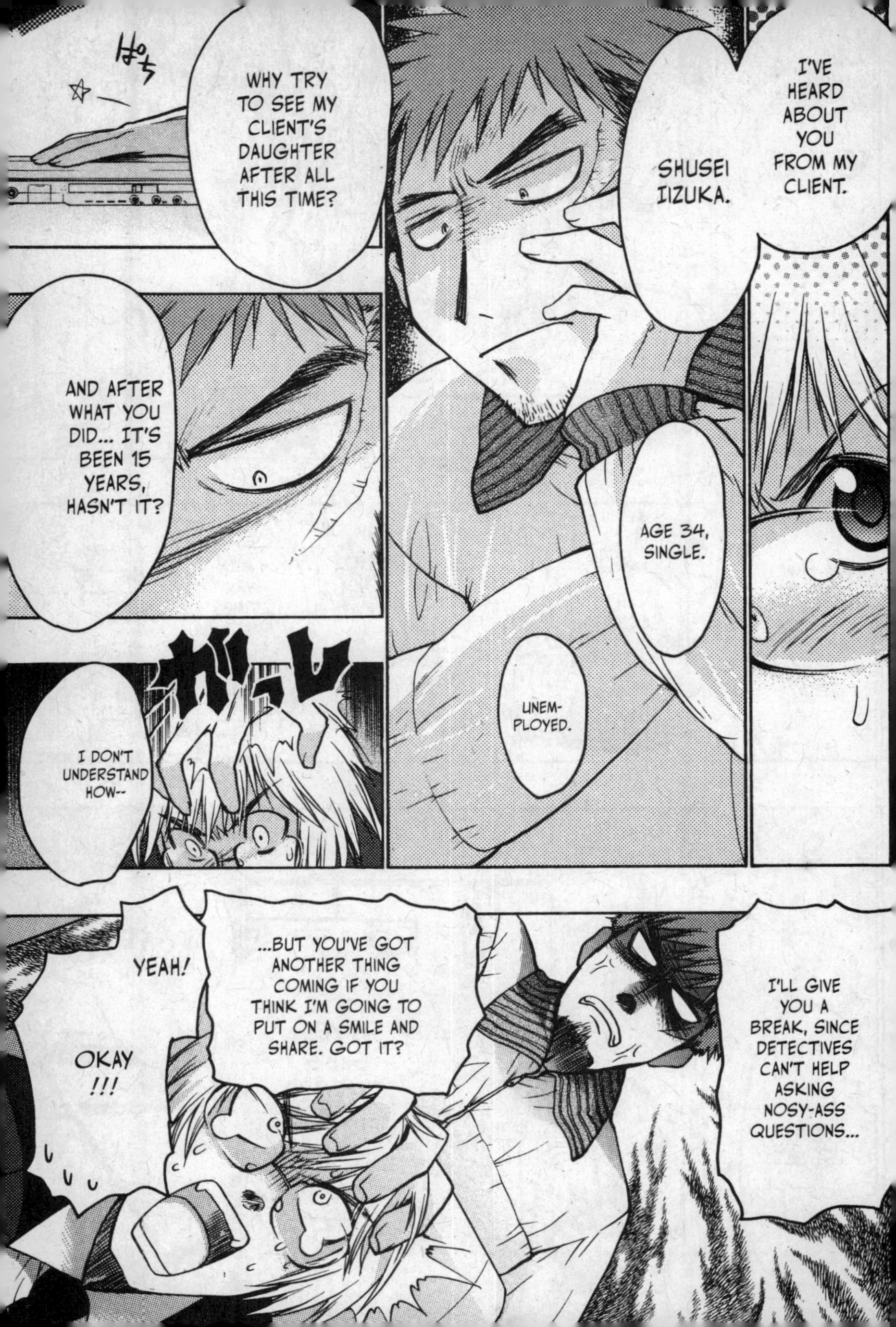
I'VE HEARD ABOUT YOU FROM MY CLIENT.
SHUSEI IIZUKA.
AGE 34, SINGLE.
UNEMPLOYED.
WHY TRY TO SEE MY CLIENT'S DAUGHTER AFTER ALL THIS TIME?
AND AFTER WHAT YOU DID... IT'S BEEN 15 YEARS, HASN'T IT?
I DON'T UNDERSTAND HOW--
I'LL GIVE YOU A BREAK, SINCE DETECTIVES CAN'T HELP ASKING NOSY-ASS QUESTIONS...
...BUT YOU'VE GOT ANOTHER THING COMING IF YOU THINK I'M GOING TO PUT ON A SMILE AND SHARE. GOT IT?
YEAH!
OKAY !!!

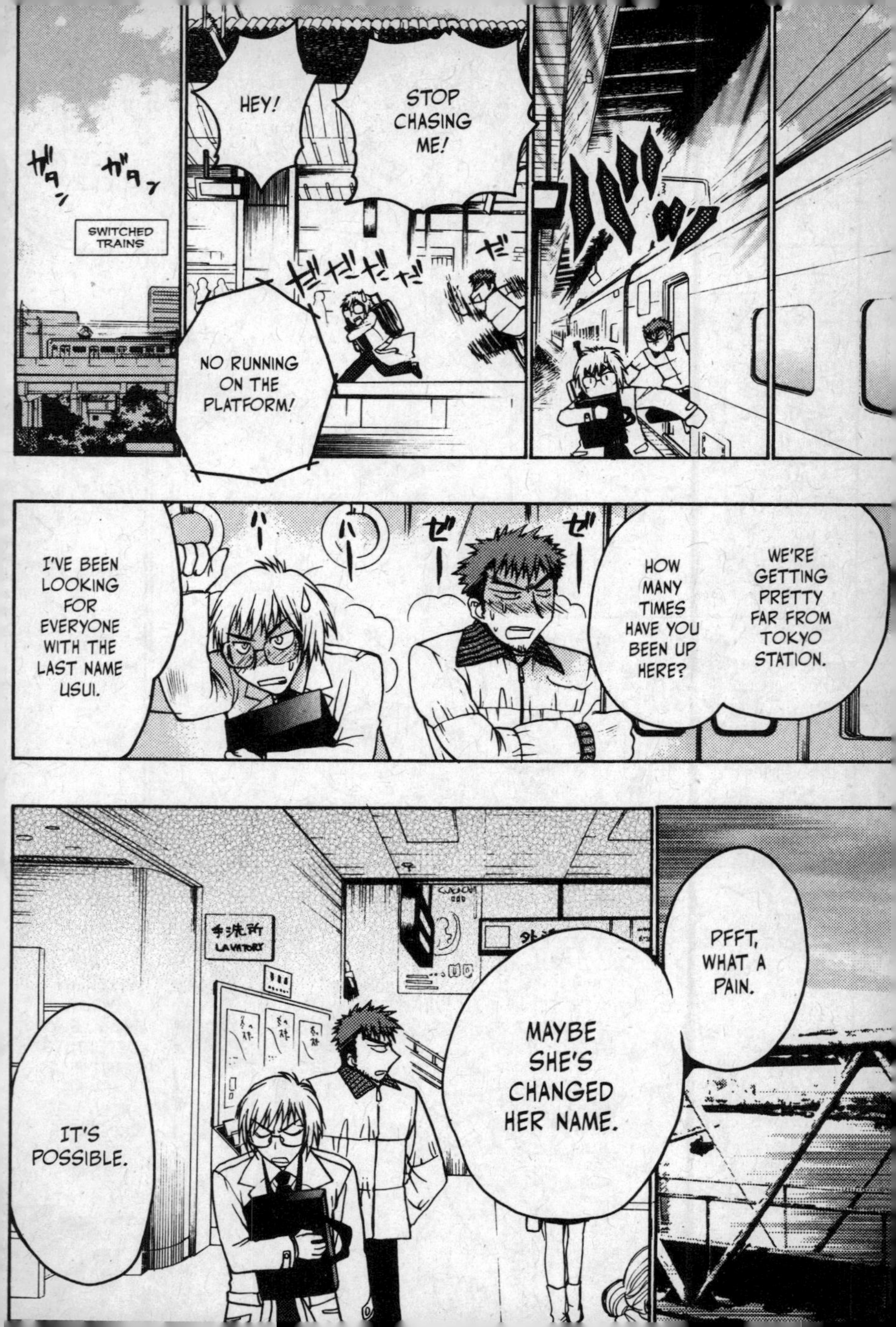
STOP CHASING ME!
HEY!
NO RUNNING ON THE PLATFORM!
SWITCHED TRAINS
WE'RE GETTING PRETTY FAR FROM TOKYO STATION.
HOW MANY TIMES HAVE YOU BEEN UP HERE?
I'VE BEEN LOOKING FOR EVERYONE WITH THE LAST NAME USUI.
PFFT, WHAT A PAIN.
MAYBE SHE'S CHANGED HER NAME.
手洗所
LAVATORY
IT'S POSSIBLE.

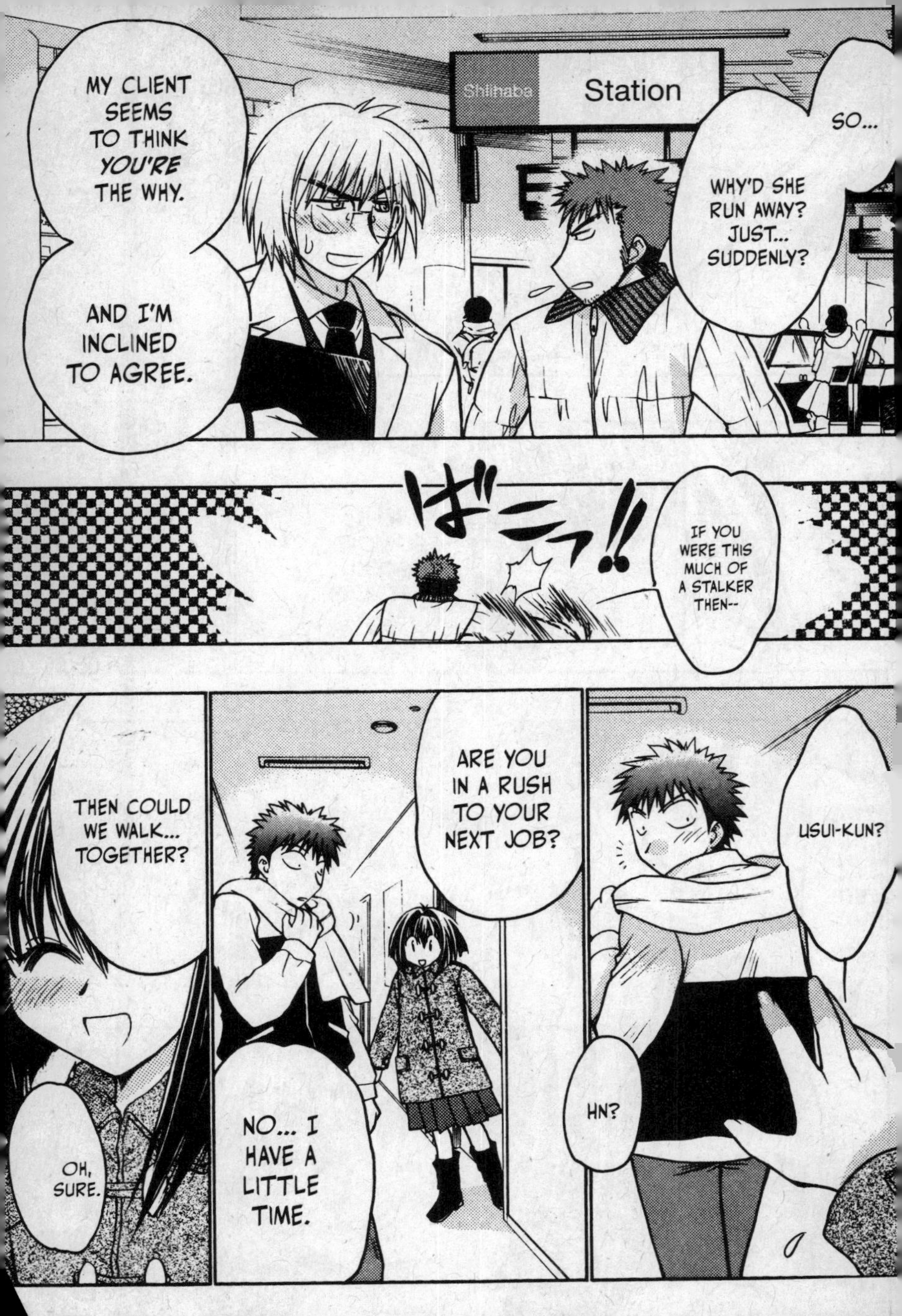
Shiihaba Station
SO...
WHY'D SHE RUN AWAY? JUST... SUDDENLY?
MY CLIENT SEEMS TO THINK *YOU'RE* THE WHY.
AND I'M INCLINED TO AGREE.
ばーッ!!
IF YOU WERE THIS MUCH OF A STALKER THEN--
USUI-KUN?
HN?
ARE YOU IN A RUSH TO YOUR NEXT JOB?
NO... I HAVE A LITTLE TIME.
THEN COULD WE WALK... TOGETHER?
OH, SURE.

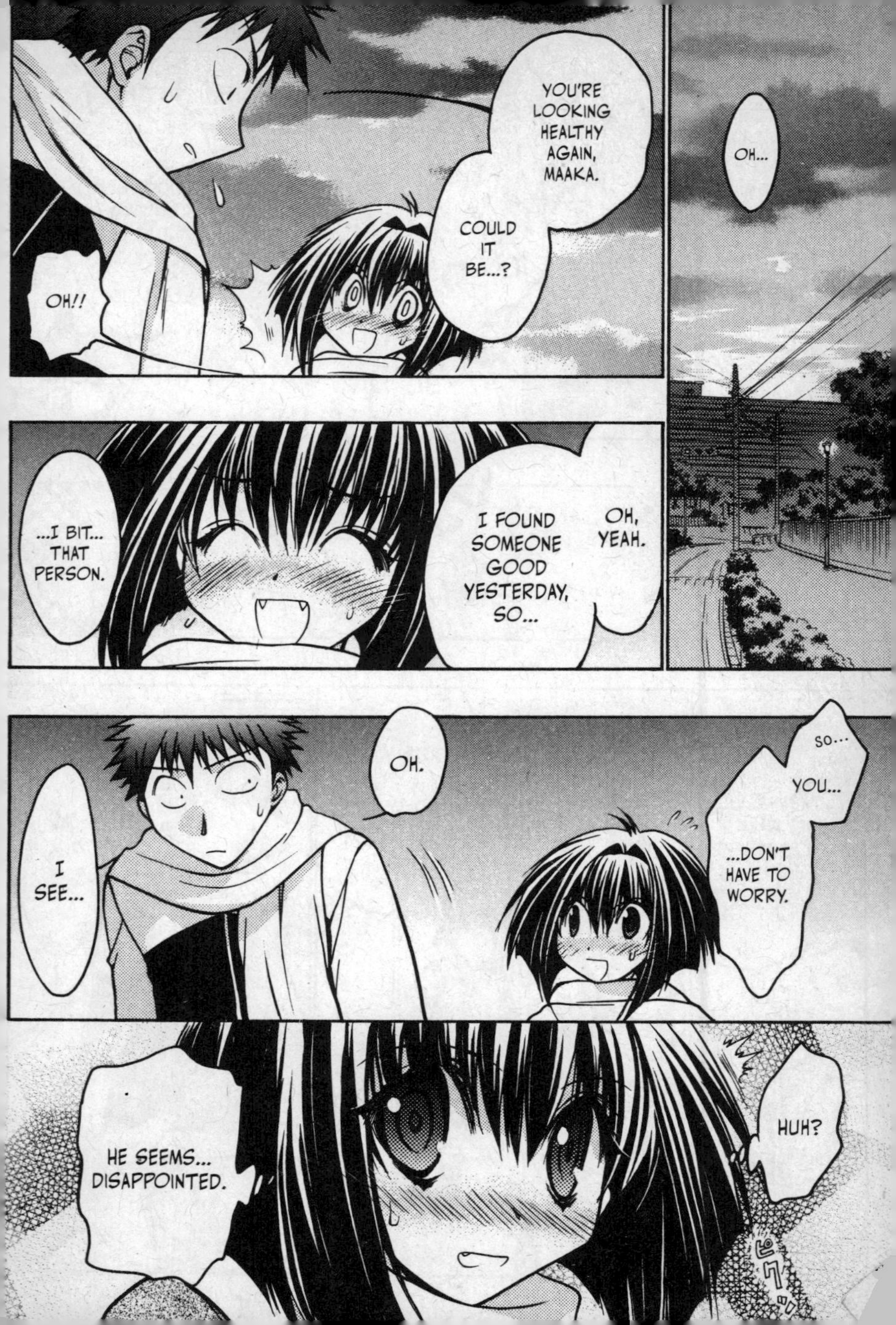
OH...
YOU'RE LOOKING HEALTHY AGAIN, MAAKA.
COULD IT BE...?
OH!!
OH, YEAH.
I FOUND SOMEONE GOOD YESTERDAY, SO...
...I BIT... THAT PERSON.
SO...
YOU...
...DON'T HAVE TO WORRY.
OH.
I SEE...
HUH?
HE SEEMS... DISAPPOINTED.

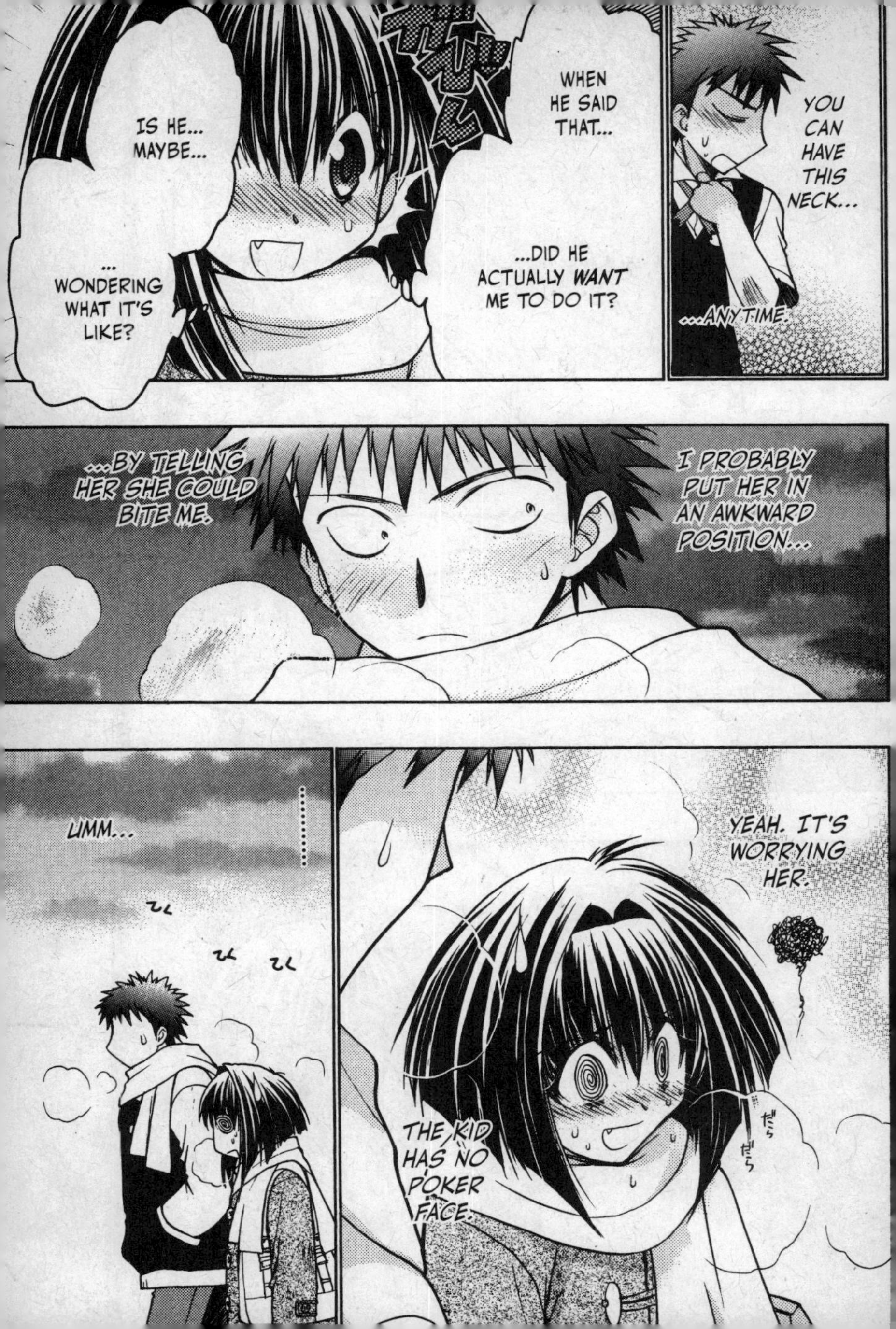
YOU CAN HAVE THIS NECK...
...ANYTIME.
WHEN HE SAID THAT...
...DID HE ACTUALLY *WANT* ME TO DO IT?
IS HE... MAYBE...
... WONDERING WHAT IT'S LIKE?
I PROBABLY PUT HER IN AN AWKWARD POSITION...
...BY TELLING HER SHE COULD BITE ME.
YEAH. IT'S WORRYING HER.
だら だら
THE KID HAS NO POKER FACE.
......
UMM...

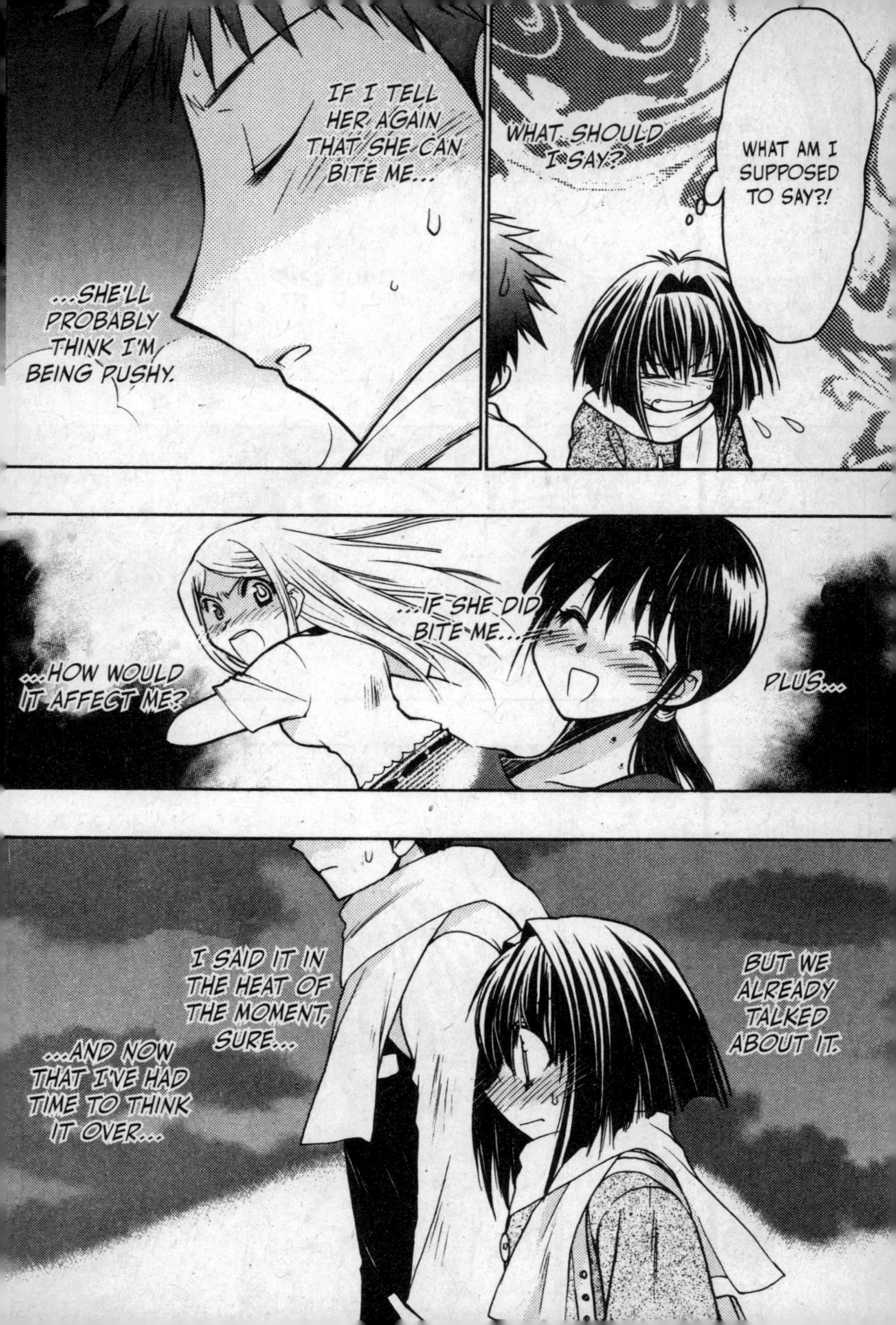
WHAT AM I SUPPOSED TO SAY?!
WHAT SHOULD I SAY?
IF I TELL HER AGAIN THAT SHE CAN BITE ME...
...SHE'LL PROBABLY THINK I'M BEING PUSHY.
PLUS...
...IF SHE DID BITE ME...
...HOW WOULD IT AFFECT ME?
BUT WE ALREADY TALKED ABOUT IT.
I SAID IT IN THE HEAT OF THE MOMENT, SURE...
...AND NOW THAT I'VE HAD TIME TO THINK IT OVER...

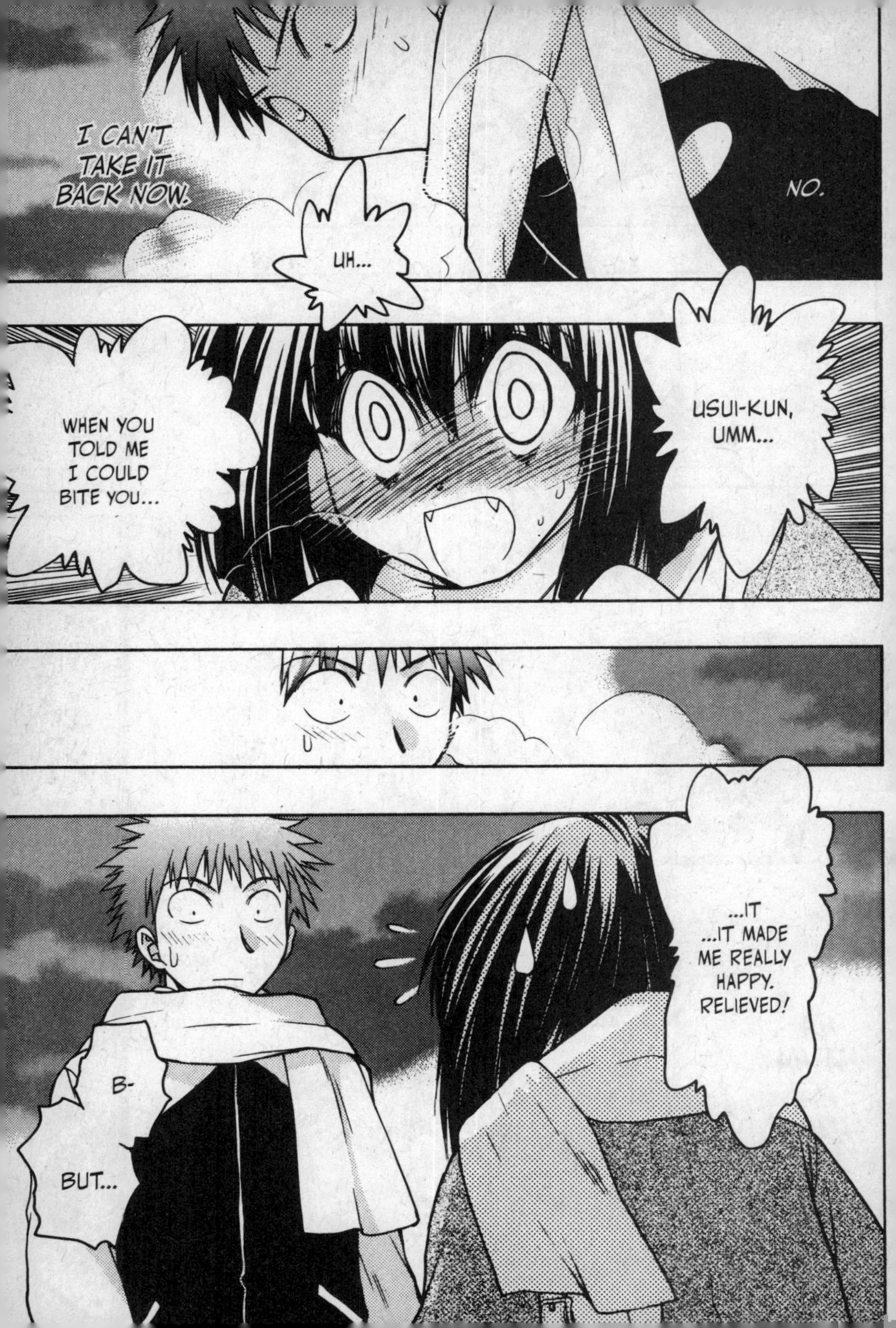
NO.
I CAN'T TAKE IT BACK NOW.
UH...
USUI-KUN, UMM...
WHEN YOU TOLD ME I COULD BITE YOU...
...IT ...IT MADE ME REALLY HAPPY. RELIEVED!
B-
BUT...

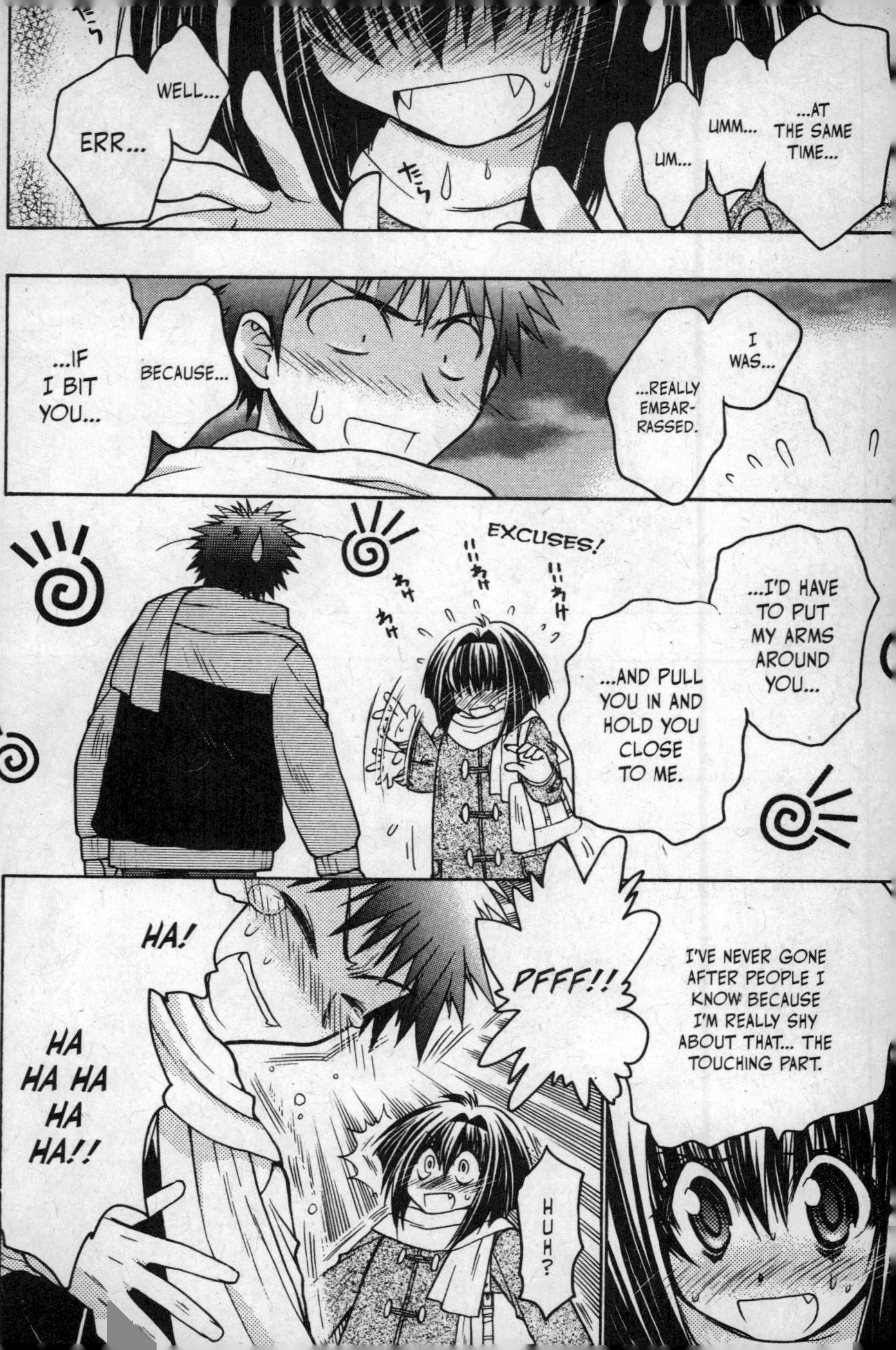
...AT THE SAME TIME...
UMM...
UM...
たら
WELL...
ERR...
たら
I WAS...
...REALLY EMBARRASSED.
BECAUSE...
...IF I BIT YOU...
...I'D HAVE TO PUT MY ARMS AROUND YOU...
...AND PULL YOU IN AND HOLD YOU CLOSE TO ME.
EXCUSES!
I'VE NEVER GONE AFTER PEOPLE I KNOW BECAUSE I'M REALLY SHY ABOUT THAT... THE TOUCHING PART.
PFFF!!
HA!
HA HA HA HA HA!!
HUH?

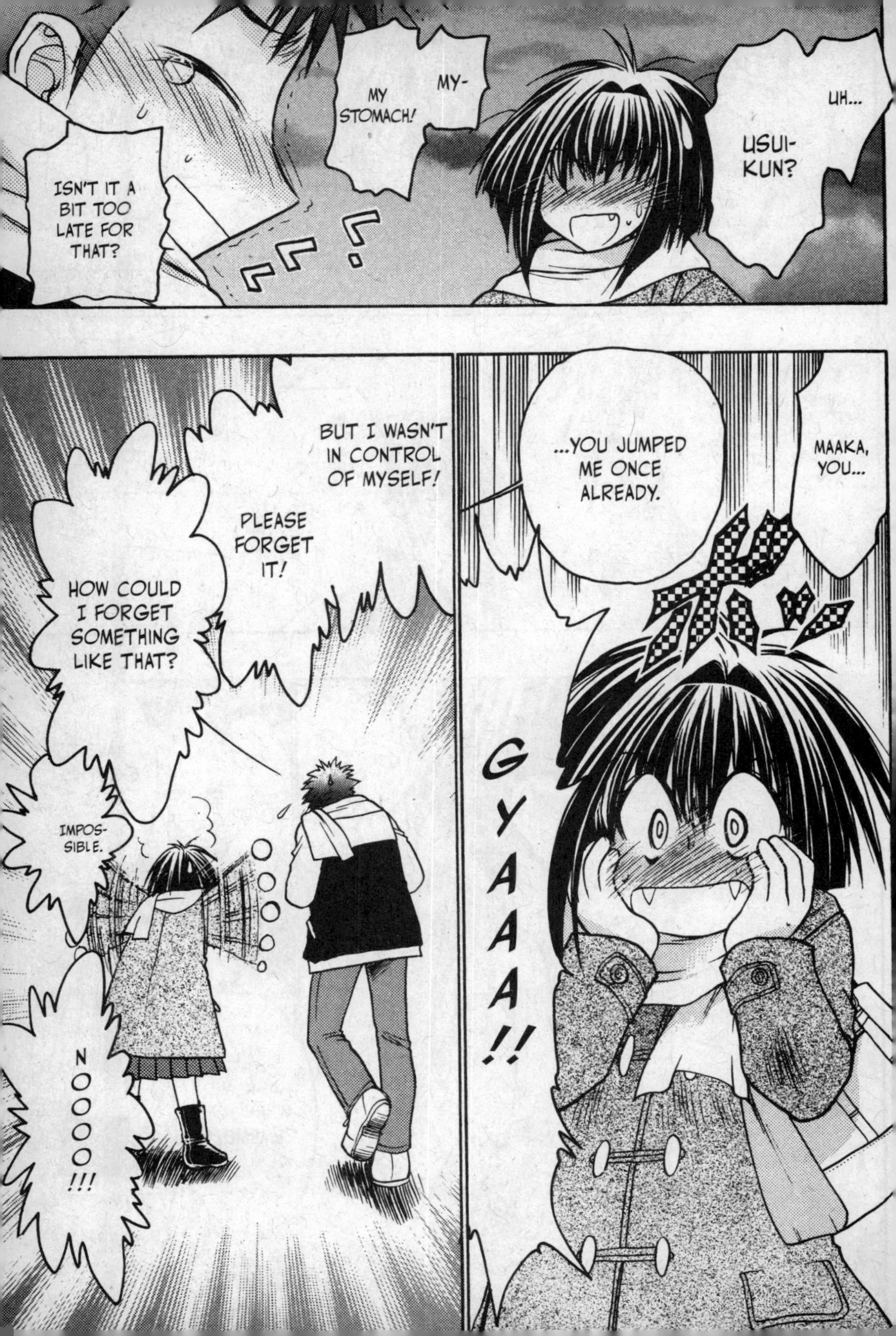
UH...
USUI-KUN?
MY-
MY STOMACH!
ISN'T IT A BIT TOO LATE FOR THAT?
MAAKA, YOU...
...YOU JUMPED ME ONCE ALREADY.
GYAAAA!!
BUT I WASN'T IN CONTROL OF MYSELF!
PLEASE FORGET IT!
HOW COULD I FORGET SOMETHING LIKE THAT?
IMPOSSIBLE.
NOOOOO!!!

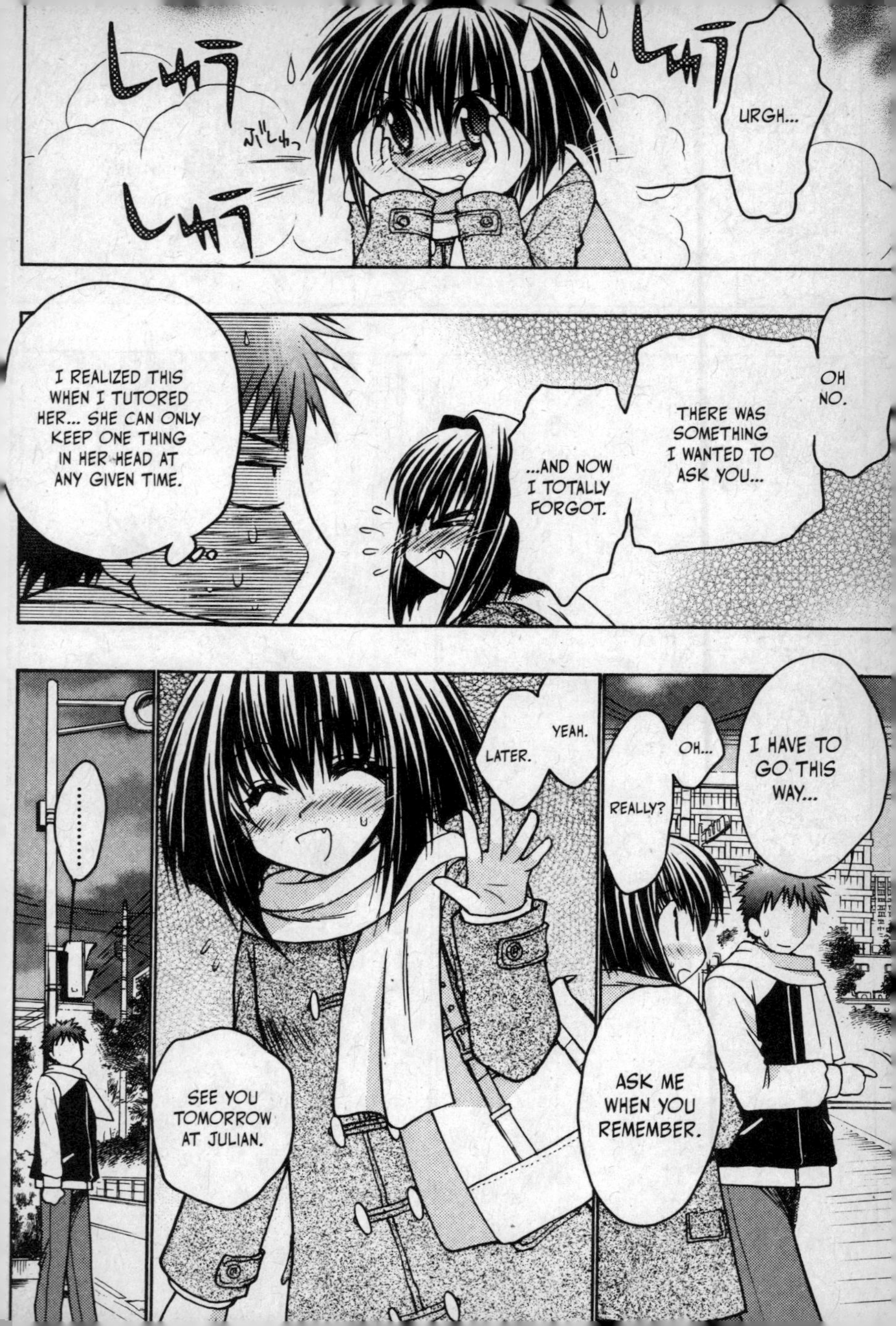
URGH...
OH NO.
THERE WAS SOMETHING I WANTED TO ASK YOU...
...AND NOW I TOTALLY FORGOT.
I REALIZED THIS WHEN I TUTORED HER... SHE CAN ONLY KEEP ONE THING IN HER HEAD AT ANY GIVEN TIME.
I HAVE TO GO THIS WAY...
OH... REALLY?
ASK ME WHEN YOU REMEMBER.
YEAH. LATER.
SEE YOU TOMORROW AT JULIAN.
......

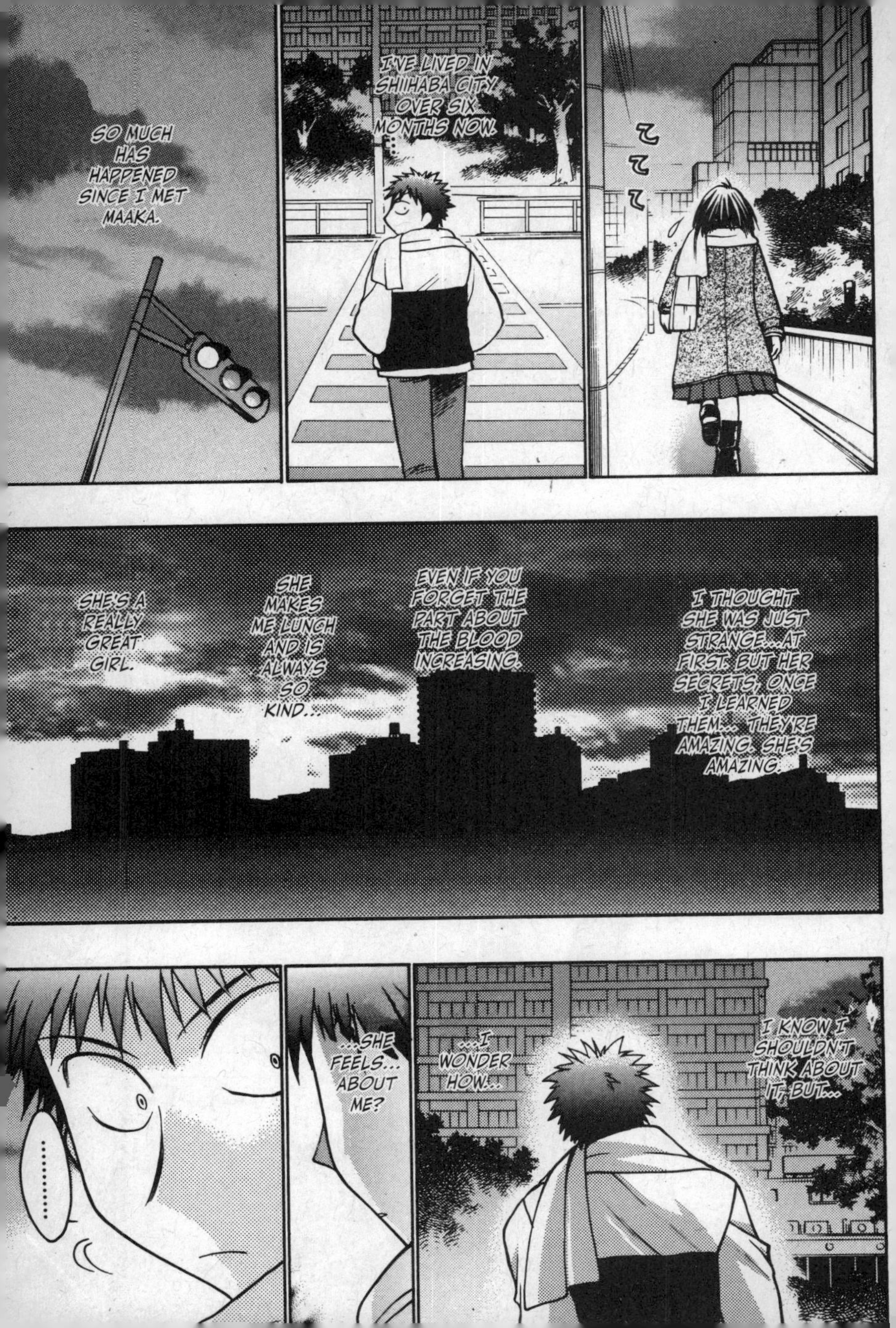
ててて
I'VE LIVED IN SHIIHABA CITY OVER SIX MONTHS NOW.
...
SO MUCH HAS HAPPENED SINCE I MET MAAKA.
I THOUGHT SHE WAS JUST STRANGE... AT FIRST. BUT HER SECRETS, ONCE I LEARNED THEM... THEY'RE AMAZING. SHE'S AMAZING.
EVEN IF YOU FORGET THE PART ABOUT THE BLOOD INCREASING.
SHE MAKES ME LUNCH AND IS ALWAYS SO KIND...
SHE'S A REALLY GREAT GIRL.
I KNOW I SHOULDN'T THINK ABOUT IT, BUT...
...I WONDER HOW...
...SHE FEELS... ABOUT ME?
......

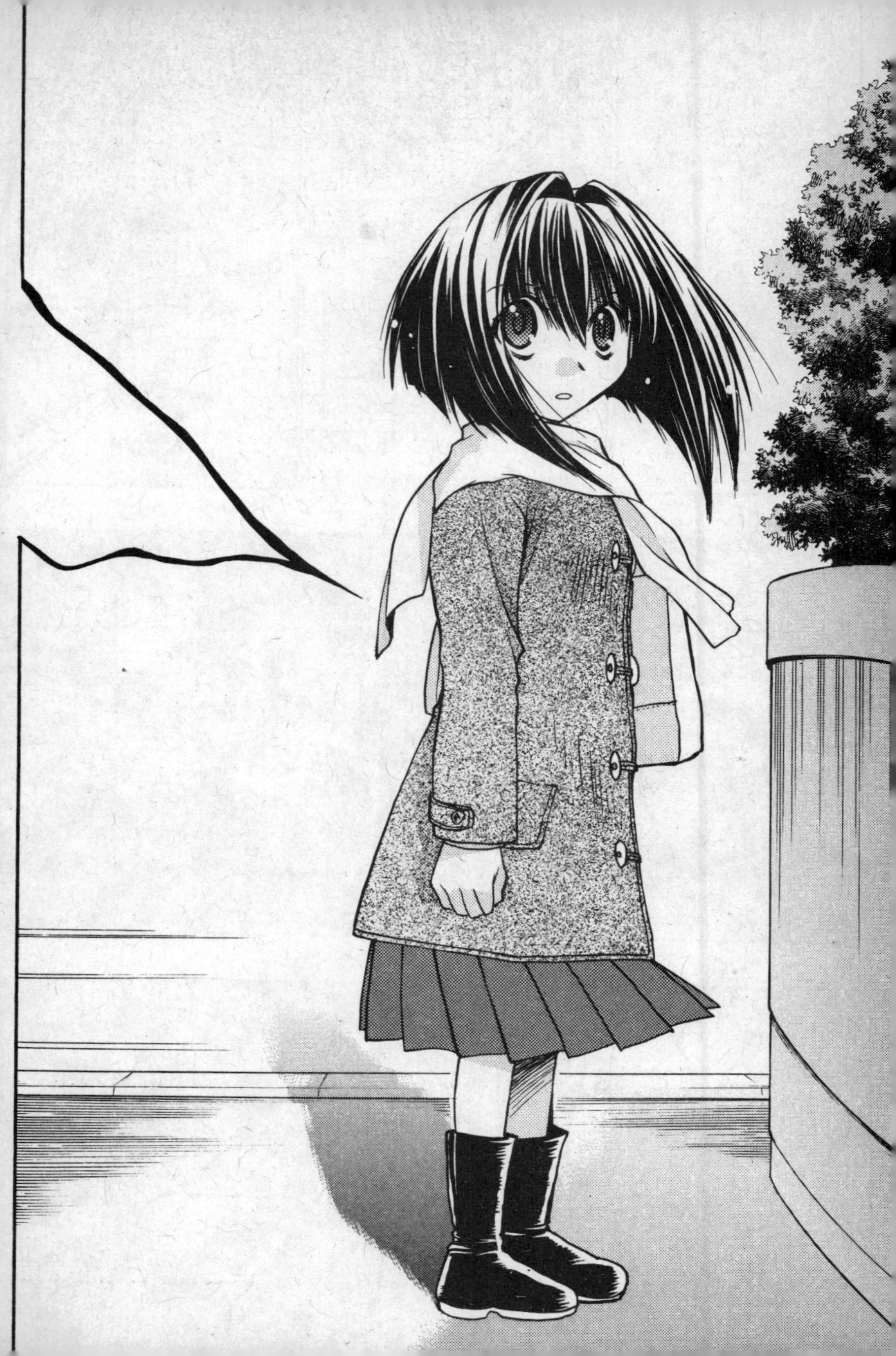

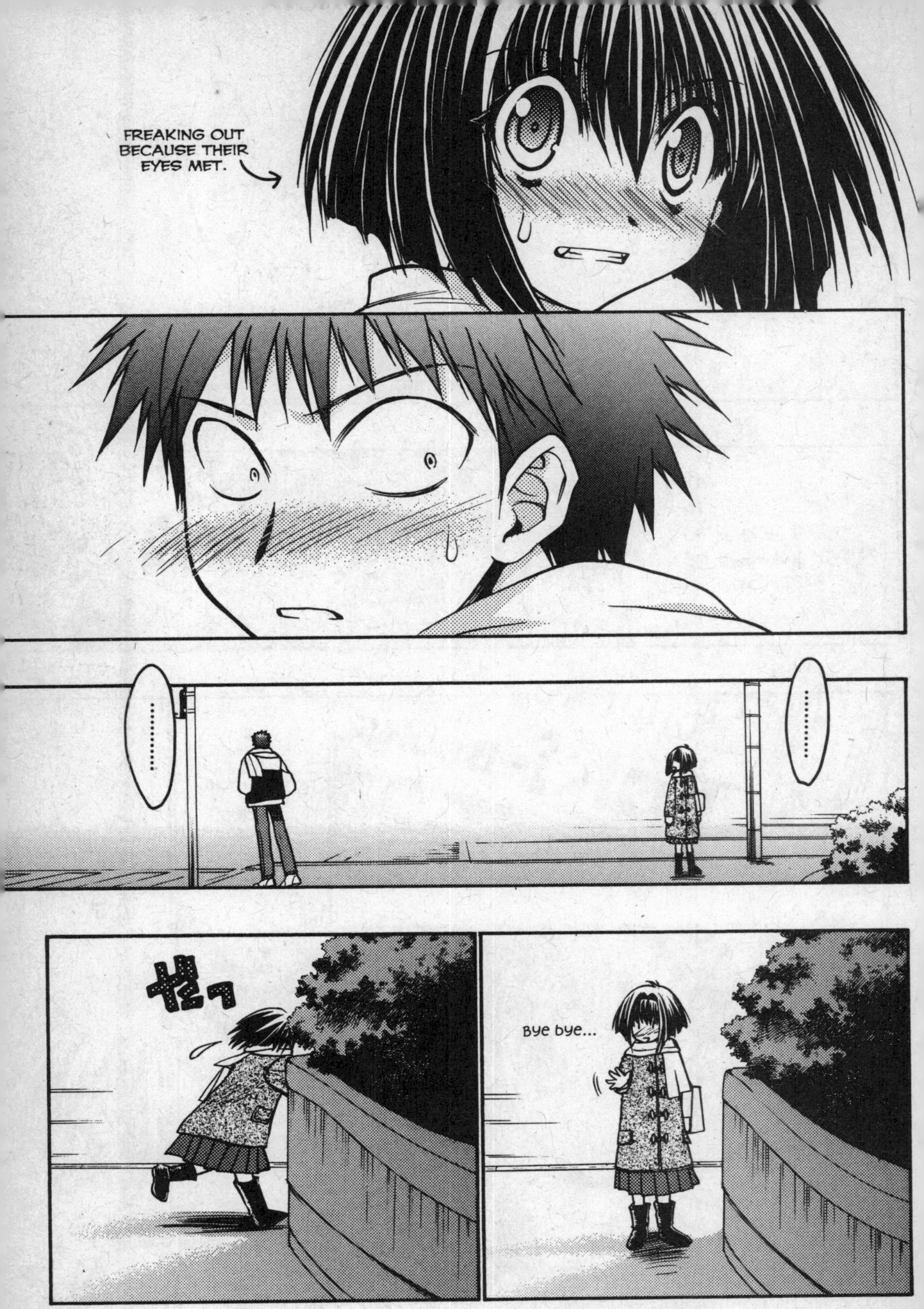
FREAKING OUT BECAUSE THEIR EYES MET.
……
……
Bye bye...
ぜっ

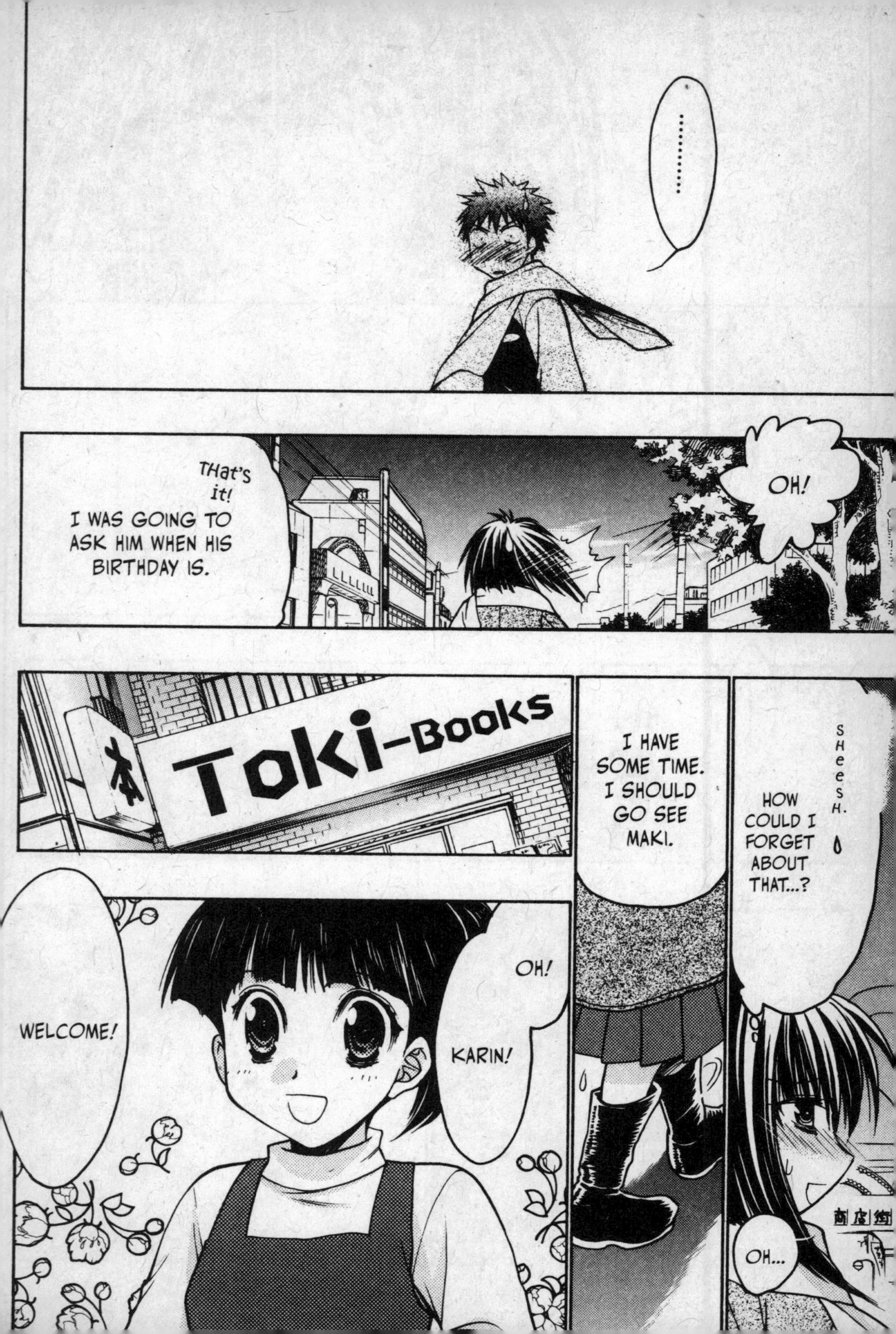
......
OH!
That's it! I WAS GOING TO ASK HIM WHEN HIS BIRTHDAY IS.
SHEESH.
HOW COULD I FORGET ABOUT THAT...?
商店街
OH...
I HAVE SOME TIME. I SHOULD GO SEE MAKI.
本
Toki-Books
OH! KARIN!
WELCOME!

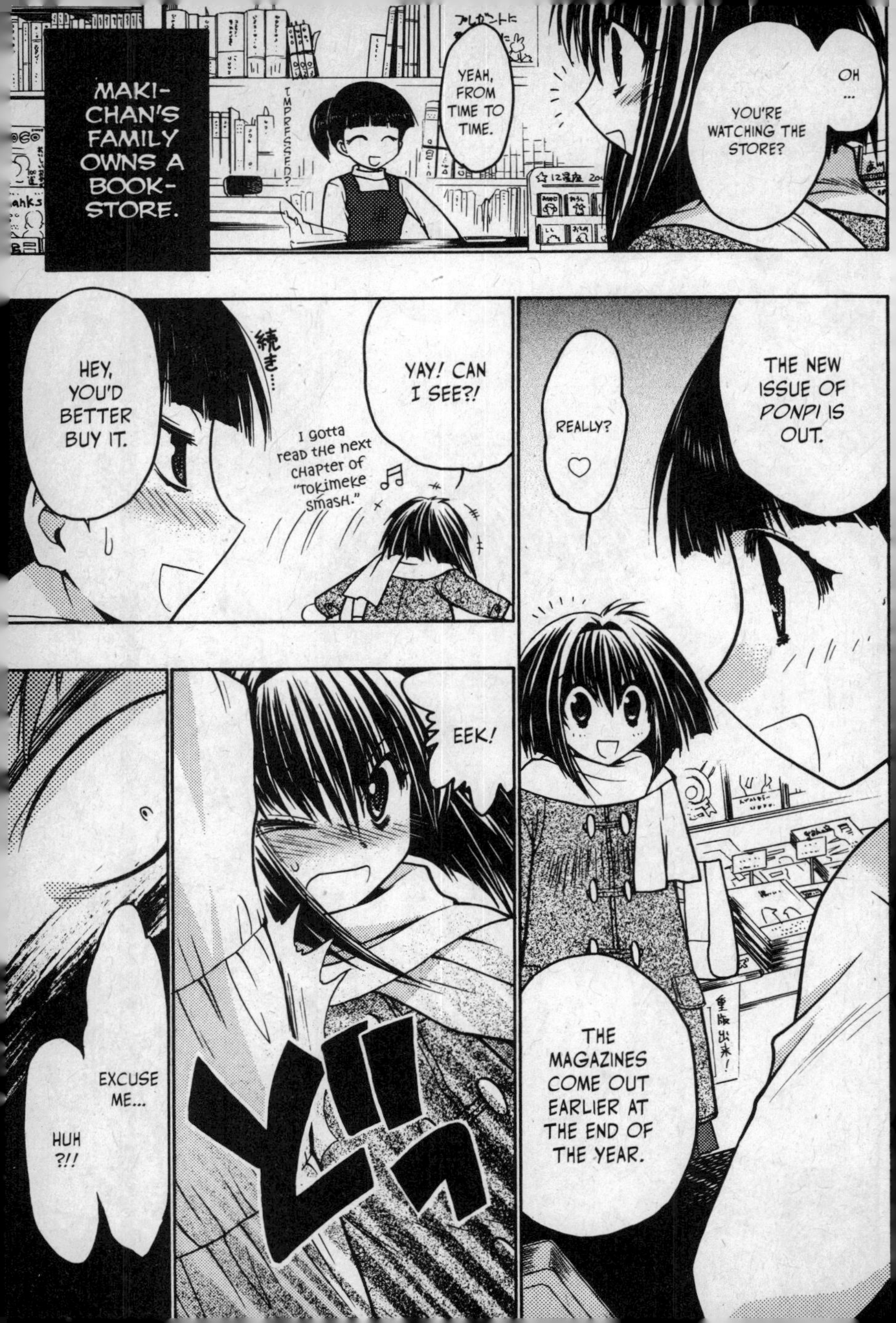
OH ... YOU'RE WATCHING THE STORE?
YEAH, FROM TIME TO TIME.
IMPRESSED?
MAKI-CHAN'S FAMILY OWNS A BOOK-STORE.
THE NEW ISSUE OF PONPI IS OUT.
REALLY? ♡
THE MAGAZINES COME OUT EARLIER AT THE END OF THE YEAR.
YAY! CAN I SEE?!
I gotta read the next chapter of "Tokimeke Smash."
続き…
HEY, YOU'D BETTER BUY IT.
EEK!
EXCUSE ME...
HUH ?!!

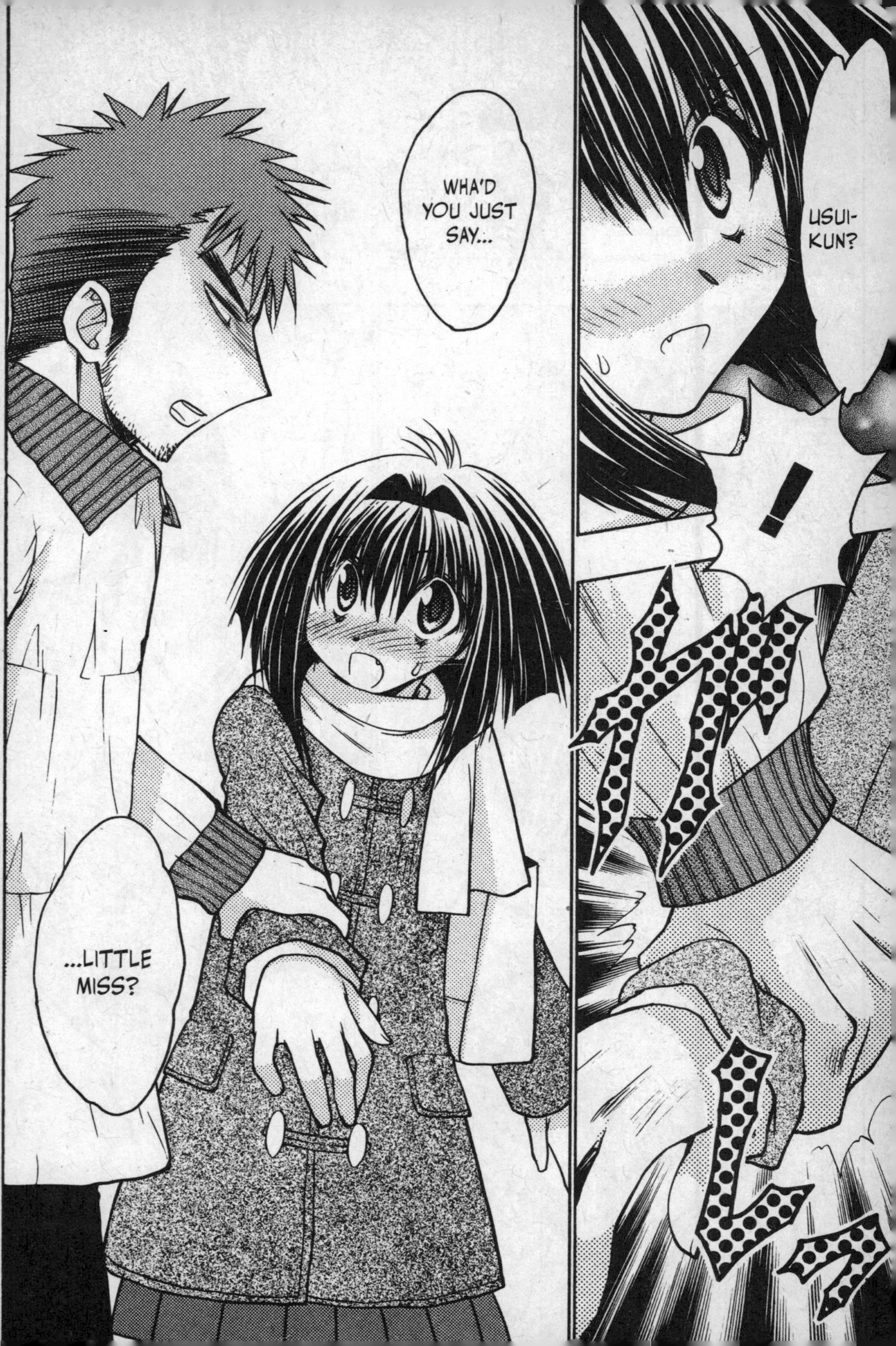
USUI-KUN?
!
WHA'D YOU JUST SAY...
...LITTLE MISS?

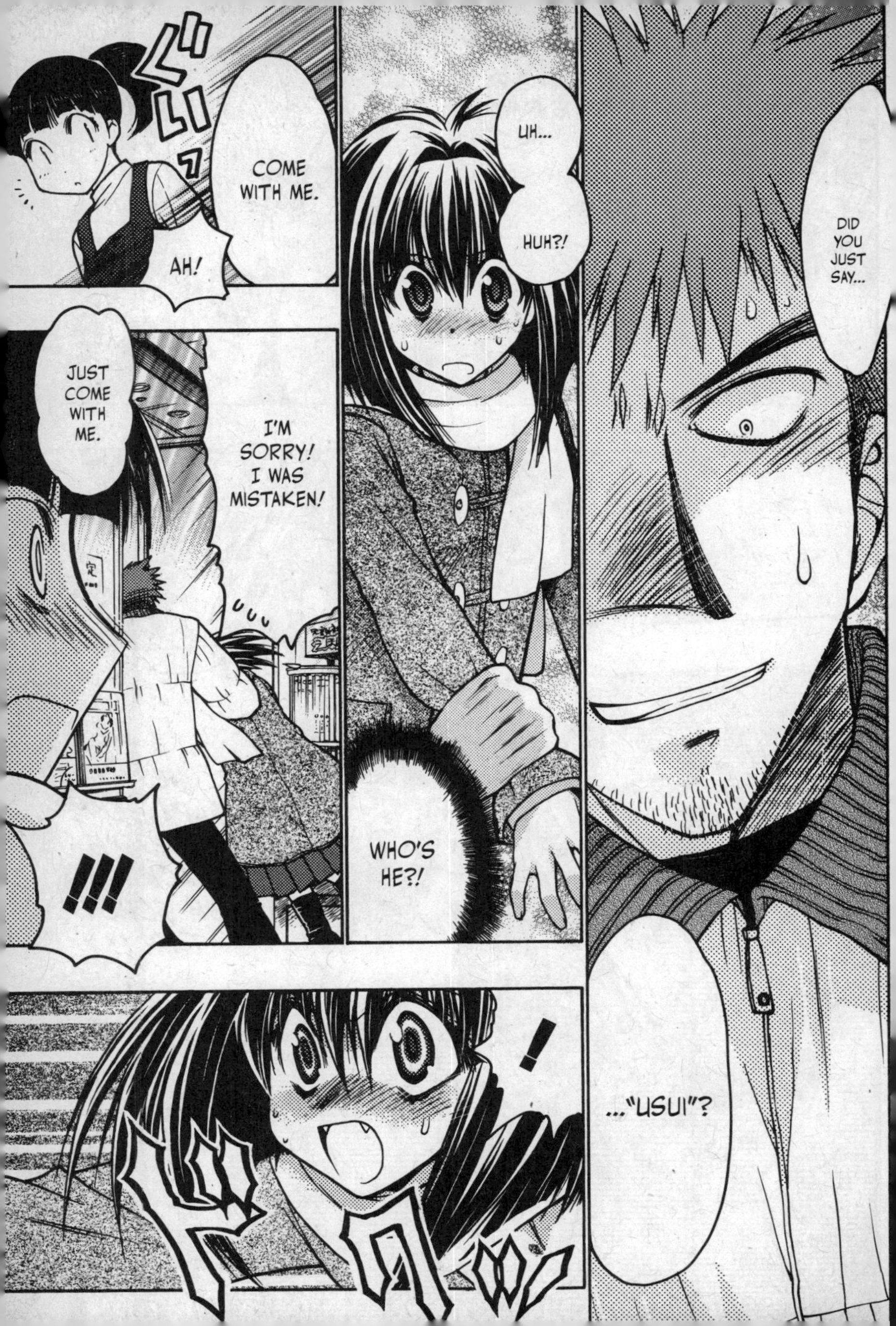
DID YOU JUST SAY...
..."USUI"?
UH...
HUH?!
WHO'S HE?!
COME WITH ME.
AH!
JUST COME WITH ME.
I'M SORRY! I WAS MISTAKEN!
!!!
!

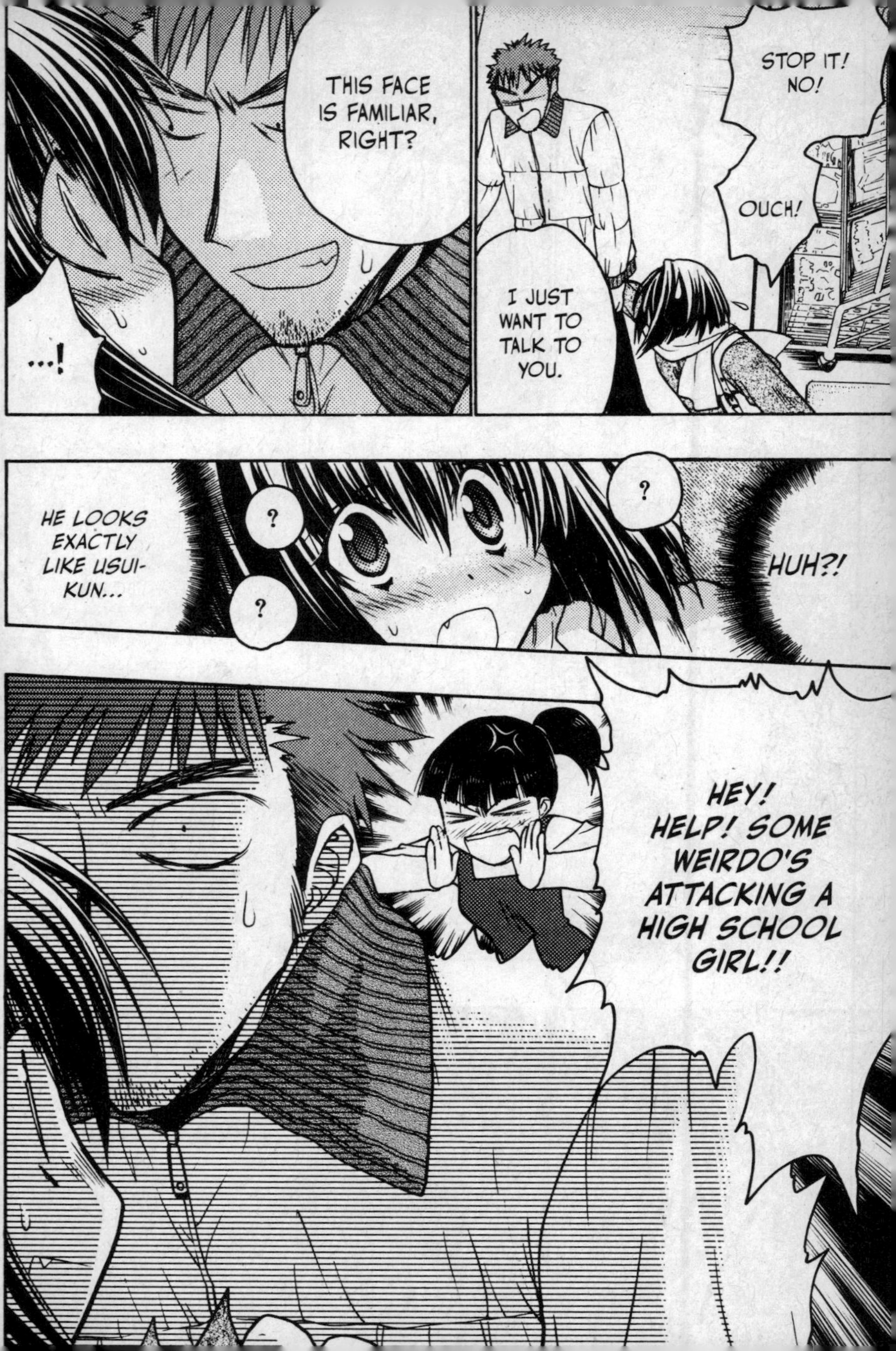
STOP IT! NO!
OUCH!
I JUST WANT TO TALK TO YOU.
THIS FACE IS FAMILIAR, RIGHT?
...!
?
?
?
HUH?!
HE LOOKS EXACTLY LIKE USUI-KUN...
HEY! HELP! SOME WEIRDO'S ATTACKING A HIGH SCHOOL GIRL!!

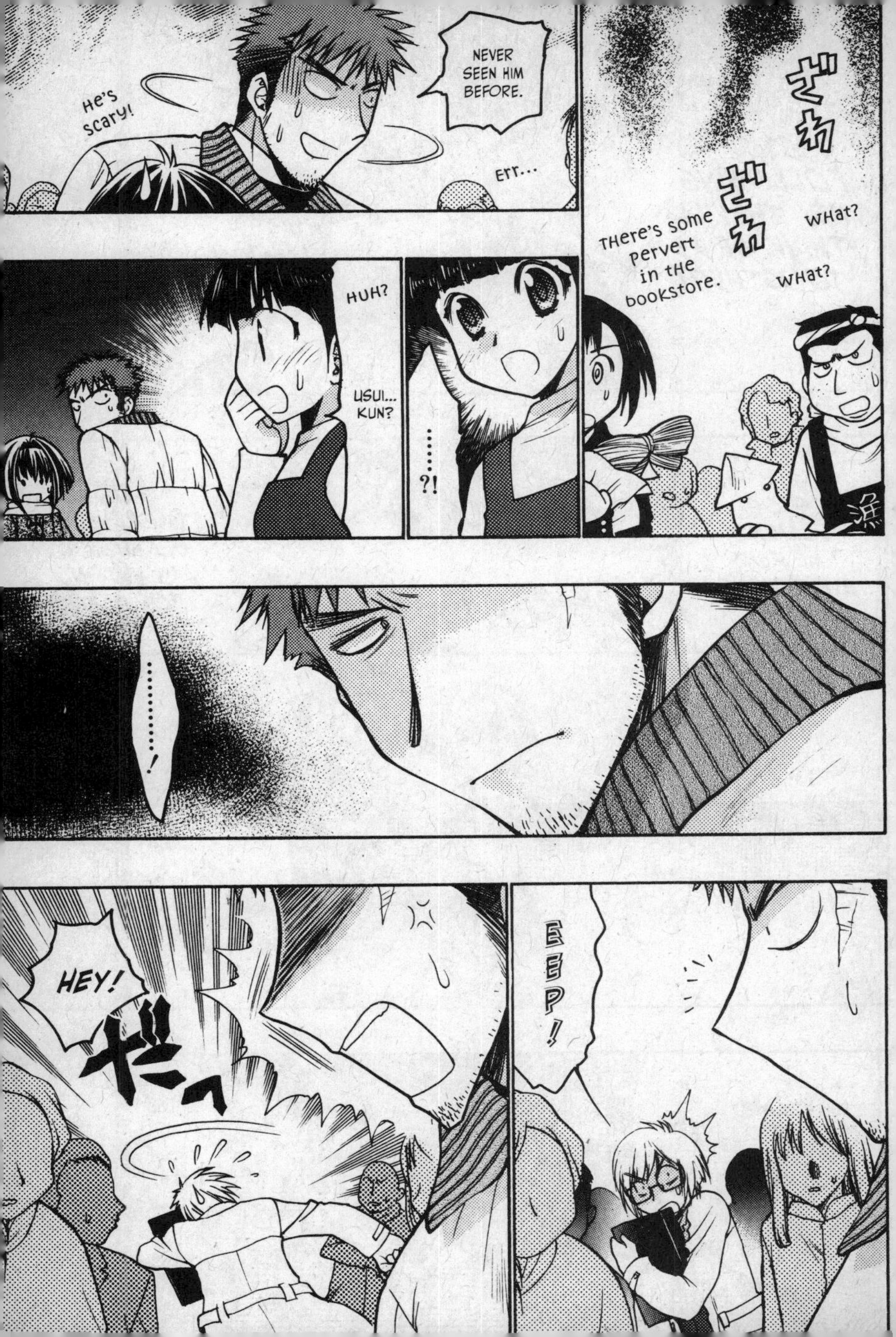

ざわ
ざわ
What?
There's some pervert in the bookstore.
What?
Never seen him before.
Err...
He's scary!
……?!
Huh?
Usui... kun?
……!
EEP!
HEY!

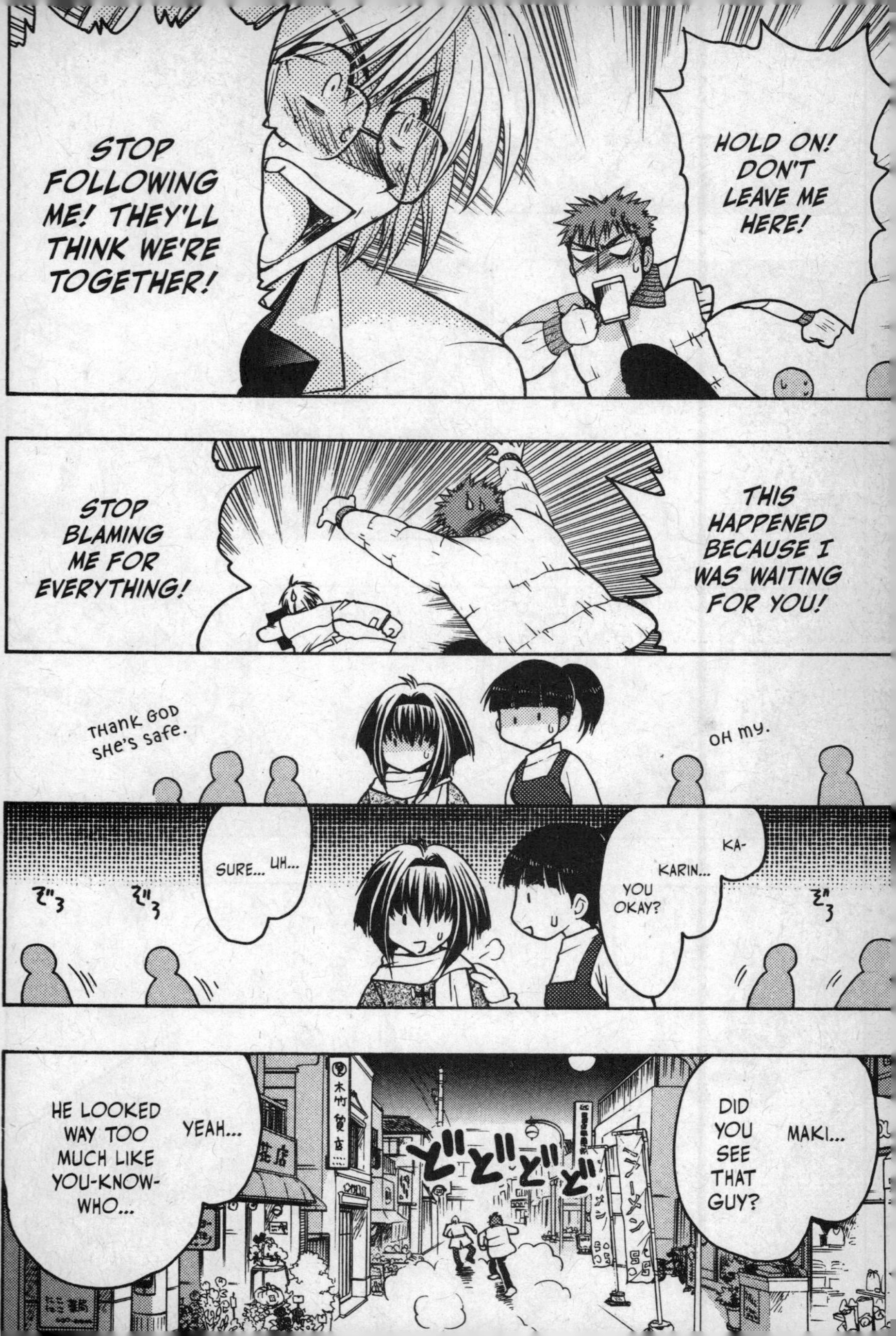
HOLD ON! DON'T LEAVE ME HERE!
STOP FOLLOWING ME! THEY'LL THINK WE'RE TOGETHER!
THIS HAPPENED BECAUSE I WAS WAITING FOR YOU!
STOP BLAMING ME FOR EVERYTHING!
OH MY.
THANK GOD SHE'S SAFE.
KA- KARIN... YOU OKAY?
SURE... UH...
MAKI... DID YOU SEE THAT GUY?
YEAH... HE LOOKED WAY TOO MUCH LIKE YOU-KNOW-WHO...
どどどど

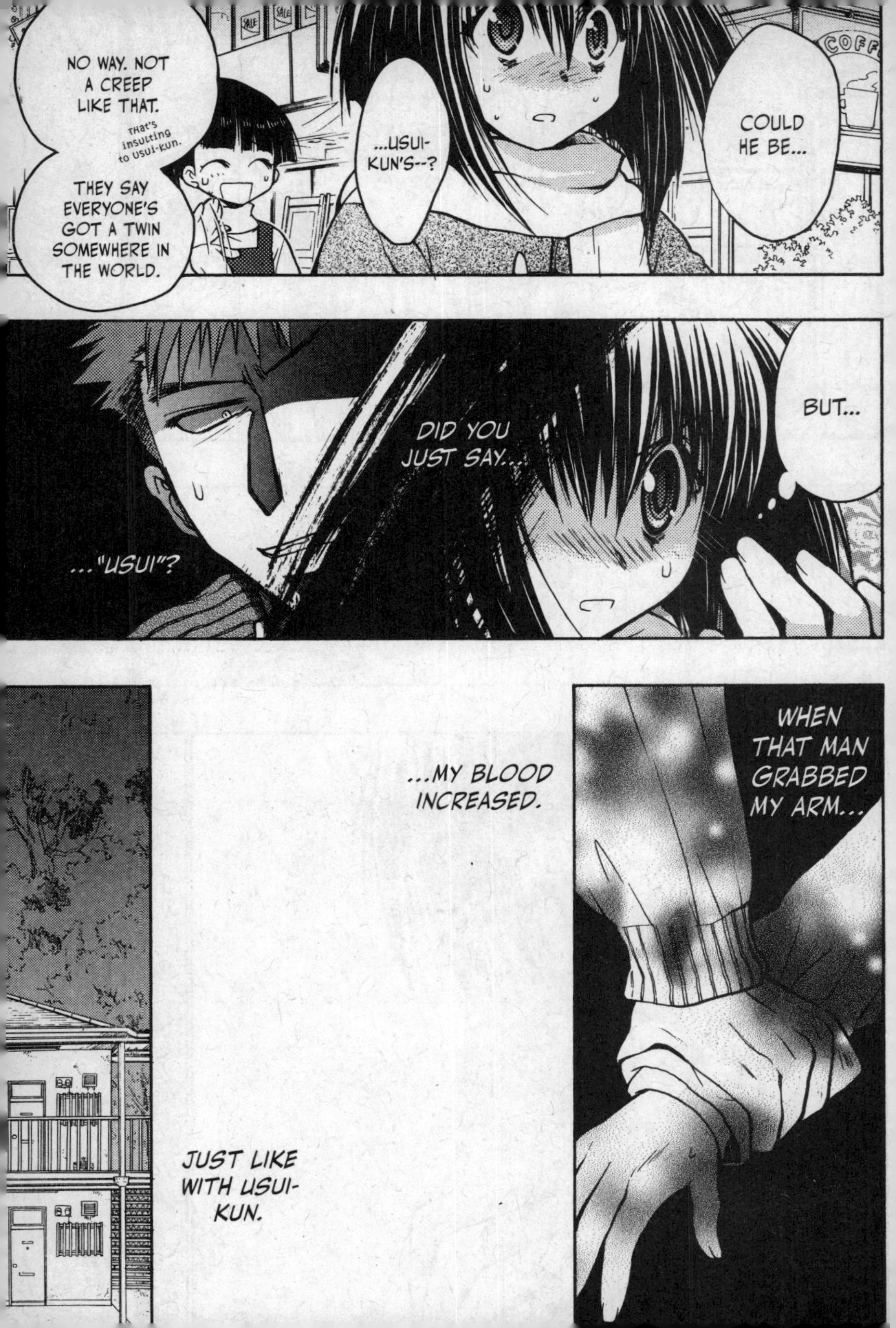
COULD HE BE...
...USUI-KUN'S--?
NO WAY. NOT A CREEP LIKE THAT.
That's insulting to Usui-kun.
THEY SAY EVERYONE'S GOT A TWIN SOMEWHERE IN THE WORLD.
BUT...
DID YOU JUST SAY...
..."USUI"?
WHEN THAT MAN GRABBED MY ARM...
...MY BLOOD INCREASED.
JUST LIKE WITH USUI-KUN.

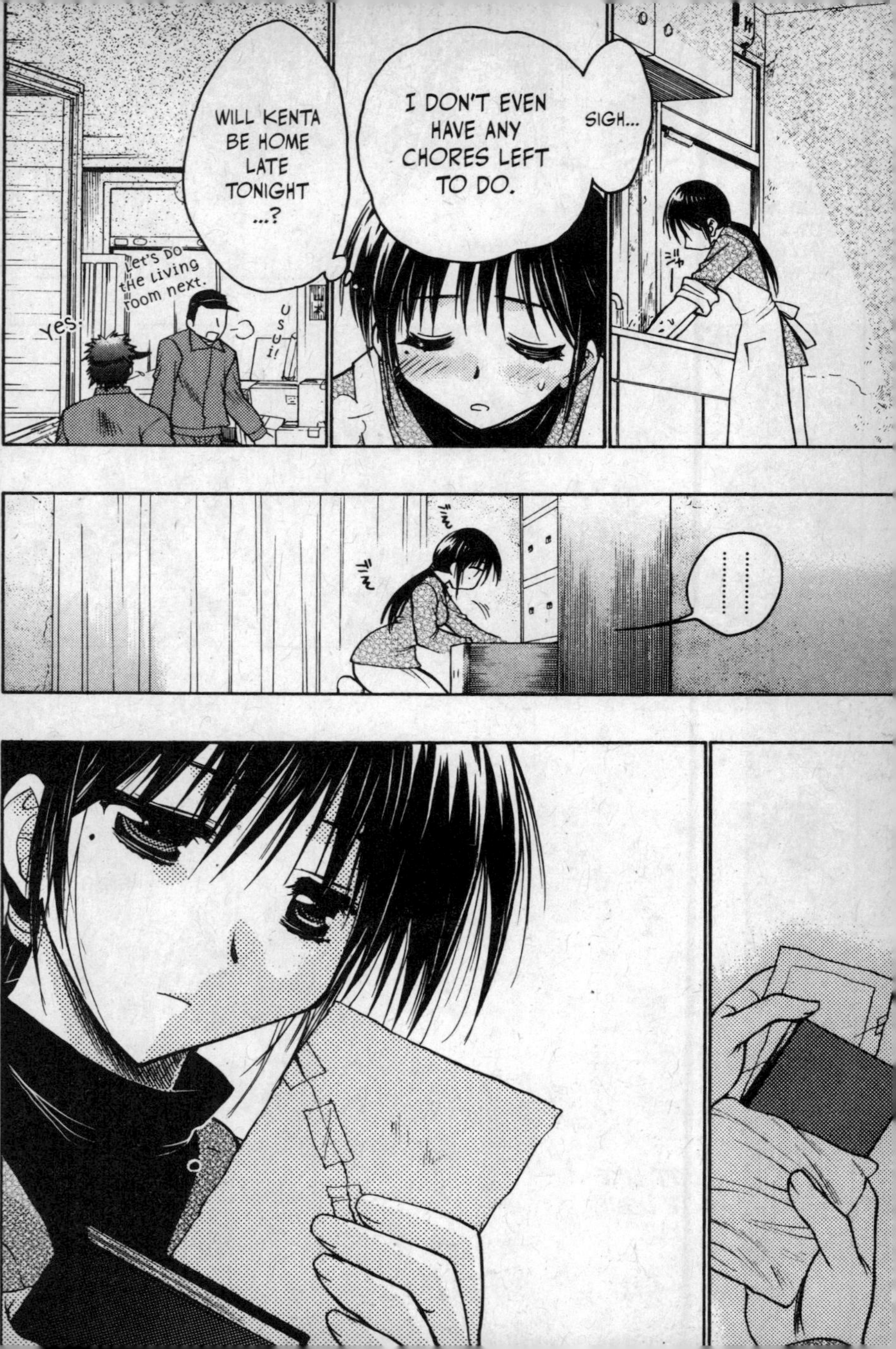
SIGH...
ジャ
I DON'T EVEN HAVE ANY CHORES LEFT TO DO.
WILL KENTA BE HOME LATE TONIGHT ...?
Let's do the living room next.
USUI!
Yes.
......

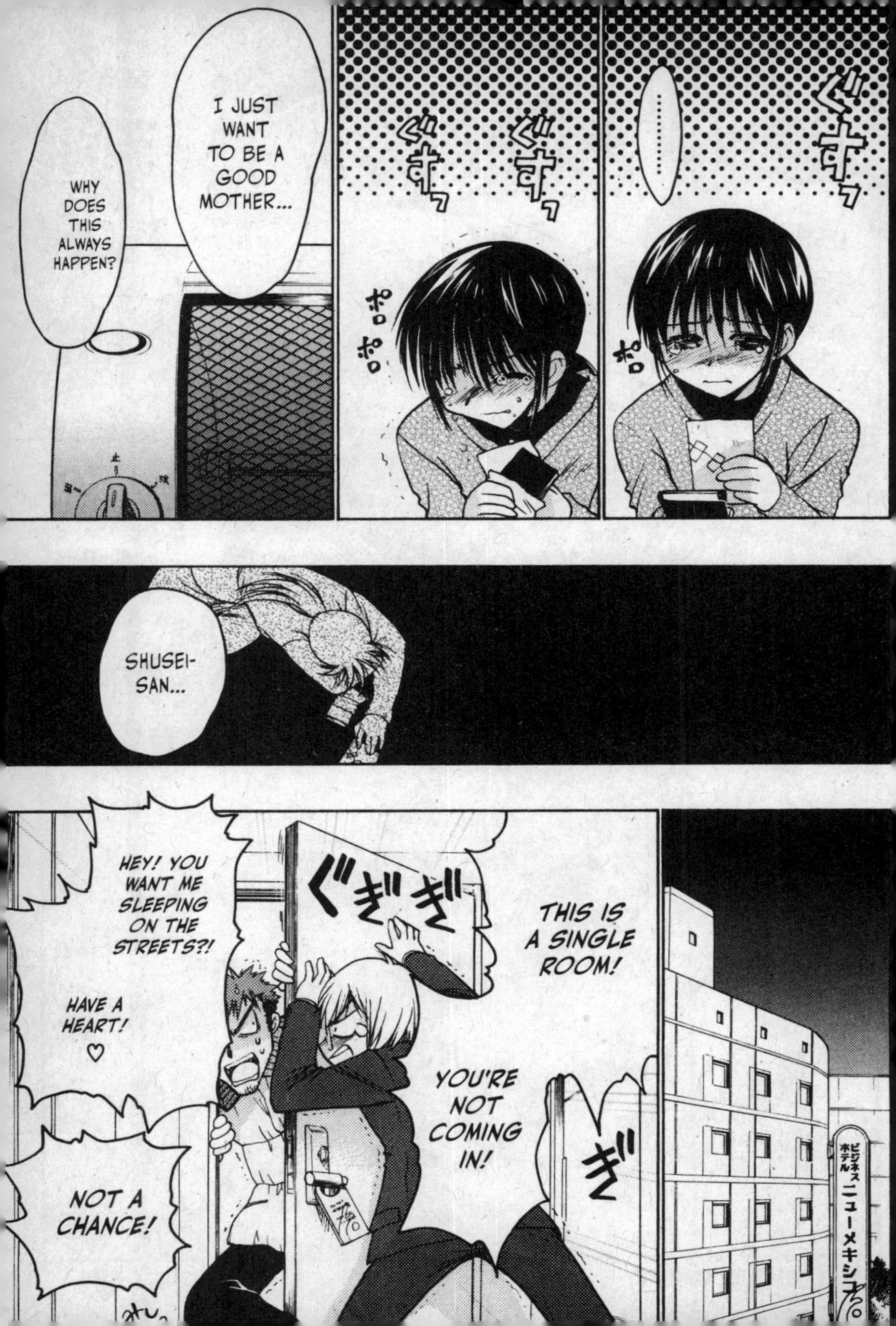

ぐすっ
......
ポロ
ぐすっ
ぐすっ
ポロポロ
I JUST WANT TO BE A GOOD MOTHER...
WHY DOES THIS ALWAYS HAPPEN?
SHUSEI-SAN...
ビジネスホテル ニューメキシコ
THIS IS A SINGLE ROOM!
ぐぎぎ
HEY! YOU WANT ME SLEEPING ON THE STREETS?!
YOU'RE NOT COMING IN!
ぎ
HAVE A HEART! ♡
NOT A CHANCE!

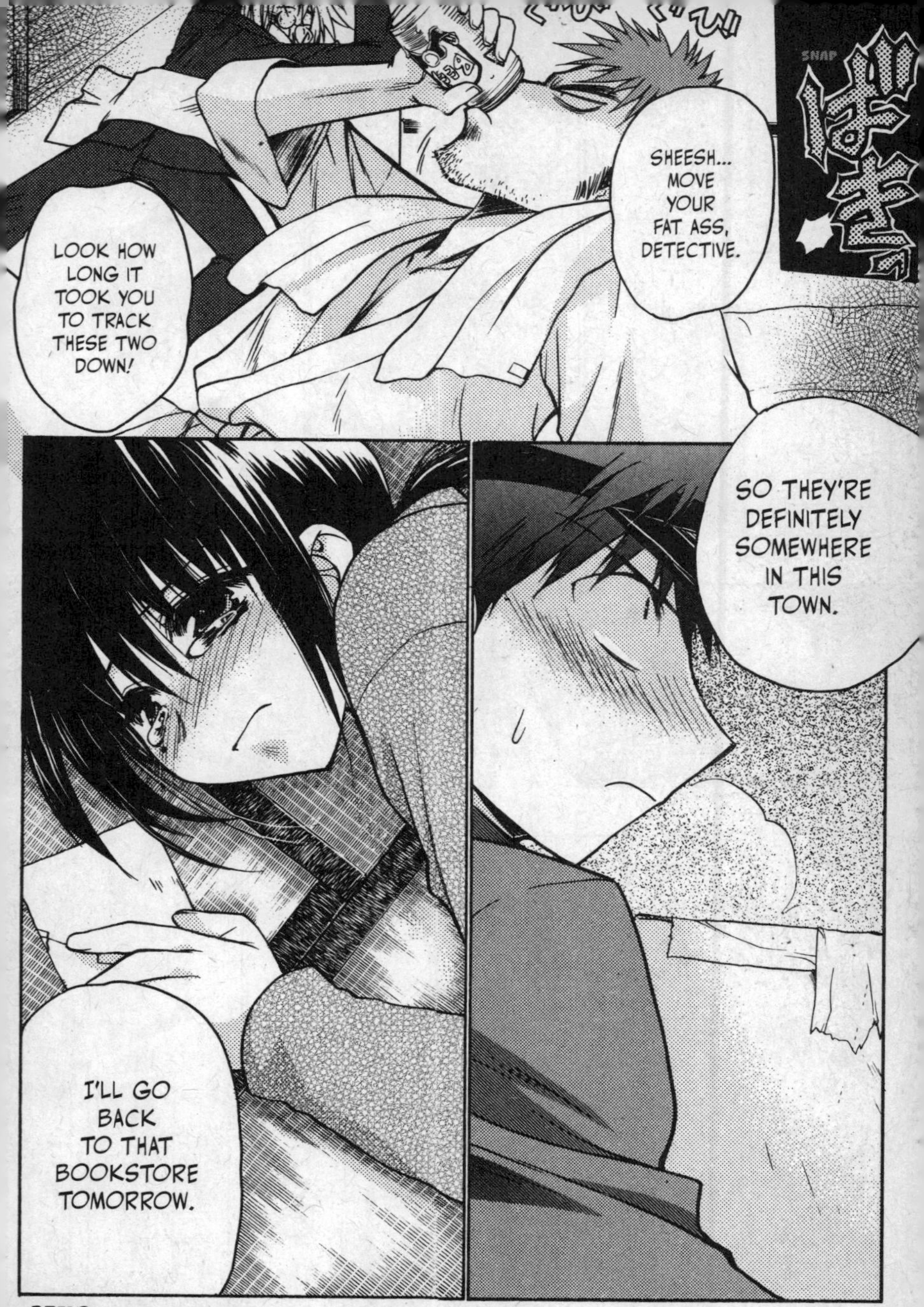
SNAP
SHEESH... MOVE YOUR FAT ASS, DETECTIVE.
LOOK HOW LONG IT TOOK YOU TO TRACK THESE TWO DOWN!
SO THEY'RE DEFINITELY SOMEWHERE IN THIS TOWN.
I'LL GO BACK TO THAT BOOKSTORE TOMORROW.

23RD EMBARRASSMENT

END

24th Embarrassment) Usui-kun's Panic and Fumio's Unrest
~ Embarrassment ~

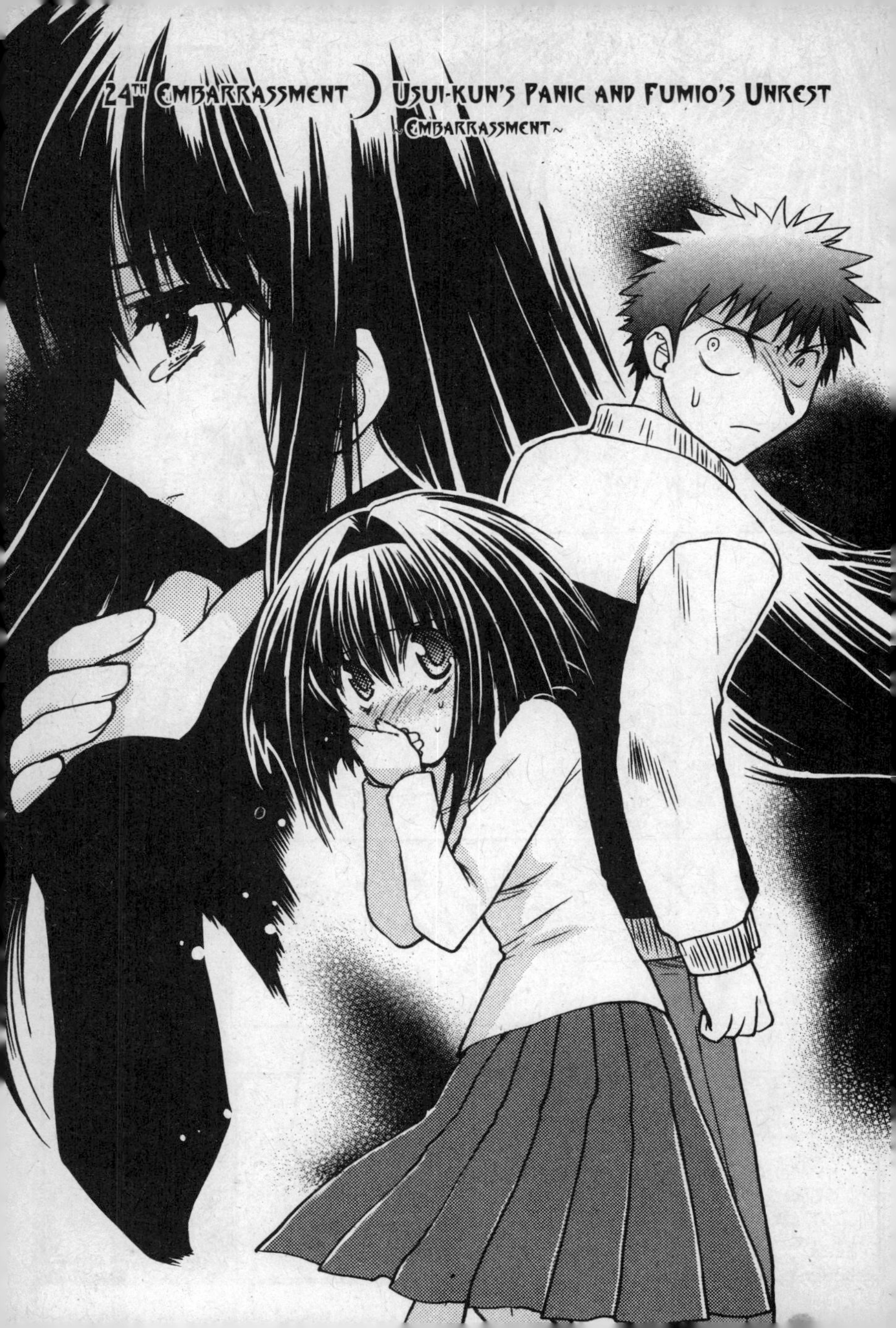

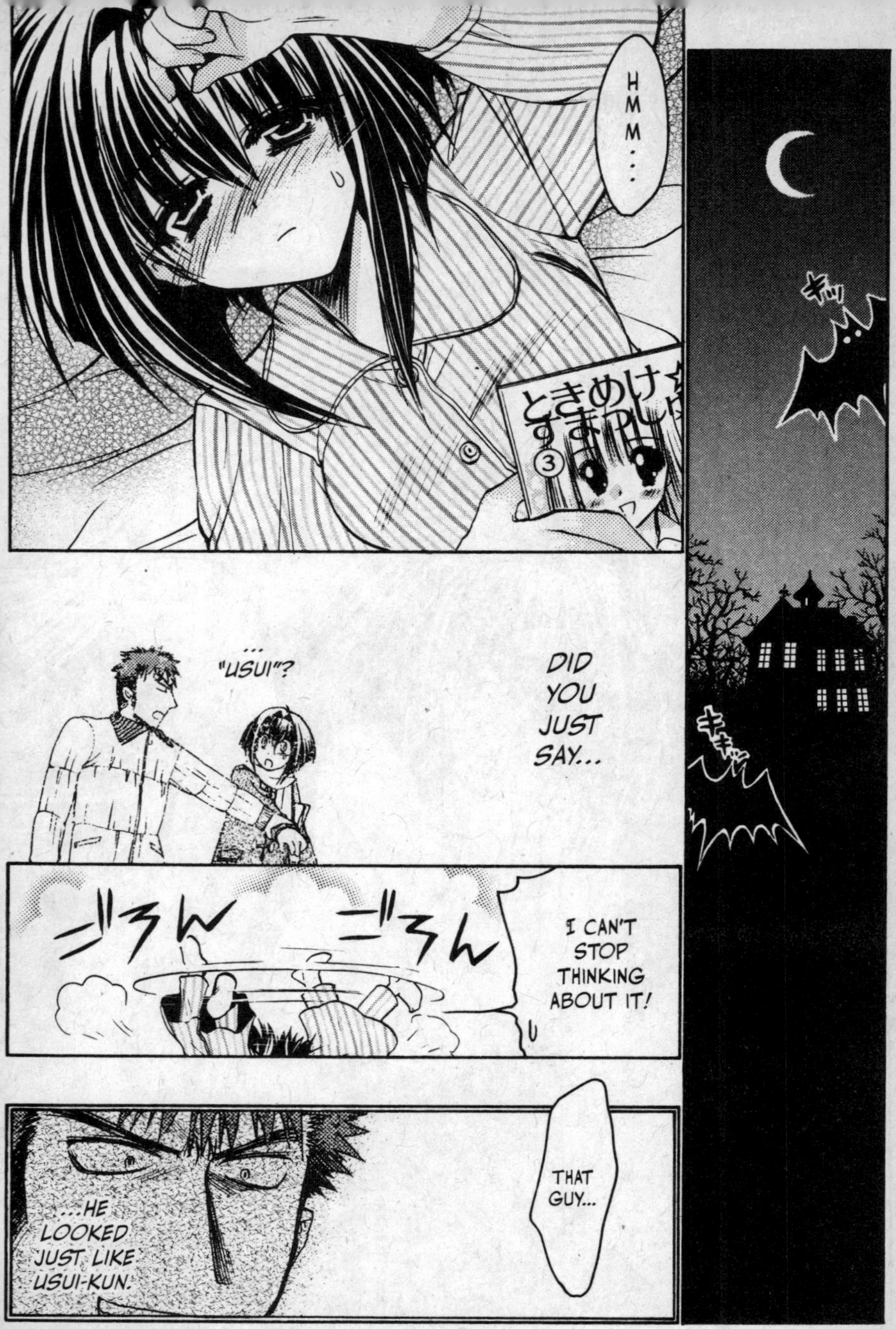
HMM...
DID YOU JUST SAY...
... "USUI"?
I CAN'T STOP THINKING ABOUT IT!
ごろん
ごろん
THAT GUY...
...HE LOOKED JUST LIKE USUI-KUN.

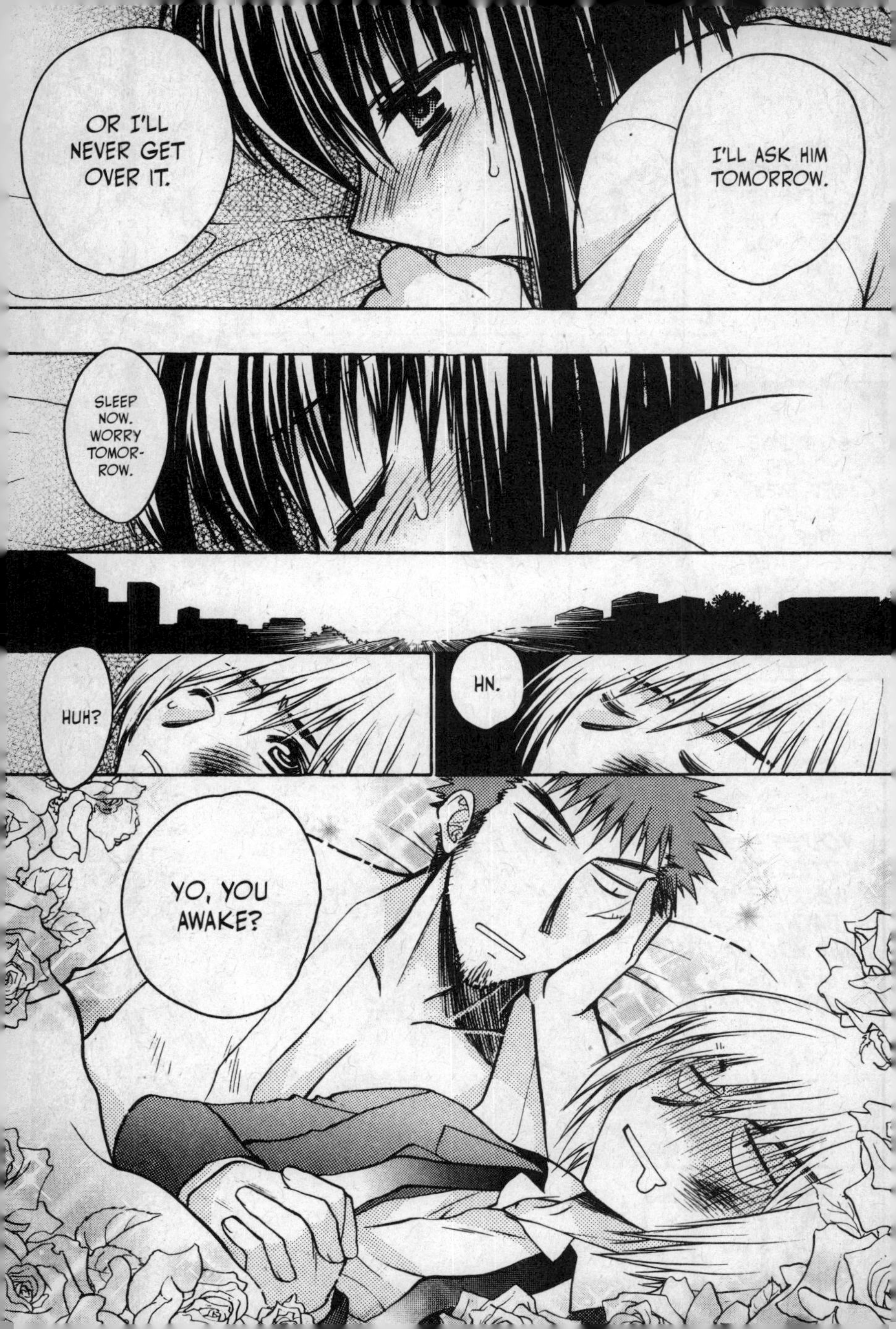
I'LL ASK HIM TOMORROW.
OR I'LL NEVER GET OVER IT.
SLEEP NOW. WORRY TOMOR-ROW.
HN.
HUH?
YO, YOU AWAKE?

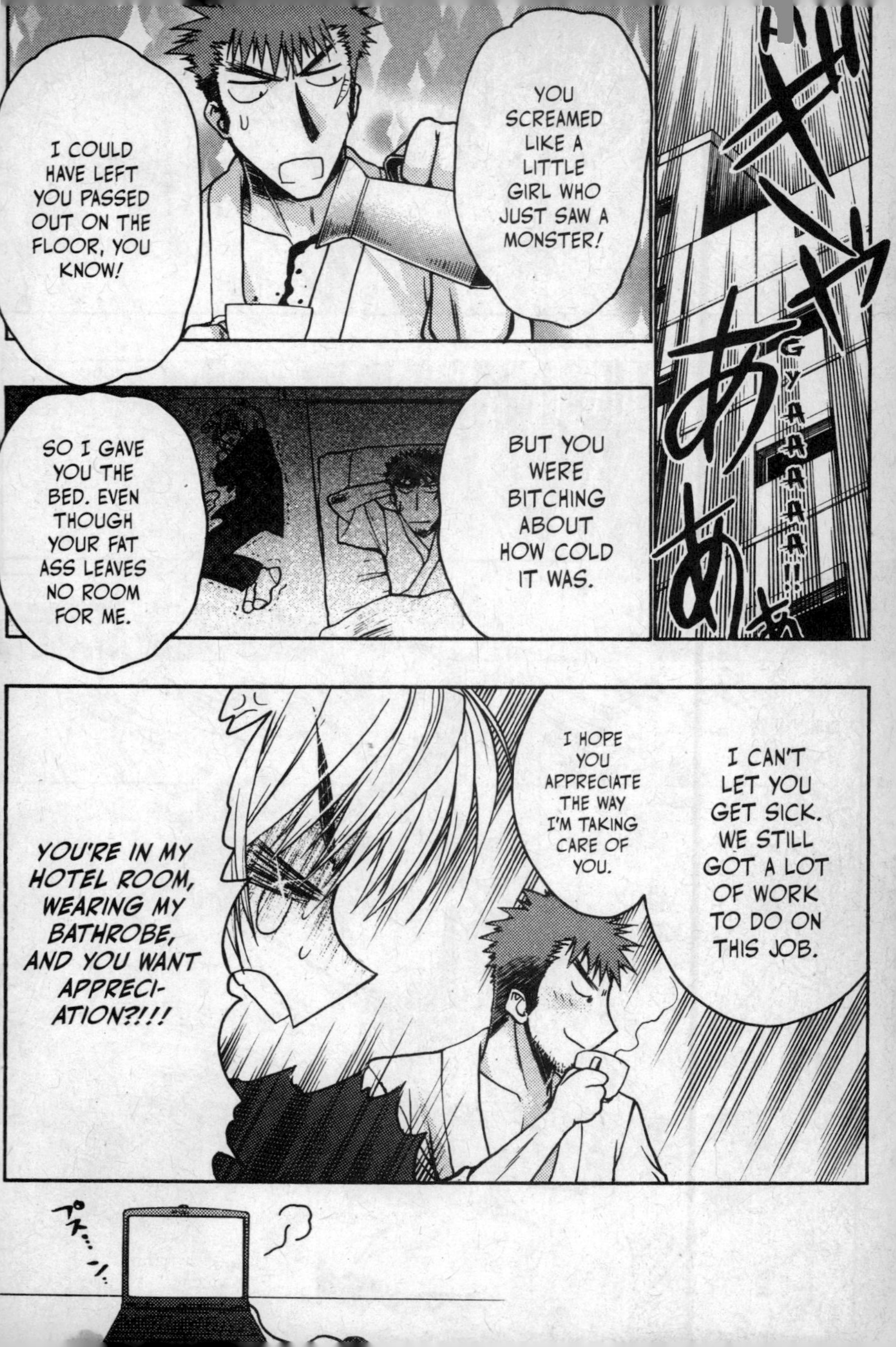
ぎゃああ
GYAAAAAA!!
YOU SCREAMED LIKE A LITTLE GIRL WHO JUST SAW A MONSTER!
I COULD HAVE LEFT YOU PASSED OUT ON THE FLOOR, YOU KNOW!
BUT YOU WERE BITCHING ABOUT HOW COLD IT WAS.
SO I GAVE YOU THE BED. EVEN THOUGH YOUR FAT ASS LEAVES NO ROOM FOR ME.
I CAN'T LET YOU GET SICK. WE STILL GOT A LOT OF WORK TO DO ON THIS JOB.
I HOPE YOU APPRECIATE THE WAY I'M TAKING CARE OF YOU.
YOU'RE IN MY HOTEL ROOM, WEARING MY BATHROBE, AND YOU WANT APPRECIATION?!!!
プス…ーン!

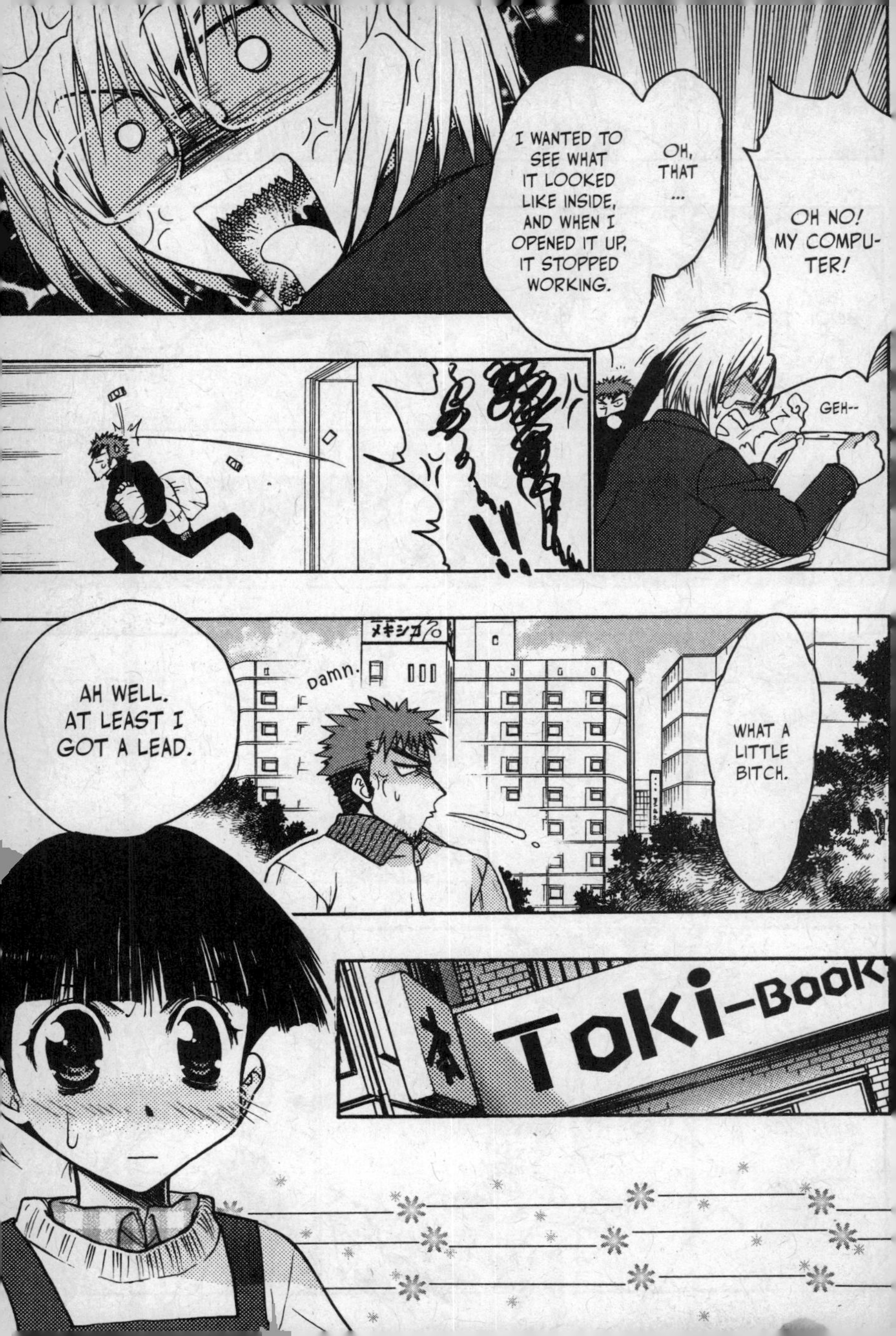
OH NO! MY COMPUTER!
OH, THAT ...
I WANTED TO SEE WHAT IT LOOKED LIKE INSIDE, AND WHEN I OPENED IT UP, IT STOPPED WORKING.
GEH--
WHAT A LITTLE BITCH.
Damn.
AH WELL. AT LEAST I GOT A LEAD.
Toki-Book

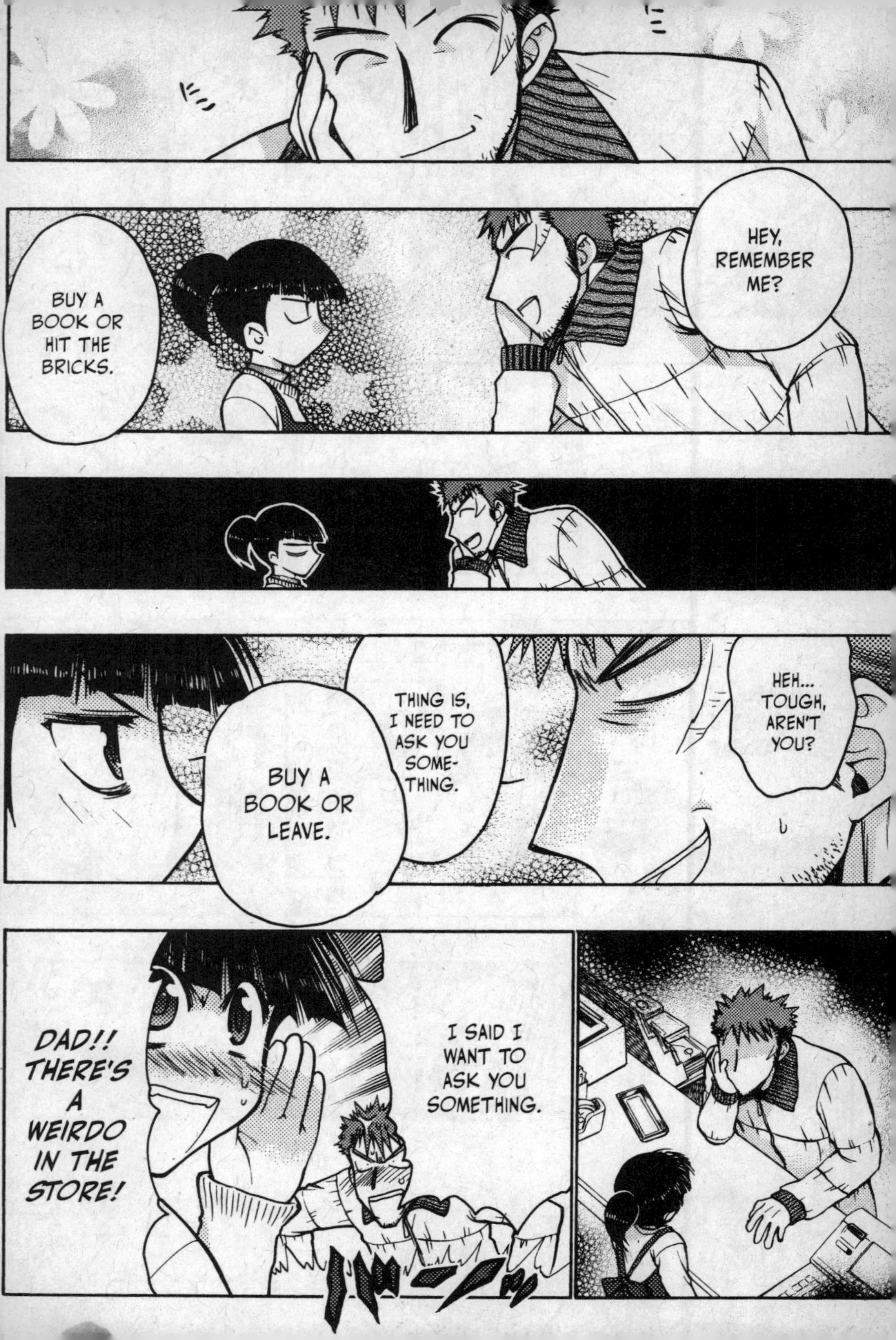
HEY, REMEMBER ME?
BUY A BOOK OR HIT THE BRICKS.
HEH... TOUGH, AREN'T YOU?
THING IS, I NEED TO ASK YOU SOME-THING.
BUY A BOOK OR LEAVE.
I SAID I WANT TO ASK YOU SOMETHING.
DAD!! THERE'S A WEIRDO IN THE STORE!

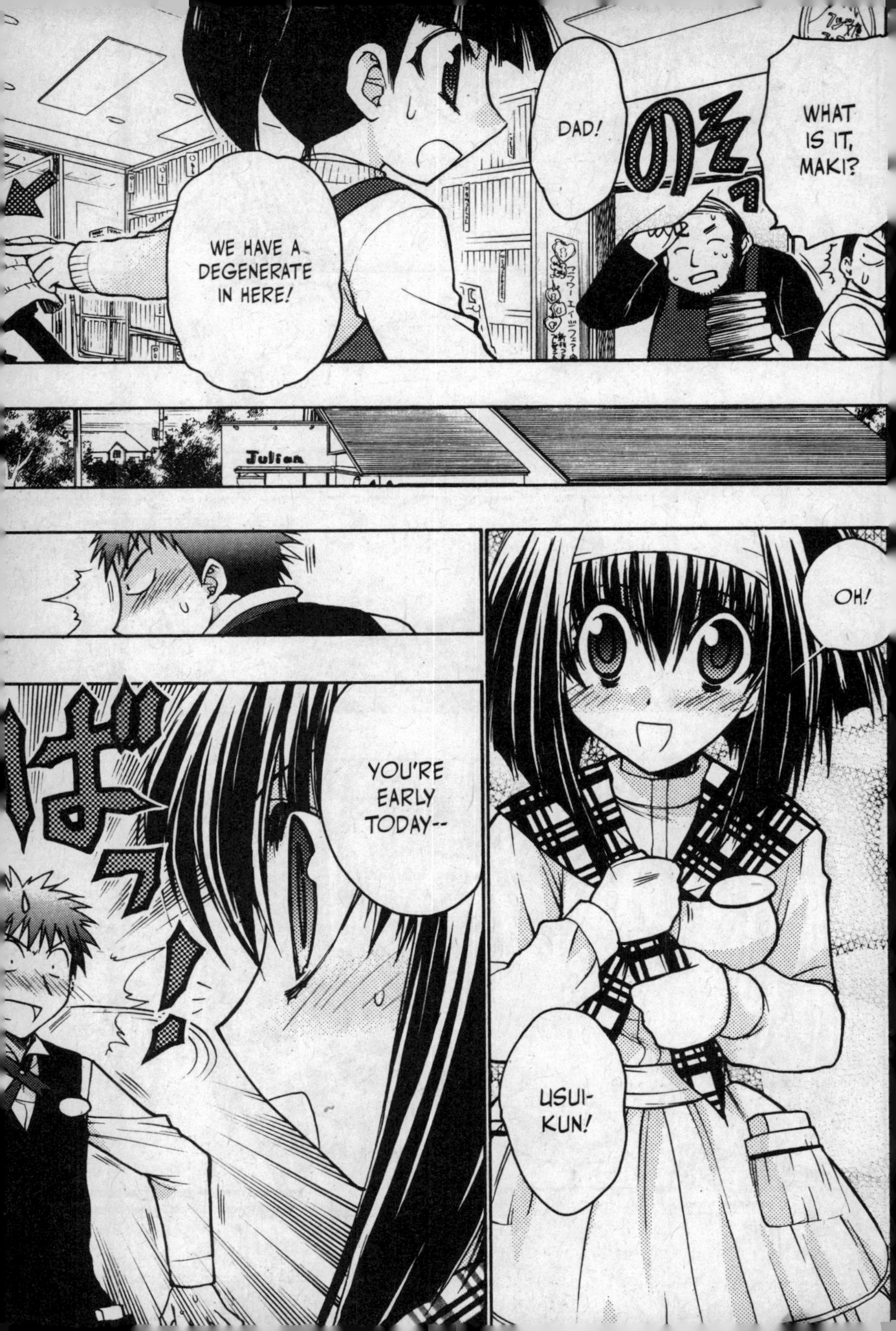
DAD!
WHAT IS IT, MAKI?
WE HAVE A DEGENERATE IN HERE!
Julian
OH!
USUI-KUN!
YOU'RE EARLY TODAY--

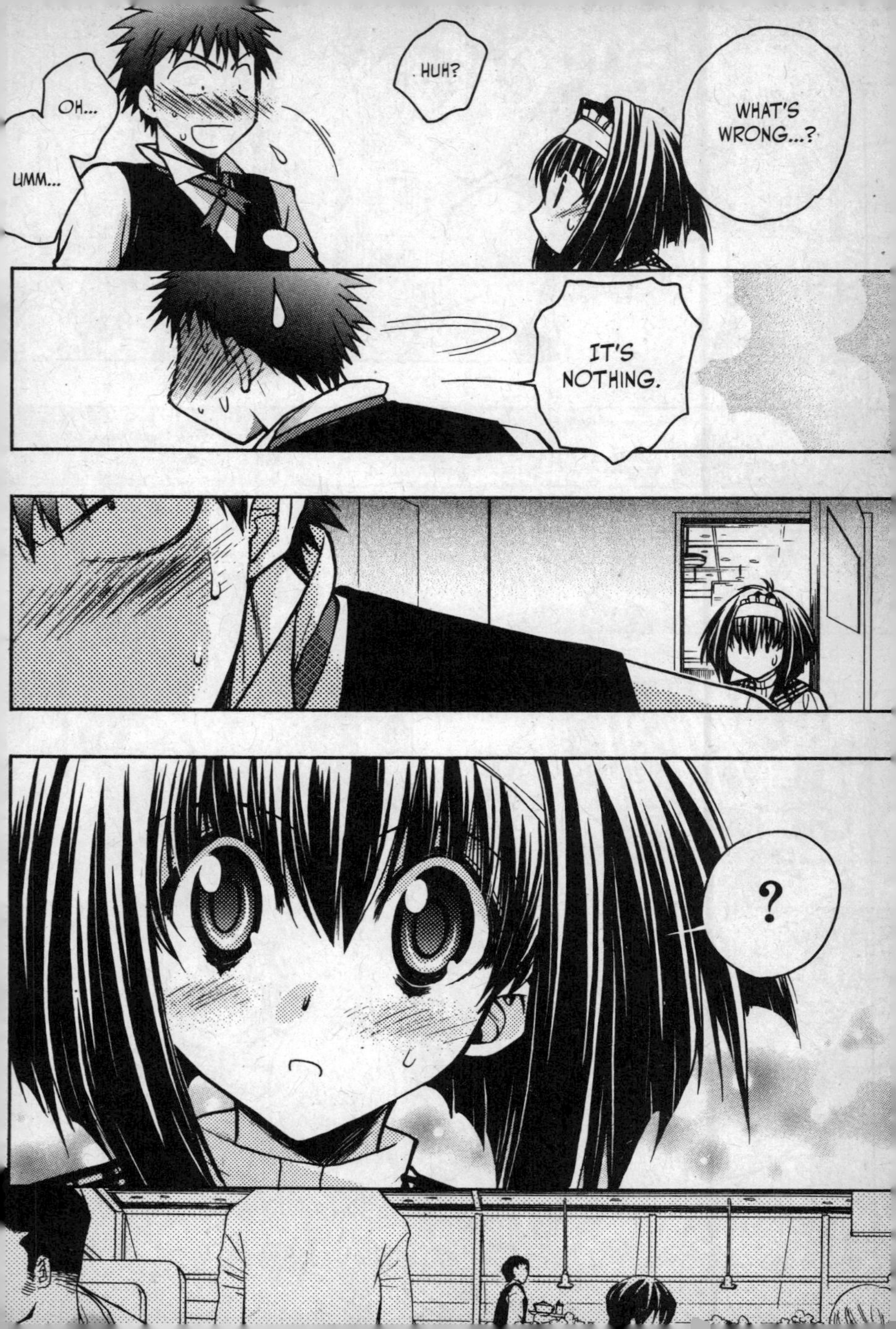
WHAT'S WRONG...?
HUH?
OH...
UMM...
IT'S NOTHING.
?

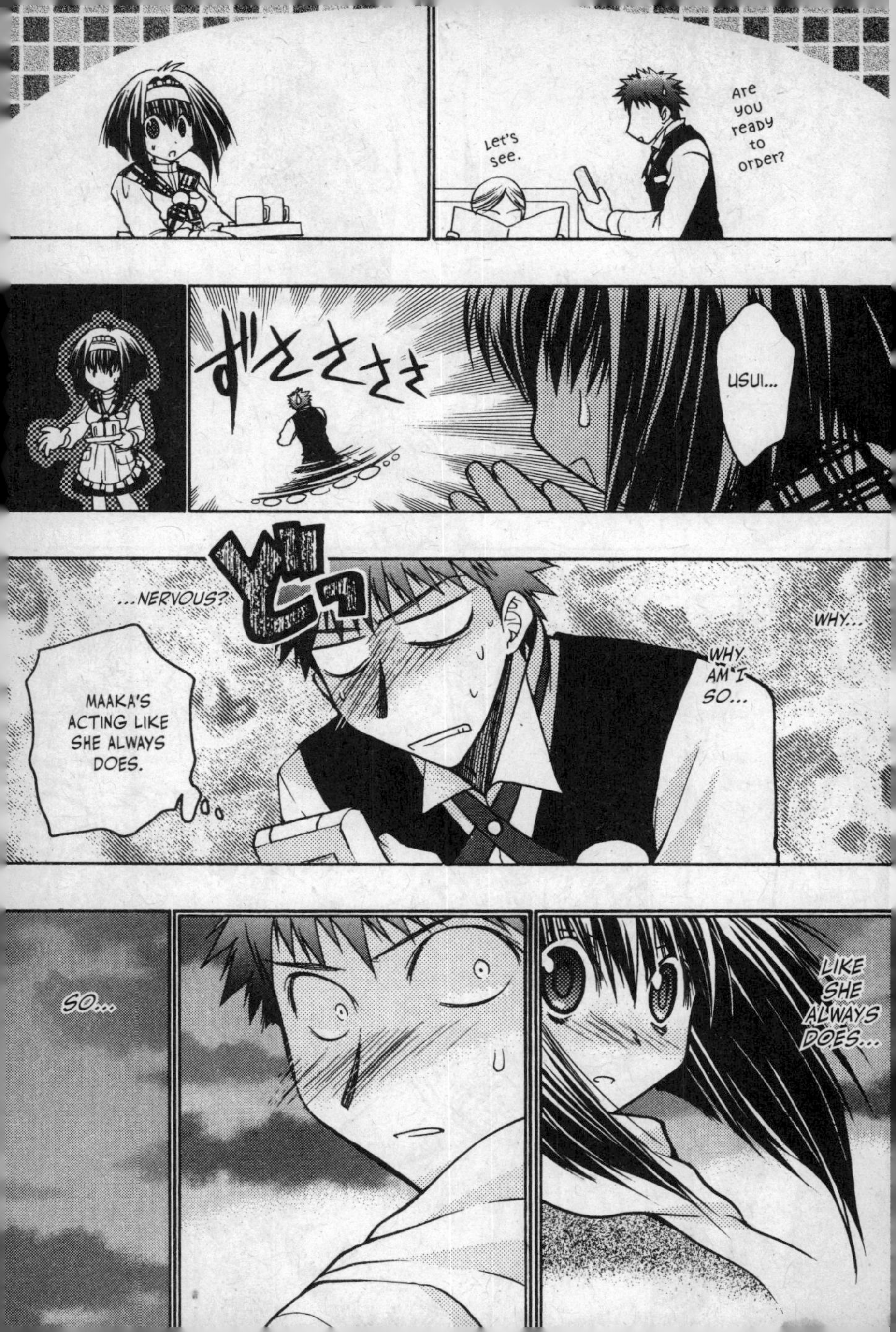
Are you ready to order?
Let's see.
USUI...
ずささささ
WHY...
WHY AM I SO...
...NERVOUS?
MAAKA'S ACTING LIKE SHE ALWAYS DOES.
LIKE SHE ALWAYS DOES...
SO...

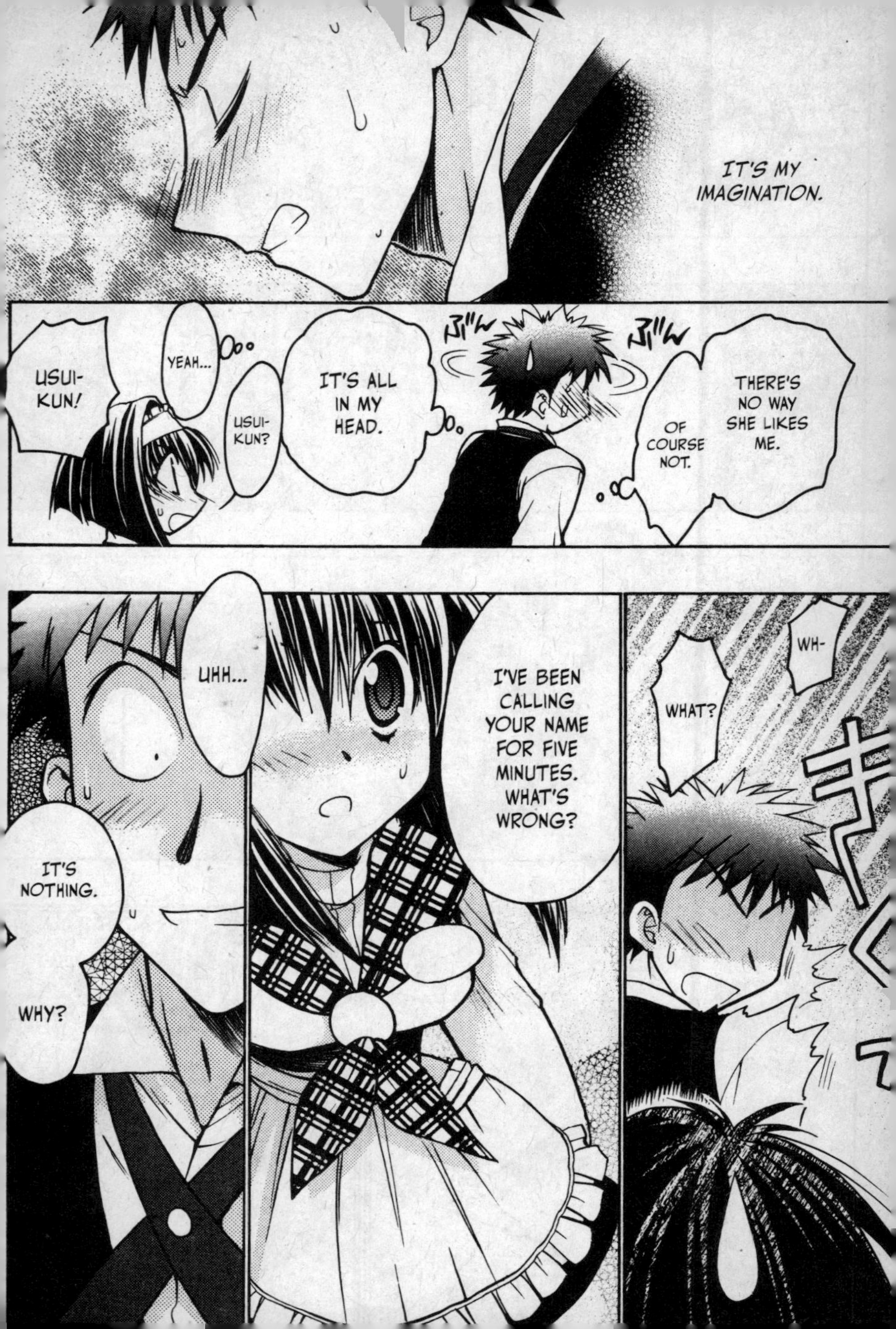
IT'S MY IMAGINATION.
THERE'S NO WAY SHE LIKES ME.
OF COURSE NOT.
IT'S ALL IN MY HEAD.
USUI-KUN?
YEAH...
USUI-KUN!
WH-
WHAT?
I'VE BEEN CALLING YOUR NAME FOR FIVE MINUTES. WHAT'S WRONG?
UHH...
IT'S NOTHING.
WHY?

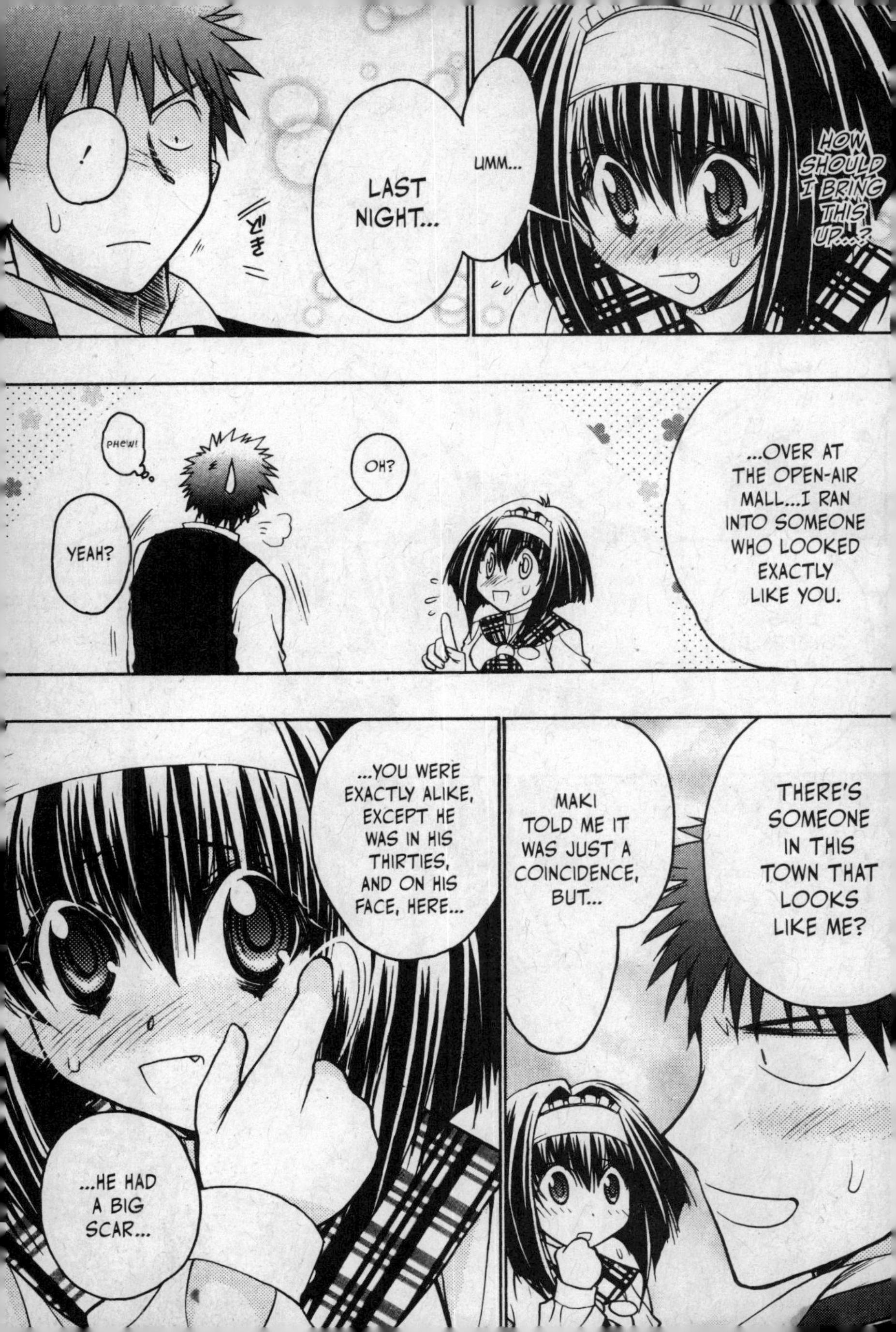
HOW SHOULD I BRING THIS UP...?
UMM...
LAST NIGHT...
!
どき
...OVER AT THE OPEN-AIR MALL...I RAN INTO SOMEONE WHO LOOKED EXACTLY LIKE YOU.
OH?
PHEW!
YEAH?
THERE'S SOMEONE IN THIS TOWN THAT LOOKS LIKE ME?
MAKI TOLD ME IT WAS JUST A COINCIDENCE, BUT...
...YOU WERE EXACTLY ALIKE, EXCEPT HE WAS IN HIS THIRTIES, AND ON HIS FACE, HERE...
...HE HAD A BIG SCAR...

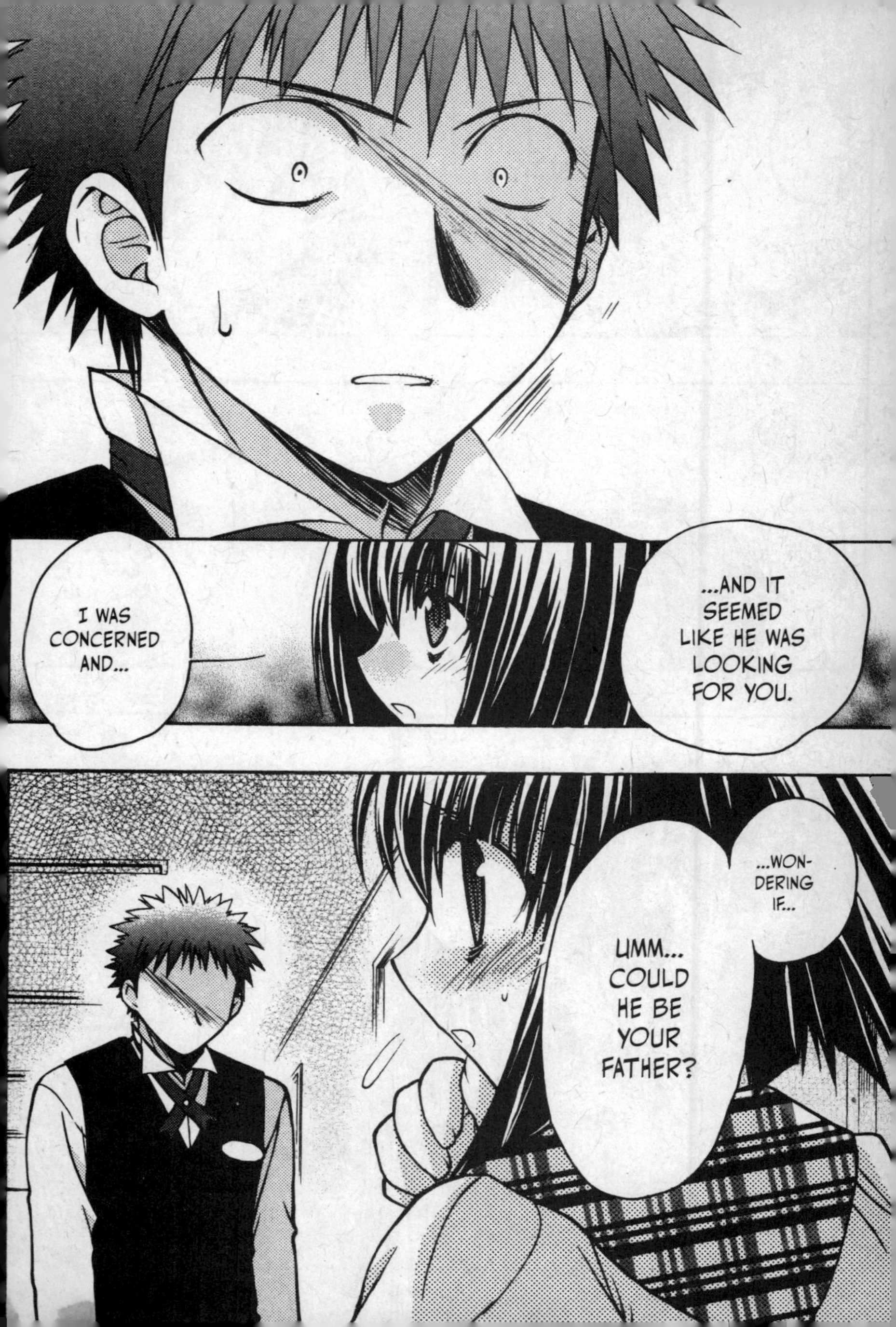
...AND IT SEEMED LIKE HE WAS LOOKING FOR YOU.
I WAS CONCERNED AND...
...WON-DERING IF...
UMM... COULD HE BE YOUR FATHER?

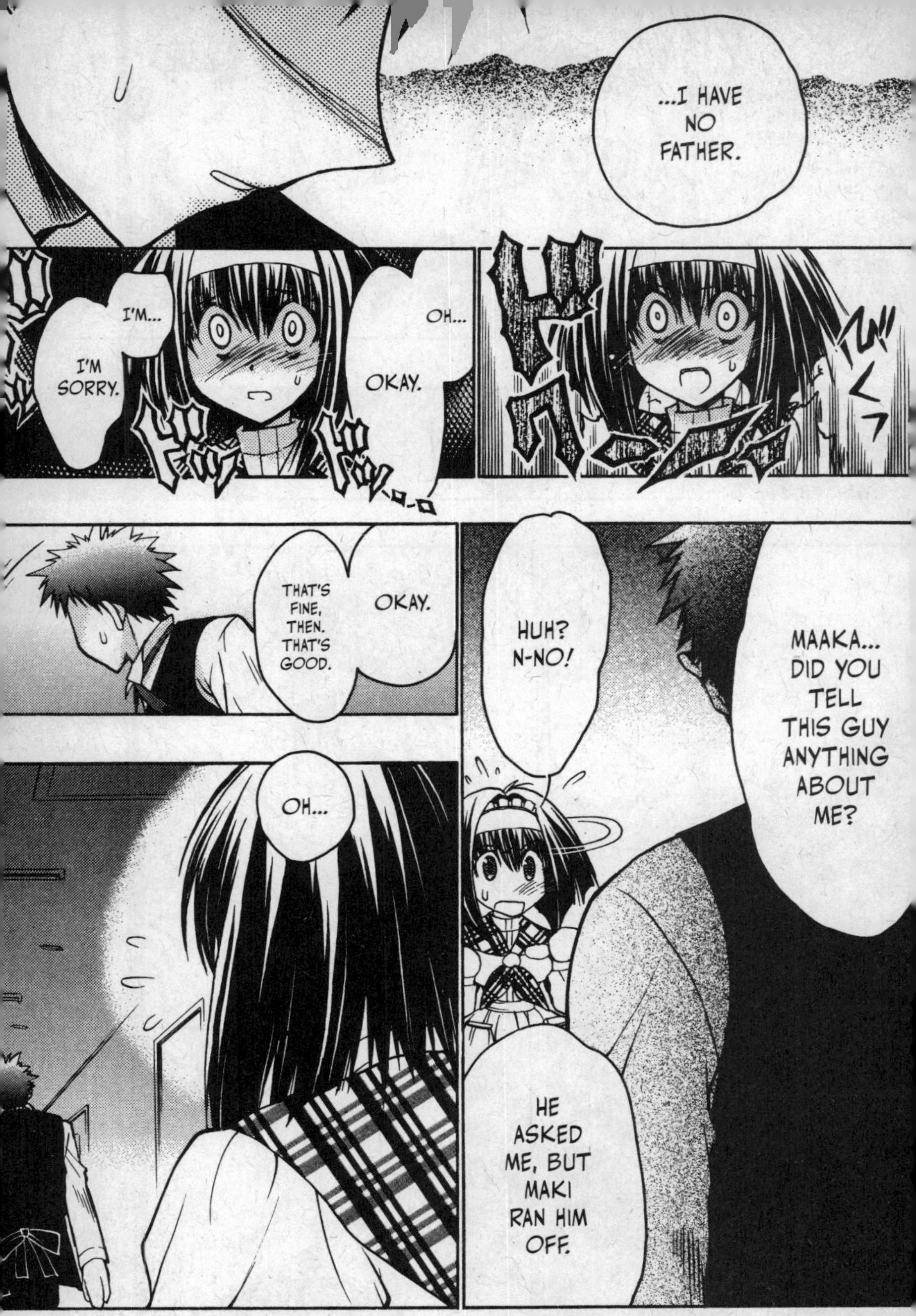
...I HAVE NO FATHER.
OH...
OKAY.
I'M...
I'M SORRY.
MAAKA... DID YOU TELL THIS GUY ANYTHING ABOUT ME?
HUH? N-NO!
HE ASKED ME, BUT MAKI RAN HIM OFF.
OKAY.
THAT'S FINE, THEN. THAT'S GOOD.
OH...

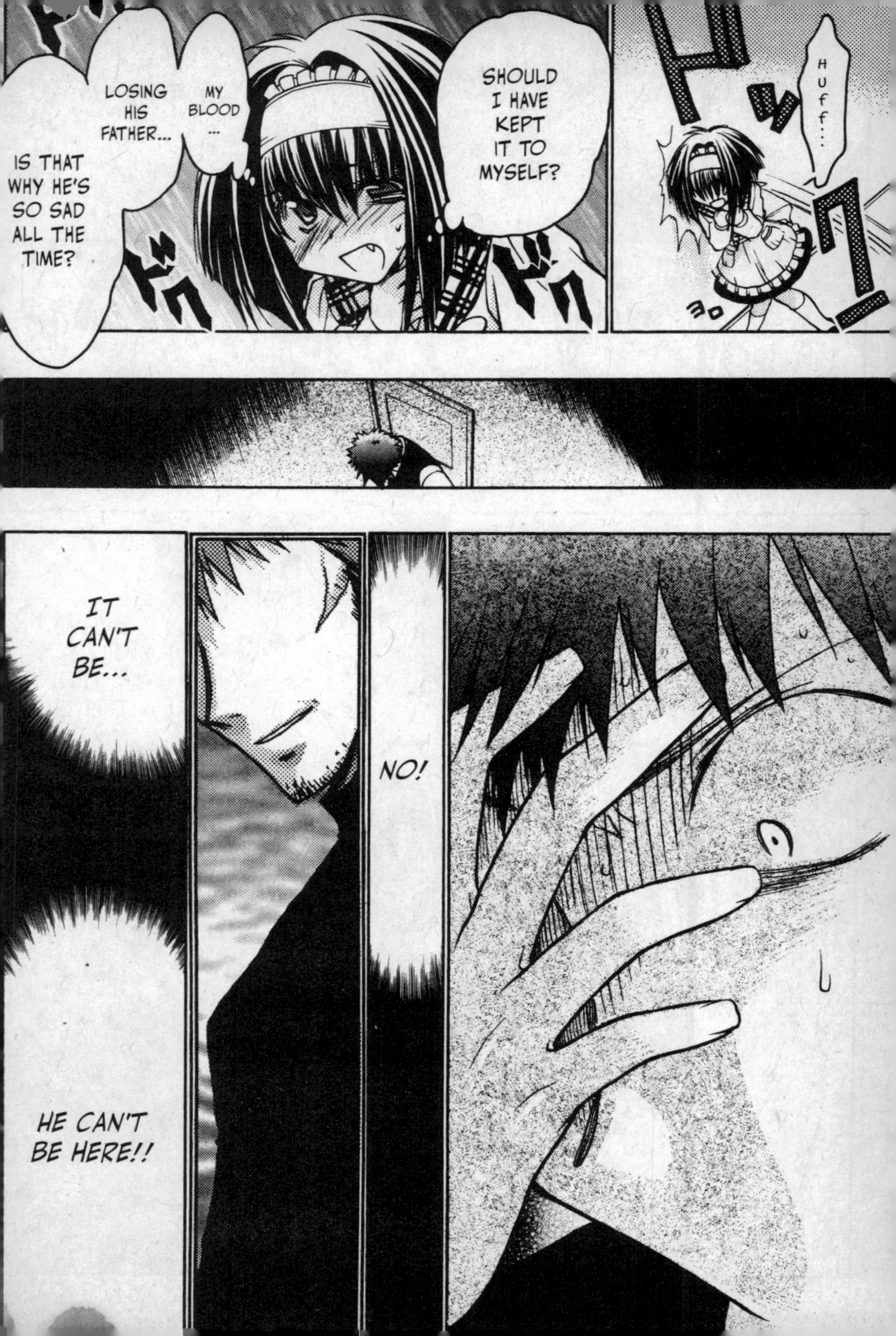
Huff...
SHOULD I HAVE KEPT IT TO MYSELF?
MY BLOOD ...
LOSING HIS FATHER...
IS THAT WHY HE'S SO SAD ALL THE TIME?
NO!
IT CAN'T BE...
HE CAN'T BE HERE!!

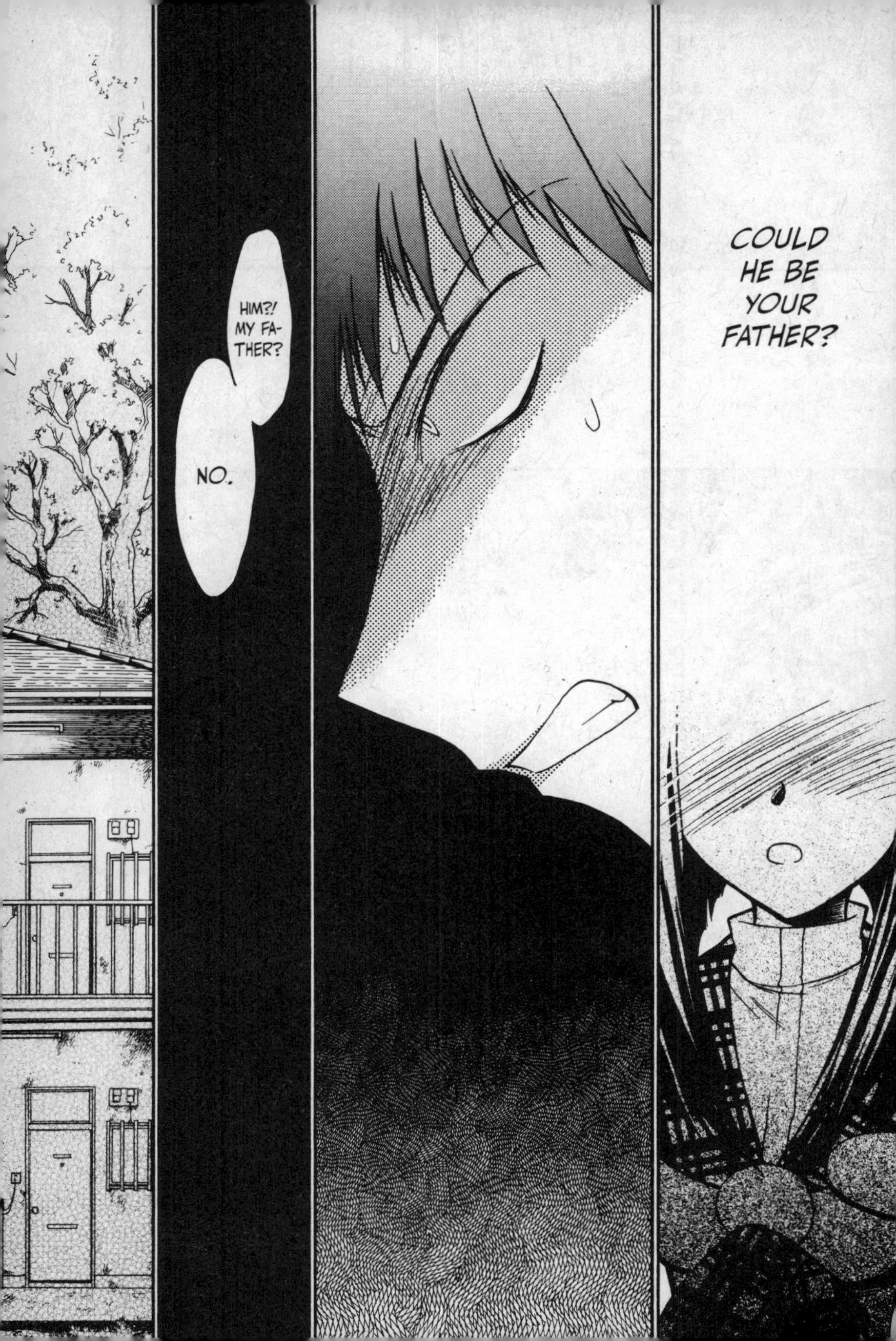
COULD HE BE YOUR FATHER?
HIM?! MY FA-THER?
NO.

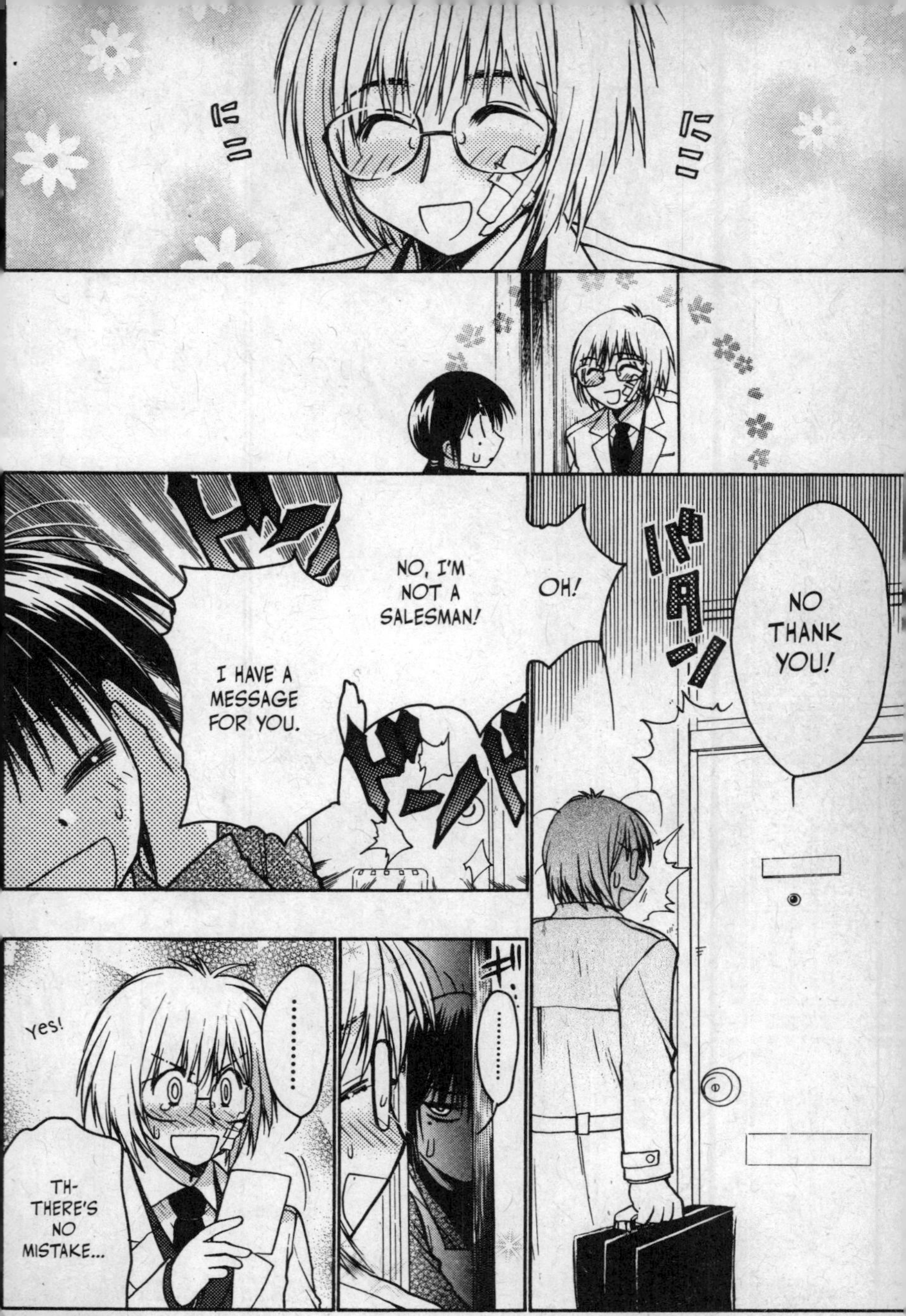
NO THANK YOU!
OH!
NO, I'M NOT A SALESMAN!
I HAVE A MESSAGE FOR YOU.
....
....
Yes!
TH- THERE'S NO MISTAKE...

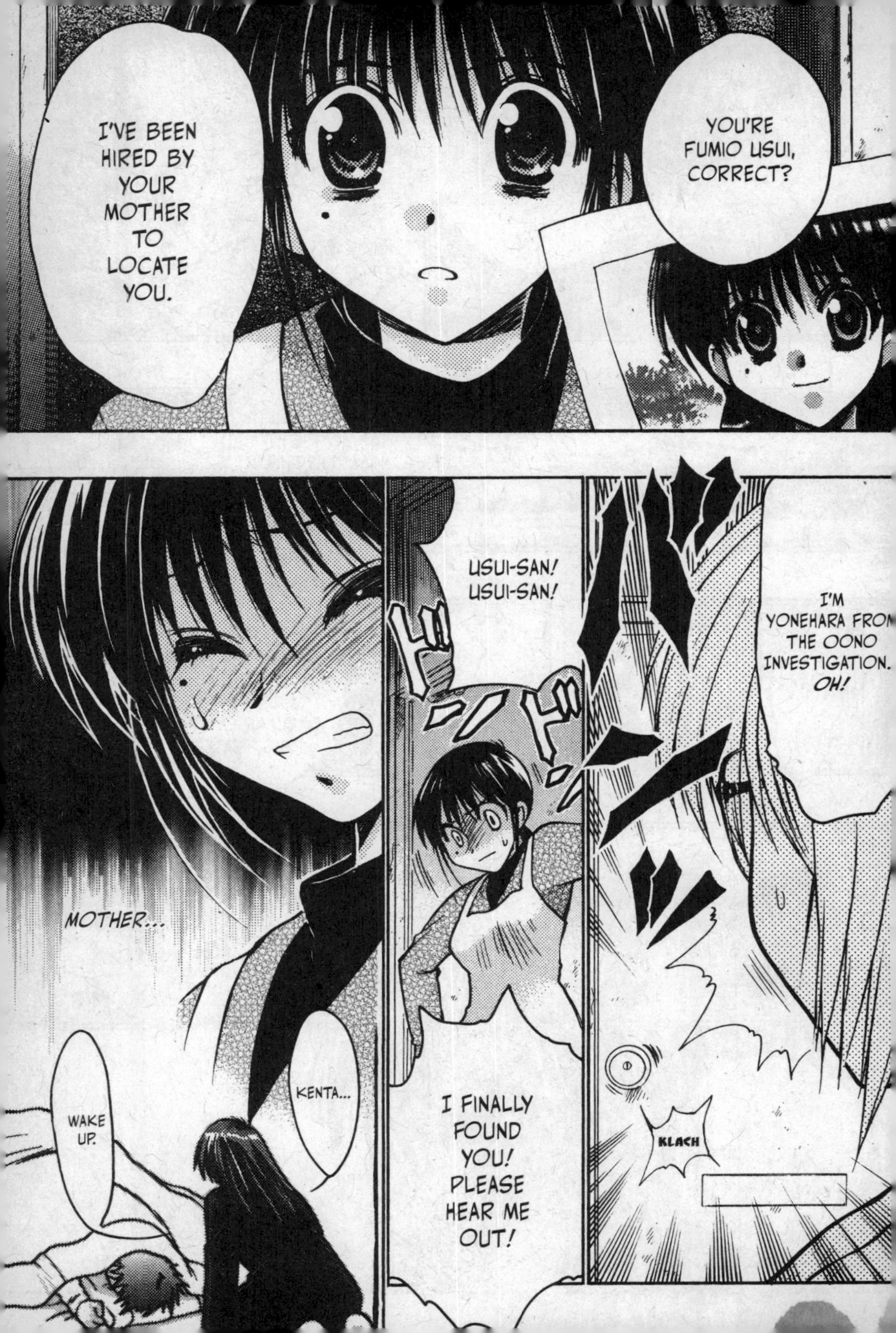

YOU'RE FUMIO USUI, CORRECT?
I'VE BEEN HIRED BY YOUR MOTHER TO LOCATE YOU.
I'M YONEHARA FROM THE OONO INVESTIGATION. OH!
KLACH
USUI-SAN! USUI-SAN!
I FINALLY FOUND YOU! PLEASE HEAR ME OUT!
MOTHER...
KENTA...
WAKE UP.

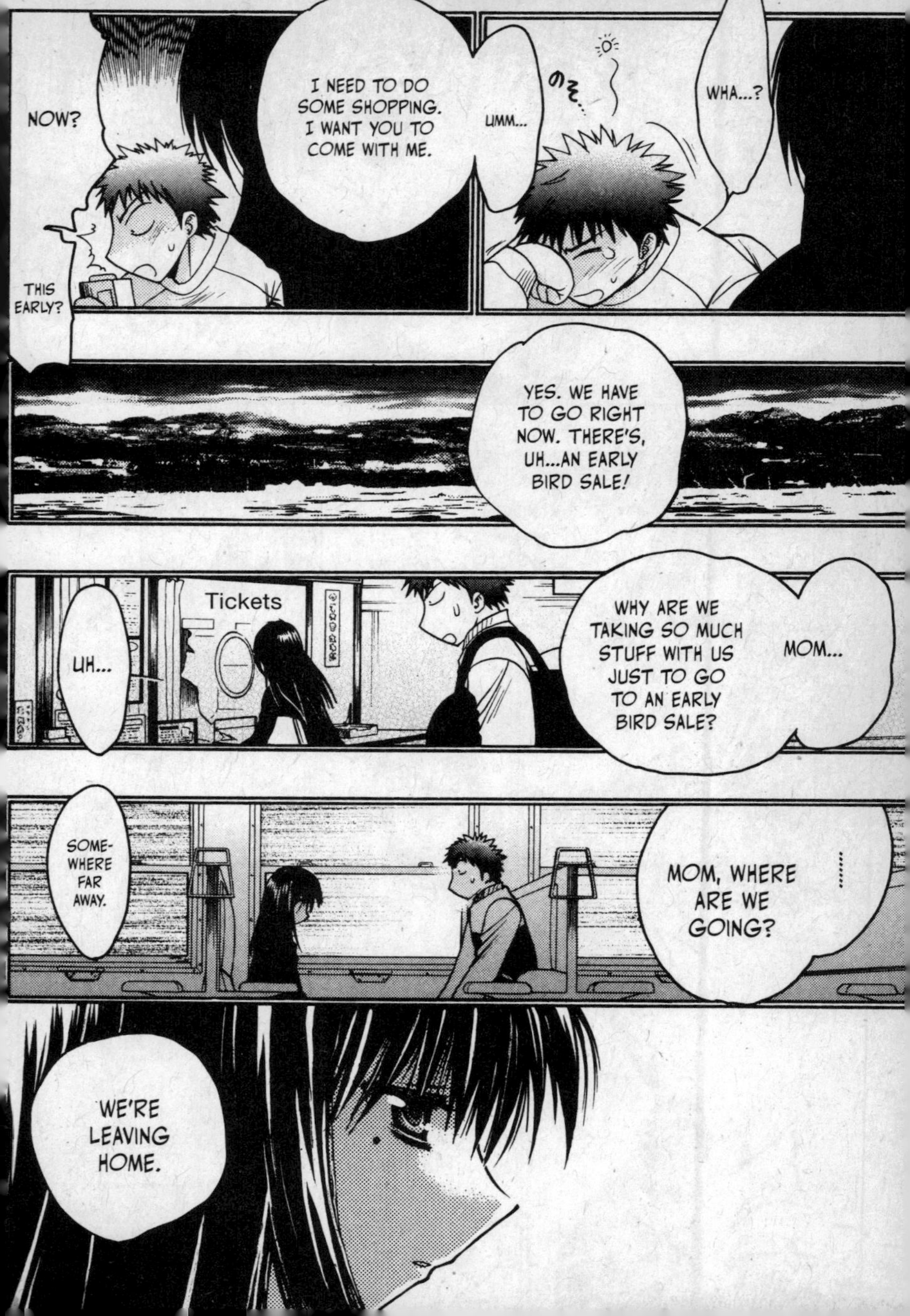
WHA...?
UMM...
I NEED TO DO SOME SHOPPING. I WANT YOU TO COME WITH ME.
NOW?
THIS EARLY?
YES. WE HAVE TO GO RIGHT NOW. THERE'S, UH...AN EARLY BIRD SALE!
MOM...
WHY ARE WE TAKING SO MUCH STUFF WITH US JUST TO GO TO AN EARLY BIRD SALE?
Tickets
UH...
......
MOM, WHERE ARE WE GOING?
SOME-WHERE FAR AWAY.
WE'RE LEAVING HOME.

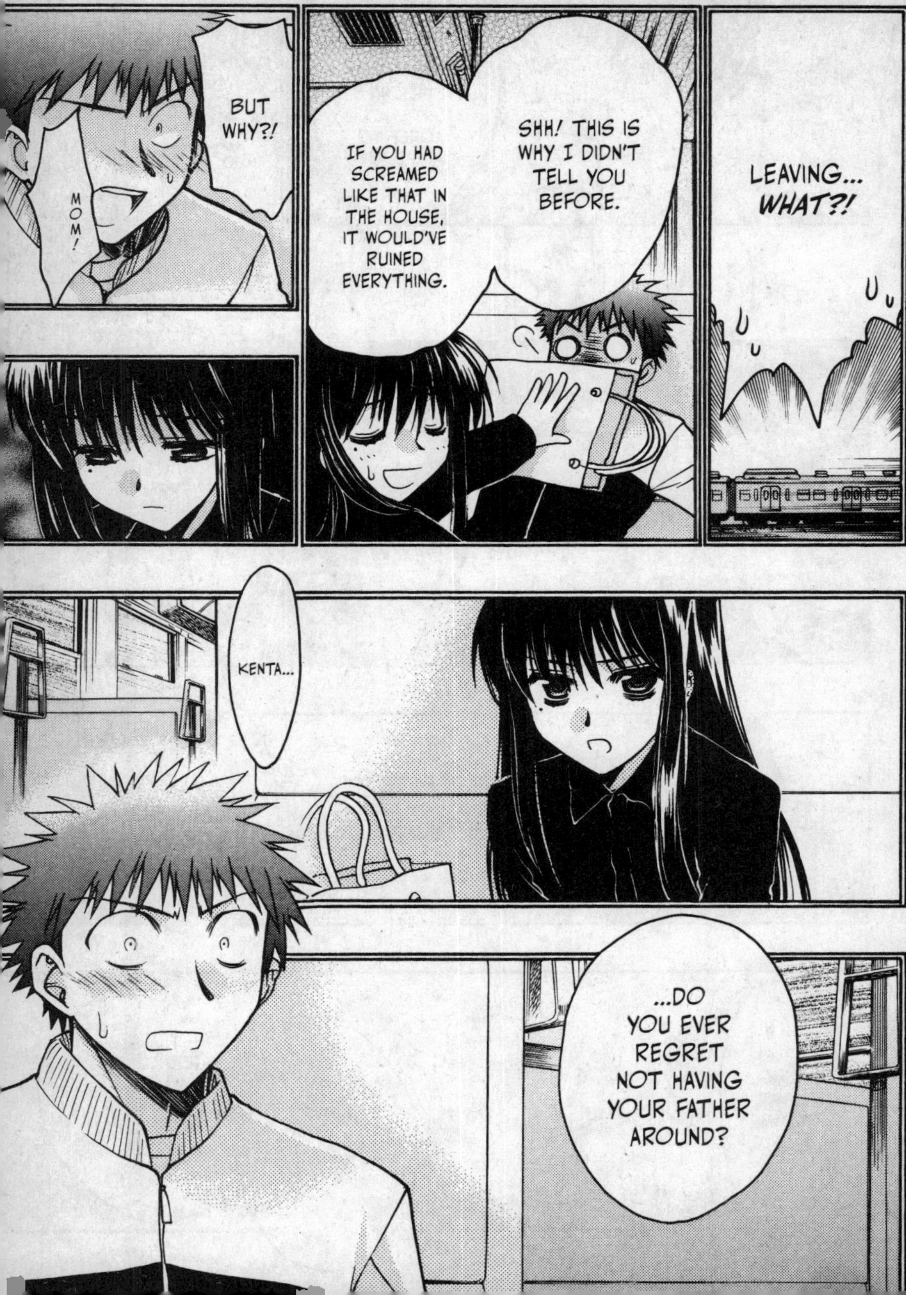
LEAVING... WHAT?!
SHH! THIS IS WHY I DIDN'T TELL YOU BEFORE.
IF YOU HAD SCREAMED LIKE THAT IN THE HOUSE, IT WOULD'VE RUINED EVERYTHING.
BUT WHY?!
MOM!
KENTA...
...DO YOU EVER REGRET NOT HAVING YOUR FATHER AROUND?

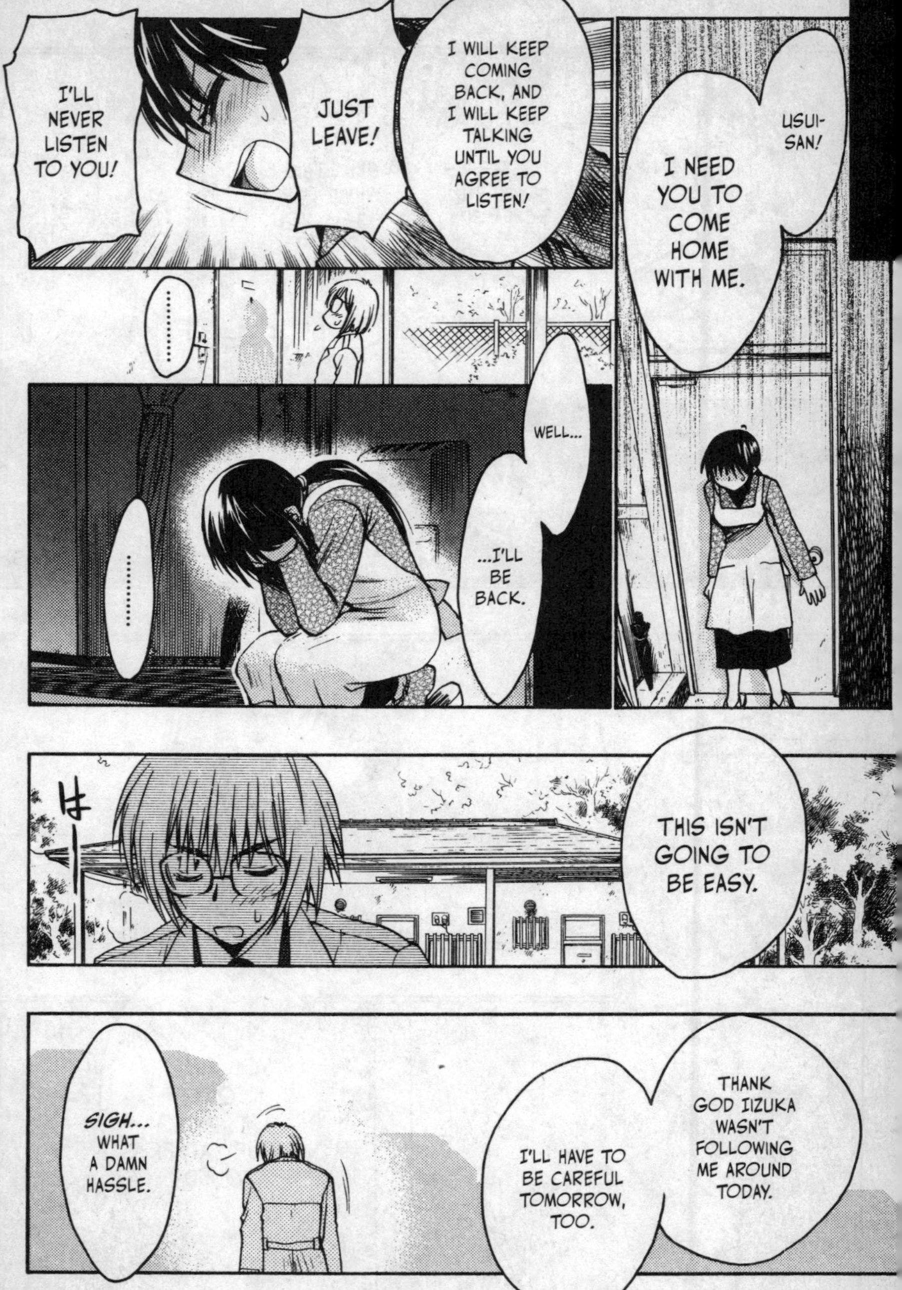
USUI-SAN!
I NEED YOU TO COME HOME WITH ME.
I WILL KEEP COMING BACK, AND I WILL KEEP TALKING UNTIL YOU AGREE TO LISTEN!
JUST LEAVE!
I'LL NEVER LISTEN TO YOU!
......
WELL...
...I'LL BE BACK.
......
THIS ISN'T GOING TO BE EASY.
はー
THANK GOD IIZUKA WASN'T FOLLOWING ME AROUND TODAY.
I'LL HAVE TO BE CAREFUL TOMORROW, TOO.
SIGH... WHAT A DAMN HASSLE.

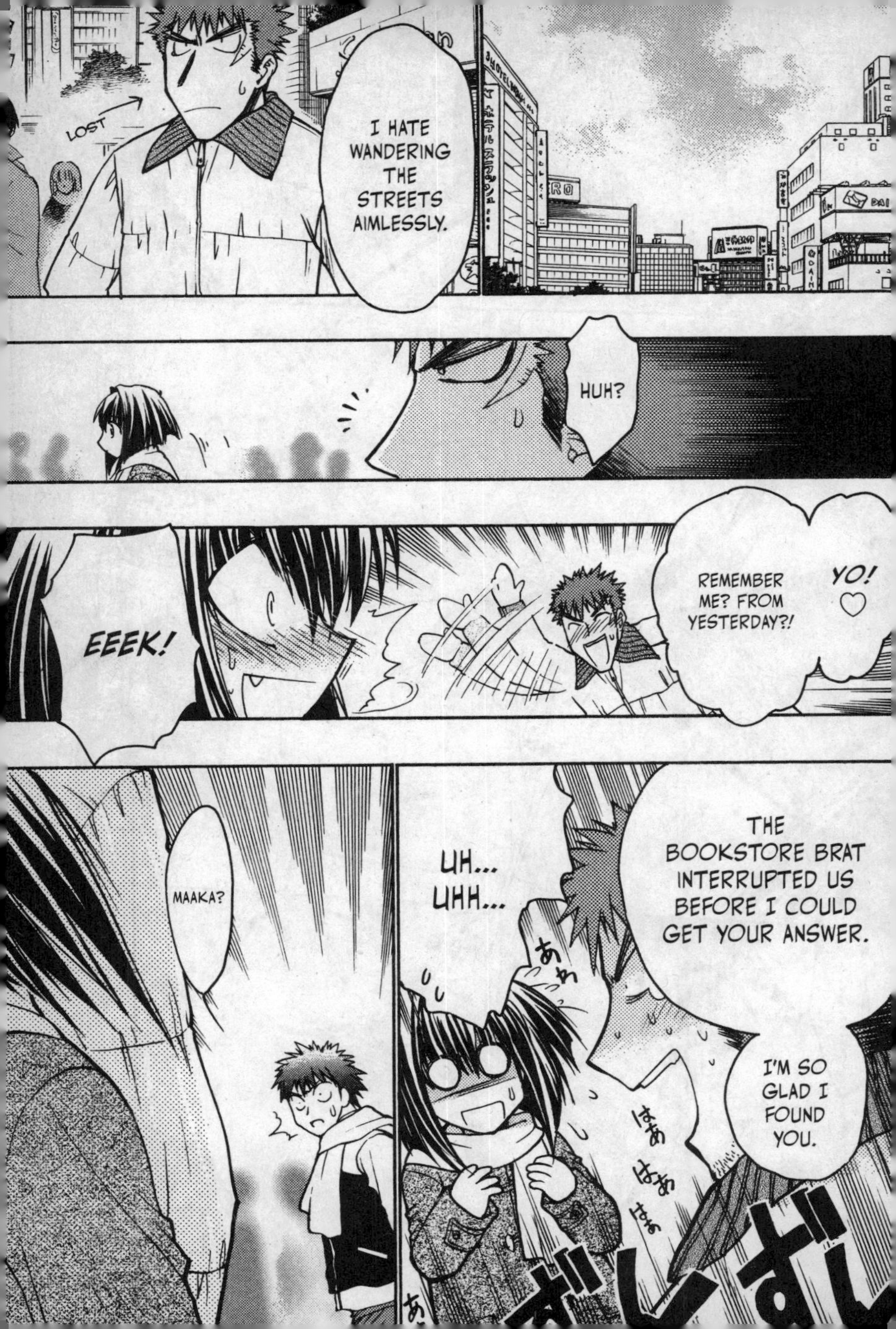
I HATE WANDERING THE STREETS AIMLESSLY.
LOST
HUH?
YO! ♡
REMEMBER ME? FROM YESTERDAY?!
EEEK!
THE BOOKSTORE BRAT INTERRUPTED US BEFORE I COULD GET YOUR ANSWER.
UH... UHH...
あれ
I'M SO GLAD I FOUND YOU.
はあ はあ はあ
MAAKA?

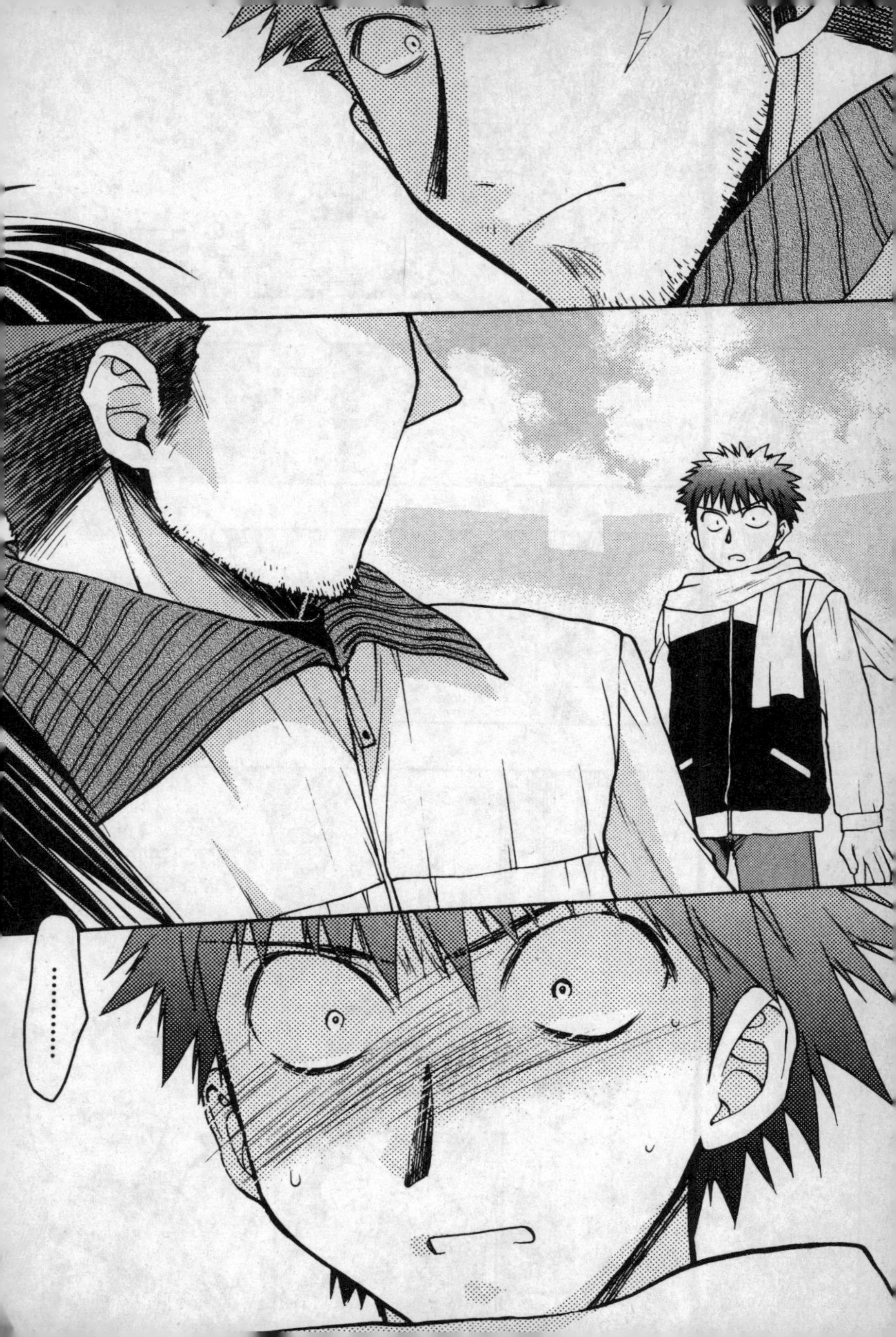
……

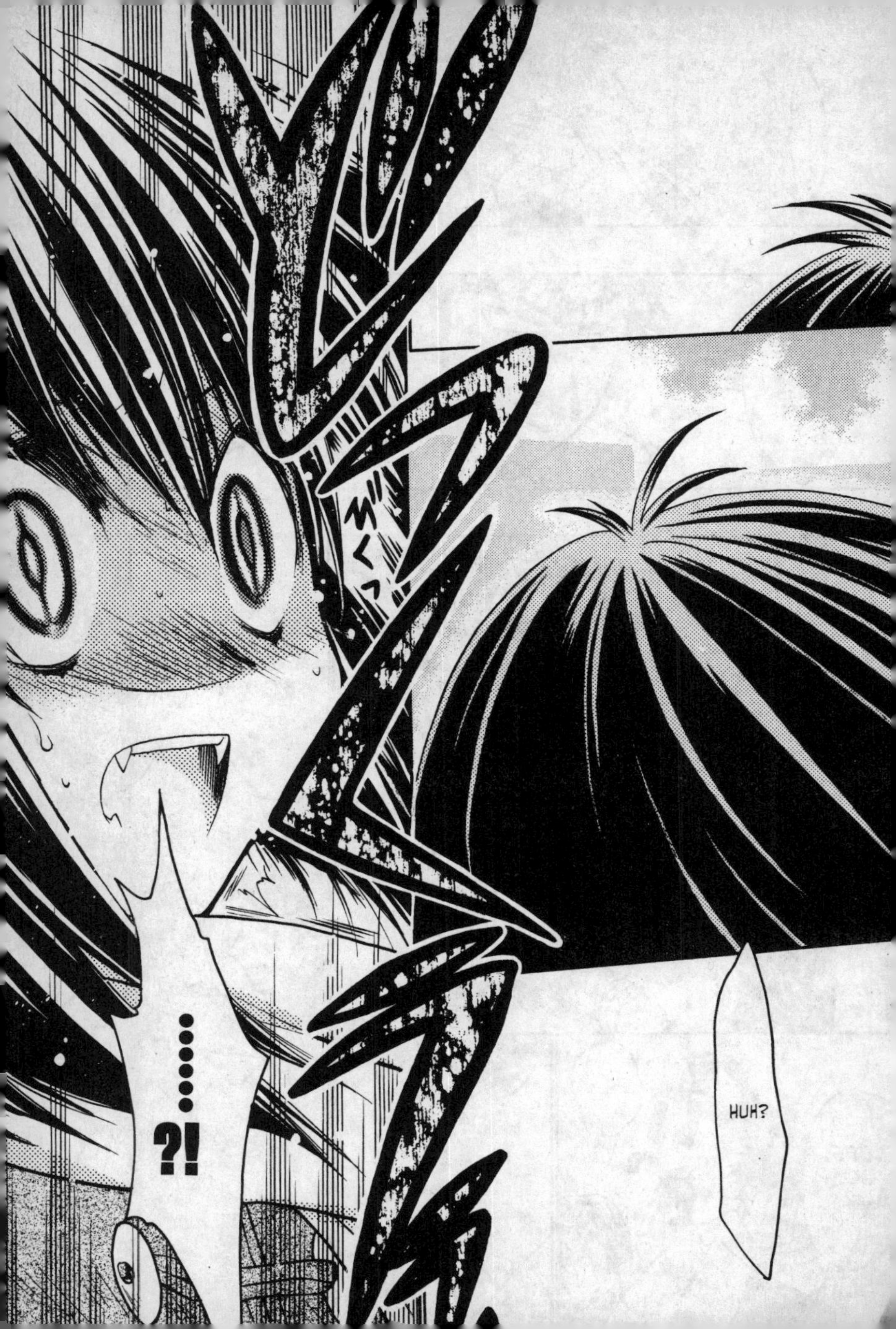
HUH?
ぎくっ
......?!

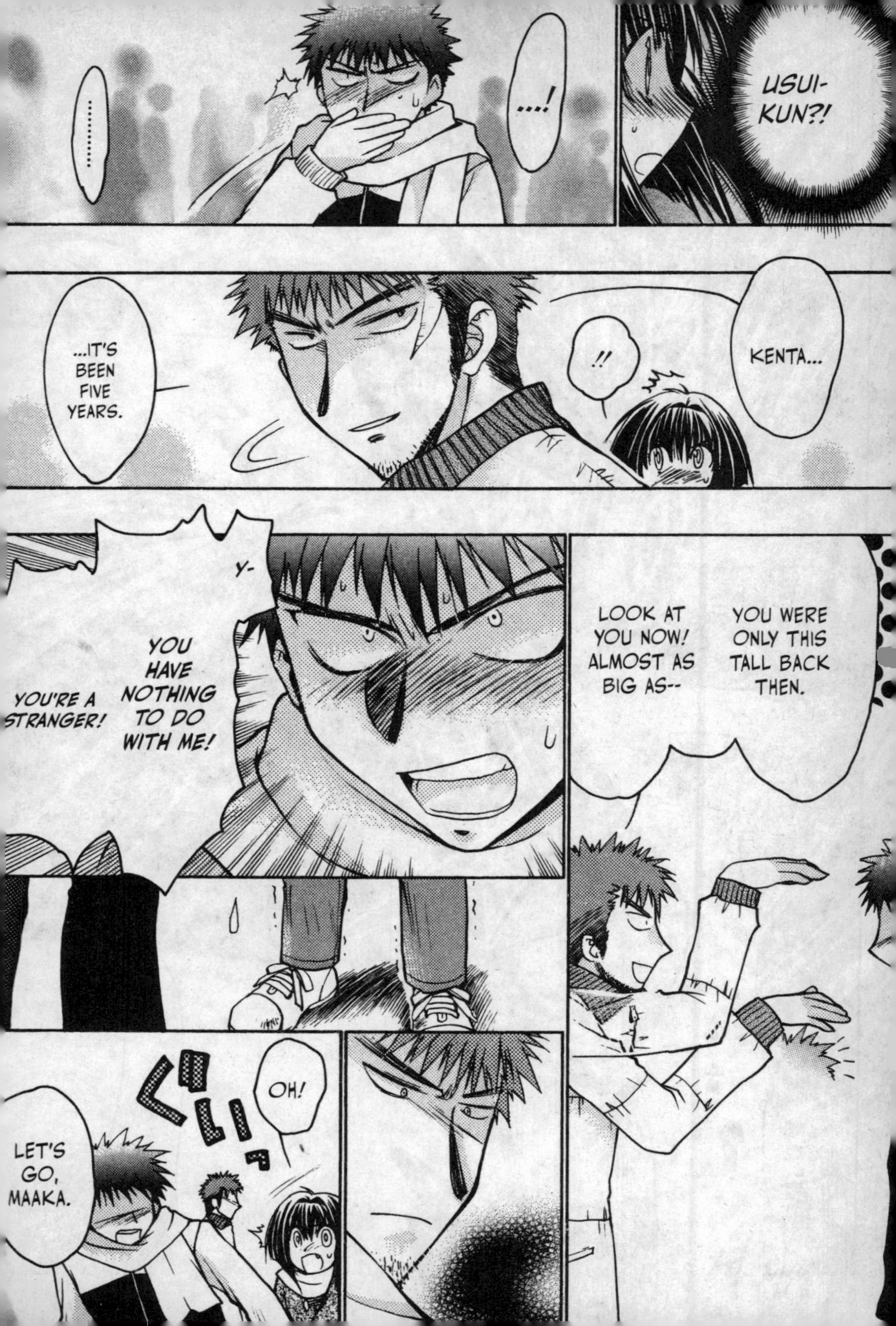
USUI-KUN?!
....!
....
KENTA...
!!
...IT'S BEEN FIVE YEARS.
YOU WERE ONLY THIS TALL BACK THEN.
LOOK AT YOU NOW! ALMOST AS BIG AS--
Y-
YOU HAVE NOTHING TO DO WITH ME!
YOU'RE A STRANGER!
OH!
LET'S GO, MAAKA.

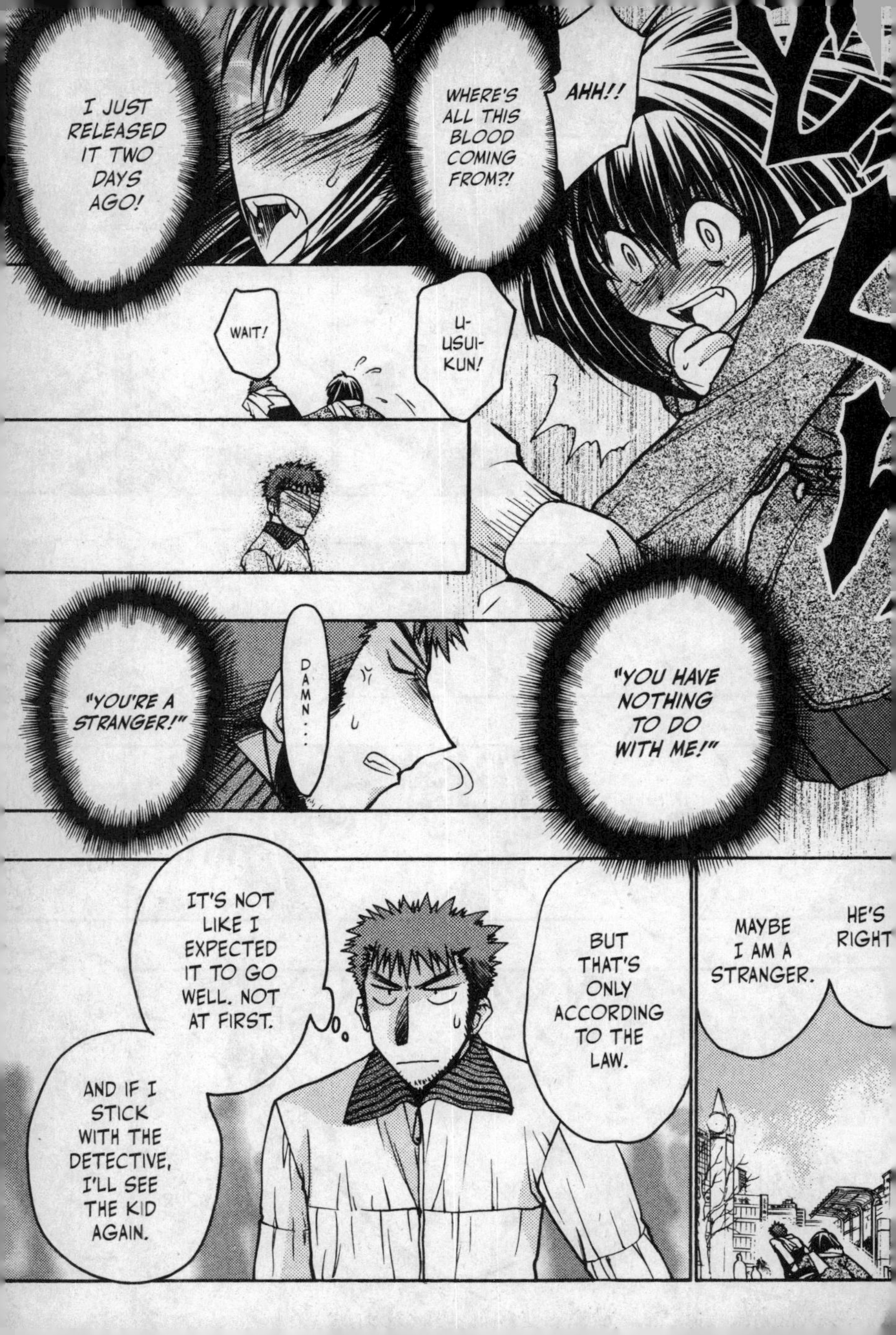
AHH!!
WHERE'S ALL THIS BLOOD COMING FROM?!
I JUST RELEASED IT TWO DAYS AGO!
U-USUI-KUN!
WAIT!
"YOU HAVE NOTHING TO DO WITH ME!"
DAMN...
"YOU'RE A STRANGER!"
HE'S RIGHT
MAYBE I AM A STRANGER.
BUT THAT'S ONLY ACCORDING TO THE LAW.
IT'S NOT LIKE I EXPECTED IT TO GO WELL. NOT AT FIRST.
AND IF I STICK WITH THE DETECTIVE, I'LL SEE THE KID AGAIN.

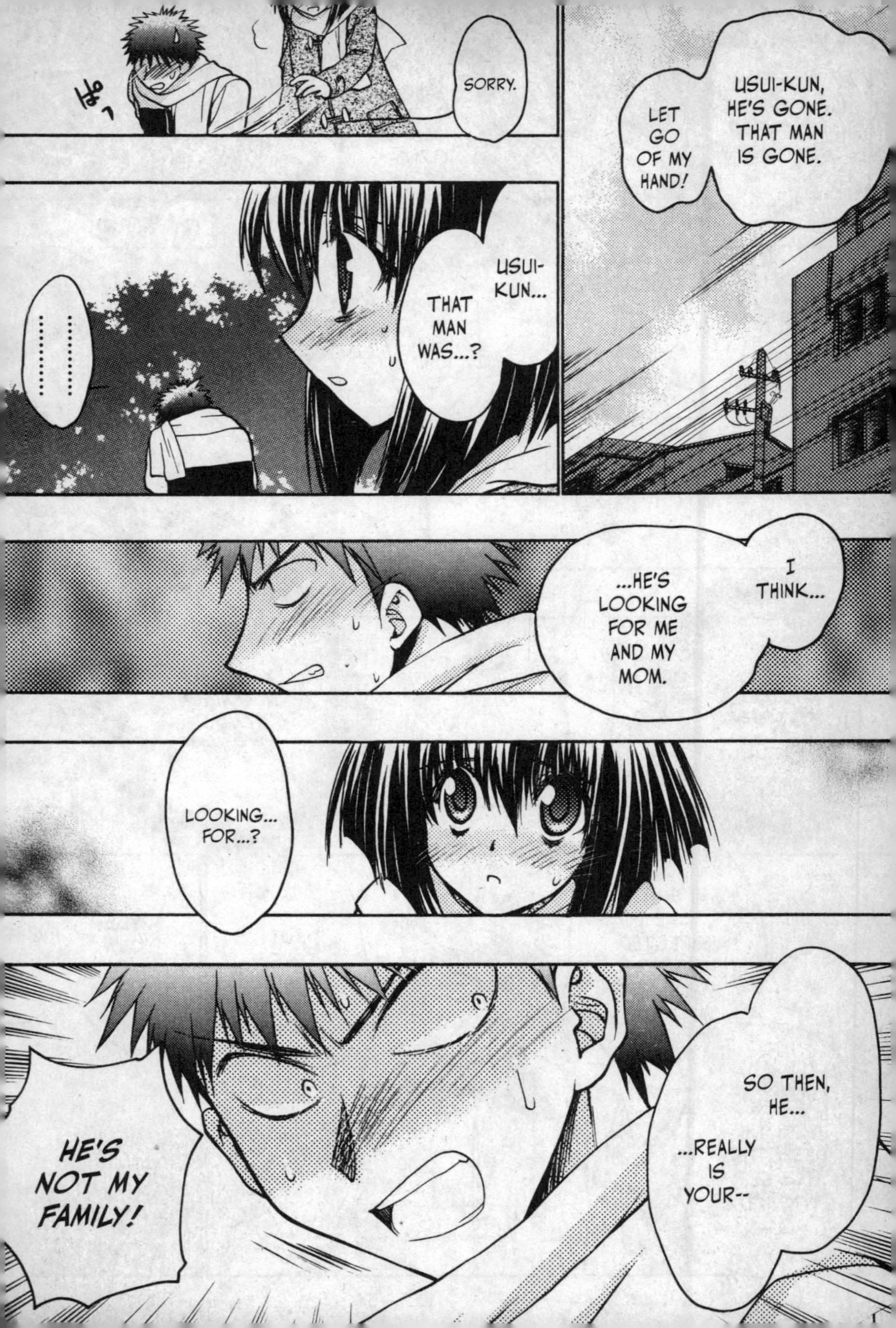
USUI-KUN, HE'S GONE. THAT MAN IS GONE.
LET GO OF MY HAND!
SORRY.
ぱっ
USUI-KUN...
THAT MAN WAS...?
......
I THINK...
...HE'S LOOKING FOR ME AND MY MOM.
LOOKING... FOR...?
SO THEN, HE...
...REALLY IS YOUR--
HE'S NOT MY FAMILY!

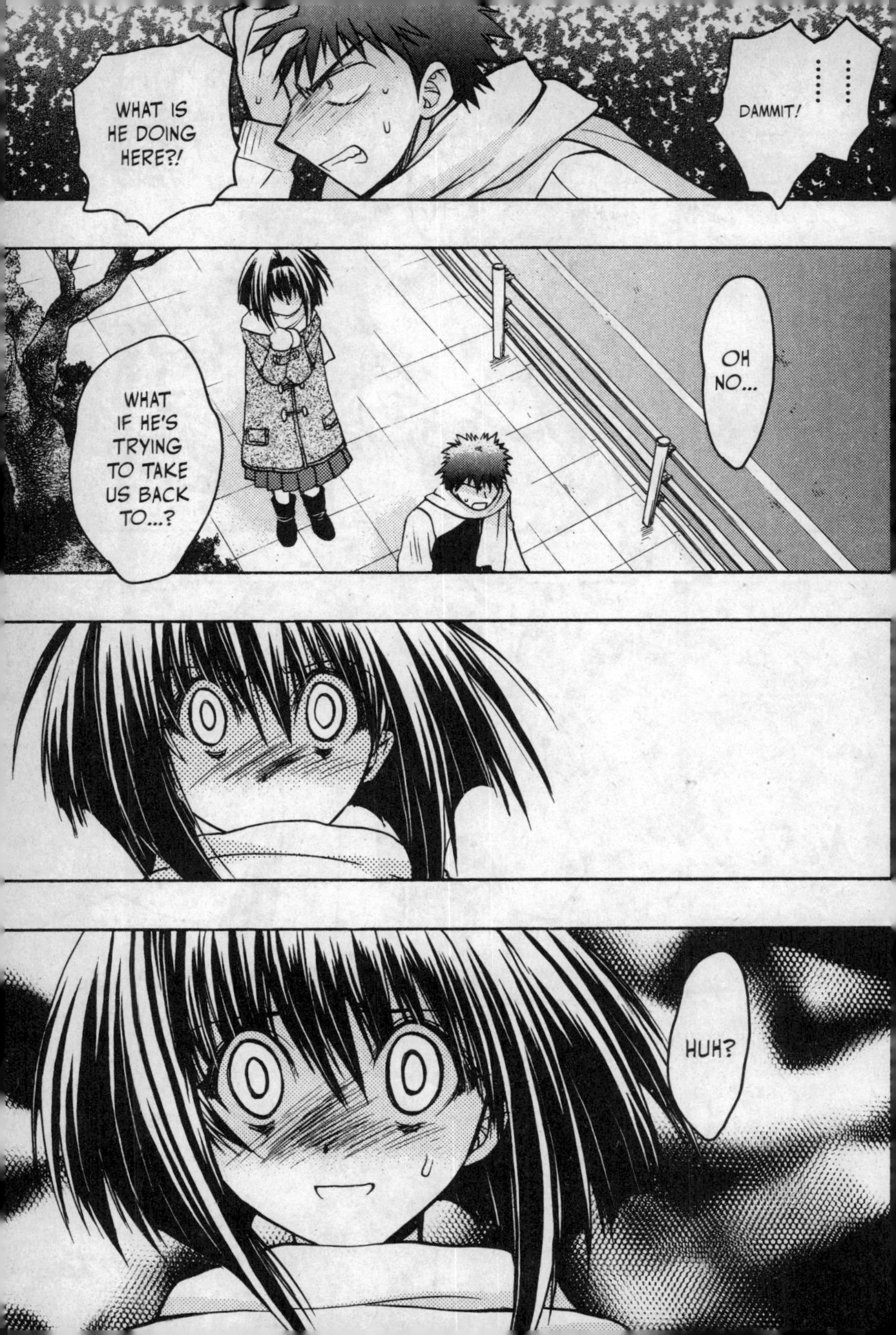
......
DAMMIT!
WHAT IS HE DOING HERE?!
OH NO...
WHAT IF HE'S TRYING TO TAKE US BACK TO...?
HUH?

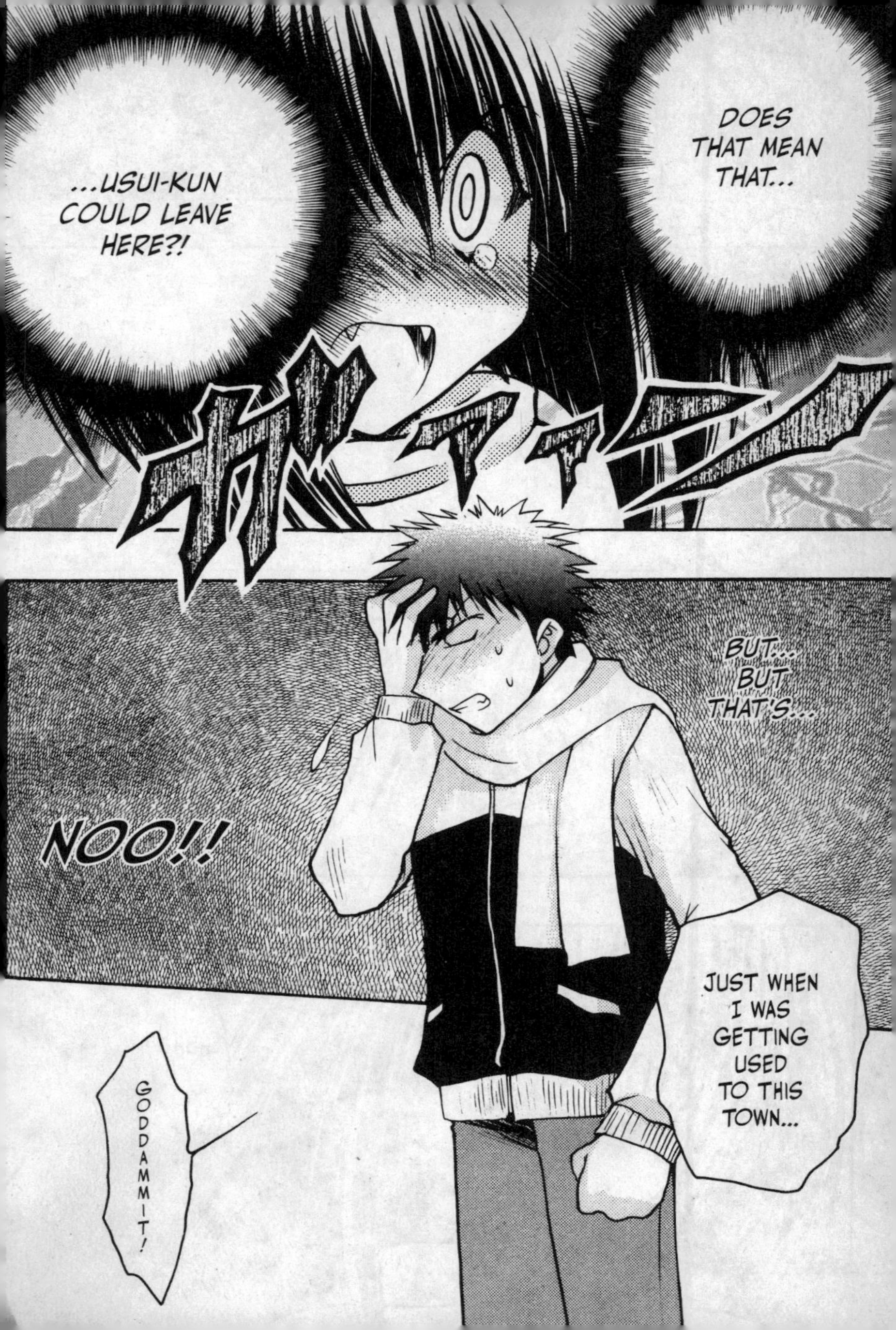
DOES THAT MEAN THAT...
...USUI-KUN COULD LEAVE HERE?!
BUT... BUT THAT'S...
NOO!!
JUST WHEN I WAS GETTING USED TO THIS TOWN...
GODDAMMIT!

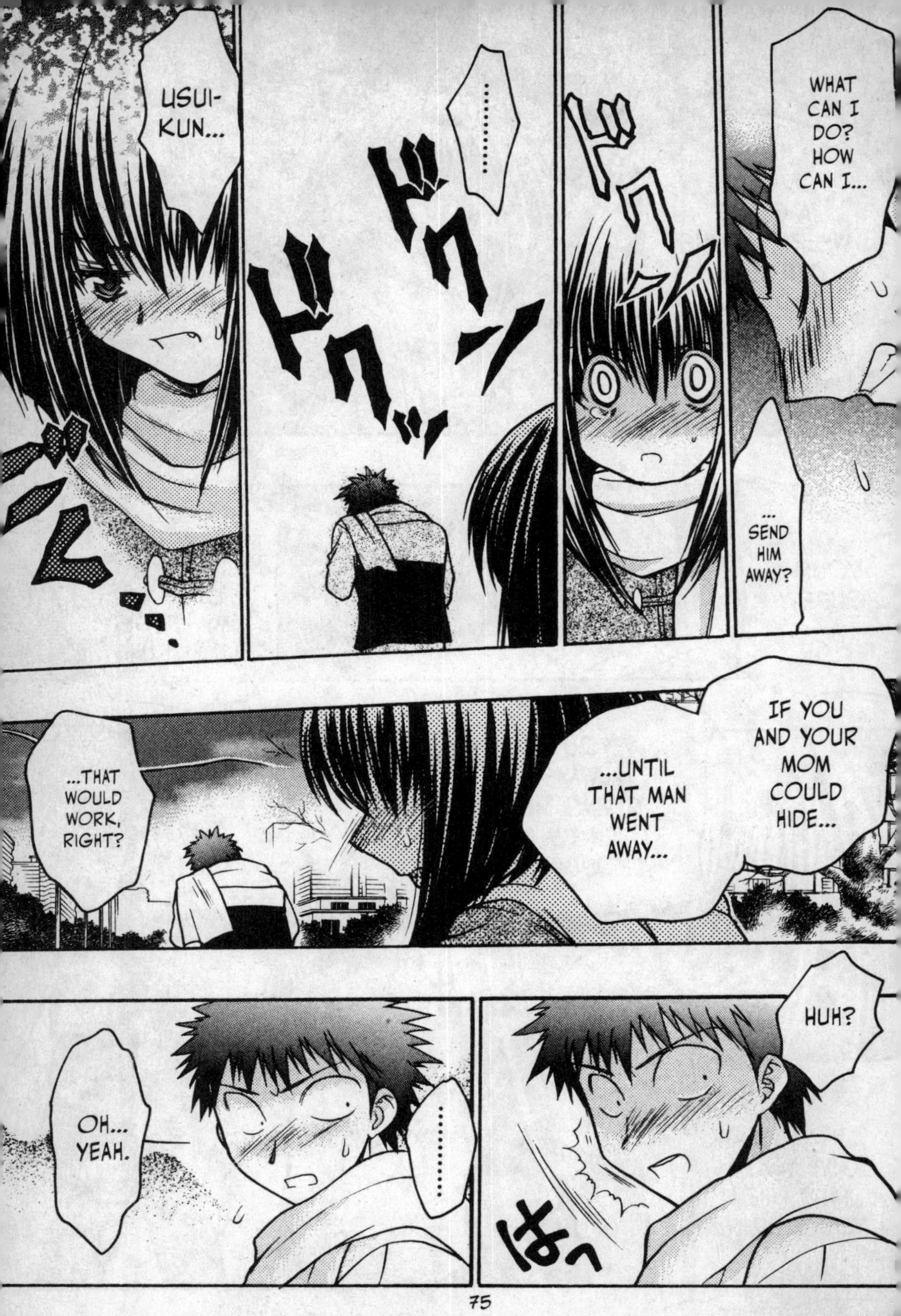
WHAT CAN I DO? HOW CAN I...
...SEND HIM AWAY?
......
USUI-KUN...
IF YOU AND YOUR MOM COULD HIDE...
...UNTIL THAT MAN WENT AWAY...
...THAT WOULD WORK, RIGHT?
HUH?
はっ
......
OH... YEAH.

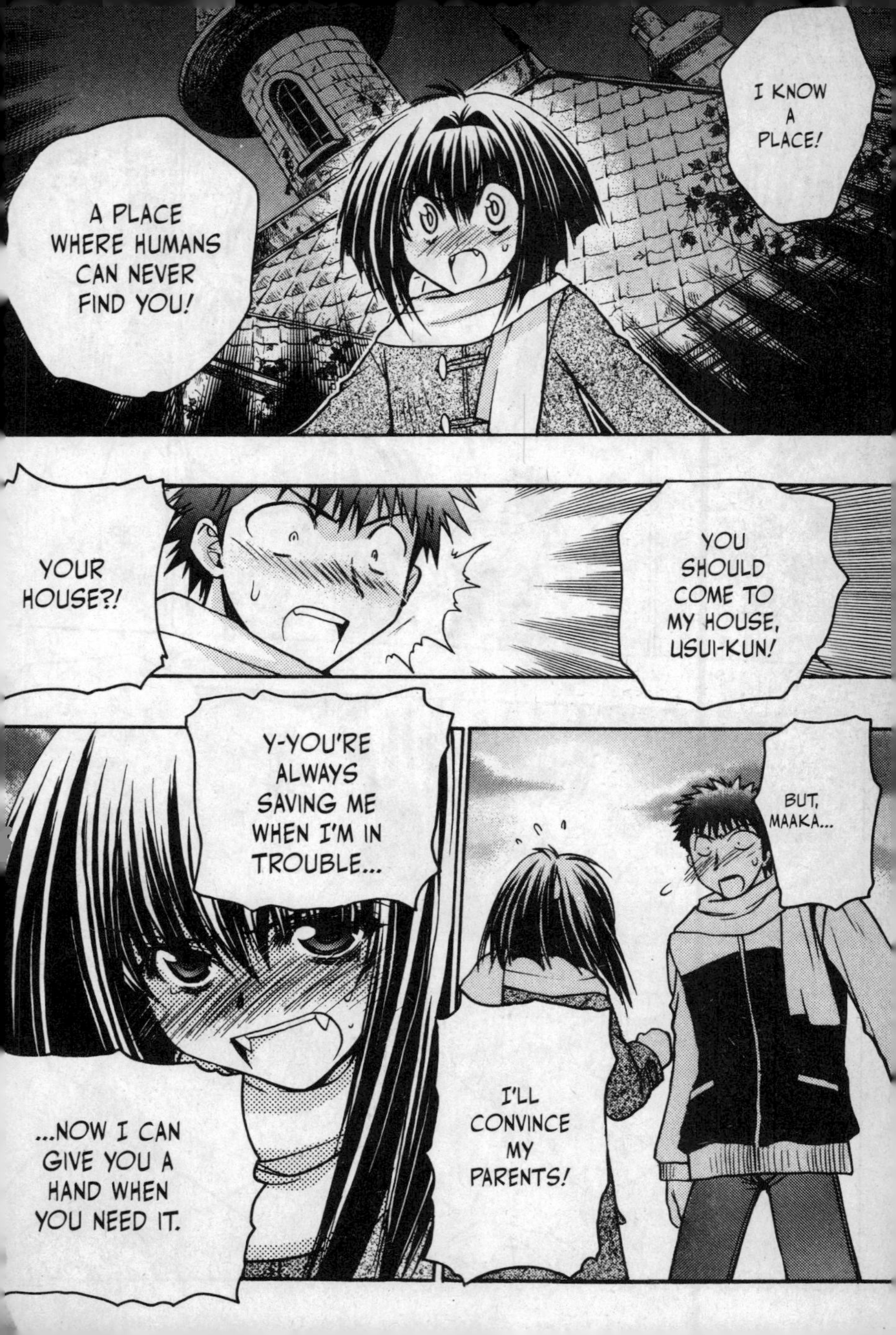
I KNOW A PLACE!
A PLACE WHERE HUMANS CAN NEVER FIND YOU!
YOU SHOULD COME TO MY HOUSE, USUI-KUN!
YOUR HOUSE?!
BUT, MAAKA...
I'LL CONVINCE MY PARENTS!
Y-YOU'RE ALWAYS SAVING ME WHEN I'M IN TROUBLE...
...NOW I CAN GIVE YOU A HAND WHEN YOU NEED IT.

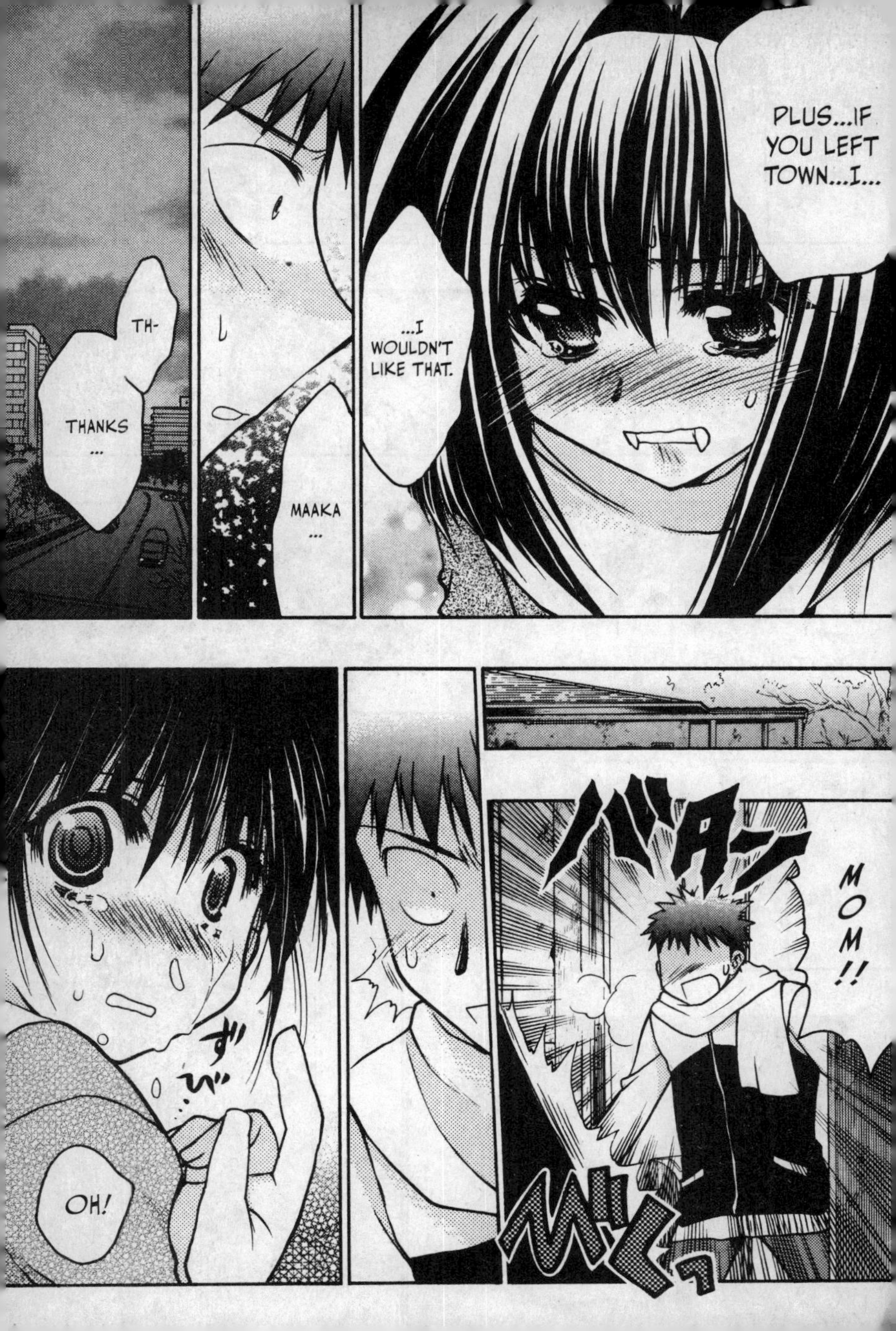
PLUS...IF YOU LEFT TOWN...I...
...I WOULDN'T LIKE THAT.
MAAKA ...
TH-
THANKS ...
MOM!!
OH!

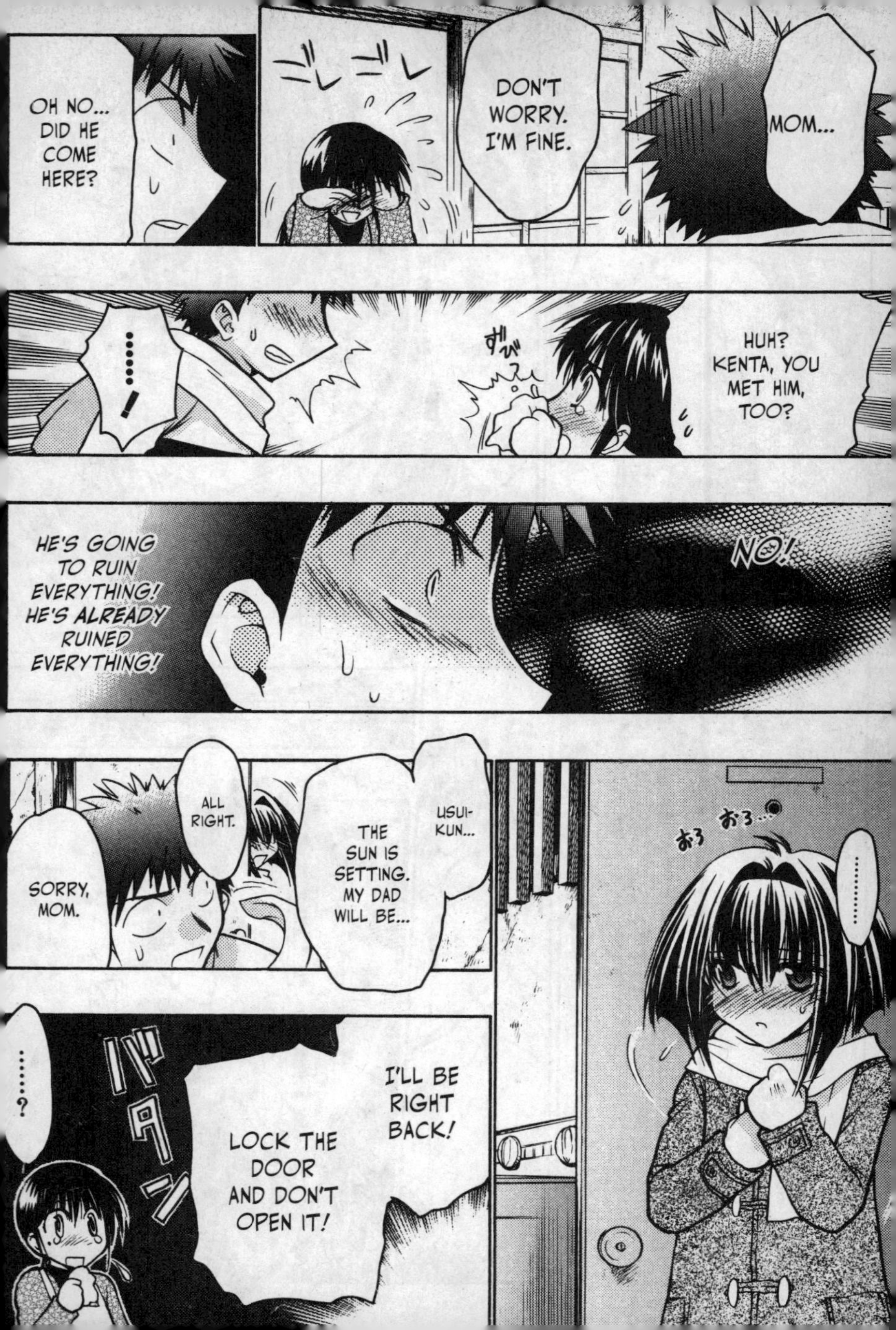
MOM...
DON'T WORRY. I'M FINE.
OH NO... DID HE COME HERE?
HUH? KENTA, YOU MET HIM, TOO?
ずび
......!
NO!
HE'S GOING TO RUIN EVERYTHING! HE'S ALREADY RUINED EVERYTHING!
......
おろ おろ...
USUI-KUN...
THE SUN IS SETTING. MY DAD WILL BE...
ALL RIGHT.
SORRY, MOM.
I'LL BE RIGHT BACK!
LOCK THE DOOR AND DON'T OPEN IT!
バタン
......?

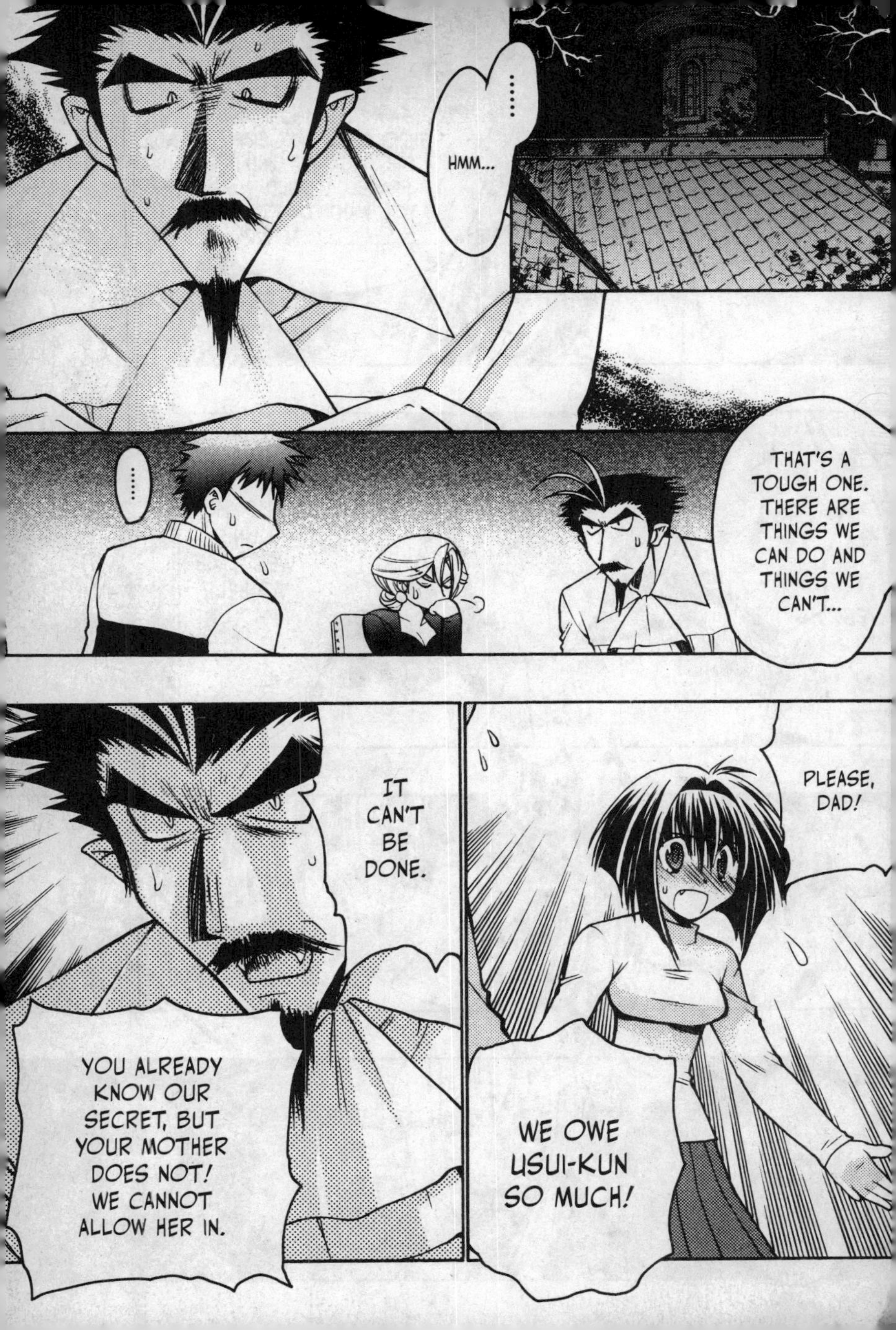
......
HMM...
THAT'S A TOUGH ONE. THERE ARE THINGS WE CAN DO AND THINGS WE CAN'T...
......
PLEASE, DAD!
WE OWE USUI-KUN SO MUCH!
IT CAN'T BE DONE.
YOU ALREADY KNOW OUR SECRET, BUT YOUR MOTHER DOES NOT! WE CANNOT ALLOW HER IN.

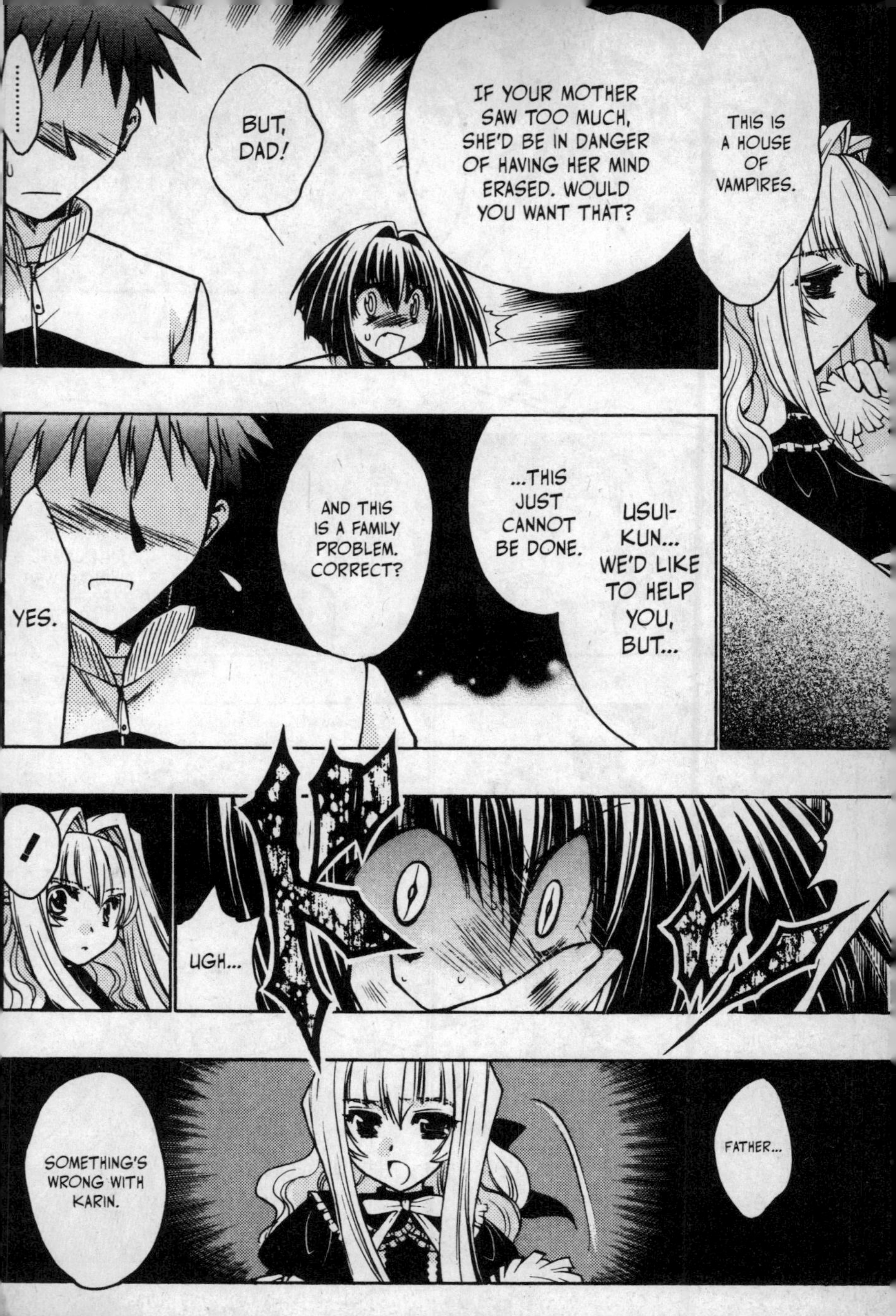
THIS IS A HOUSE OF VAMPIRES.
IF YOUR MOTHER SAW TOO MUCH, SHE'D BE IN DANGER OF HAVING HER MIND ERASED. WOULD YOU WANT THAT?
BUT, DAD!
......
USUI-KUN... WE'D LIKE TO HELP YOU, BUT...
...THIS JUST CANNOT BE DONE.
AND THIS IS A FAMILY PROBLEM. CORRECT?
YES.
UGH...
!
FATHER...
SOMETHING'S WRONG WITH KARIN.

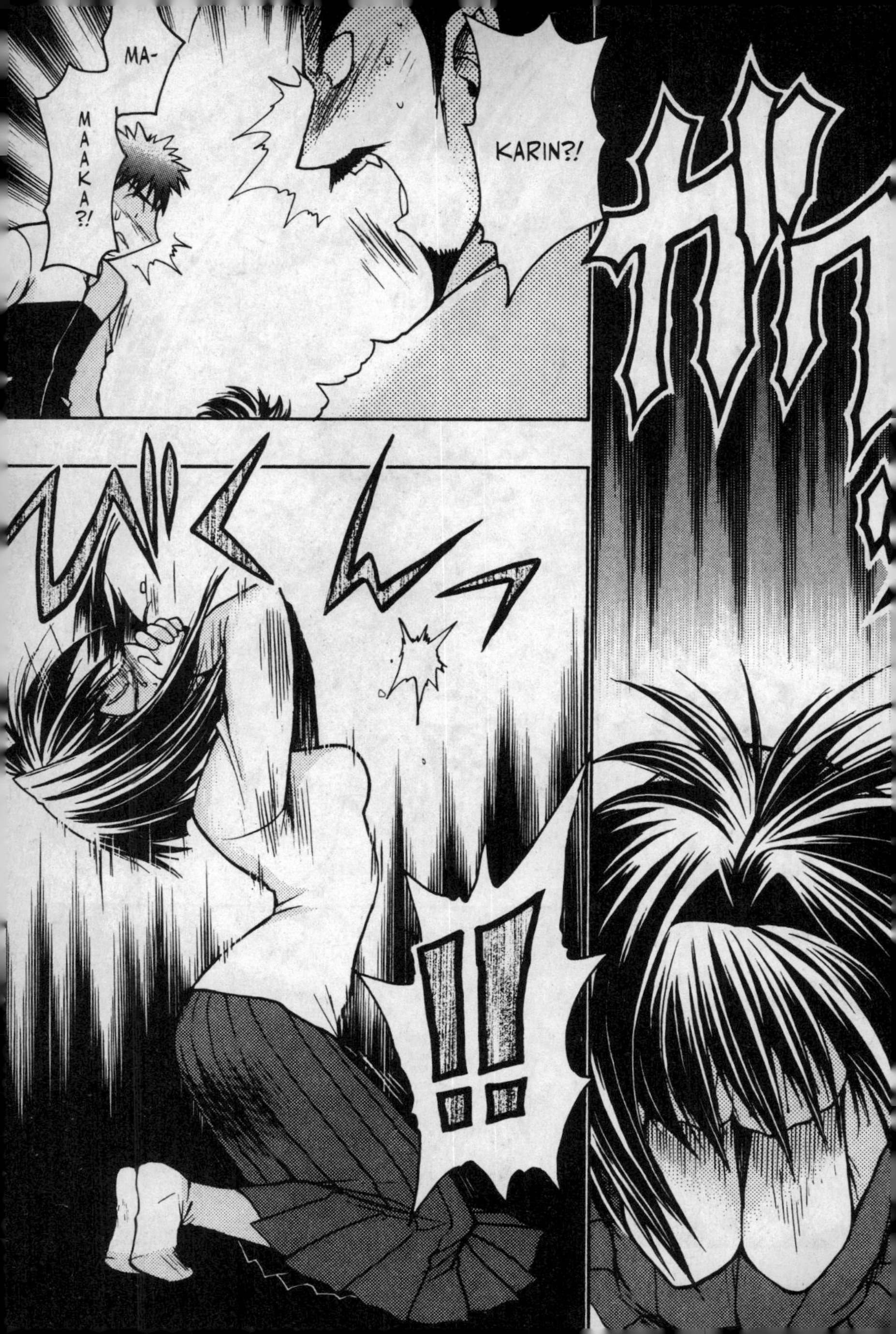
KARIN?!
MA-
MAAKA?!
!!

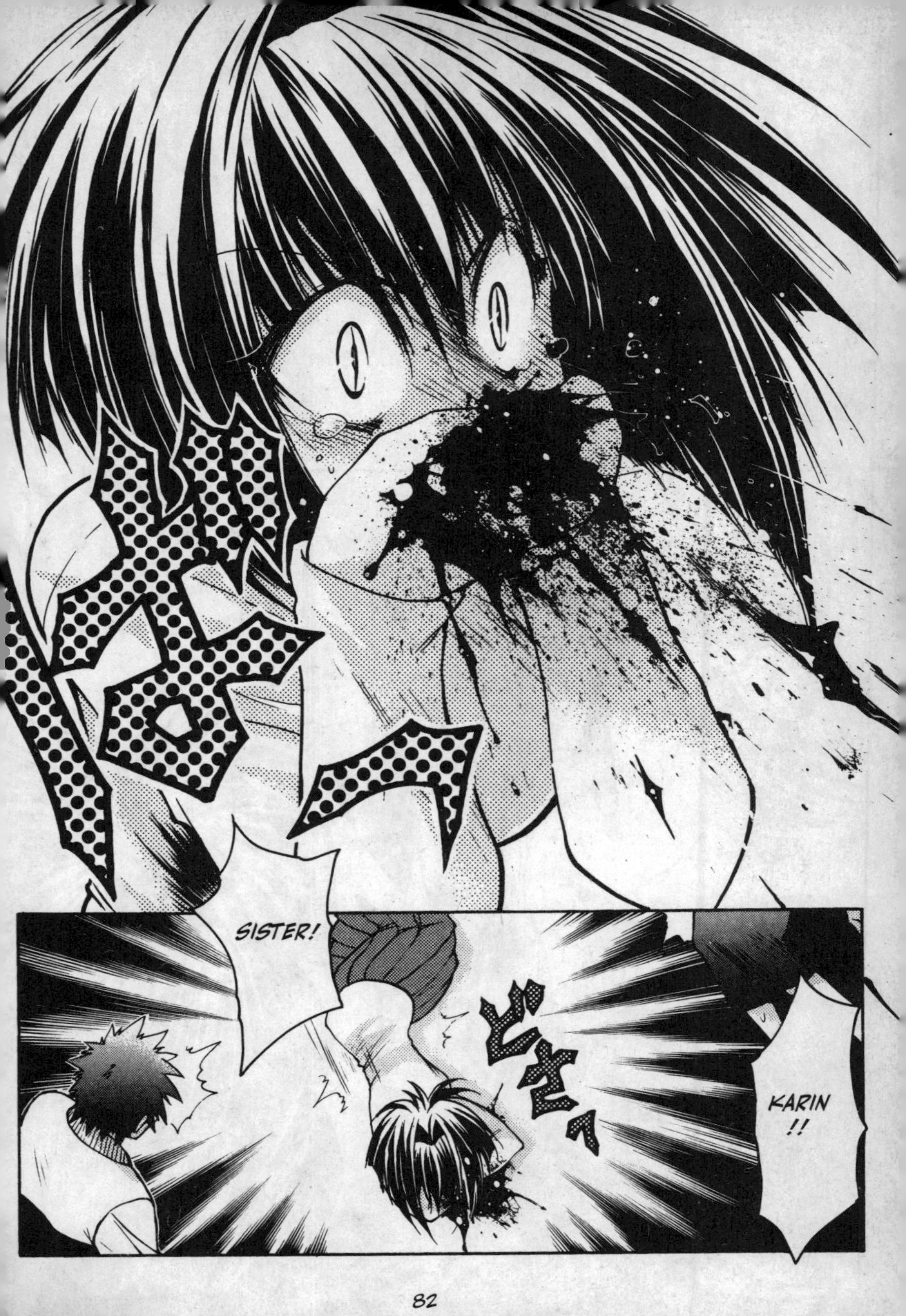
KARIN !!
SISTER!

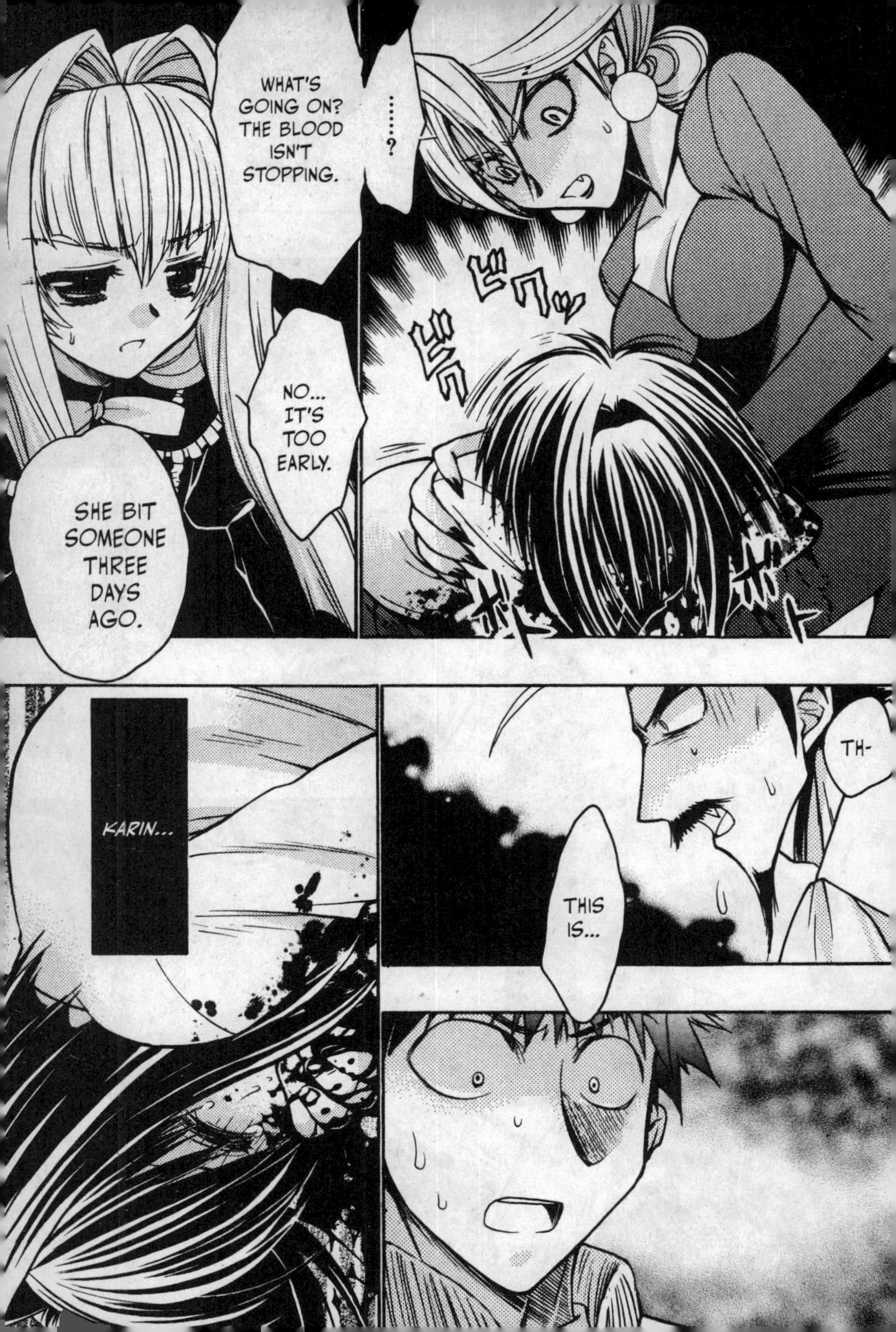

......?
WHAT'S GOING ON? THE BLOOD ISN'T STOPPING.
NO... IT'S TOO EARLY.
SHE BIT SOMEONE THREE DAYS AGO.
TH-
THIS IS...
KARIN...

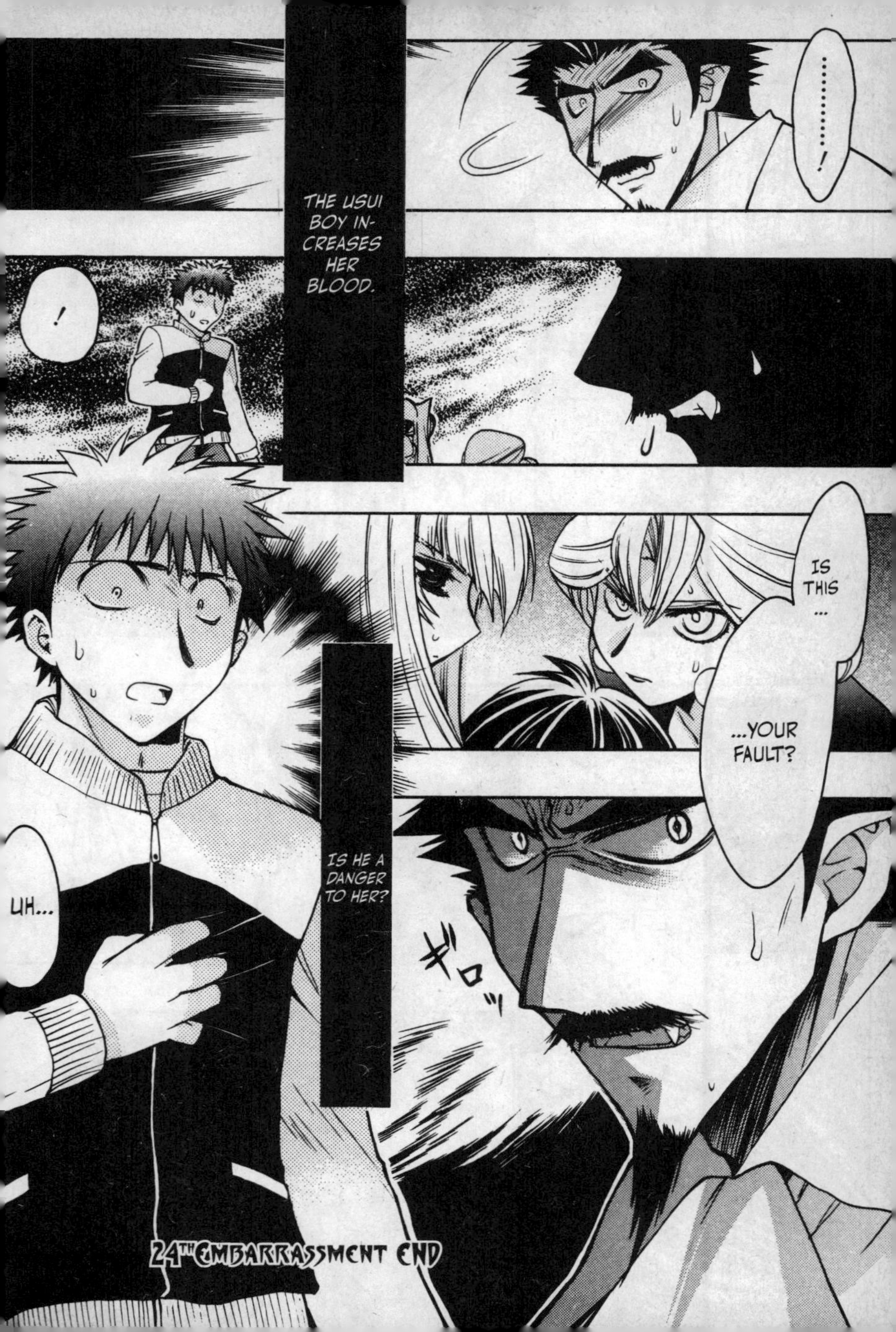

……!
THE USUI BOY INCREASES HER BLOOD.
!
IS THIS ...
...YOUR FAULT?
IS HE A DANGER TO HER?
ギロッ
UH...
24th EMBARRASSMENT END

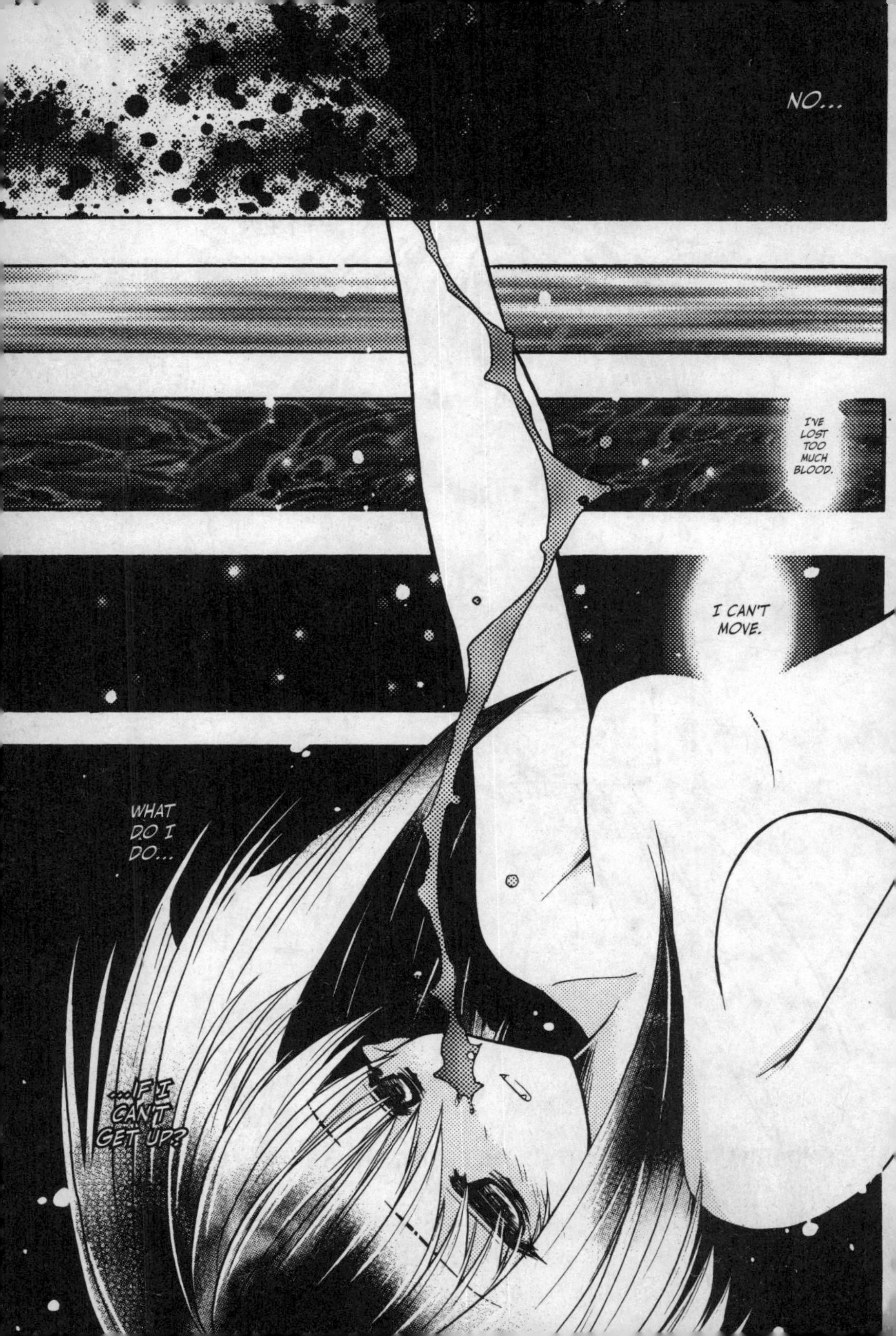
NO...
I'VE LOST TOO MUCH BLOOD.
I CAN'T MOVE.
WHAT DO I DO...
...IF I CAN'T GET UP?

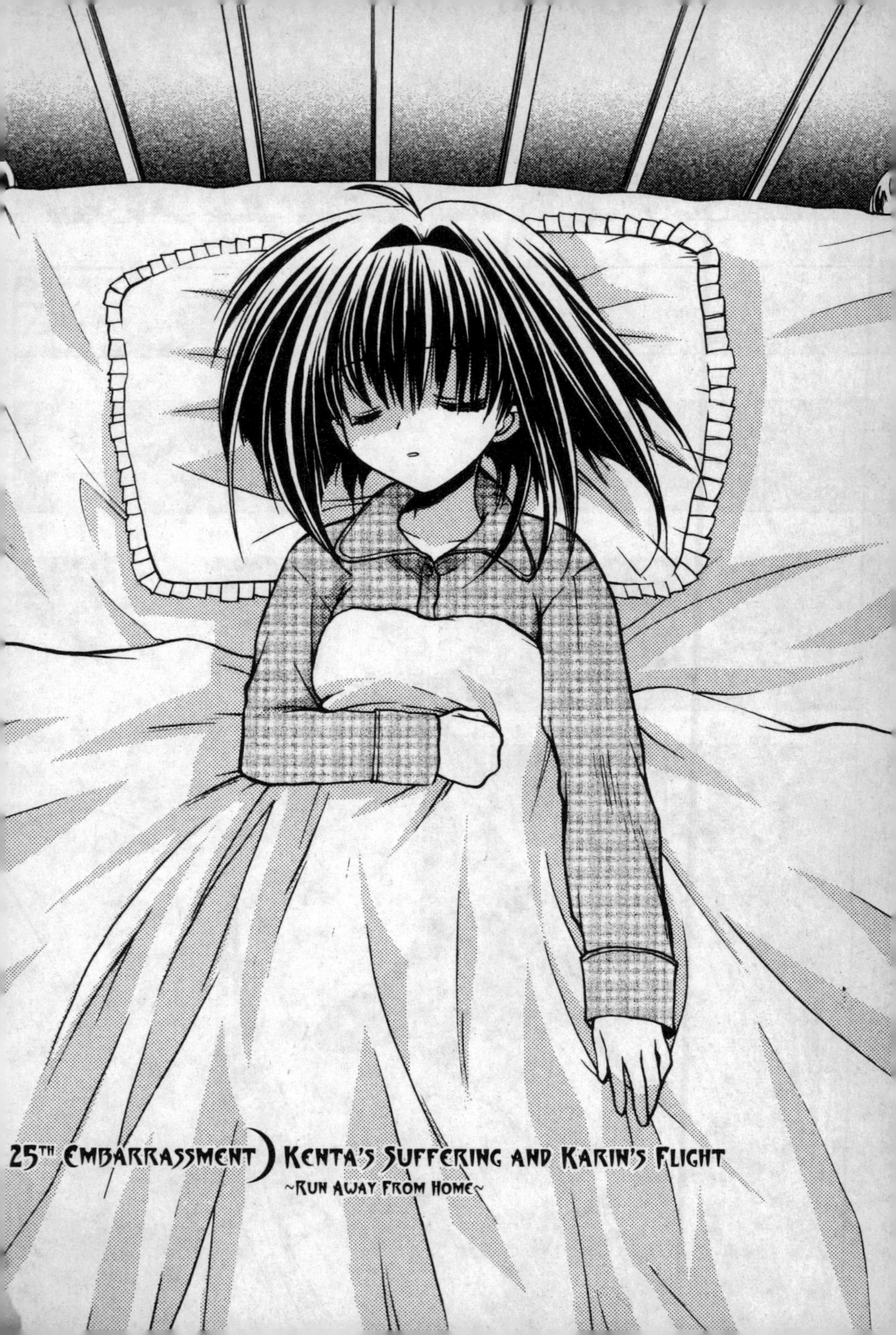
25TH EMBARRASSMENT KENTA'S SUFFERING AND KARIN'S FLIGHT
~RUN AWAY FROM HOME~

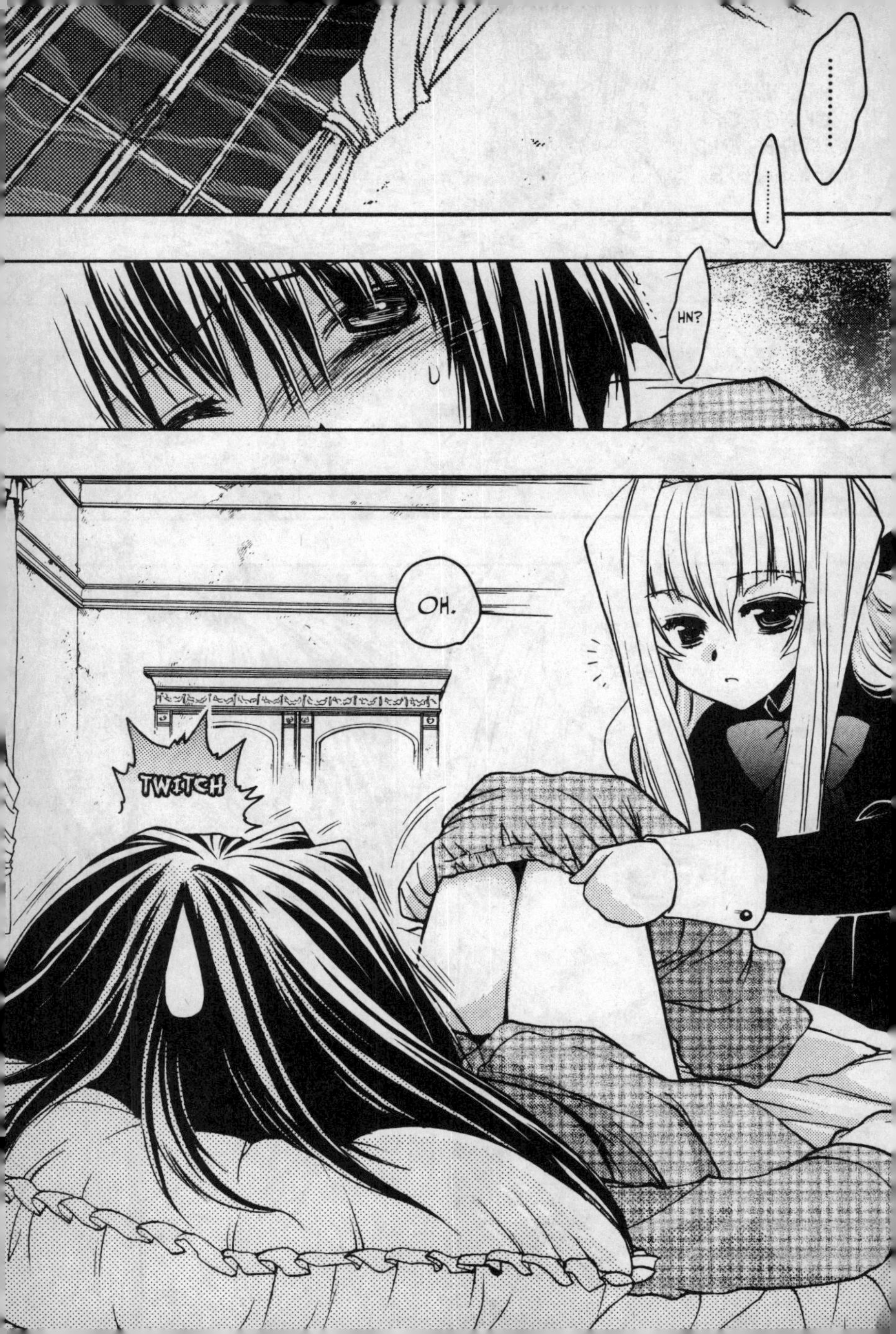

....
......
HN?
OH.
TWITCH

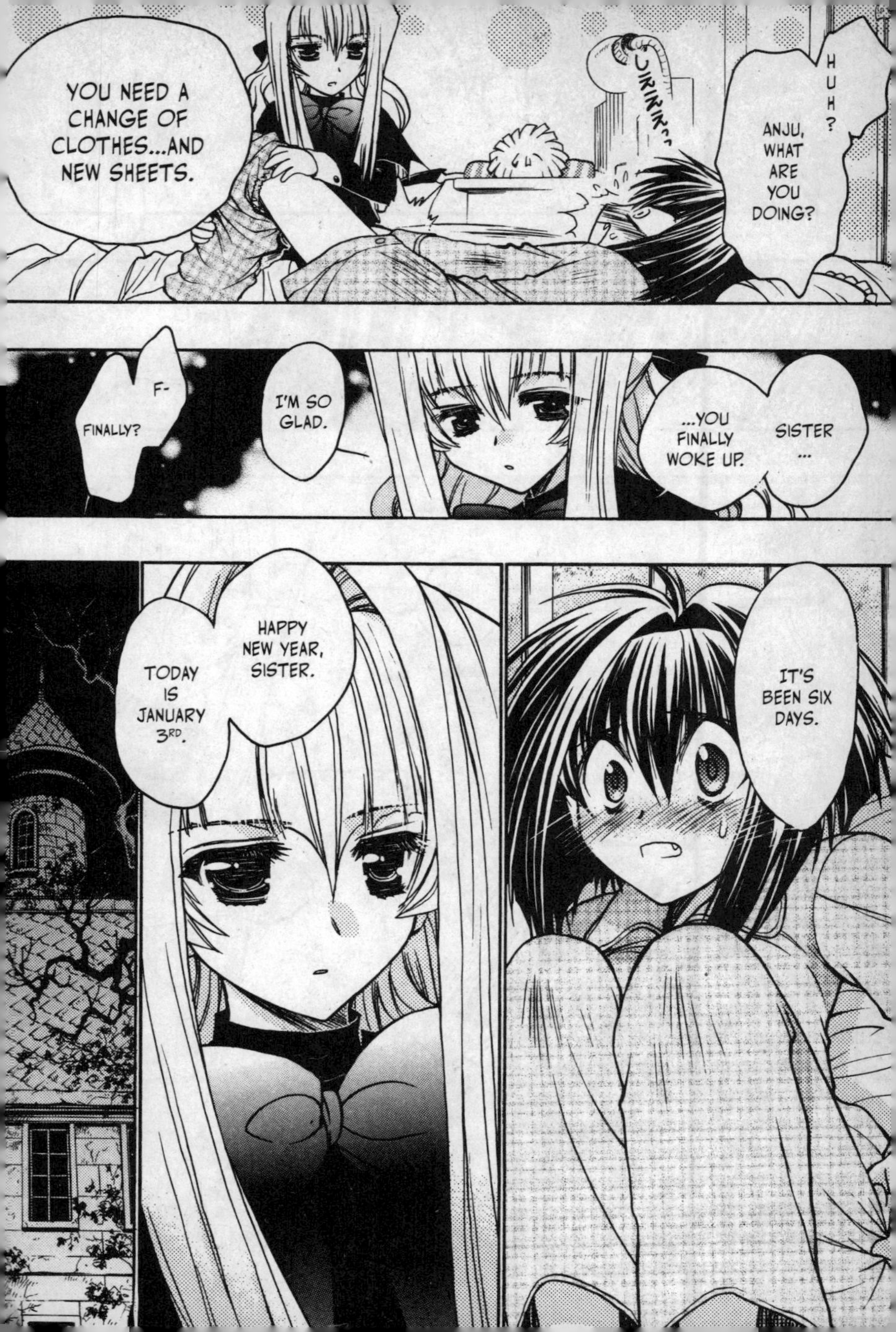
HUH?
ANJU, WHAT ARE YOU DOING?
YOU NEED A CHANGE OF CLOTHES...AND NEW SHEETS.
SISTER ...
...YOU FINALLY WOKE UP.
I'M SO GLAD.
F- FINALLY?
IT'S BEEN SIX DAYS.
HAPPY NEW YEAR, SISTER.
TODAY IS JANUARY 3RD.

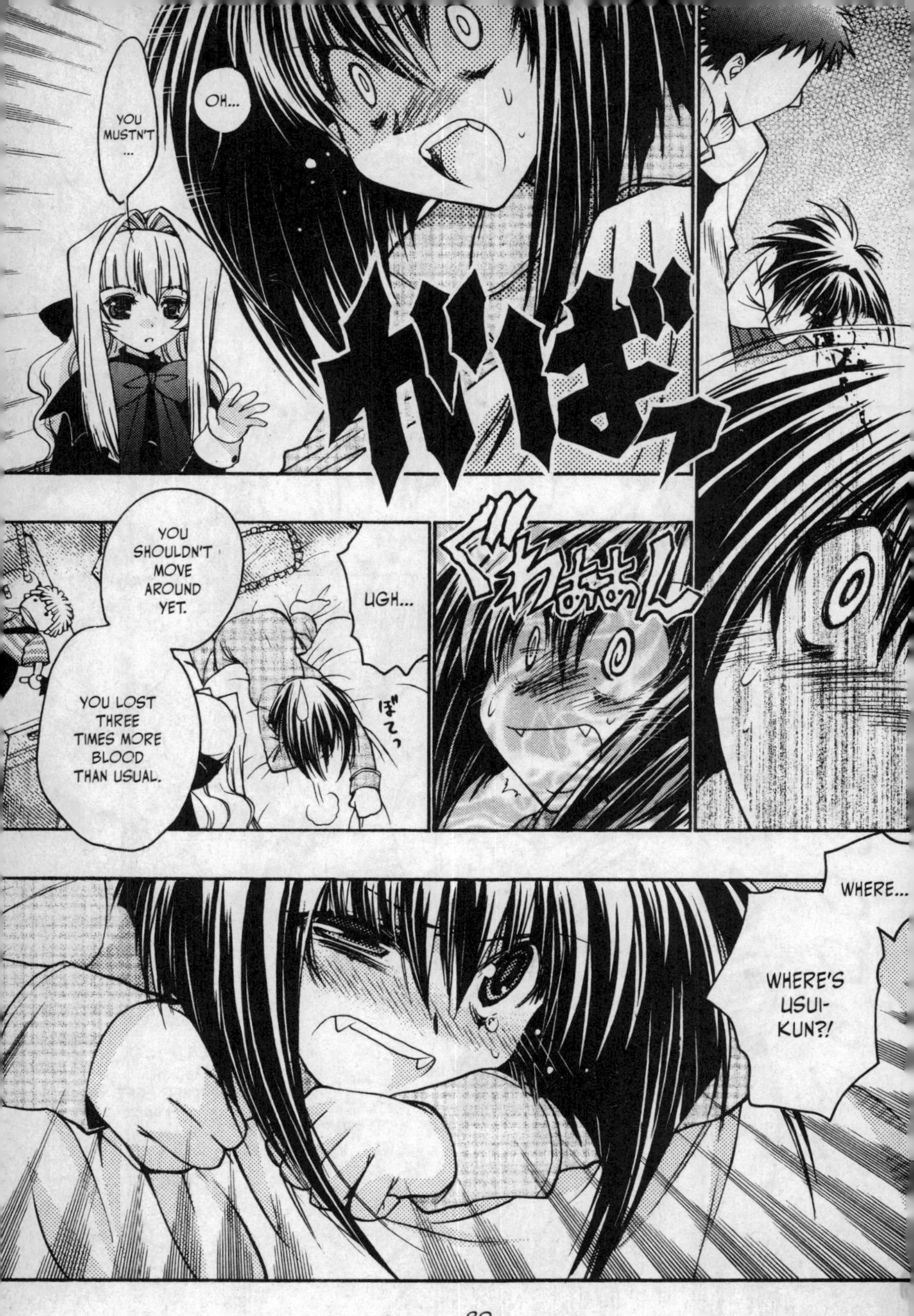
OH...
YOU MUSTN'T ...
UGH...
ぼてっ
YOU SHOULDN'T MOVE AROUND YET.
YOU LOST THREE TIMES MORE BLOOD THAN USUAL.
WHERE...
WHERE'S USUI-KUN?!

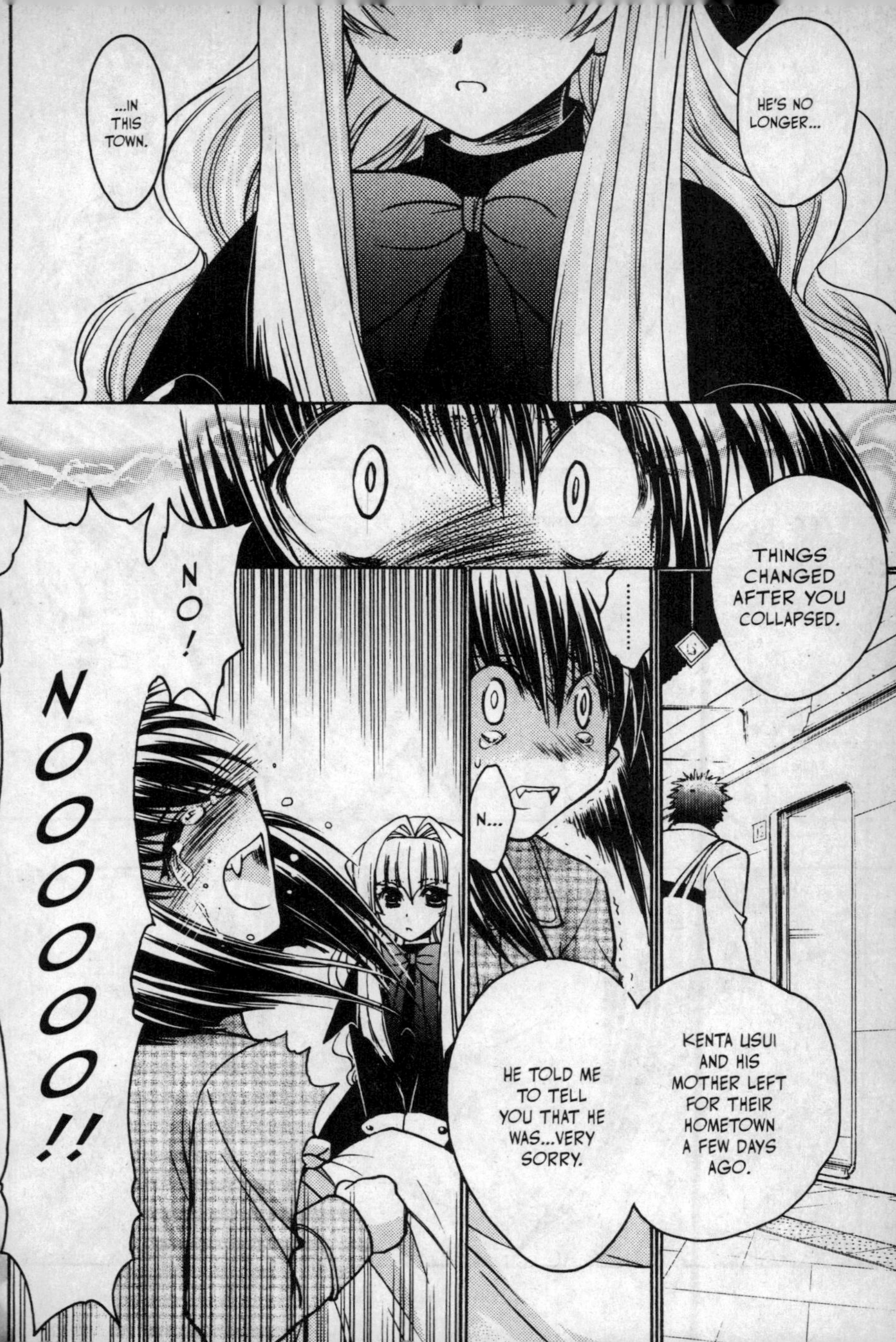

HE'S NO LONGER...
...IN THIS TOWN.
THINGS CHANGED AFTER YOU COLLAPSED.
KENTA USUI AND HIS MOTHER LEFT FOR THEIR HOMETOWN A FEW DAYS AGO.
HE TOLD ME TO TELL YOU THAT HE WAS...VERY SORRY.
......
N...
NO!
NOOOOOO!!

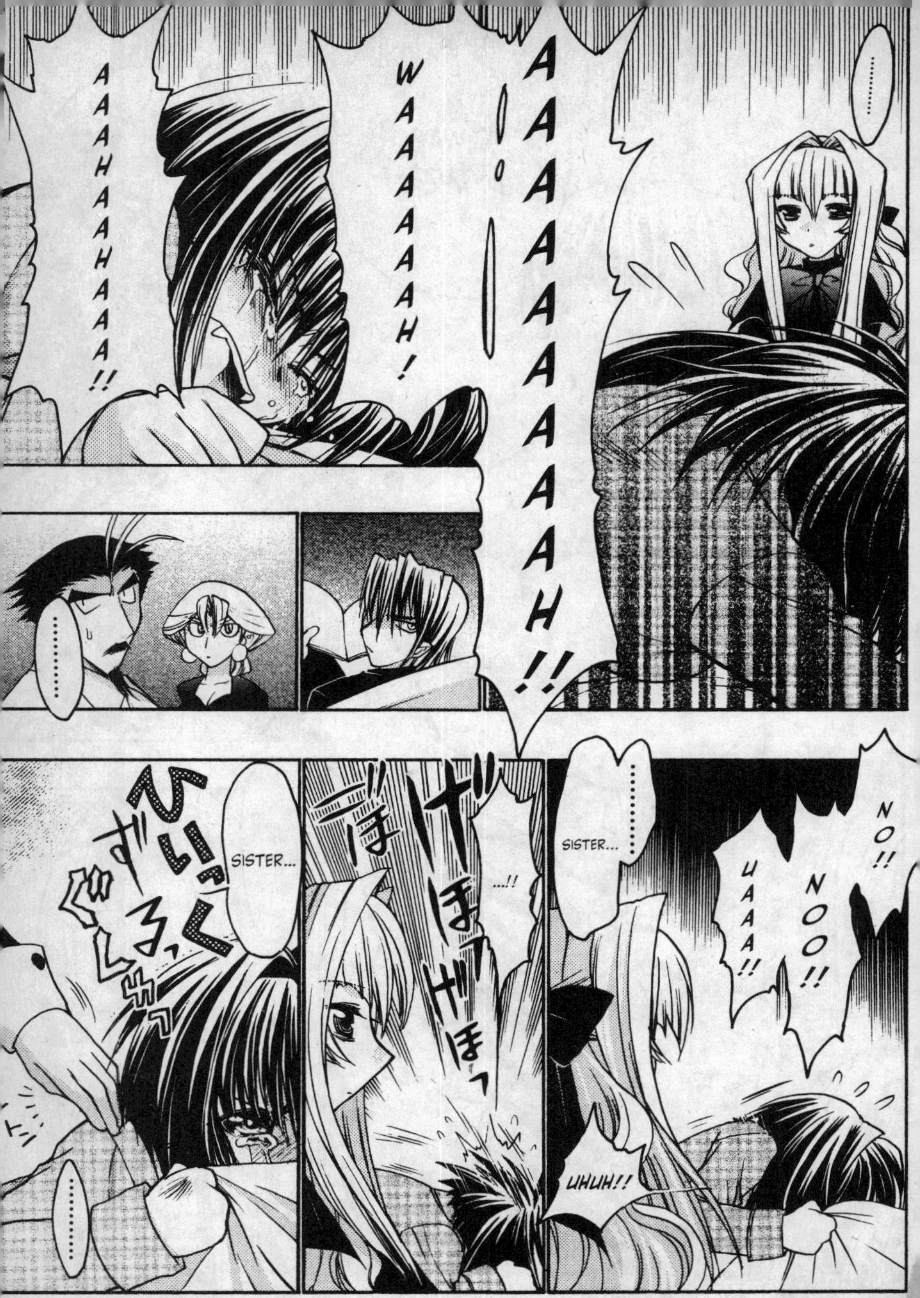
......
AAAAAAAAAAAAAAH!!
WAAAAAAAAAH!
AAAHAAAHAAAA!!
......
NO!!
NOO!!
UAAAA!!
SISTER......
UHUH!!
...!!
SISTER......
......

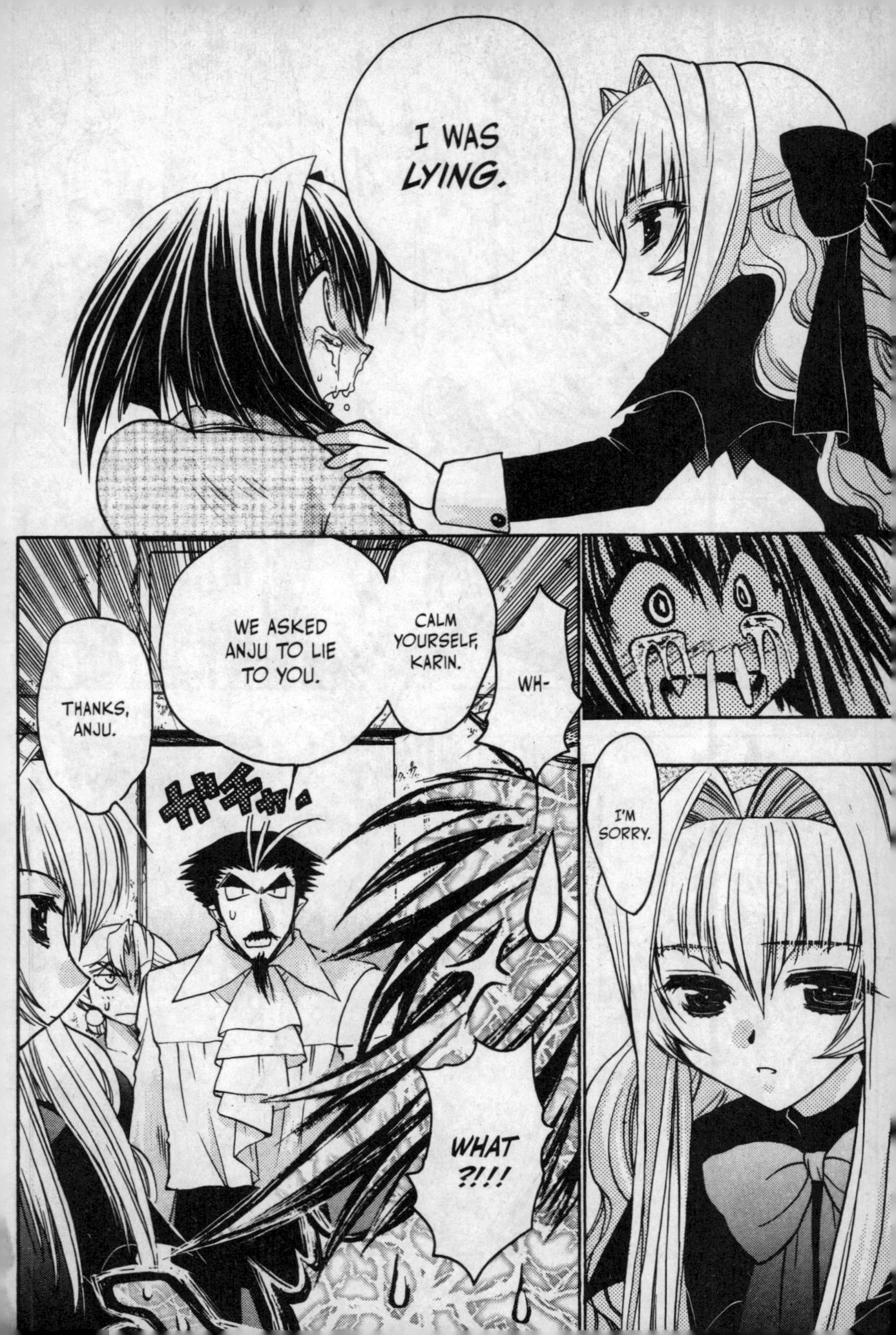
I WAS LYING.
WH-
I'M SORRY.
CALM YOURSELF, KARIN.
WE ASKED ANJU TO LIE TO YOU.
THANKS, ANJU.
ガチャ
WHAT?!!!

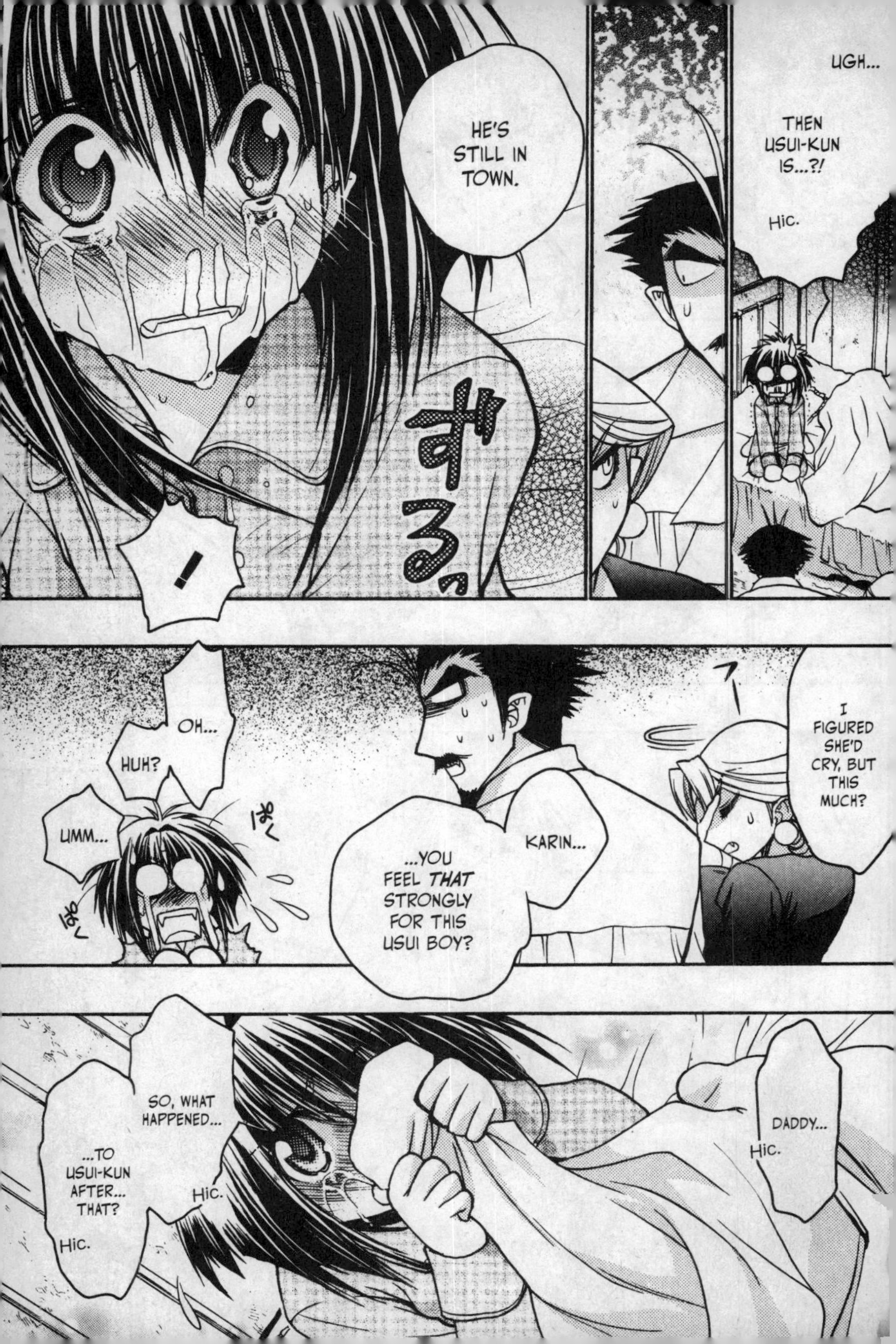
UGH...
THEN USUI-KUN IS...?!
Hic.
HE'S STILL IN TOWN.
ずるっ
!
I FIGURED SHE'D CRY, BUT THIS MUCH?
KARIN...
...YOU FEEL *THAT* STRONGLY FOR THIS USUI BOY?
OH...
HUH?
UMM...
ぱく
ぱく
DADDY...
Hic.
SO, WHAT HAPPENED...
...TO USUI-KUN AFTER... THAT?
Hic.
Hic.

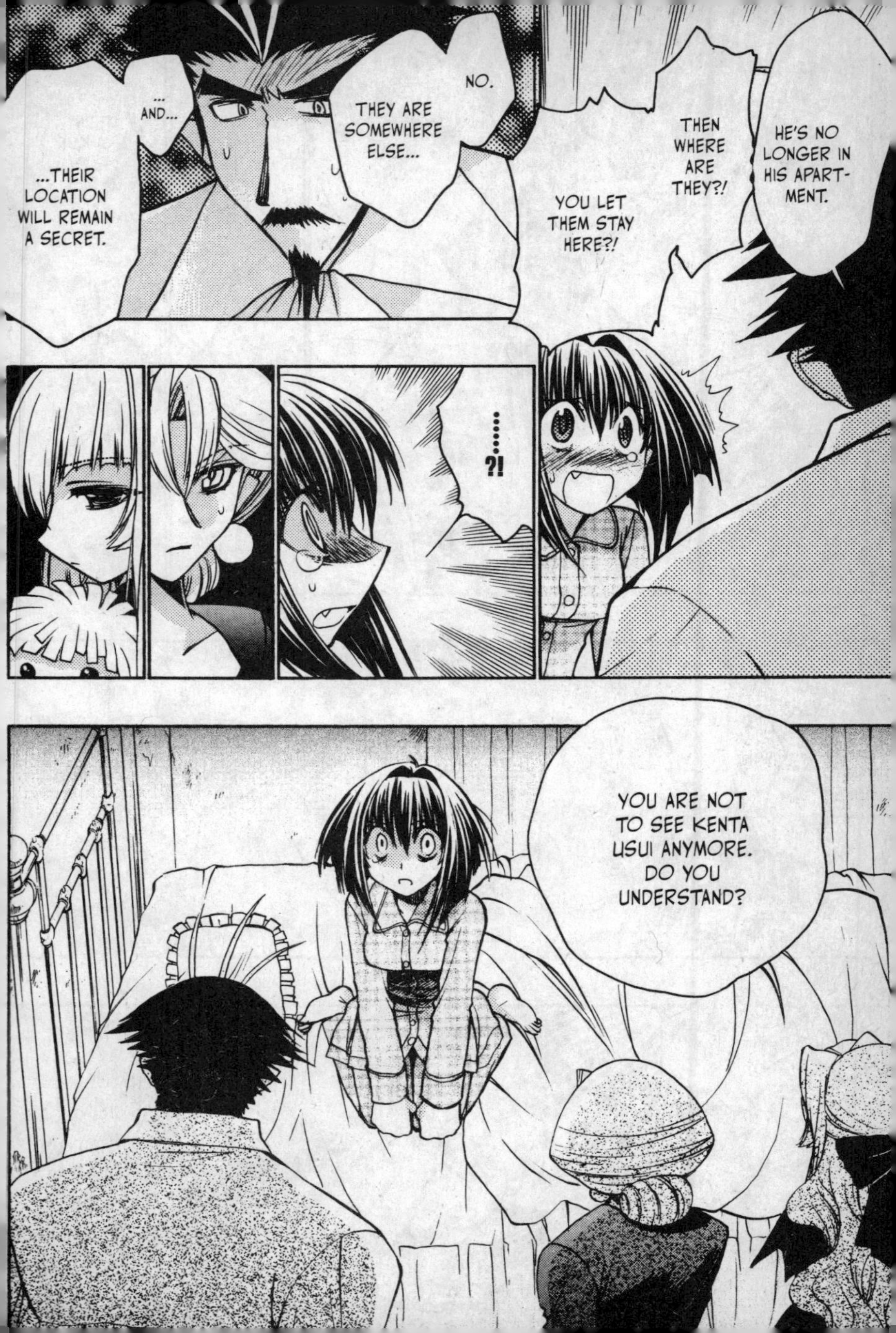
HE'S NO LONGER IN HIS APARTMENT.
THEN WHERE ARE THEY?!
YOU LET THEM STAY HERE?!
NO.
THEY ARE SOMEWHERE ELSE...
... AND...
...THEIR LOCATION WILL REMAIN A SECRET.
......?!
YOU ARE NOT TO SEE KENTA USUI ANYMORE. DO YOU UNDERSTAND?

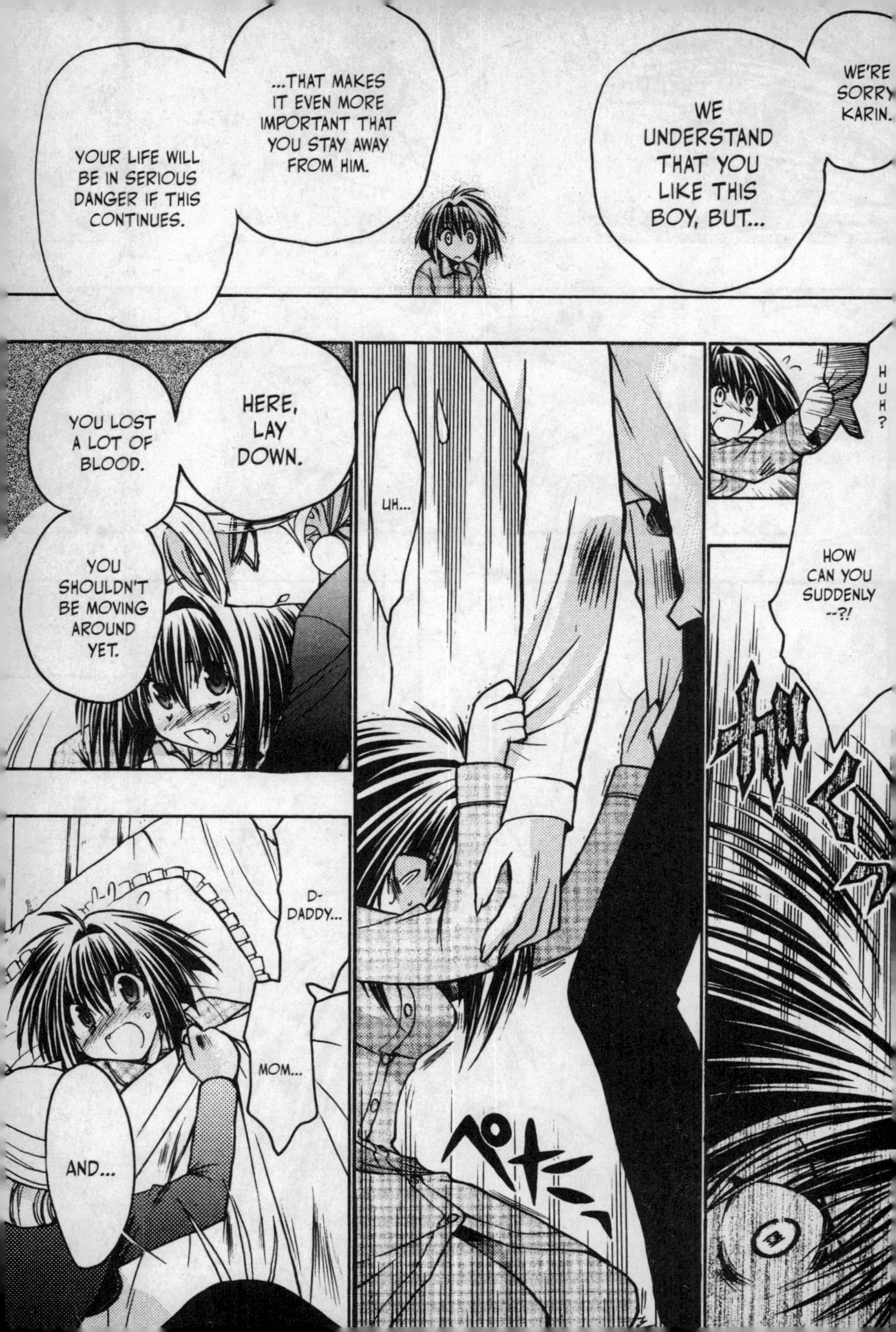
WE'RE SORRY KARIN.
WE UNDERSTAND THAT YOU LIKE THIS BOY, BUT...
...THAT MAKES IT EVEN MORE IMPORTANT THAT YOU STAY AWAY FROM HIM.
YOUR LIFE WILL BE IN SERIOUS DANGER IF THIS CONTINUES.
HUH?
HOW CAN YOU SUDDENLY --?!
UH...
HERE, LAY DOWN.
YOU LOST A LOT OF BLOOD.
YOU SHOULDN'T BE MOVING AROUND YET.
D-DADDY...
MOM...
AND...

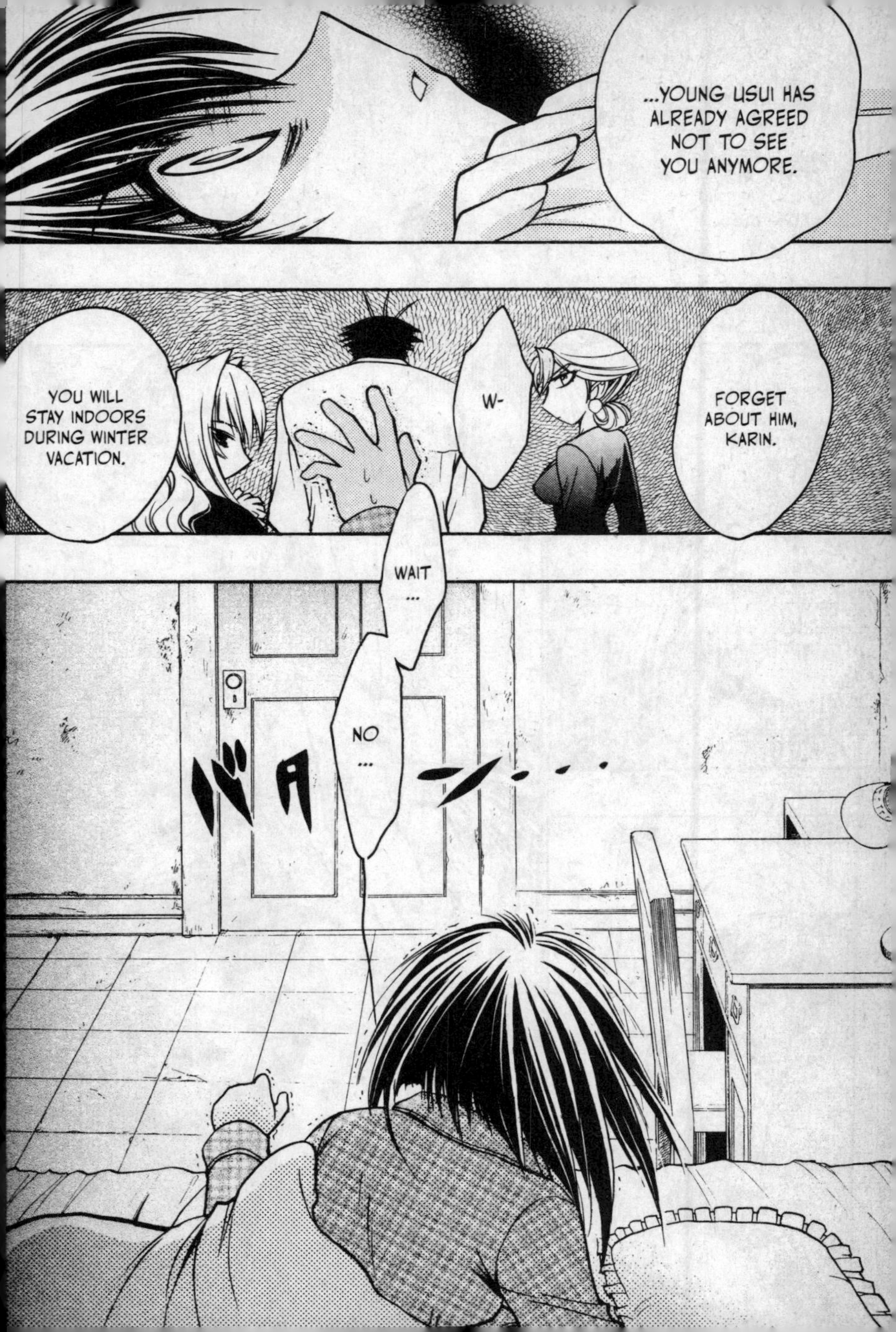
...YOUNG USUI HAS ALREADY AGREED NOT TO SEE YOU ANYMORE.
FORGET ABOUT HIM, KARIN.
W-
YOU WILL STAY INDOORS DURING WINTER VACATION.
WAIT ...
NO ...
バタン...

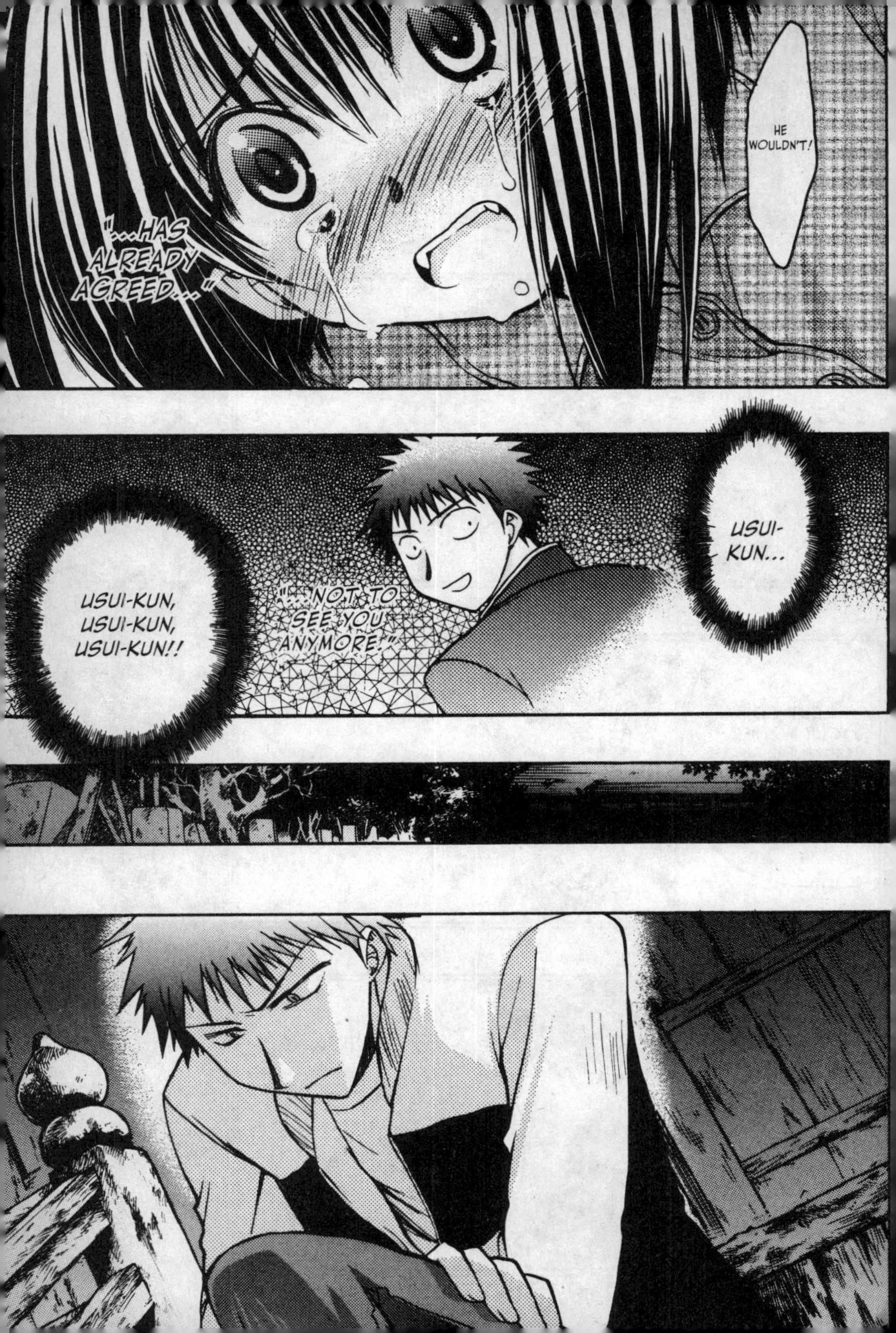
HE WOULDN'T!
"...HAS ALREADY AGREED..."
USUI-KUN...
"...NOT TO SEE YOU ANYMORE."
USUI-KUN, USUI-KUN, USUI-KUN!!

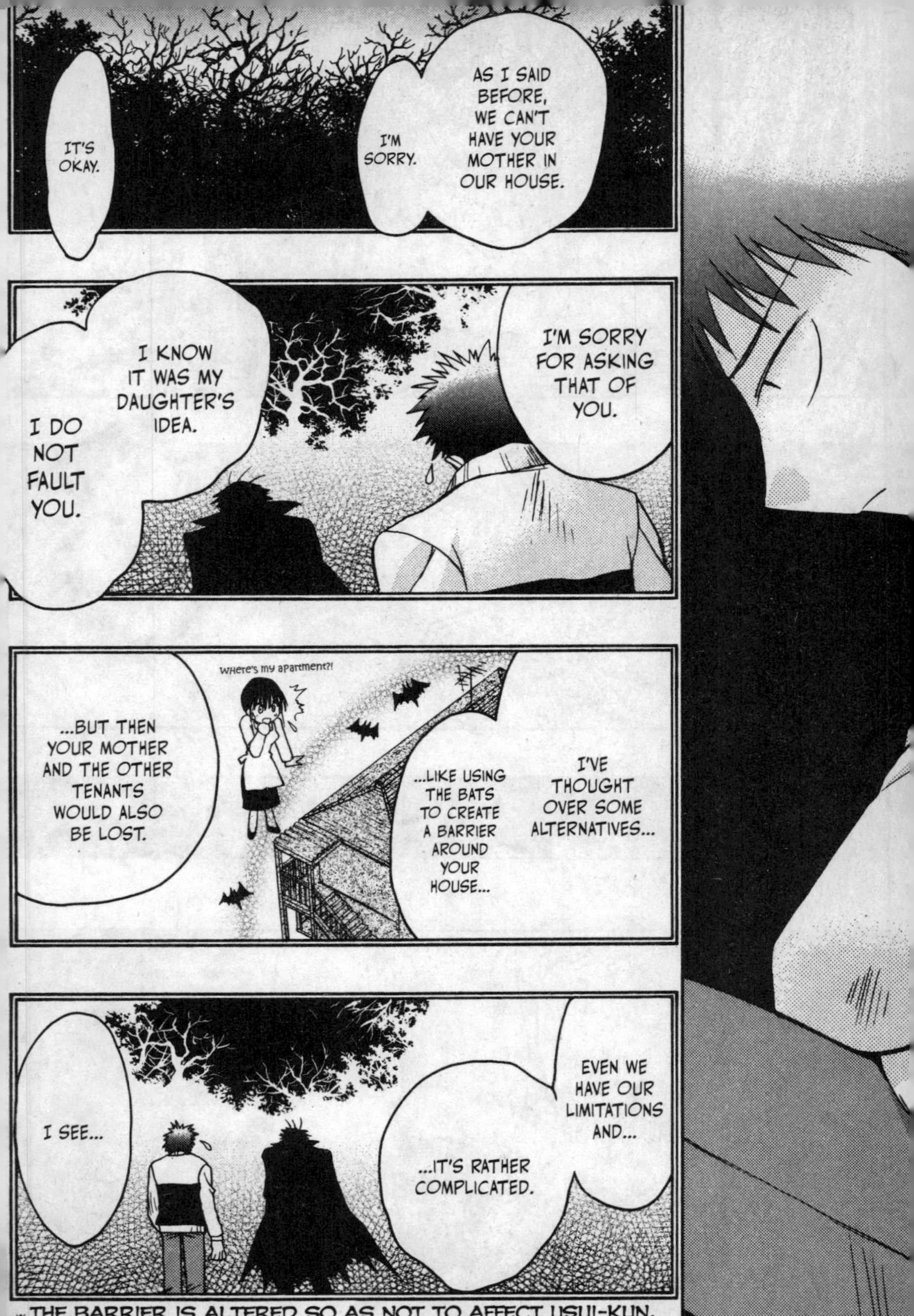
AS I SAID BEFORE, WE CAN'T HAVE YOUR MOTHER IN OUR HOUSE.
I'M SORRY.
IT'S OKAY.
I'M SORRY FOR ASKING THAT OF YOU.
I KNOW IT WAS MY DAUGHTER'S IDEA.
I DO NOT FAULT YOU.
I'VE THOUGHT OVER SOME ALTERNATIVES...
...LIKE USING THE BATS TO CREATE A BARRIER AROUND YOUR HOUSE...
Where's my apartment?!
...BUT THEN YOUR MOTHER AND THE OTHER TENANTS WOULD ALSO BE LOST.
EVEN WE HAVE OUR LIMITATIONS AND...
...IT'S RATHER COMPLICATED.
I SEE...

※ THE BARRIER IS ALTERED SO AS NOT TO AFFECT USUI-KUN.

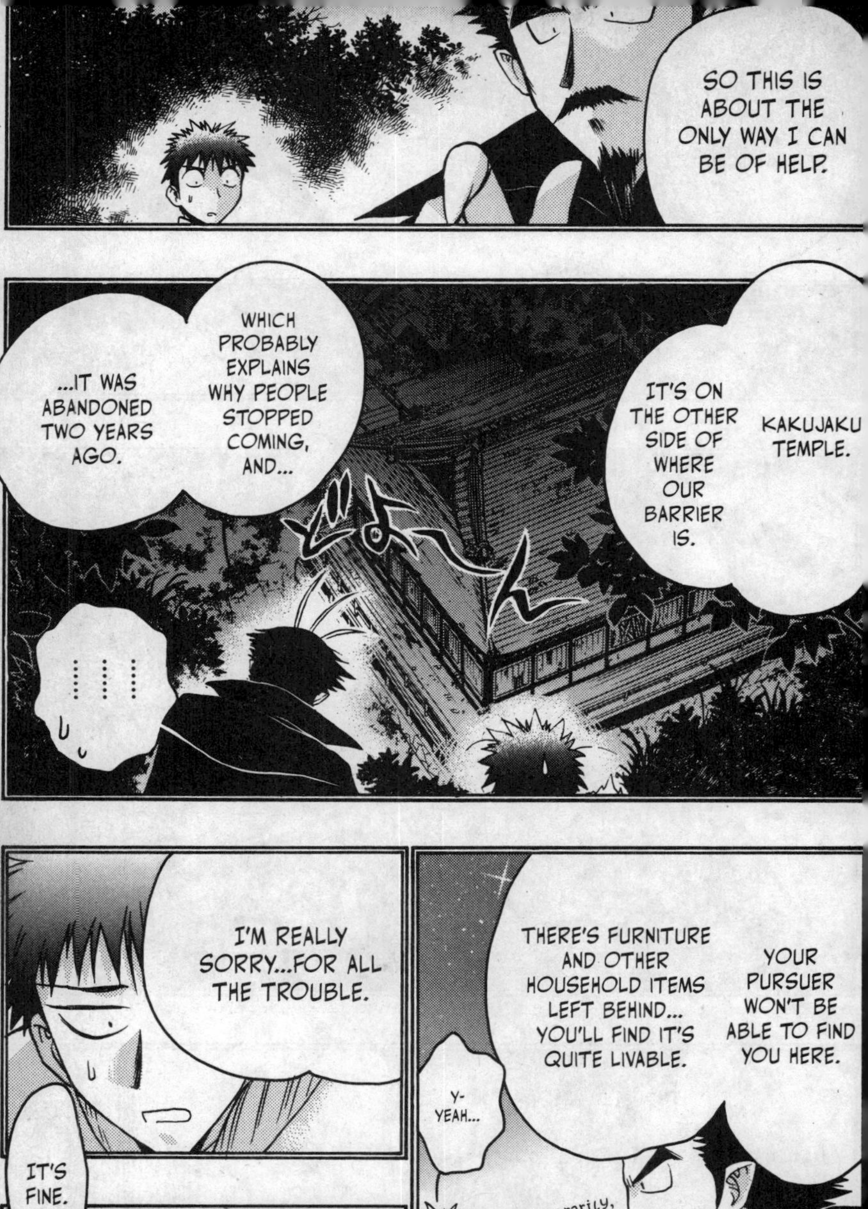
SO THIS IS ABOUT THE ONLY WAY I CAN BE OF HELP.
KAKUJAKU TEMPLE.
IT'S ON THE OTHER SIDE OF WHERE OUR BARRIER IS.
WHICH PROBABLY EXPLAINS WHY PEOPLE STOPPED COMING, AND...
...IT WAS ABANDONED TWO YEARS AGO.
......
YOUR PURSUER WON'T BE ABLE TO FIND YOU HERE.
THERE'S FURNITURE AND OTHER HOUSEHOLD ITEMS LEFT BEHIND... YOU'LL FIND IT'S QUITE LIVABLE.
Y-YEAH...
Temporarily, of course.
I'M REALLY SORRY...FOR ALL THE TROUBLE.
IT'S FINE.

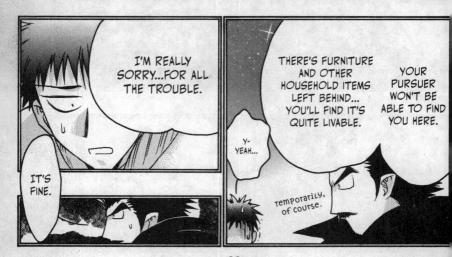

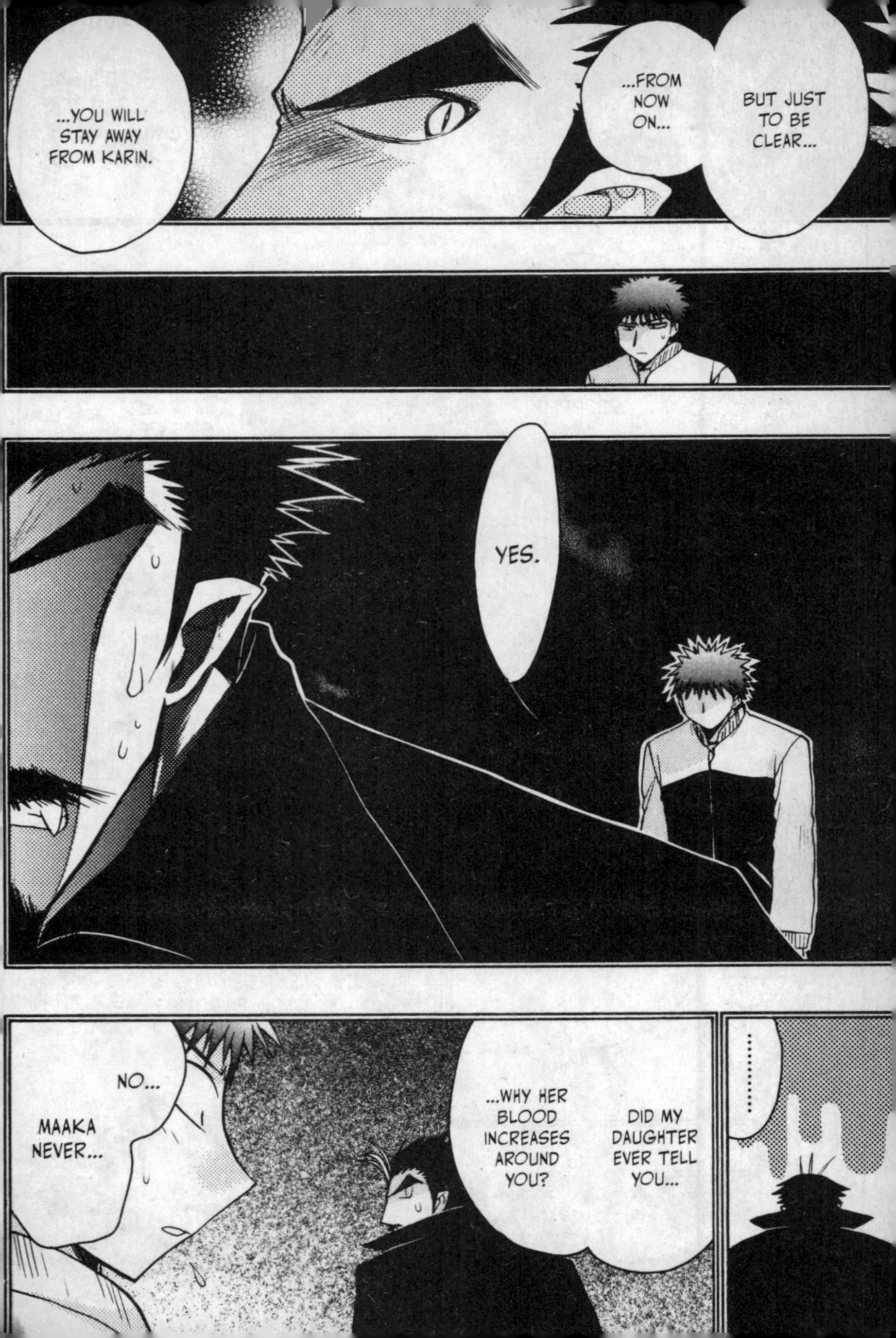
BUT JUST TO BE CLEAR...
...FROM NOW ON...
...YOU WILL STAY AWAY FROM KARIN.
YES.
......
DID MY DAUGHTER EVER TELL YOU...
...WHY HER BLOOD INCREASES AROUND YOU?
NO...
MAAKA NEVER...

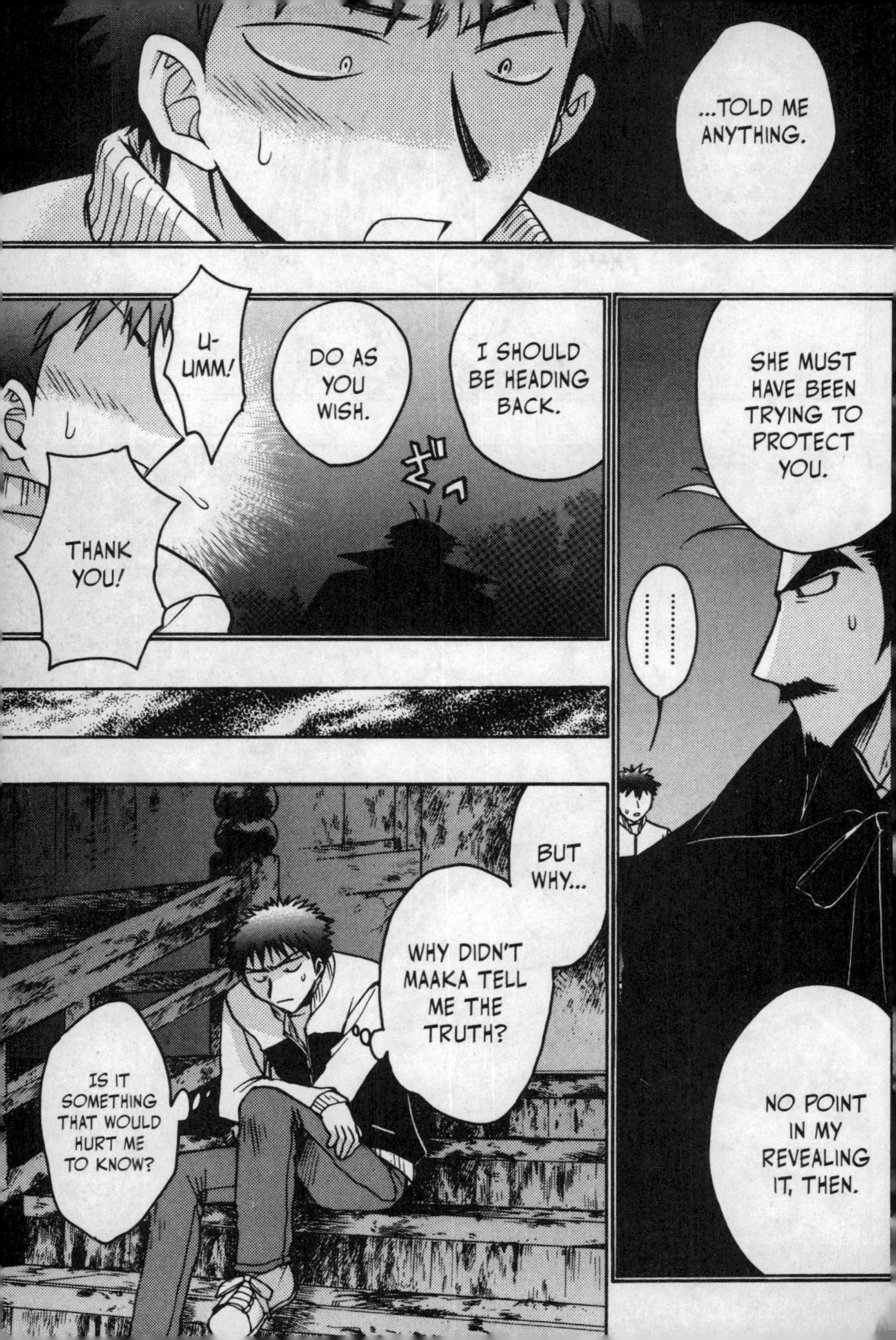
...TOLD ME ANYTHING.
SHE MUST HAVE BEEN TRYING TO PROTECT YOU.
......
NO POINT IN MY REVEALING IT, THEN.
I SHOULD BE HEADING BACK.
DO AS YOU WISH.
U-UMM!
THANK YOU!
BUT WHY...
WHY DIDN'T MAAKA TELL ME THE TRUTH?
IS IT SOMETHING THAT WOULD HURT ME TO KNOW?

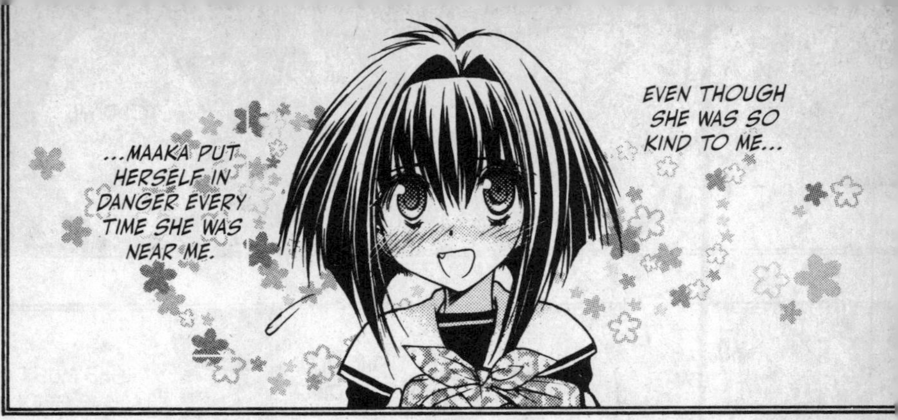
EVEN THOUGH SHE WAS SO KIND TO ME...
...MAAKA PUT HERSELF IN DANGER EVERY TIME SHE WAS NEAR ME.

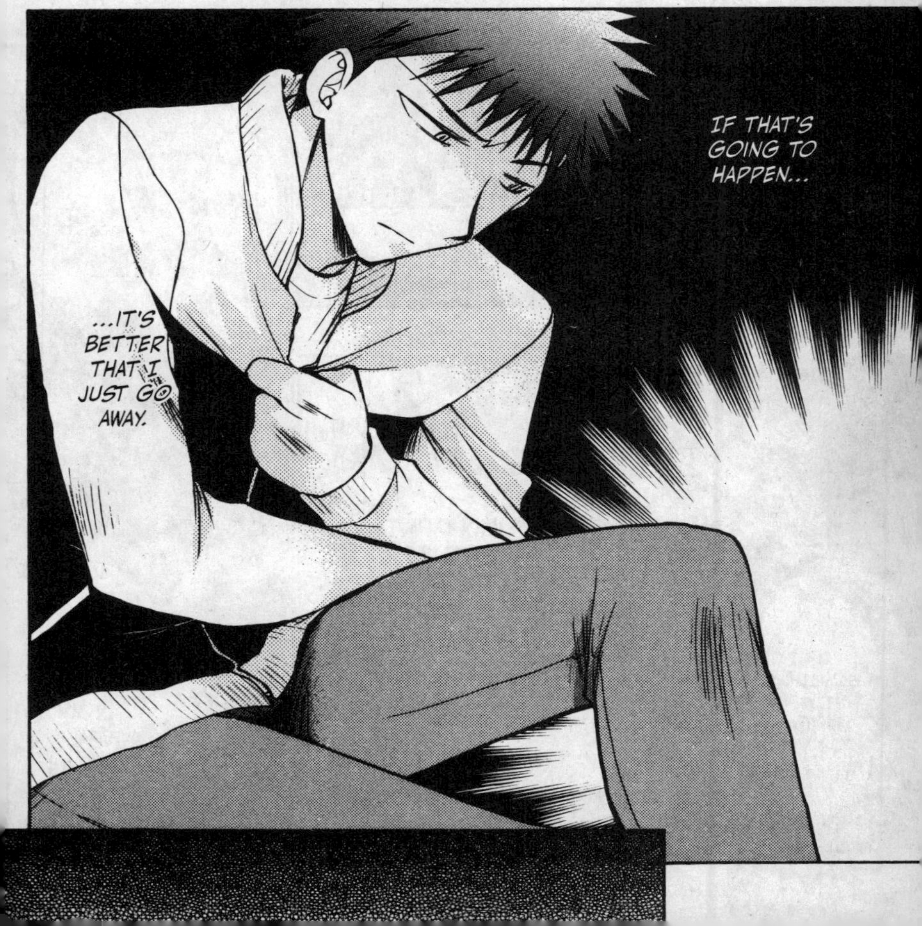
IF THAT'S GOING TO HAPPEN...
...IT'S BETTER THAT I JUST GO AWAY.

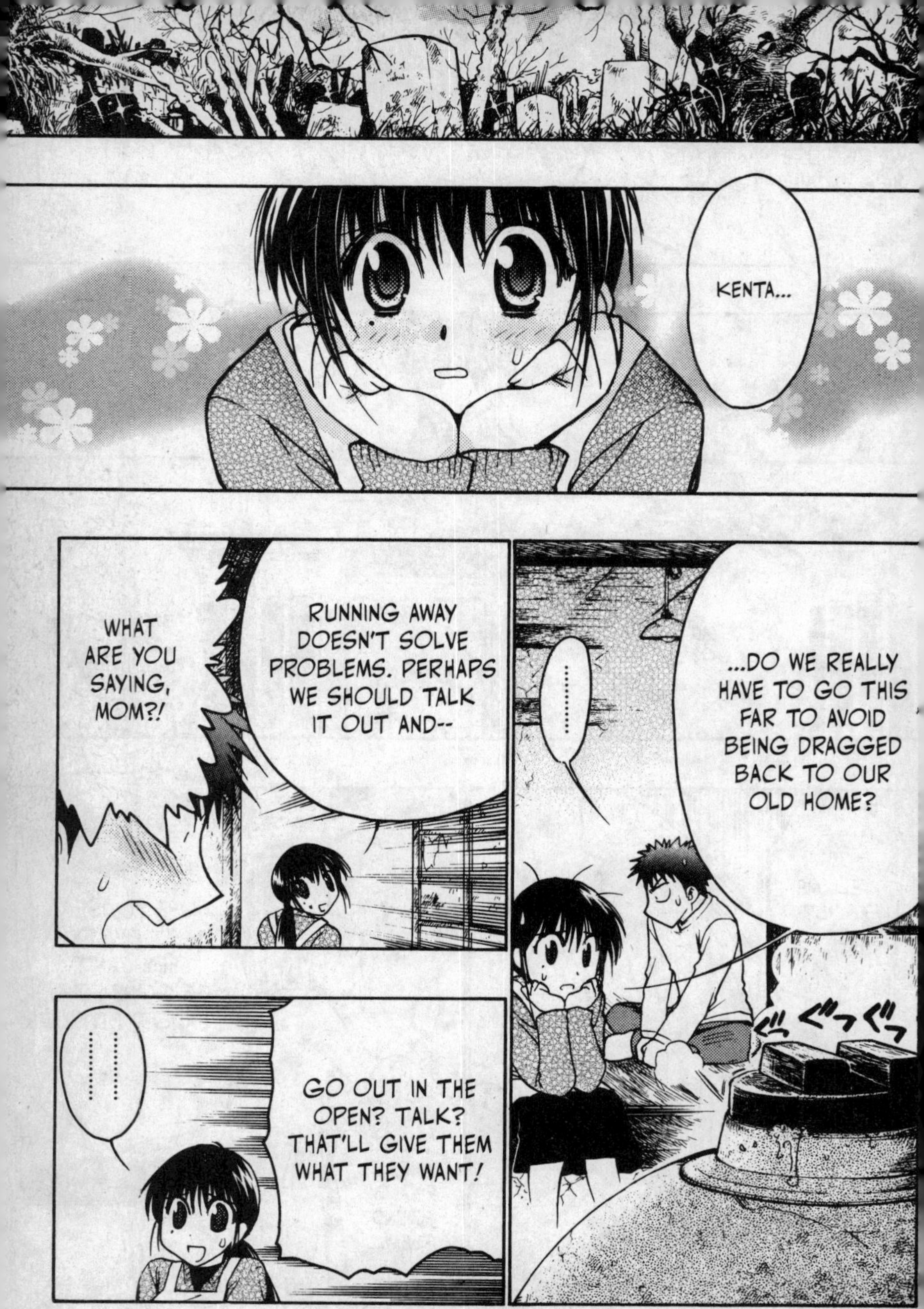
KENTA...
...DO WE REALLY HAVE TO GO THIS FAR TO AVOID BEING DRAGGED BACK TO OUR OLD HOME?
......
ぐっぐっぐっ
RUNNING AWAY DOESN'T SOLVE PROBLEMS. PERHAPS WE SHOULD TALK IT OUT AND--
WHAT ARE YOU SAYING, MOM?!
GO OUT IN THE OPEN? TALK? THAT'LL GIVE THEM WHAT THEY WANT!
......

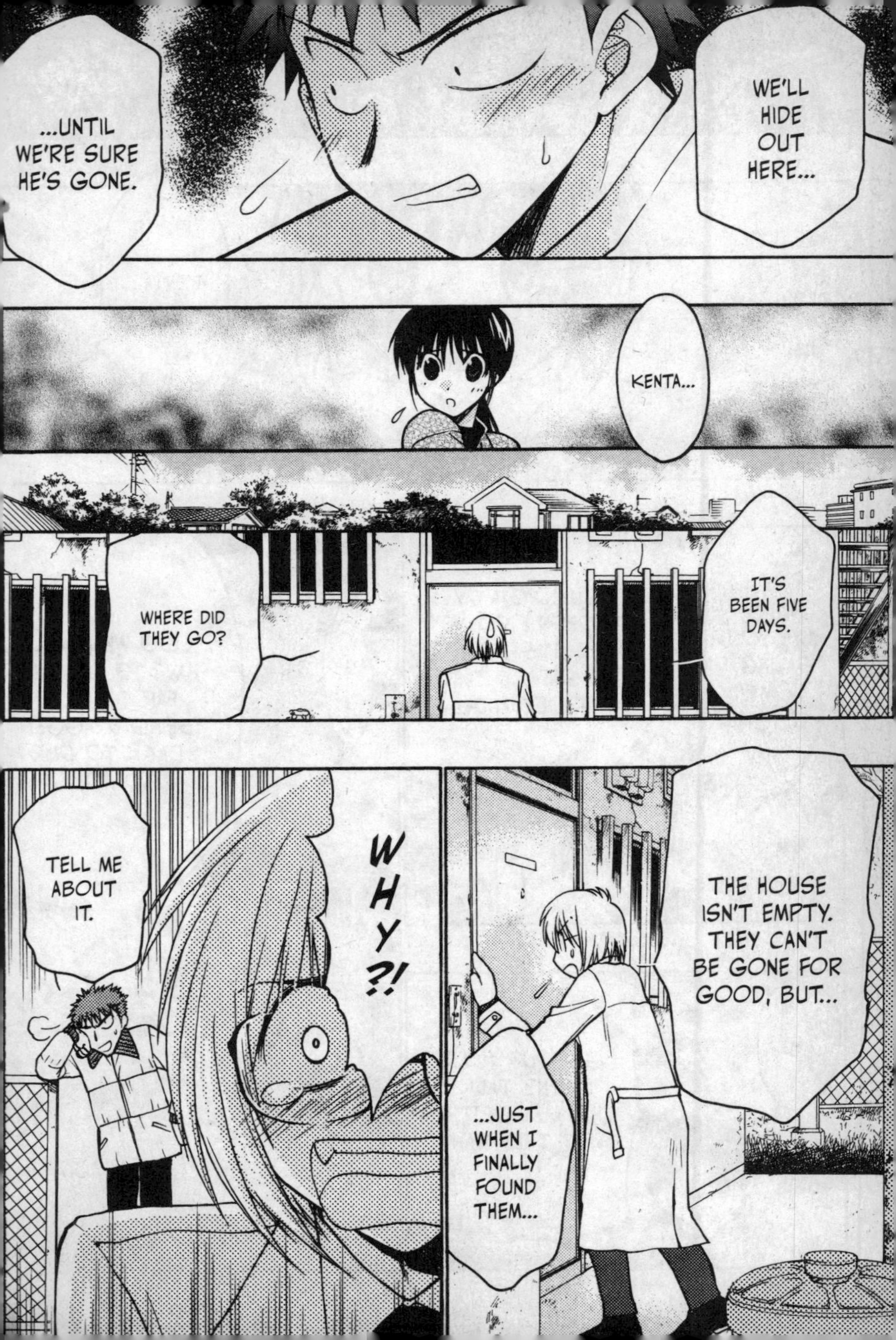
WE'LL HIDE OUT HERE...
...UNTIL WE'RE SURE HE'S GONE.
KENTA...
IT'S BEEN FIVE DAYS.
WHERE DID THEY GO?
THE HOUSE ISN'T EMPTY. THEY CAN'T BE GONE FOR GOOD, BUT...
...JUST WHEN I FINALLY FOUND THEM...
WHY?!
TELL ME ABOUT IT.

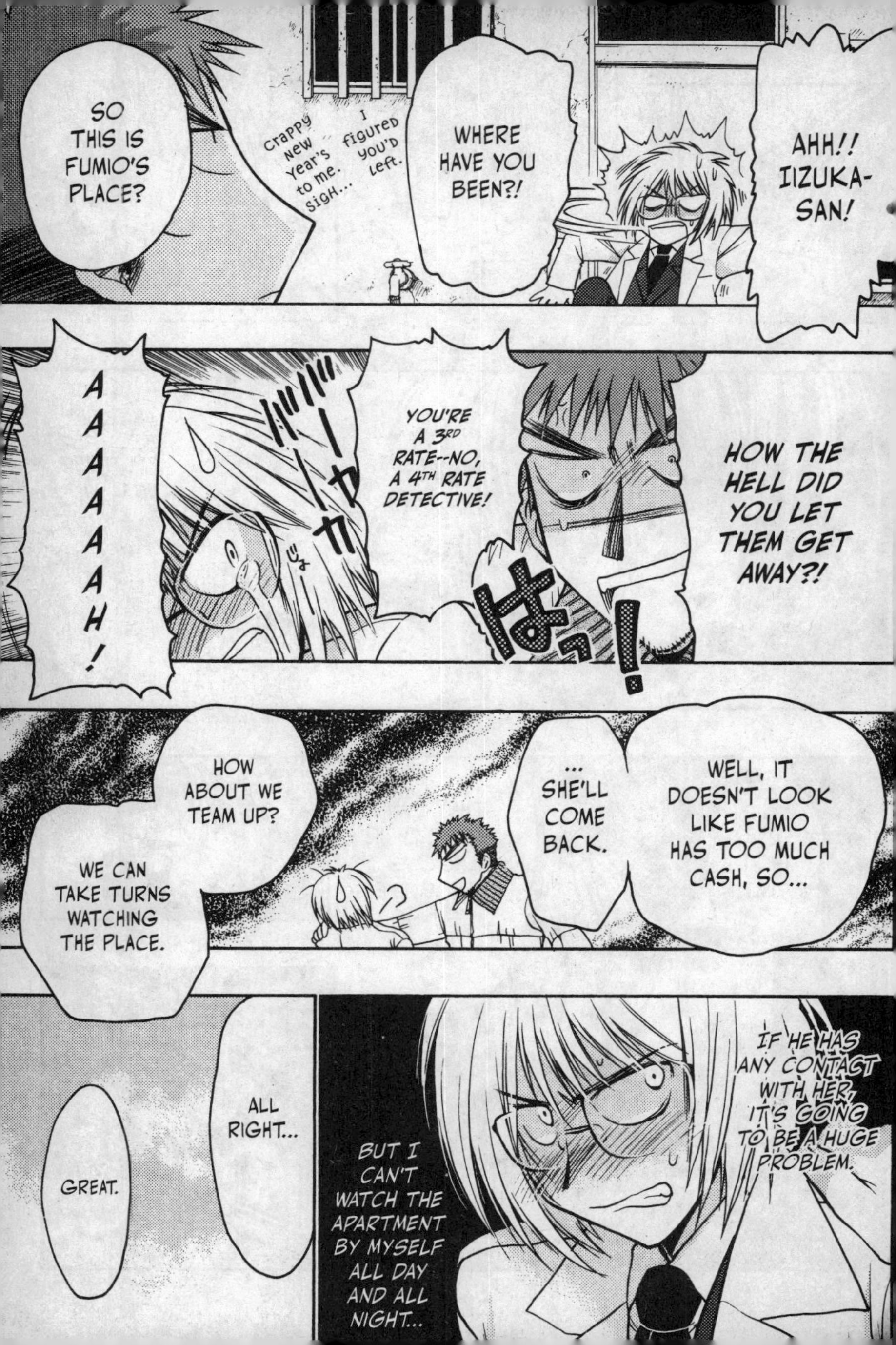
AHH!! IIZUKA-SAN!
WHERE HAVE YOU BEEN?!
I figured YOU'D left.
Crappy New Year's to me. SIGH...
SO THIS IS FUMIO'S PLACE?
HOW THE HELL DID YOU LET THEM GET AWAY?!
はっ!
YOU'RE A 3RD RATE--NO, A 4TH RATE DETECTIVE!
AAAAAAH!
WELL, IT DOESN'T LOOK LIKE FUMIO HAS TOO MUCH CASH, SO...
... SHE'LL COME BACK.
HOW ABOUT WE TEAM UP?
WE CAN TAKE TURNS WATCHING THE PLACE.
IF HE HAS ANY CONTACT WITH HER, IT'S GOING TO BE A HUGE PROBLEM.
BUT I CAN'T WATCH THE APARTMENT BY MYSELF ALL DAY AND ALL NIGHT...
ALL RIGHT...
GREAT.

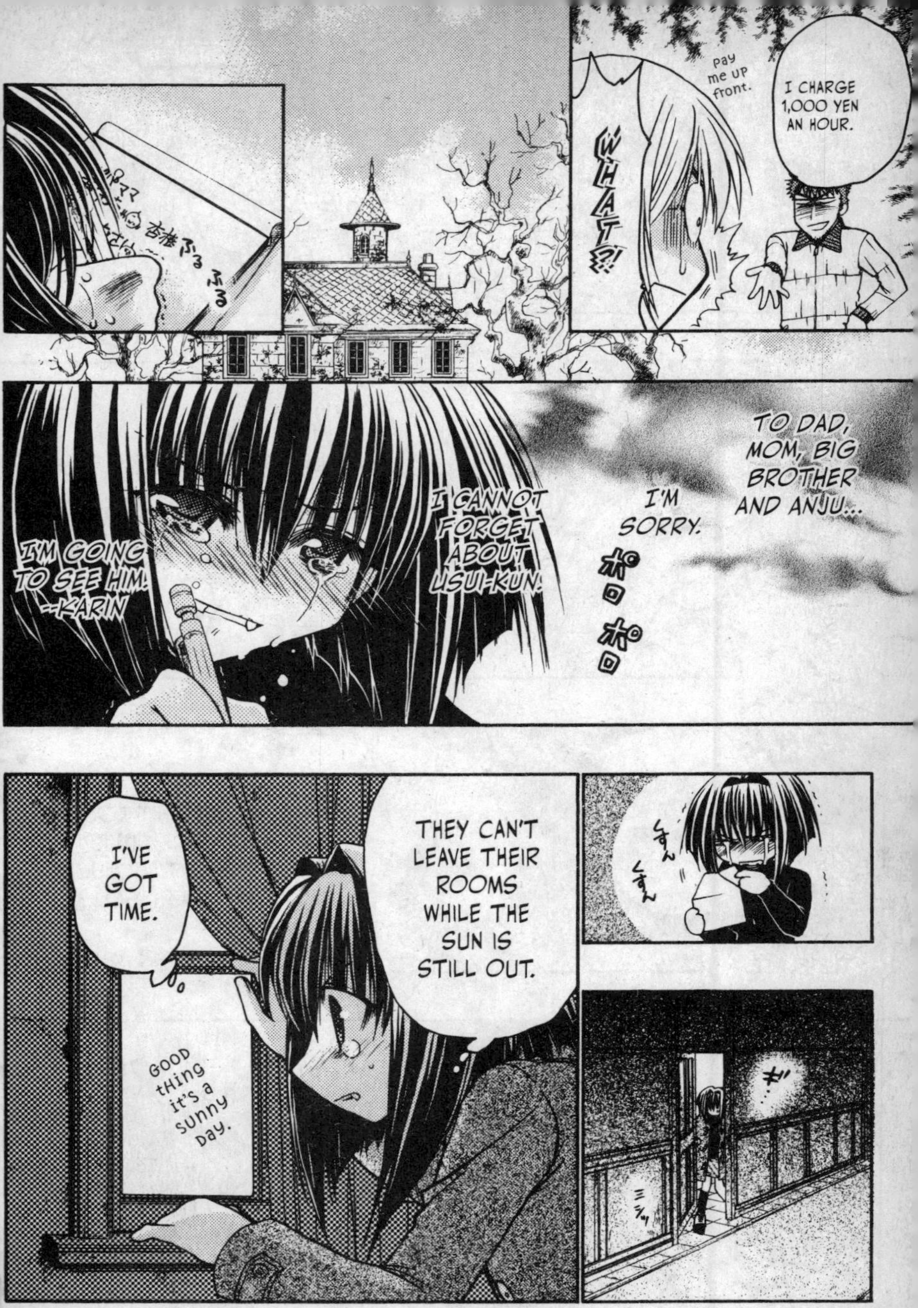
I CHARGE 1,000 YEN AN HOUR.
Pay me up front.
WHAT?!
ふる ふる
TO DAD, MOM, BIG BROTHER AND ANJU...
I'M SORRY.
ポロ ポロ
I CANNOT FORGET ABOUT USUI-KUN!
I'M GOING TO SEE HIM! --KARIN
くすん くすん
ギ
ミシッ
THEY CAN'T LEAVE THEIR ROOMS WHILE THE SUN IS STILL OUT.
I'VE GOT TIME.
GOOD THING it's a SUNNY DAY.

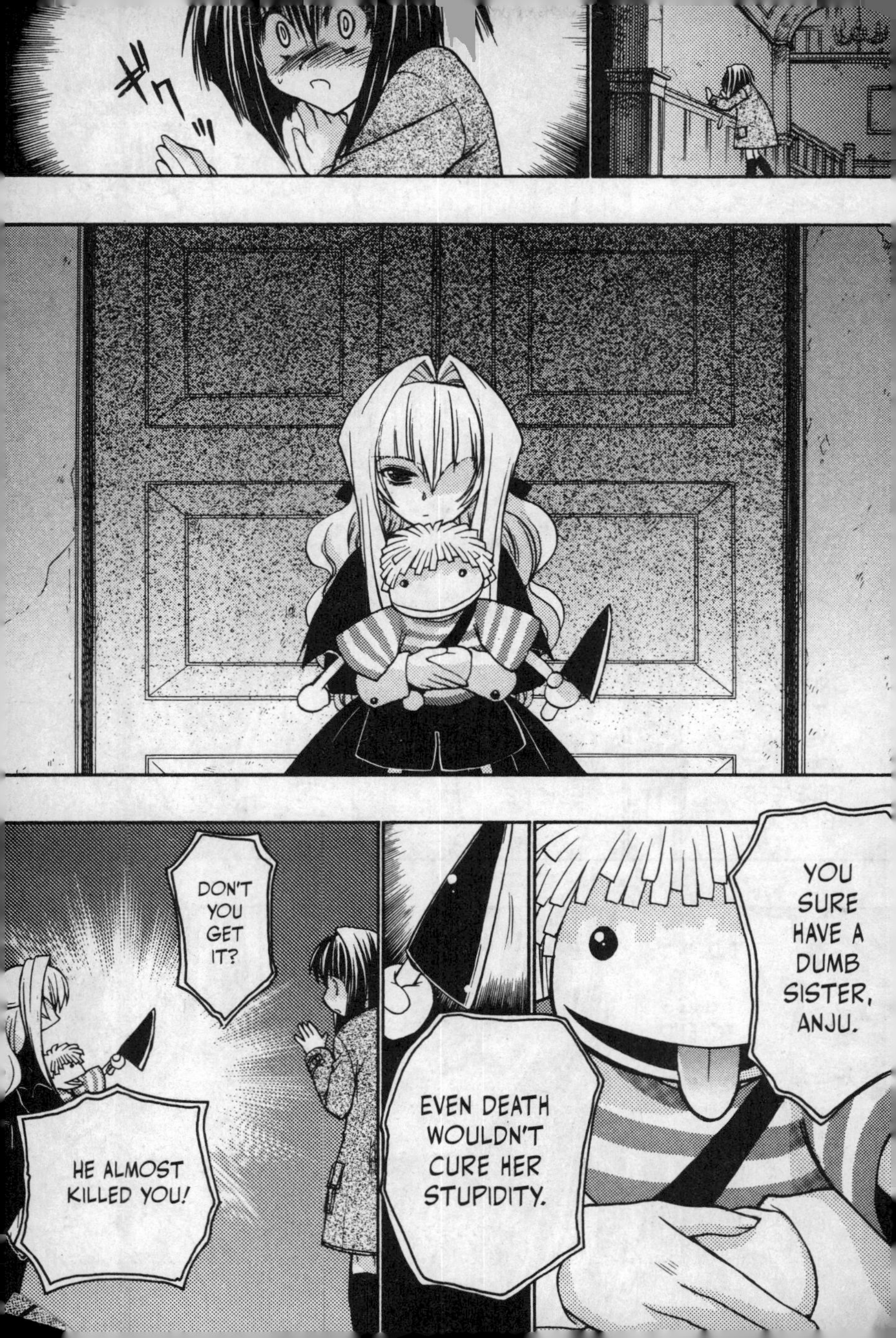
ギクッ
YOU SURE HAVE A DUMB SISTER, ANJU.
EVEN DEATH WOULDN'T CURE HER STUPIDITY.
DON'T YOU GET IT?
HE ALMOST KILLED YOU!

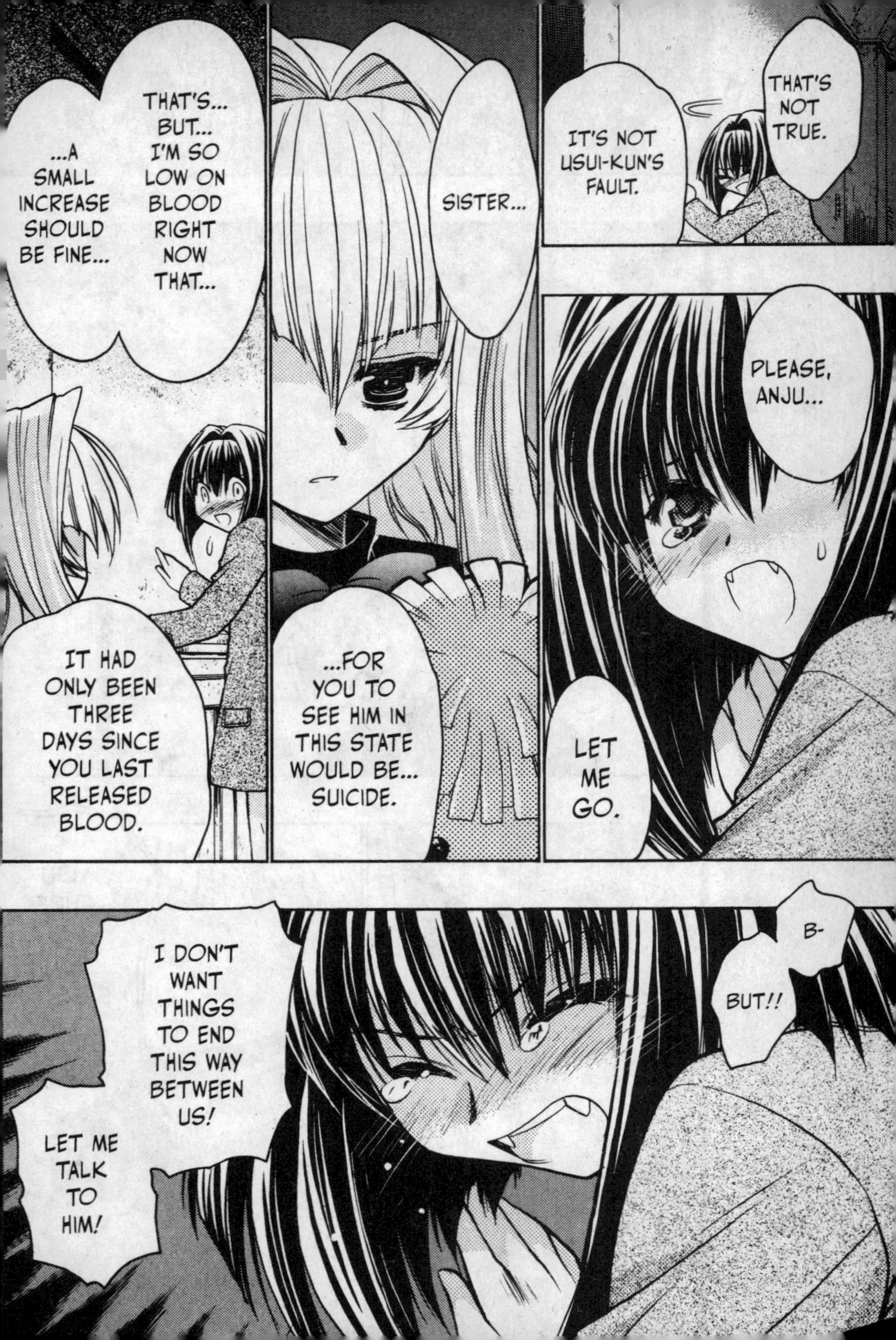
THAT'S NOT TRUE.
IT'S NOT USUI-KUN'S FAULT.
PLEASE, ANJU...
LET ME GO.
SISTER...
...FOR YOU TO SEE HIM IN THIS STATE WOULD BE... SUICIDE.
THAT'S... BUT... I'M SO LOW ON BLOOD RIGHT NOW THAT...
...A SMALL INCREASE SHOULD BE FINE...
IT HAD ONLY BEEN THREE DAYS SINCE YOU LAST RELEASED BLOOD.
B-
BUT!!
I DON'T WANT THINGS TO END THIS WAY BETWEEN US!
LET ME TALK TO HIM!

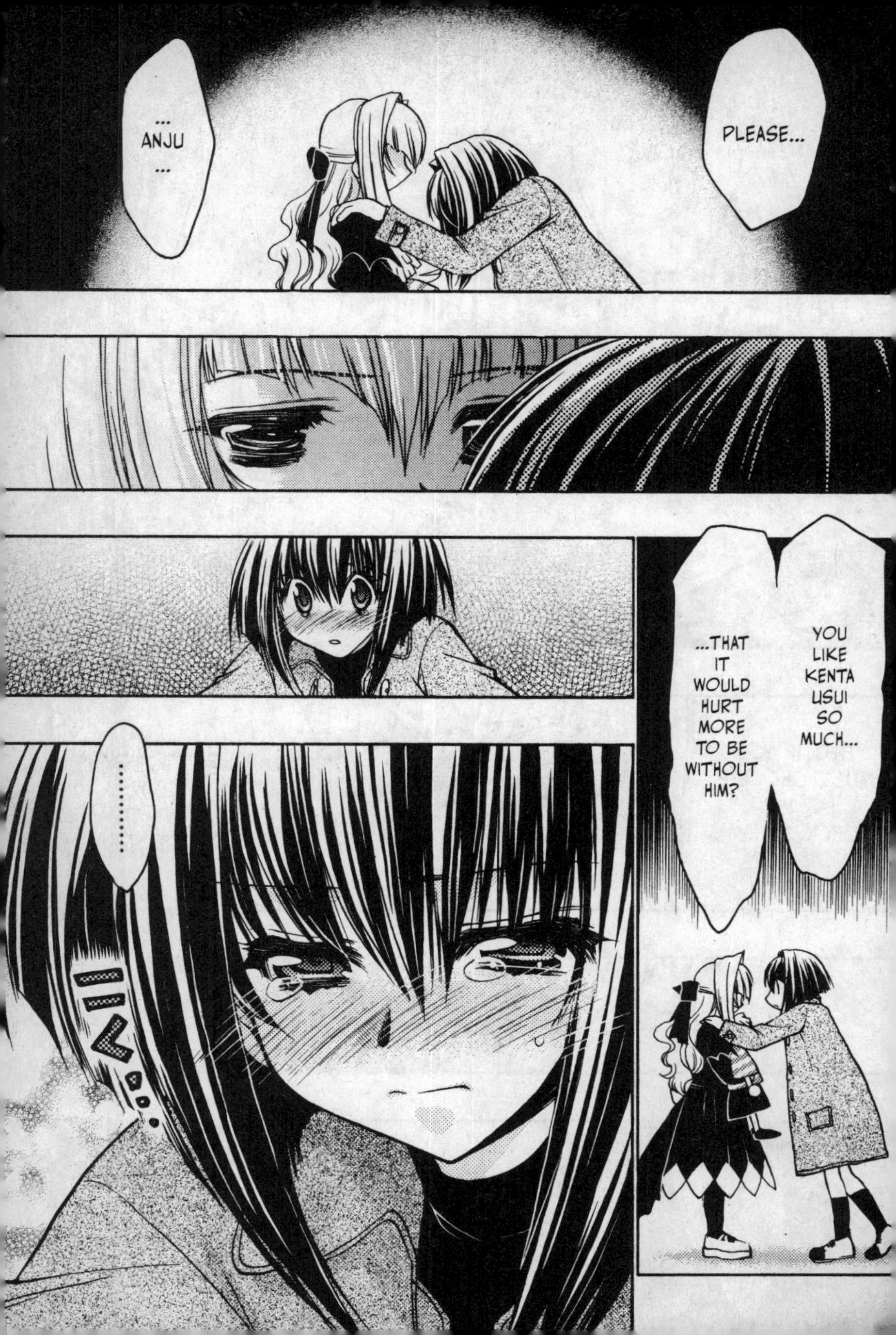
PLEASE...
... ANJU ...
YOU LIKE KENTA USUI SO MUCH...
...THAT IT WOULD HURT MORE TO BE WITHOUT HIM?
....

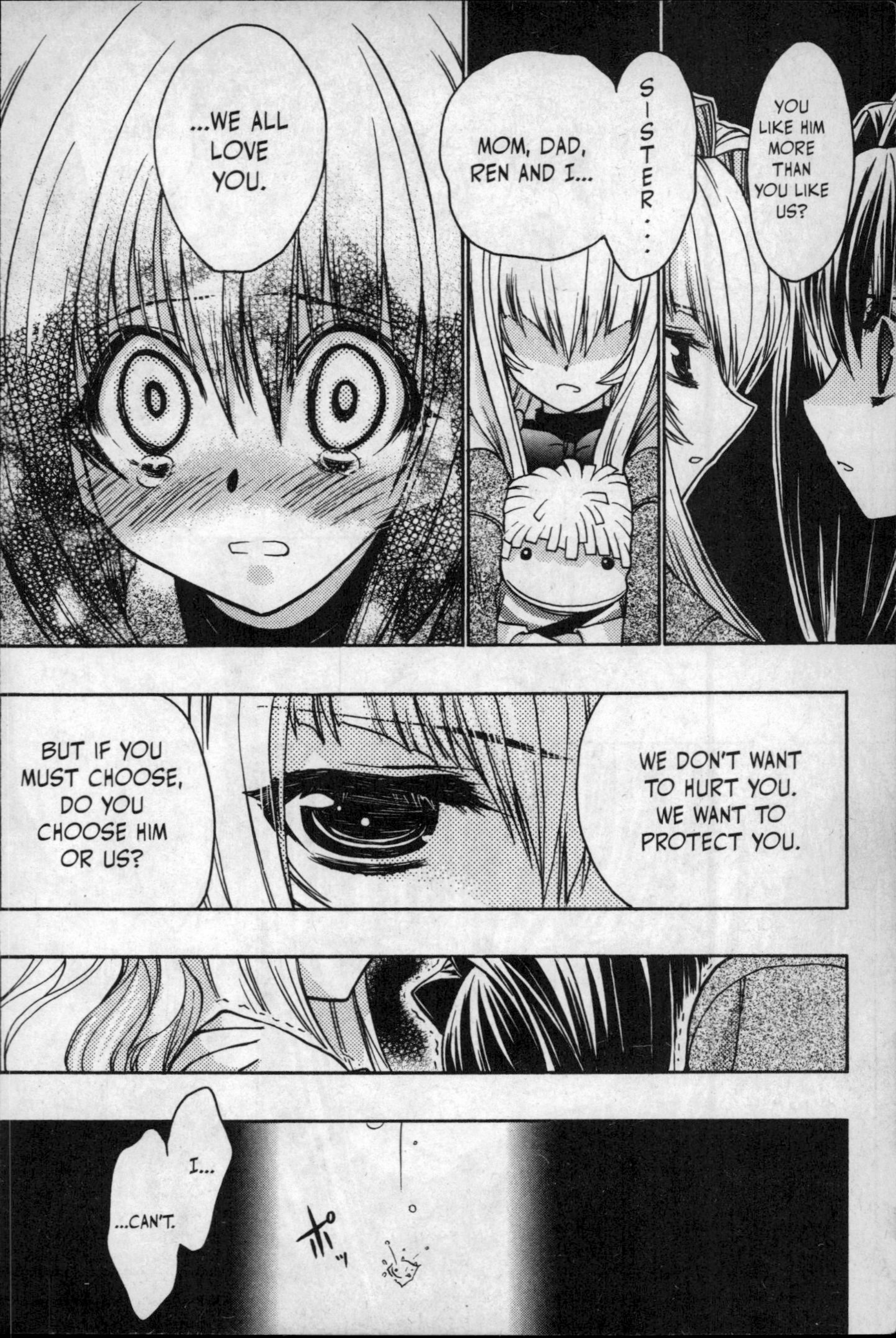
YOU LIKE HIM MORE THAN YOU LIKE US?
SISTER...
MOM, DAD, REN AND I...
...WE ALL LOVE YOU.
WE DON'T WANT TO HURT YOU. WE WANT TO PROTECT YOU.
BUT IF YOU MUST CHOOSE, DO YOU CHOOSE HIM OR US?
I...
...CAN'T.

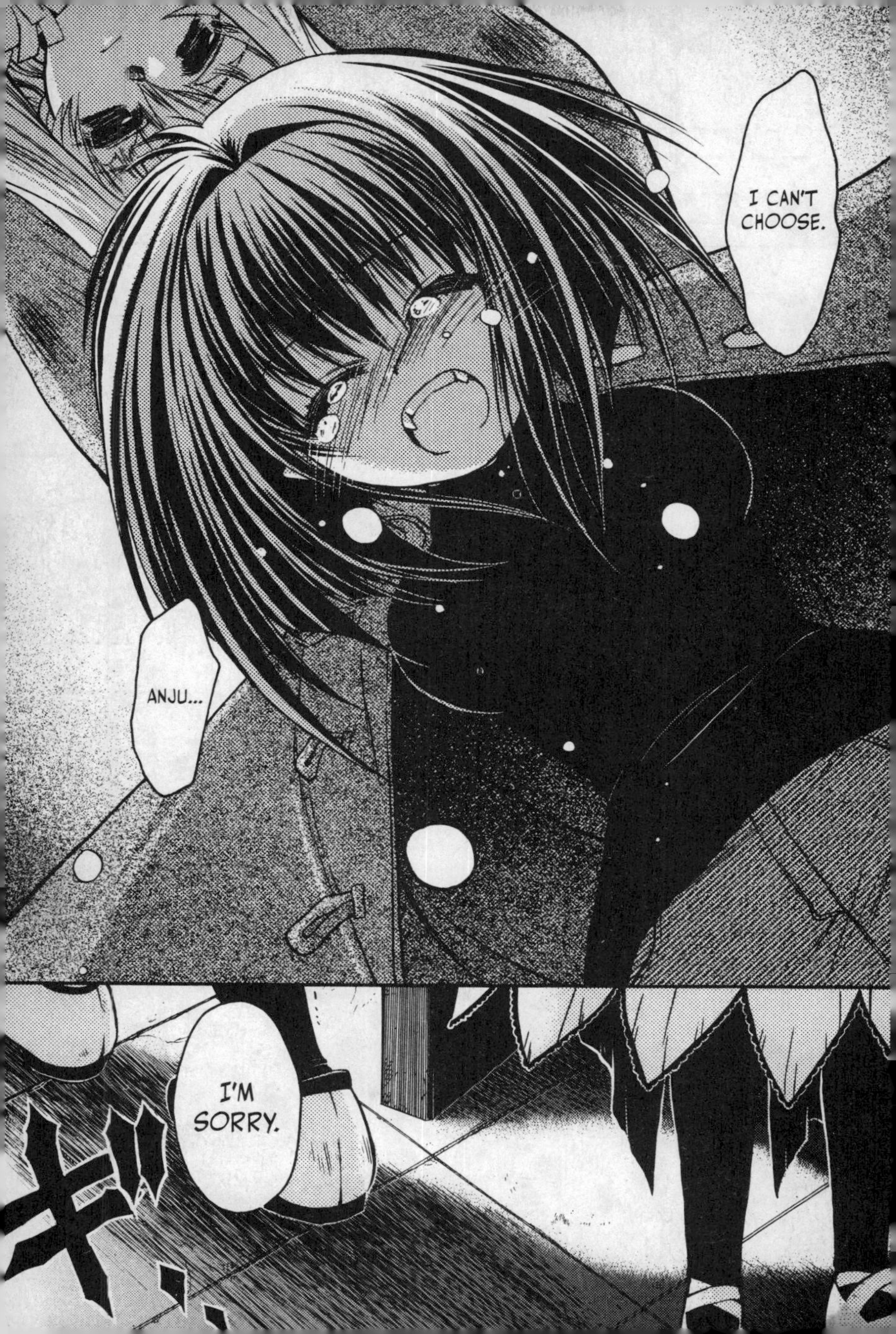
I CAN'T CHOOSE.
ANJU...
I'M SORRY.

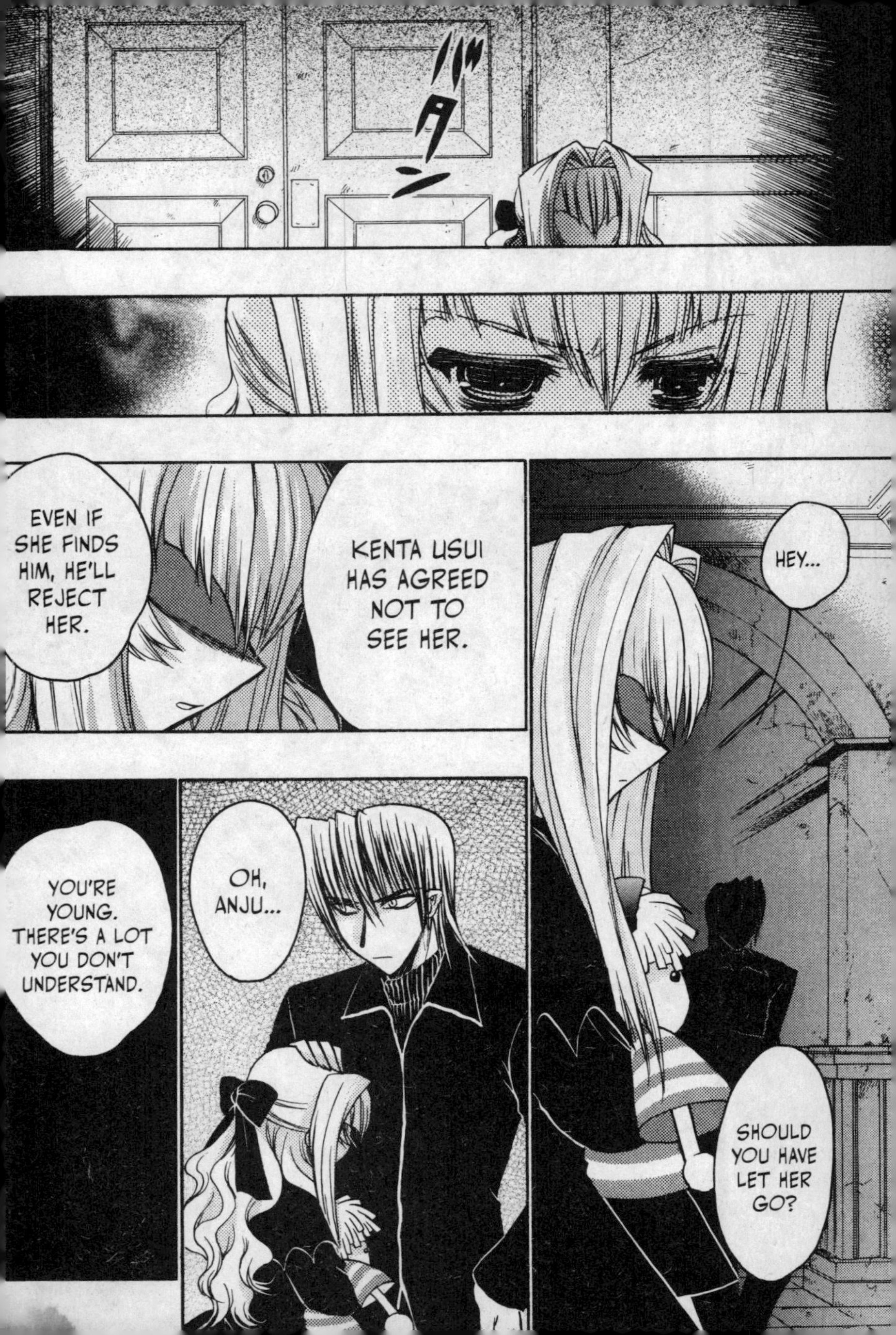
バタン
HEY...
SHOULD YOU HAVE LET HER GO?
KENTA USUI HAS AGREED NOT TO SEE HER.
EVEN IF SHE FINDS HIM, HE'LL REJECT HER.
OH, ANJU...
YOU'RE YOUNG. THERE'S A LOT YOU DON'T UNDERSTAND.

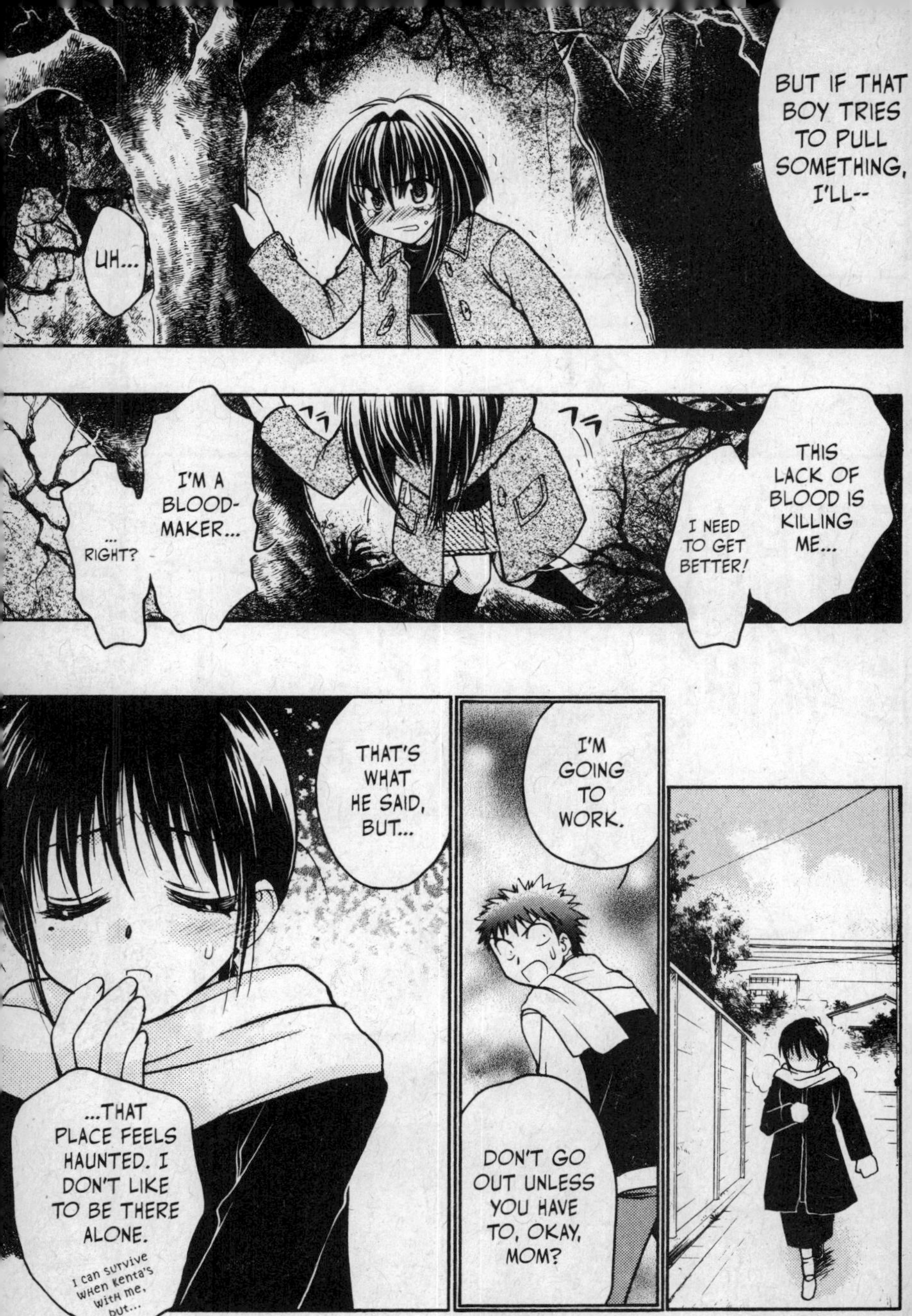
BUT IF THAT BOY TRIES TO PULL SOMETHING, I'LL--
UH...
THIS LACK OF BLOOD IS KILLING ME...
I NEED TO GET BETTER!
フラ
フラ
I'M A BLOOD-MAKER...
...RIGHT?
I'M GOING TO WORK.
DON'T GO OUT UNLESS YOU HAVE TO, OKAY, MOM?
THAT'S WHAT HE SAID, BUT...
...THAT PLACE FEELS HAUNTED. I DON'T LIKE TO BE THERE ALONE.
I can survive when Kenta's with me, but...

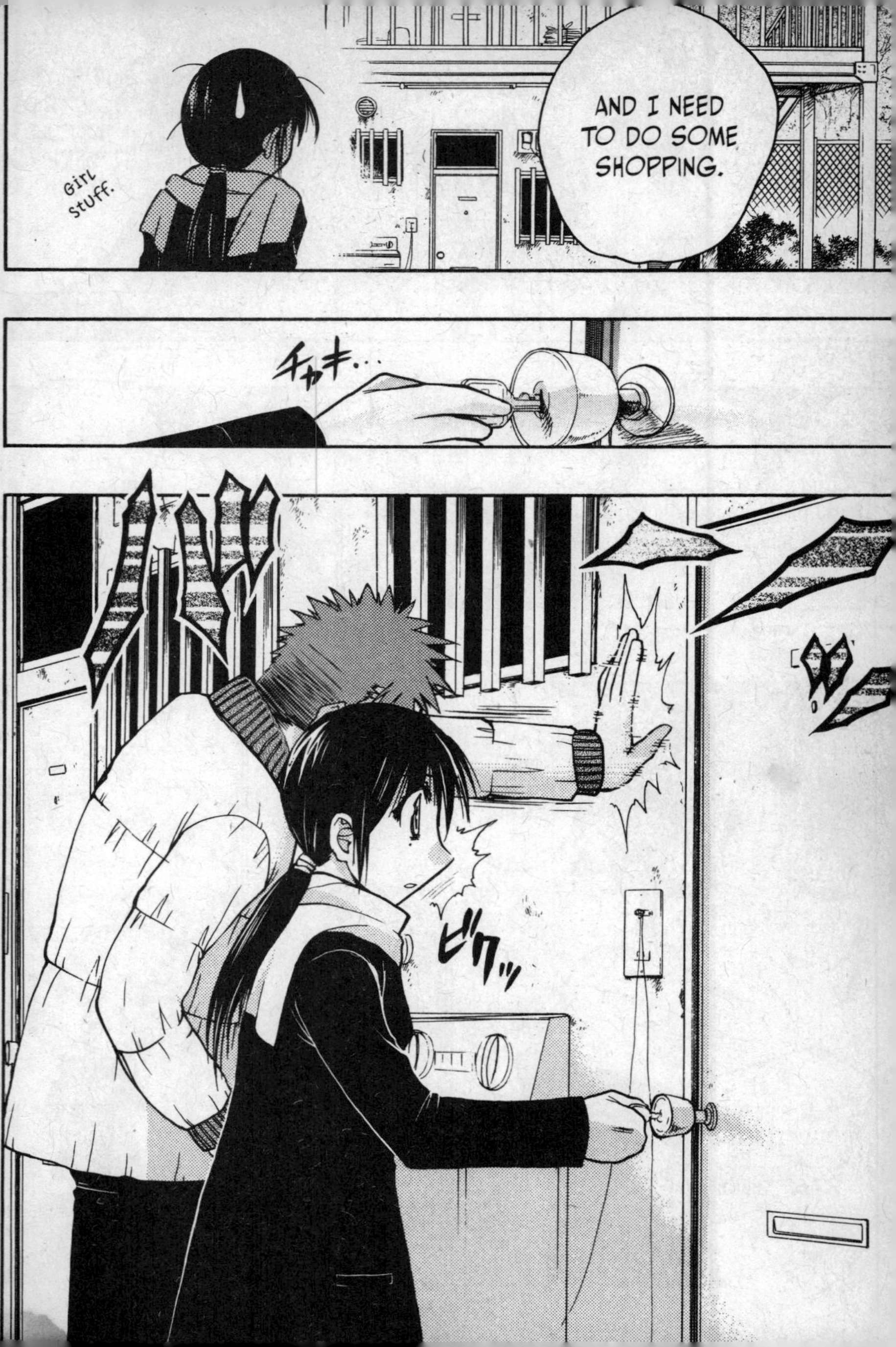
AND I NEED TO DO SOME SHOPPING.
Girl stuff.
チャキ...
ビクッ

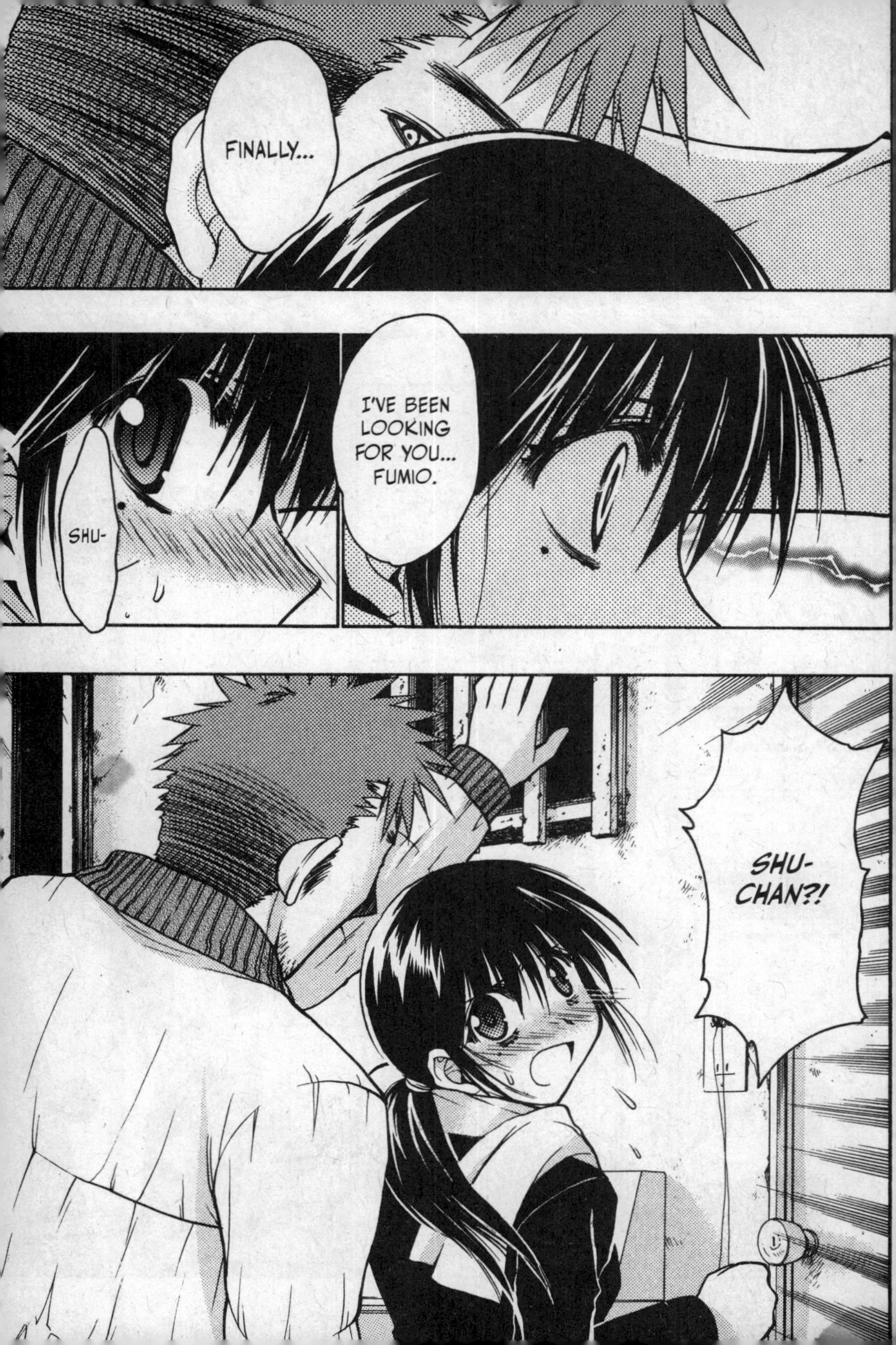
FINALLY...
I'VE BEEN LOOKING FOR YOU... FUMIO.
SHU-
SHU-CHAN?!

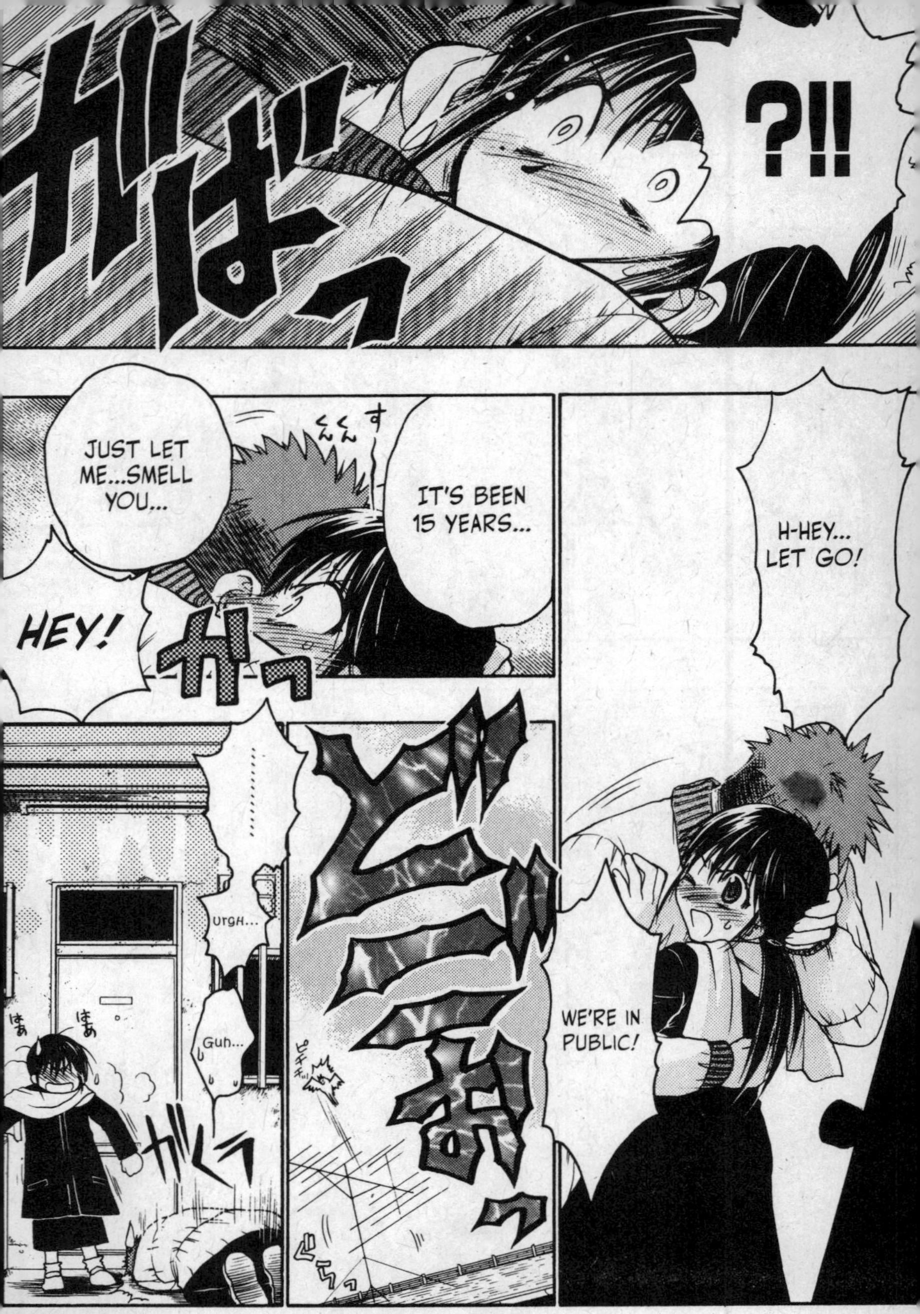

ガばっ
?!!
H-HEY... LET GO!
WE'RE IN PUBLIC!
IT'S BEEN 15 YEARS...
JUST LET ME...SMELL YOU...
HEY!
ガっ
どごおっ
......
Urgh...
Guh...
はあ はあ

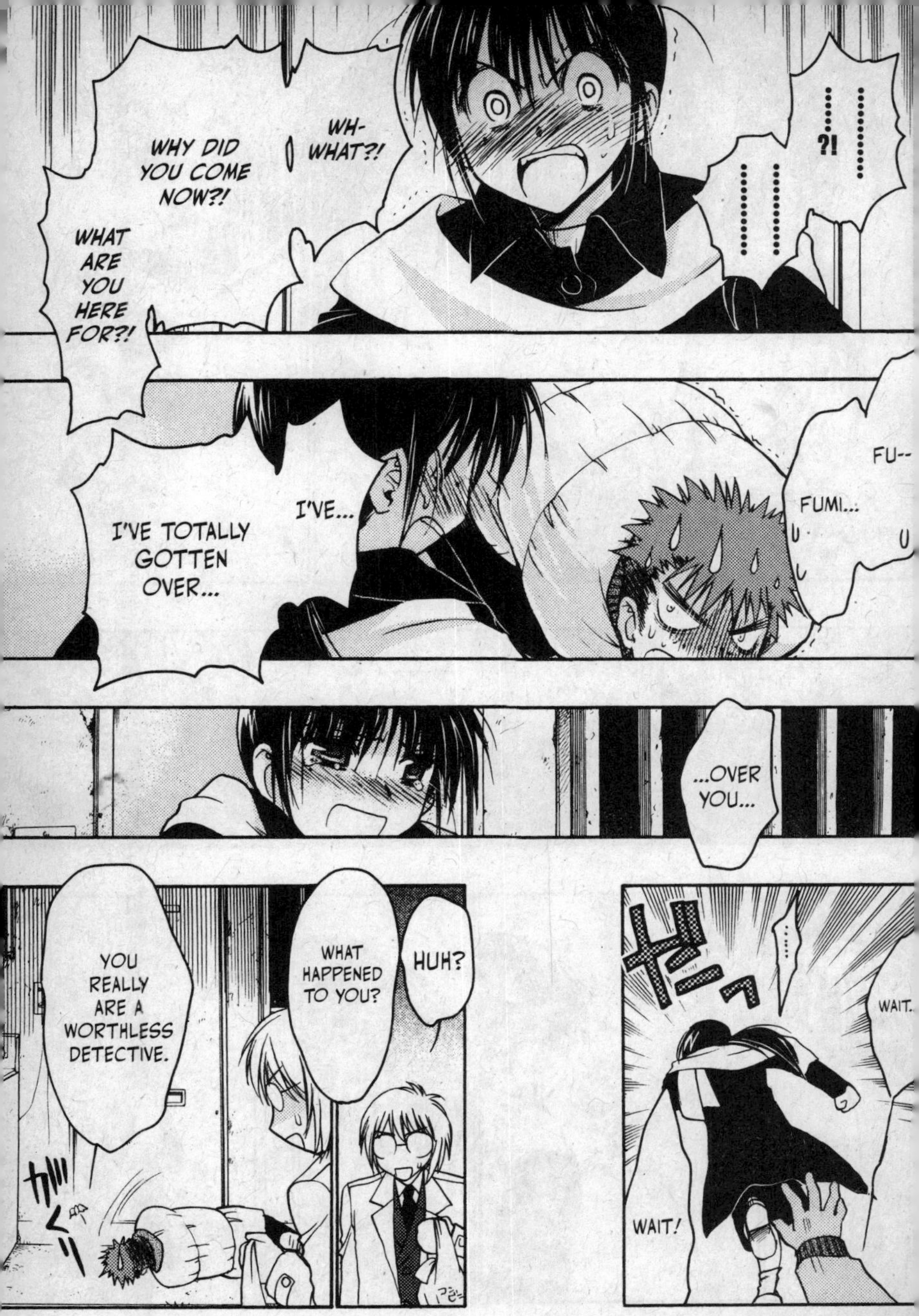
......?!......
WH- WHAT?!
WHY DID YOU COME NOW?!
WHAT ARE YOU HERE FOR?!
FU-- FUMI...
I'VE...
I'VE TOTALLY GOTTEN OVER...
...OVER YOU...
WAIT...
......
WAIT!
HUH?
WHAT HAPPENED TO YOU?
YOU REALLY ARE A WORTHLESS DETECTIVE.

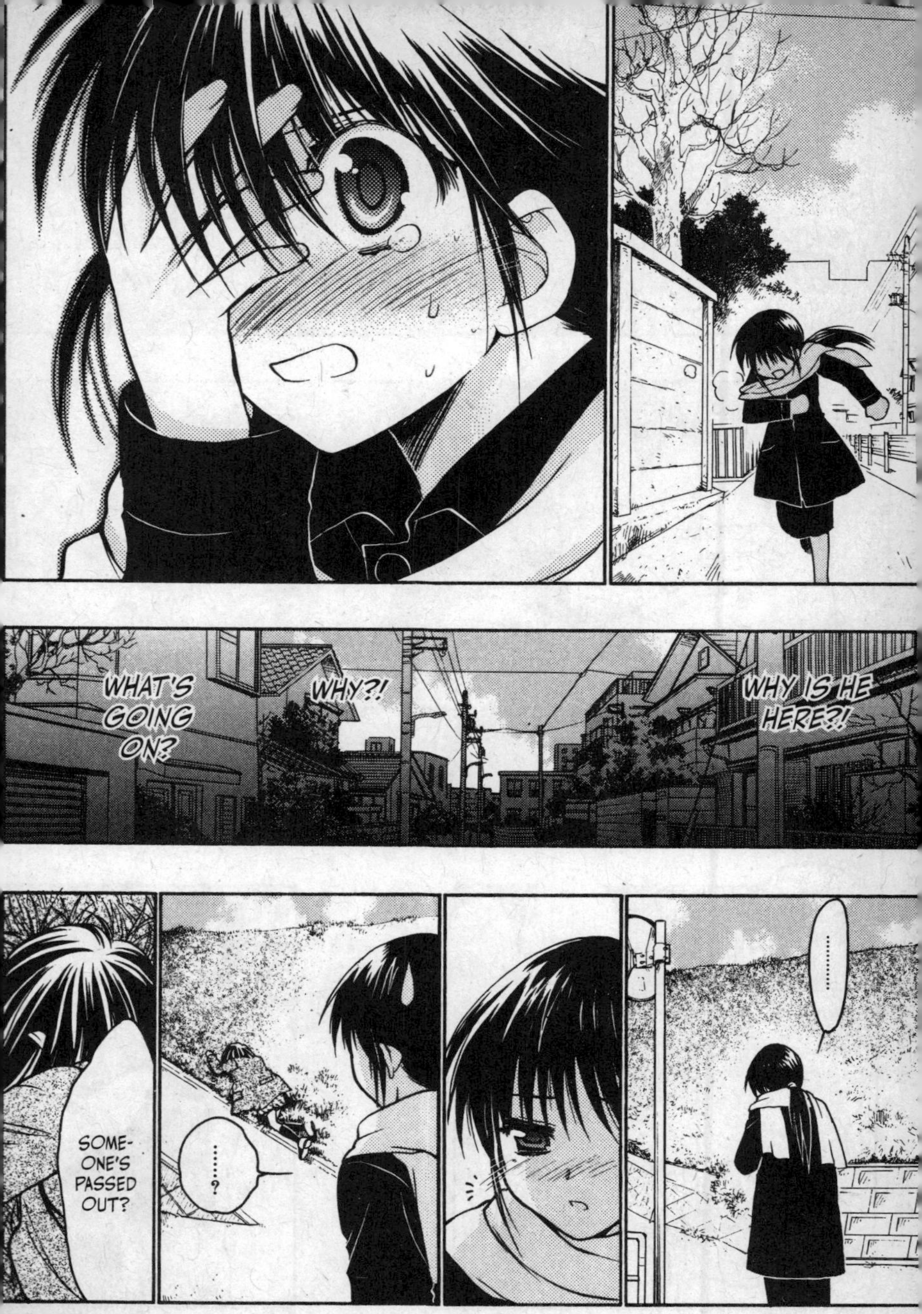

WHY IS HE HERE?!
WHY?!
WHAT'S GOING ON?
....
......?
SOME-ONE'S PASSED OUT?

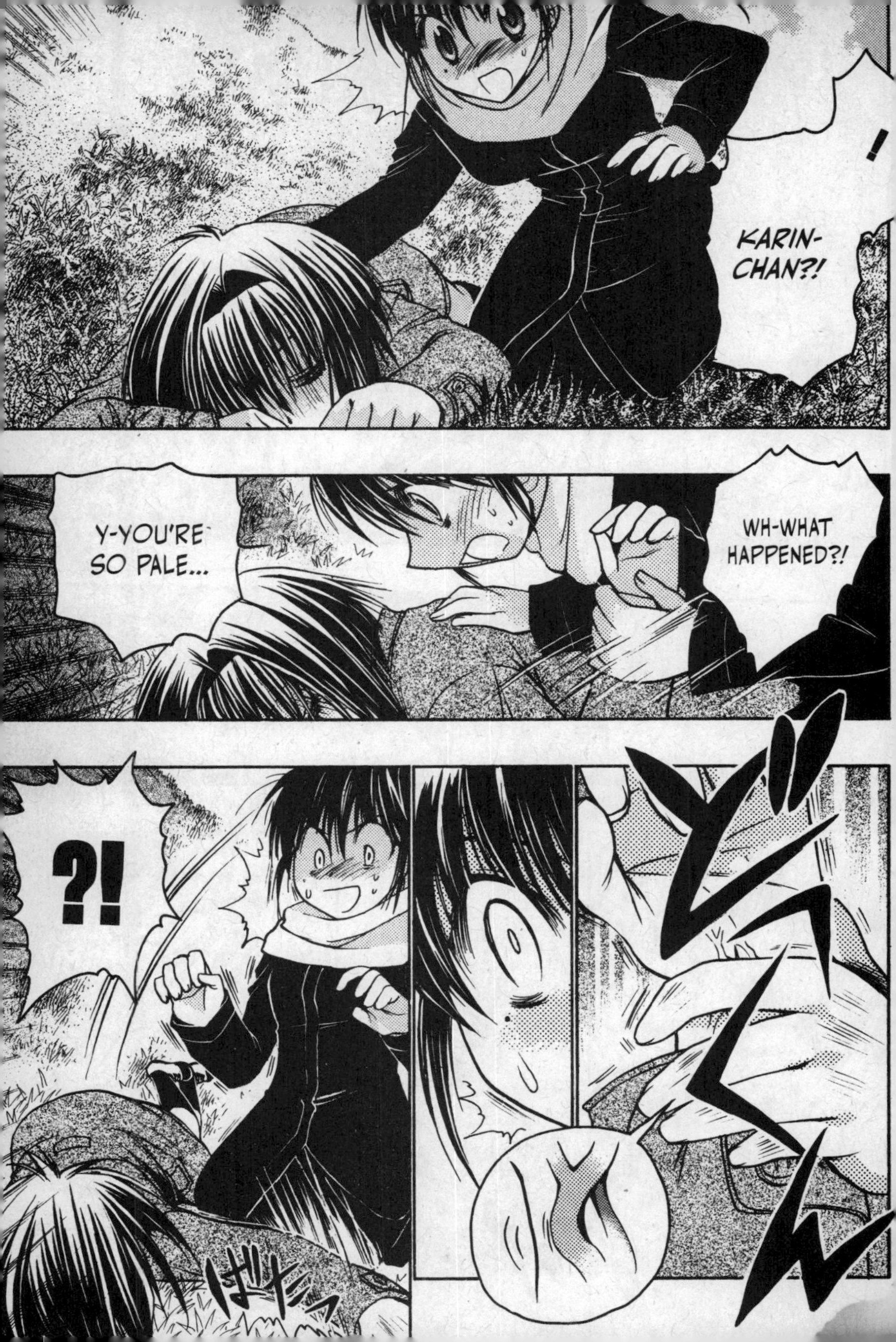
!
KARIN-CHAN?!
WH-WHAT HAPPENED?!
Y-YOU'RE SO PALE...
?!

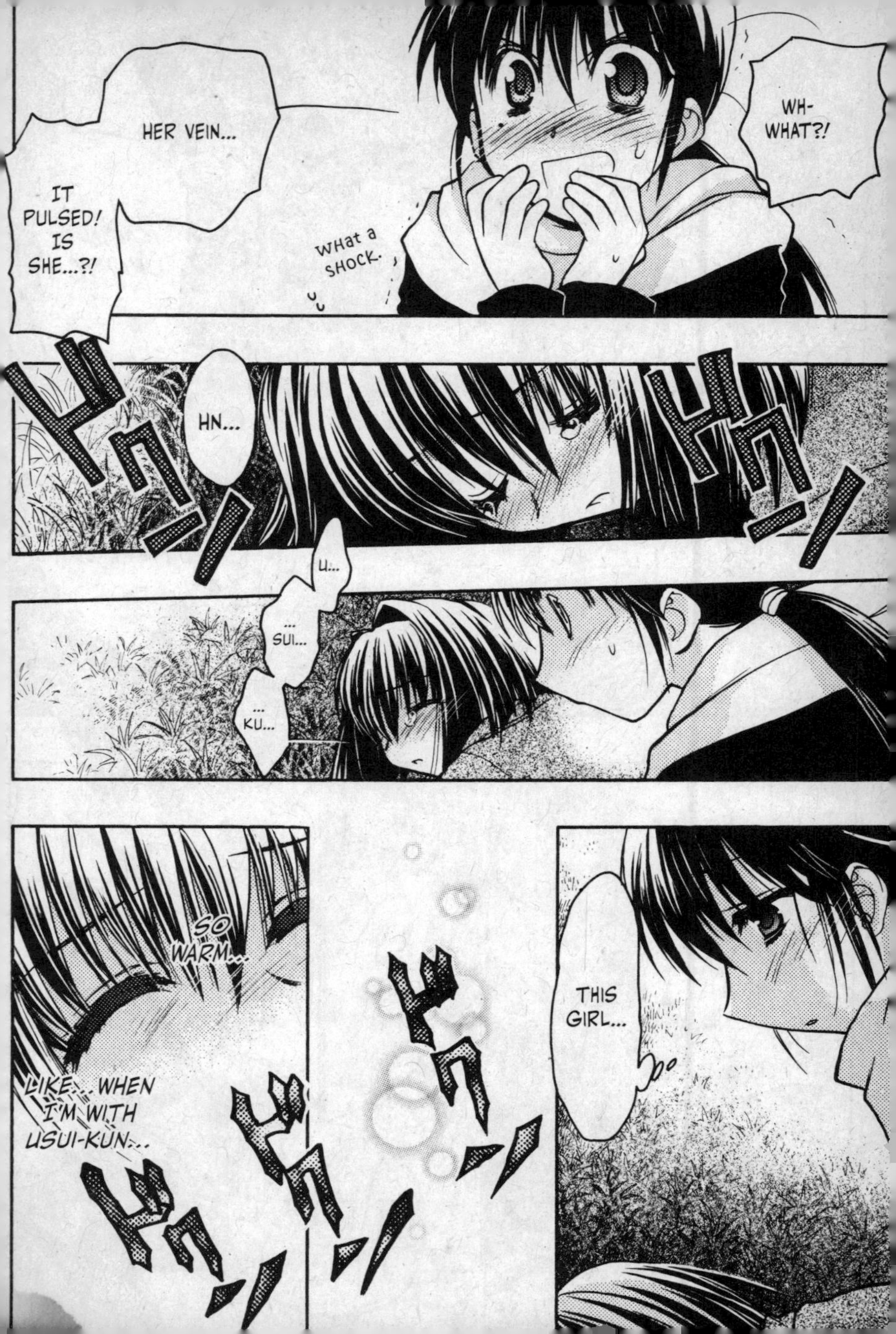
WH- WHAT?!
What a SHOCK.
HER VEIN...
IT PULSED! IS SHE...?!
HN...
U...
...SUI...
...KU...
THIS GIRL...
SO WARM...
LIKE... WHEN I'M WITH USUI-KUN...

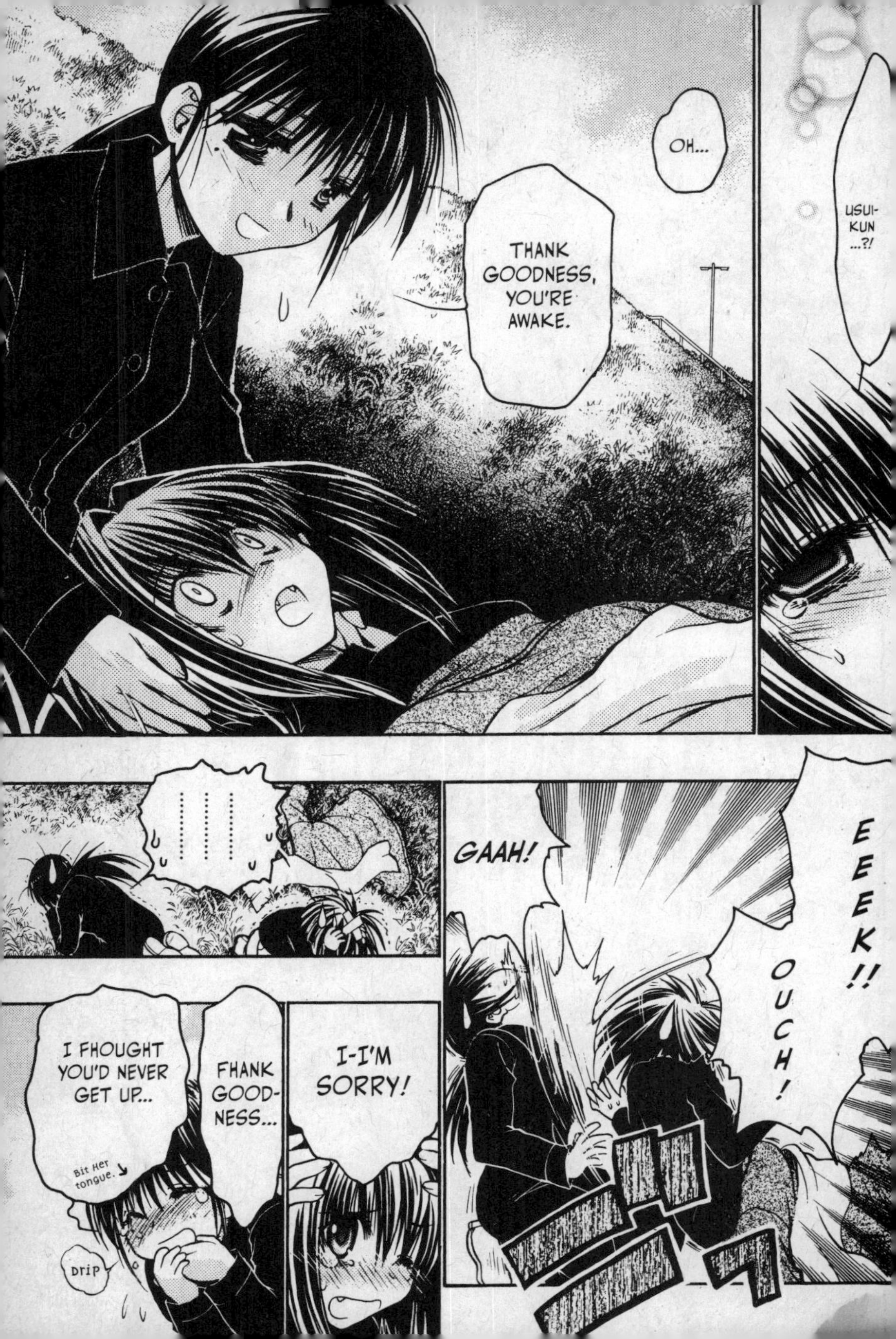
USUI-KUN ...?!
OH...
THANK GOODNESS, YOU'RE AWAKE.
EEEEK!!
OUCH!
GAAH!
......
I-I'M SORRY!
FHANK GOOD-NESS...
I FHOUGHT YOU'D NEVER GET UP...
Bit Her tongue.
Drip

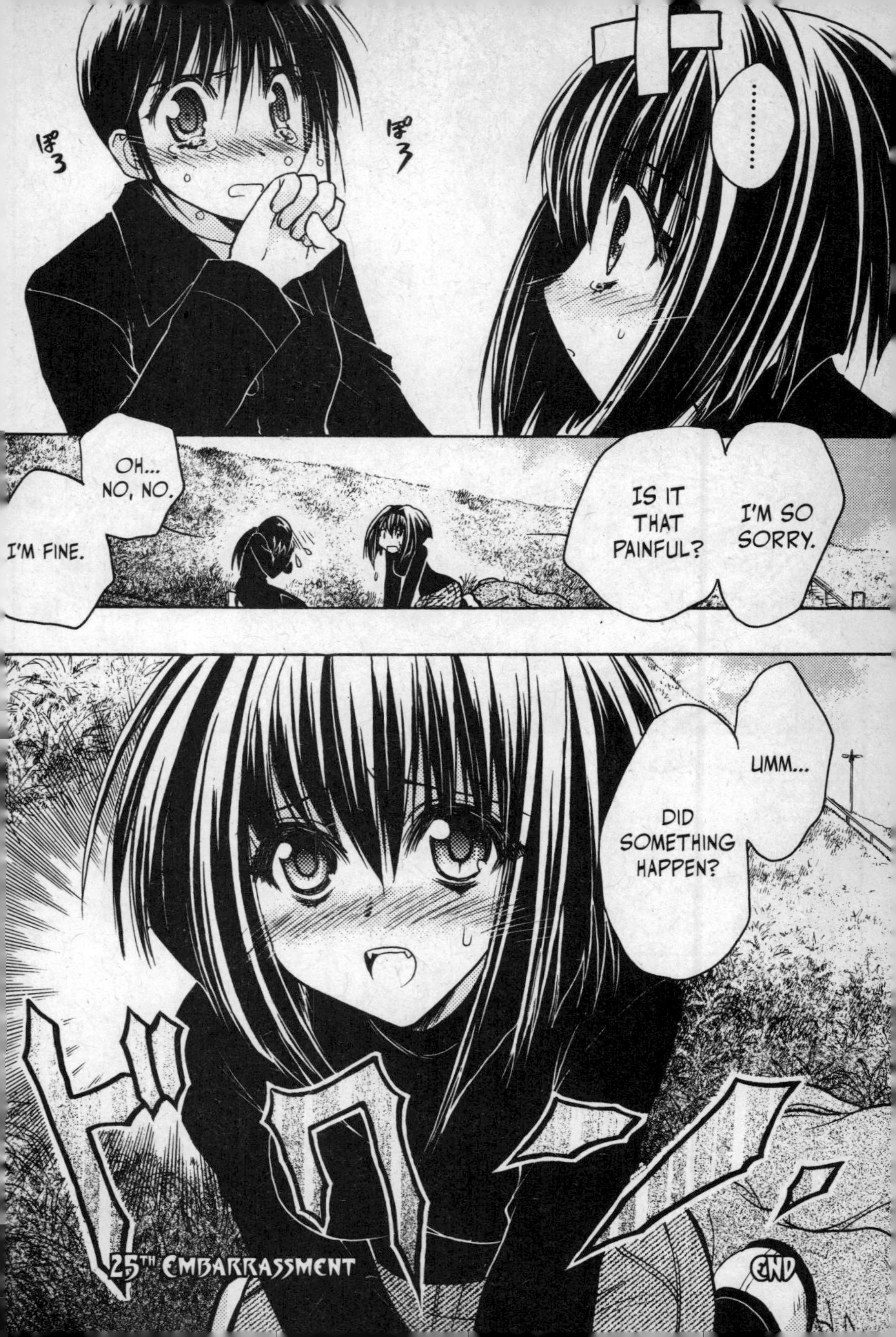
......
ぽろ
ぽろ
I'M SO SORRY.
IS IT THAT PAINFUL?
OH... NO, NO.
I'M FINE.
UMM...
DID SOMETHING HAPPEN?
END
25TH EMBARRASSMENT

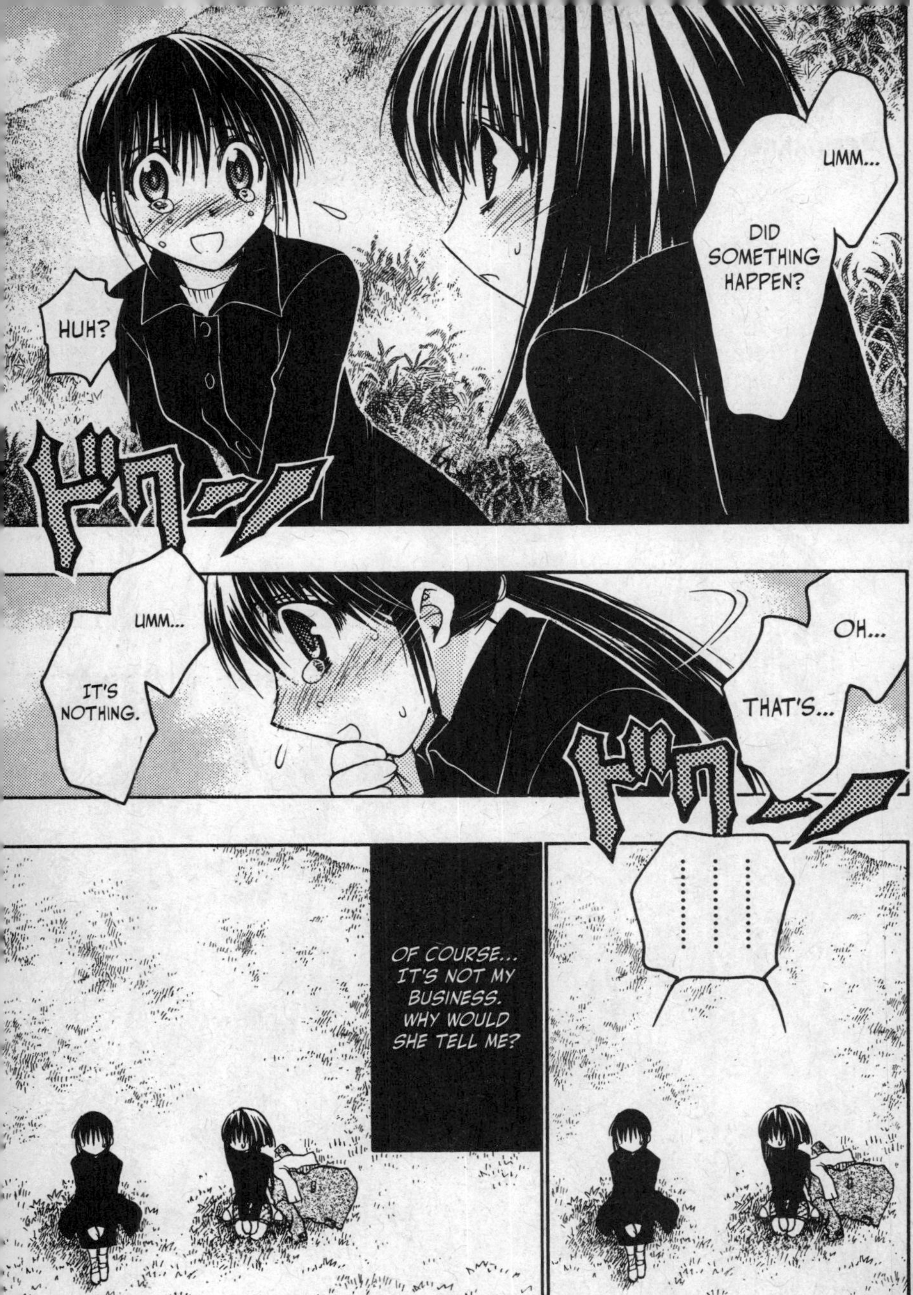
UMM... DID SOMETHING HAPPEN?
HUH?
ドクーン
OH... THAT'S...
UMM... IT'S NOTHING.
ドクン
......
OF COURSE... IT'S NOT MY BUSINESS. WHY WOULD SHE TELL ME?

26th Embarrassment) Fumio's Confession and Kenta's Rejection
~Refusal~

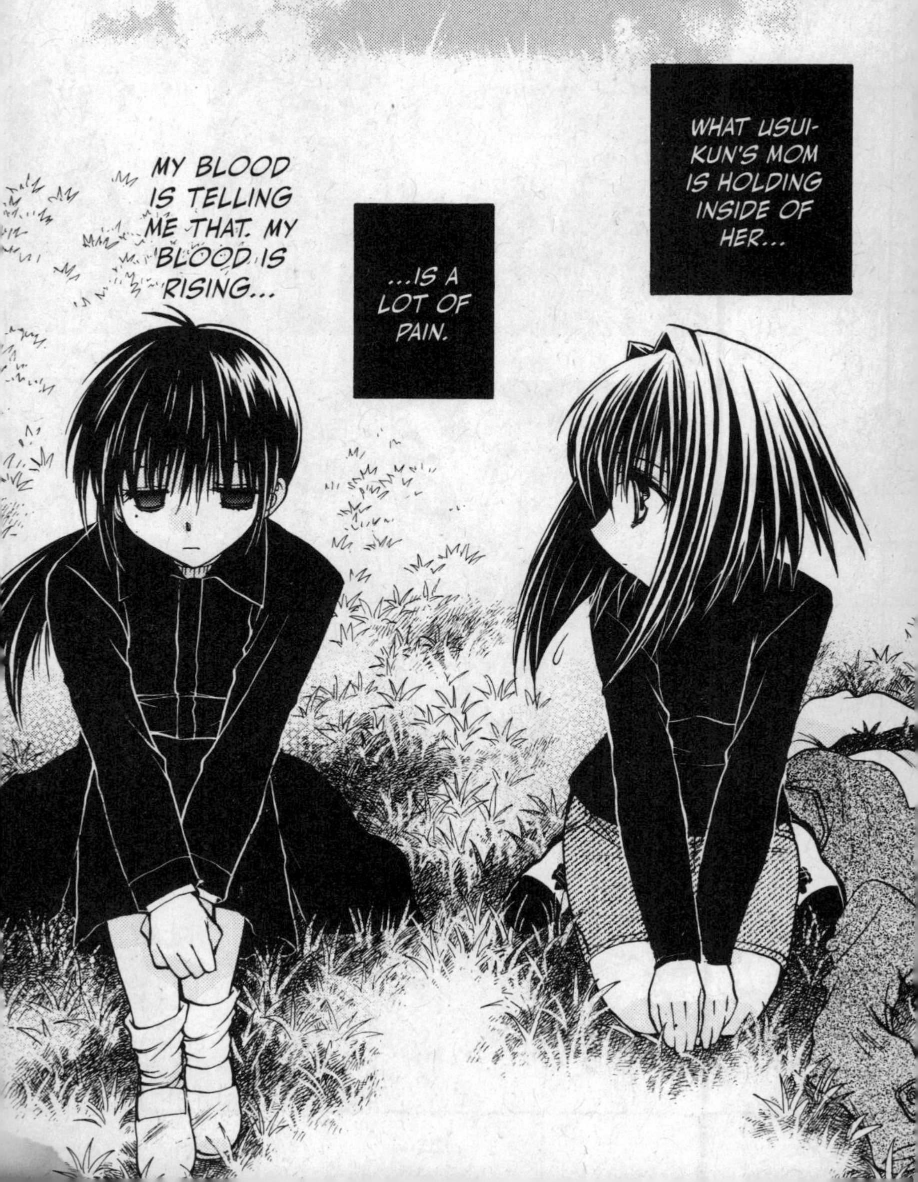
WHAT USUI-KUN'S MOM IS HOLDING INSIDE OF HER...
...IS A LOT OF PAIN.
MY BLOOD IS TELLING ME THAT. MY BLOOD IS RISING...

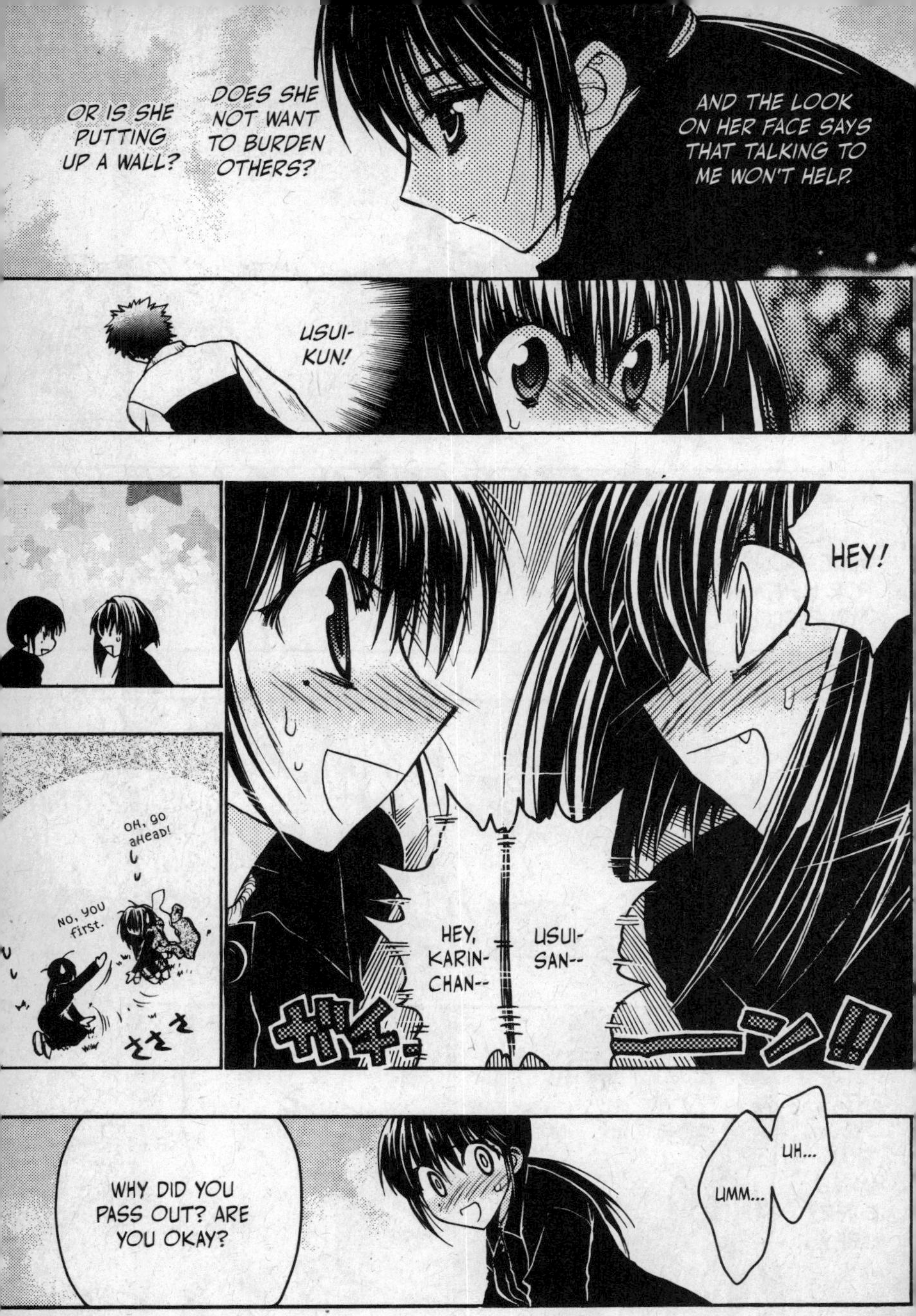

AND THE LOOK ON HER FACE SAYS THAT TALKING TO ME WON'T HELP.
DOES SHE NOT WANT TO BURDEN OTHERS?
OR IS SHE PUTTING UP A WALL?
USUI-KUN!
HEY!
USUI-SAN--
HEY, KARIN-CHAN--
OH, go aHead!
NO, YOU first.
UH...
UMM...
WHY DID YOU PASS OUT? ARE YOU OKAY?

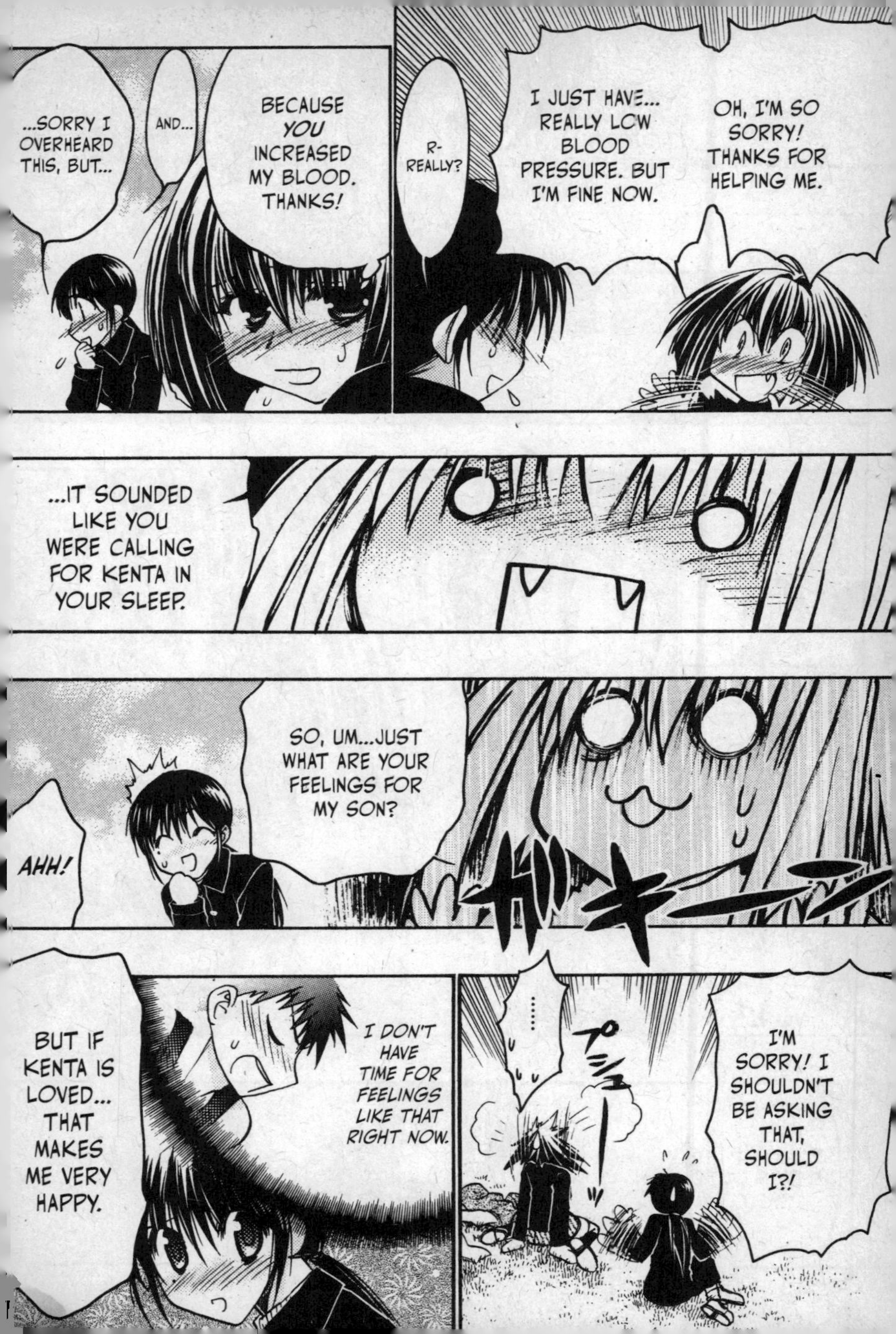
OH, I'M SO SORRY! THANKS FOR HELPING ME.
I JUST HAVE... REALLY LOW BLOOD PRESSURE. BUT I'M FINE NOW.
R-REALLY?
BECAUSE *YOU* INCREASED MY BLOOD. THANKS!
AND...
...SORRY I OVERHEARD THIS, BUT...
...IT SOUNDED LIKE YOU WERE CALLING FOR KENTA IN YOUR SLEEP.
SO, UM...JUST WHAT ARE YOUR FEELINGS FOR MY SON?
AHH!
I'M SORRY! I SHOULDN'T BE ASKING THAT, SHOULD I?!
......
I DON'T HAVE TIME FOR FEELINGS LIKE THAT RIGHT NOW.
BUT IF KENTA IS LOVED... THAT MAKES ME VERY HAPPY.

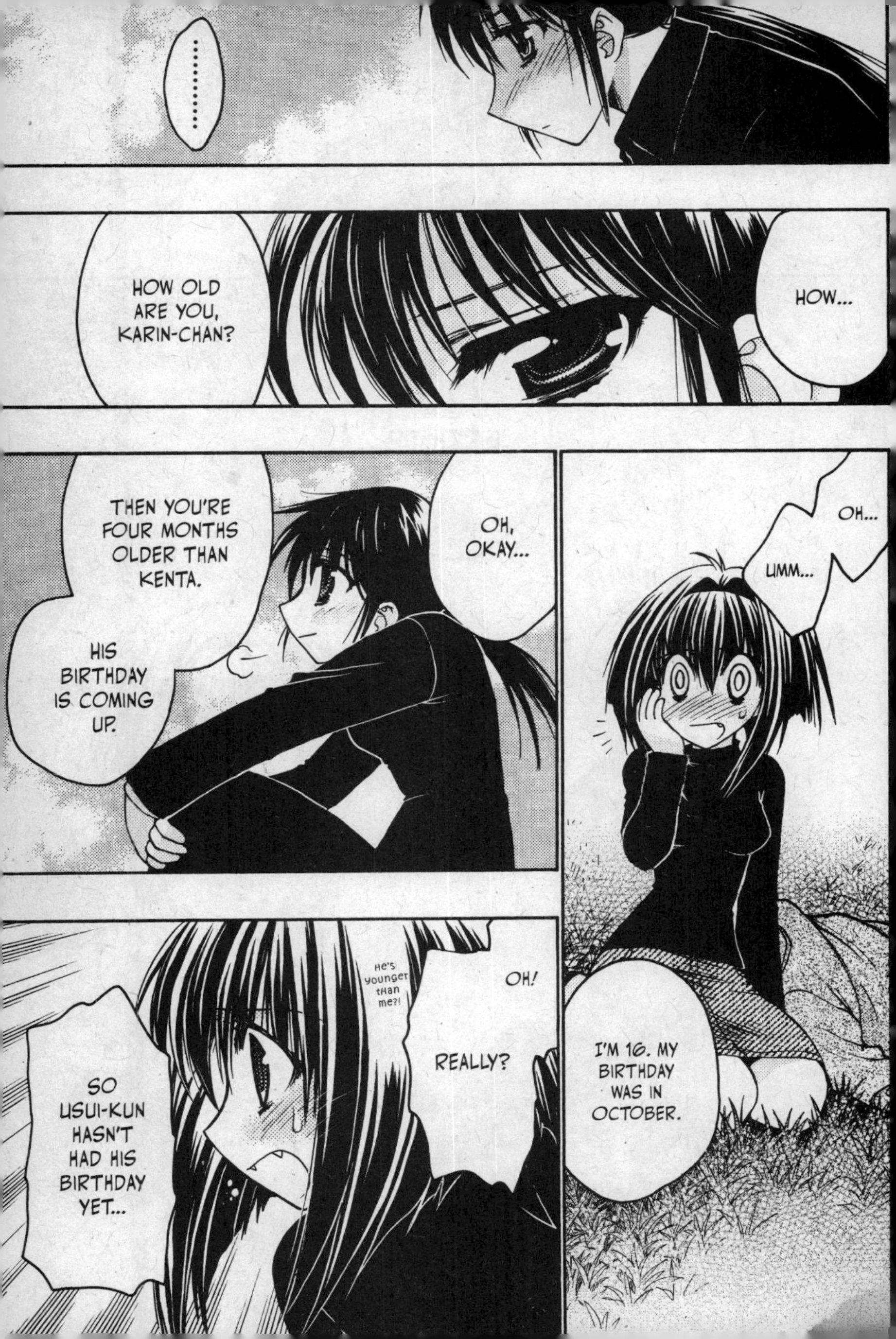
......
HOW...
HOW OLD ARE YOU, KARIN-CHAN?
OH...
UMM...
I'M 16. MY BIRTHDAY WAS IN OCTOBER.
OH, OKAY...
THEN YOU'RE FOUR MONTHS OLDER THAN KENTA.
HIS BIRTHDAY IS COMING UP.
OH!
He's younger than me?!
REALLY?
SO USUI-KUN HASN'T HAD HIS BIRTHDAY YET...

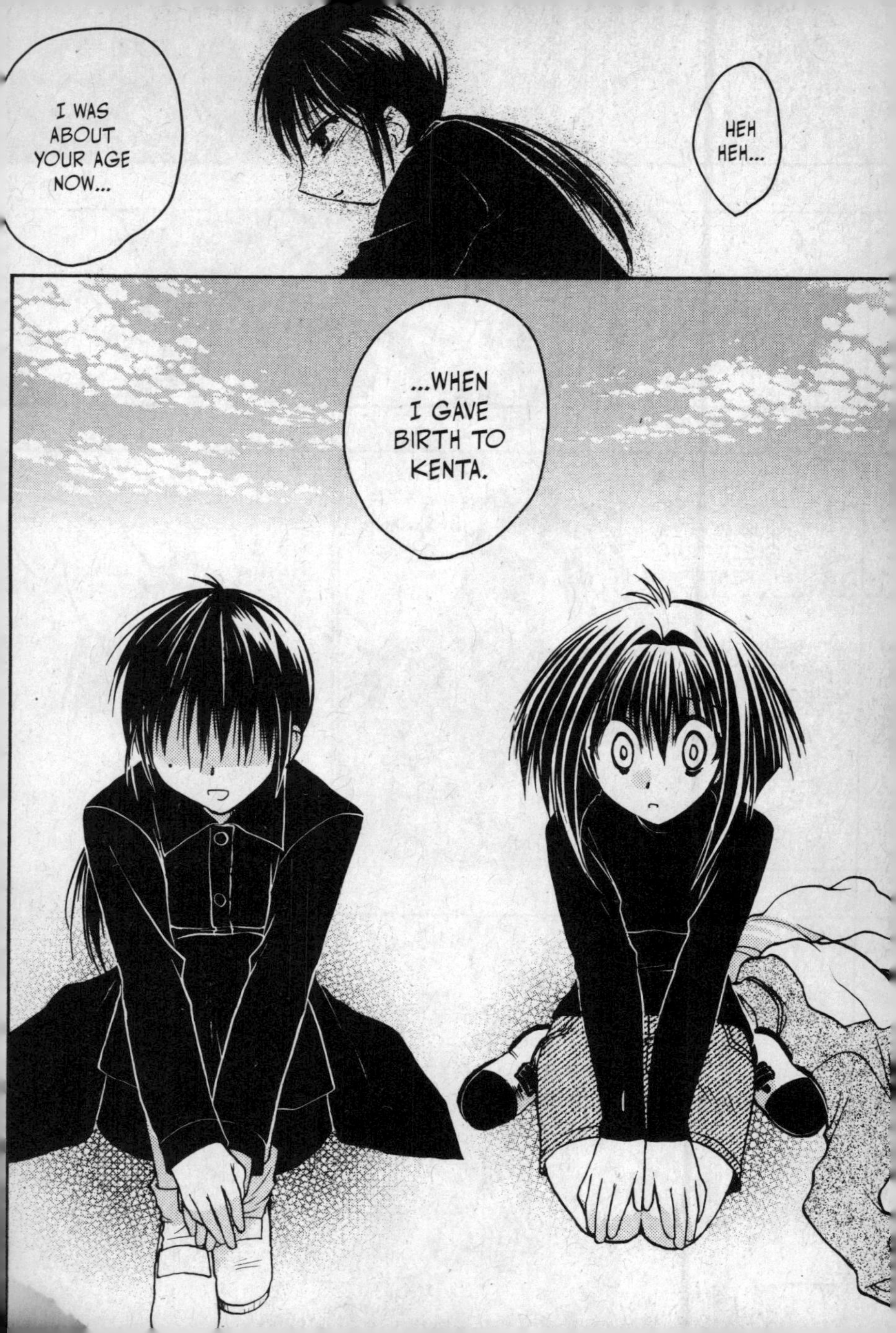
HEH HEH...
I WAS ABOUT YOUR AGE NOW...
...WHEN I GAVE BIRTH TO KENTA.

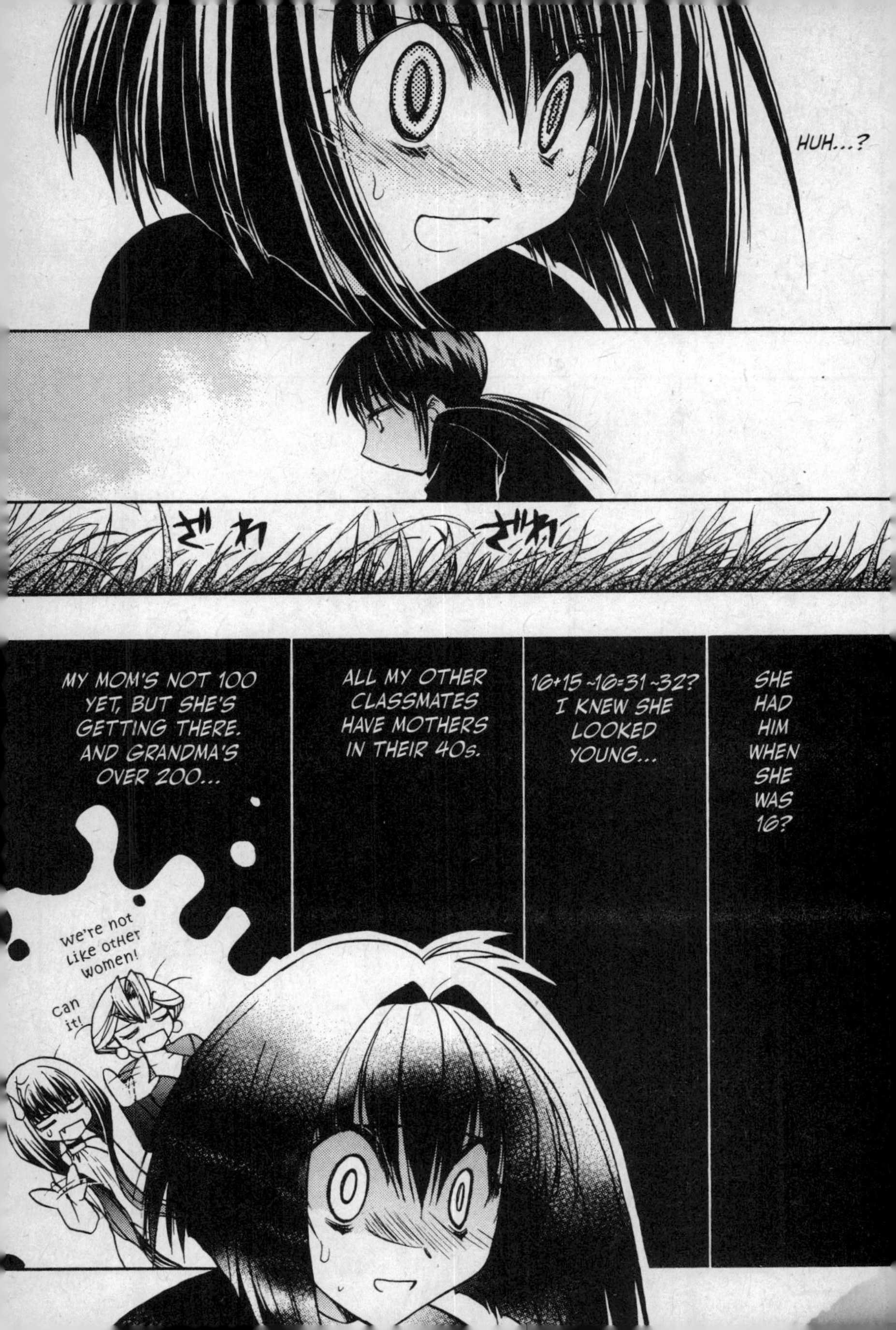
HUH...?
ざわ
ざわ
SHE HAD HIM WHEN SHE WAS 16?
16+15~16=31~32? I KNEW SHE LOOKED YOUNG...
ALL MY OTHER CLASSMATES HAVE MOTHERS IN THEIR 40s.
MY MOM'S NOT 100 YET, BUT SHE'S GETTING THERE. AND GRANDMA'S OVER 200...
We're not like other women!
Can it!

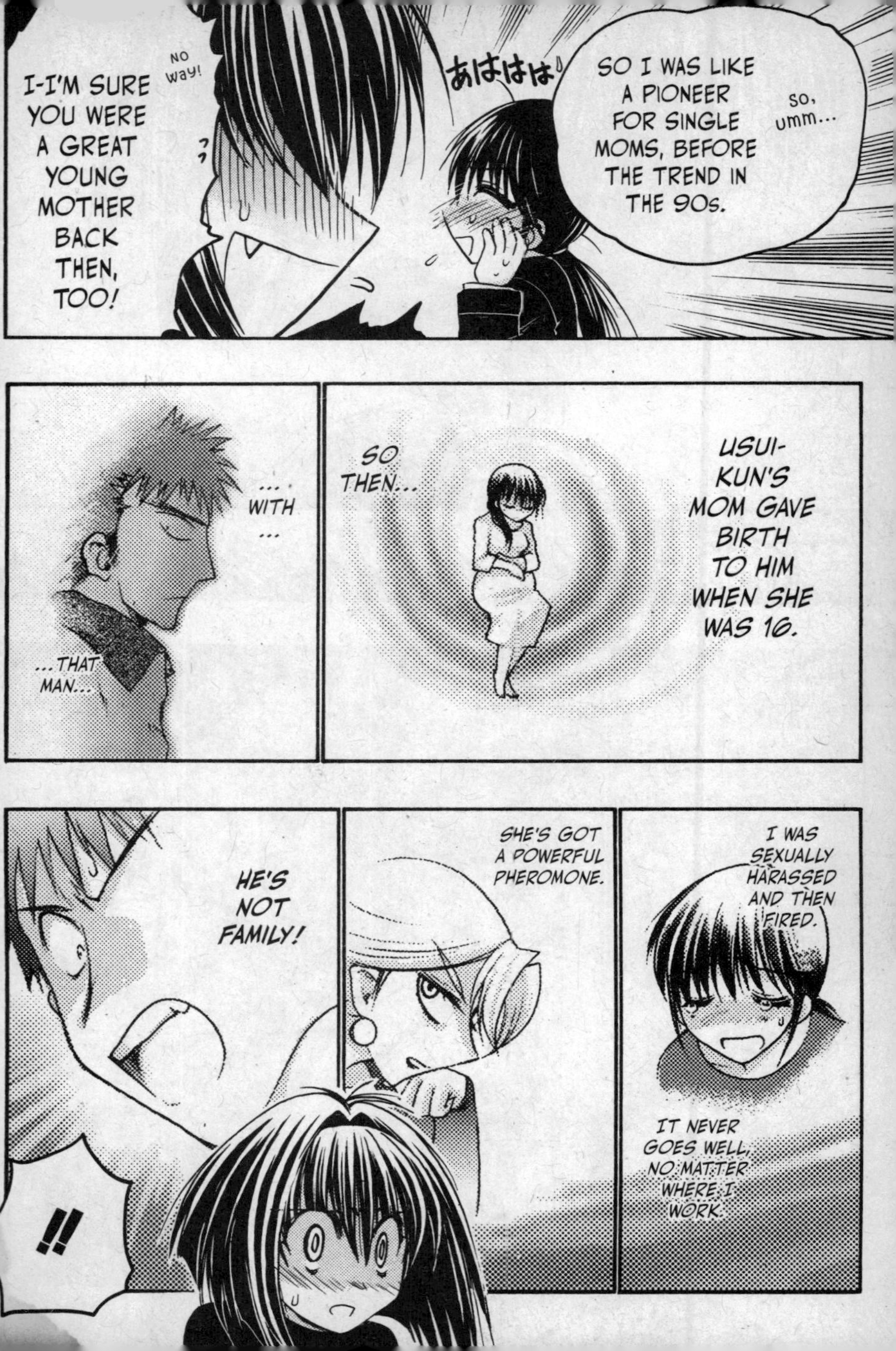
SO I WAS LIKE A PIONEER FOR SINGLE MOMS, BEFORE THE TREND IN THE 90s.
So, umm...
あはははは
No way!
I-I'M SURE YOU WERE A GREAT YOUNG MOTHER BACK THEN, TOO!
USUI-KUN'S MOM GAVE BIRTH TO HIM WHEN SHE WAS 16.
SO THEN...
... WITH ...
...THAT MAN...
I WAS SEXUALLY HARASSED AND THEN FIRED.
IT NEVER GOES WELL, NO MATTER WHERE I WORK.
SHE'S GOT A POWERFUL PHEROMONE.
HE'S NOT FAMILY!
!!

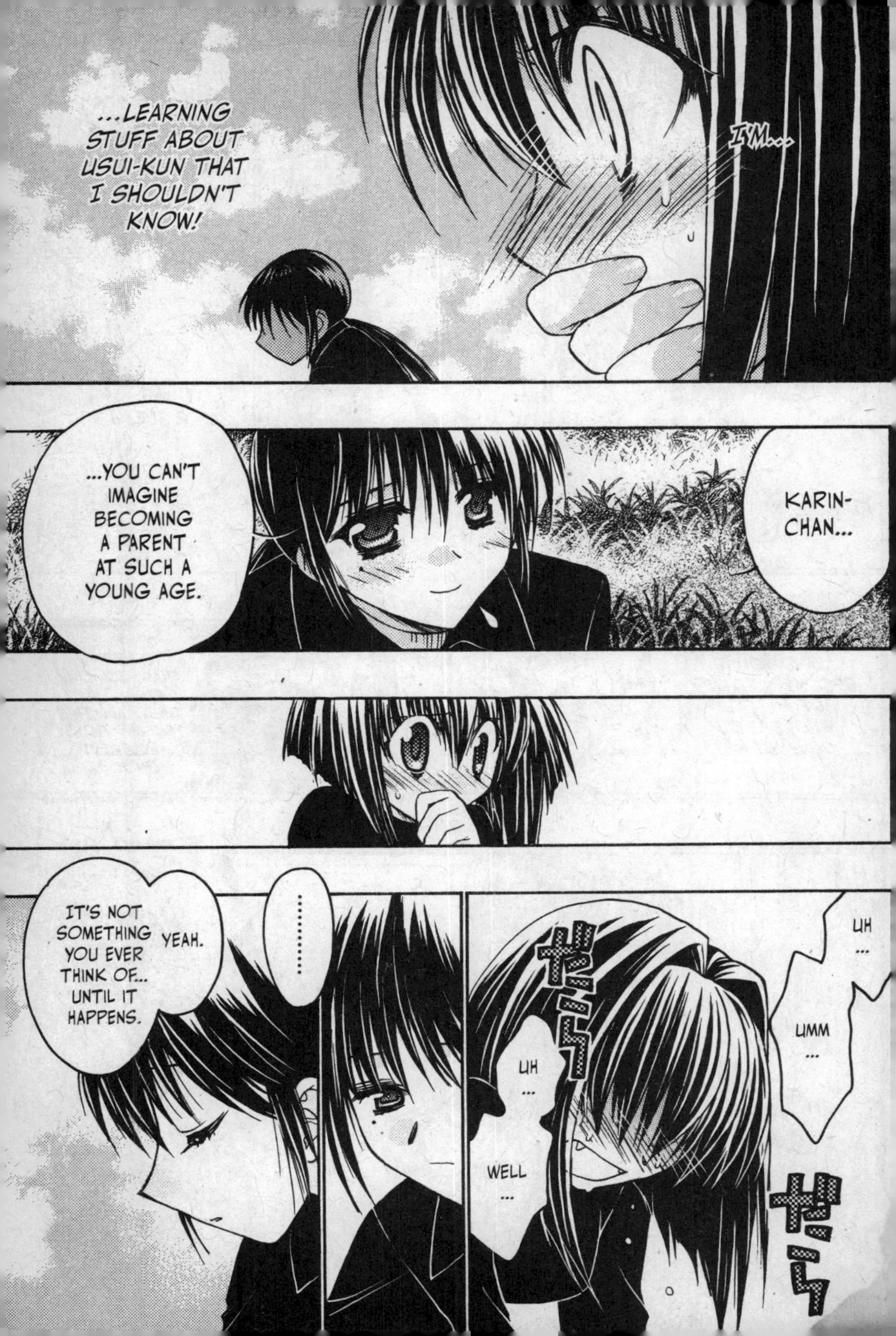
I'M...
...LEARNING STUFF ABOUT USUI-KUN THAT I SHOULDN'T KNOW!
KARIN-CHAN...
...YOU CAN'T IMAGINE BECOMING A PARENT AT SUCH A YOUNG AGE.
UH ...
UMM ...
UH ...
WELL ...
......
YEAH.
IT'S NOT SOMETHING YOU EVER THINK OF... UNTIL IT HAPPENS.

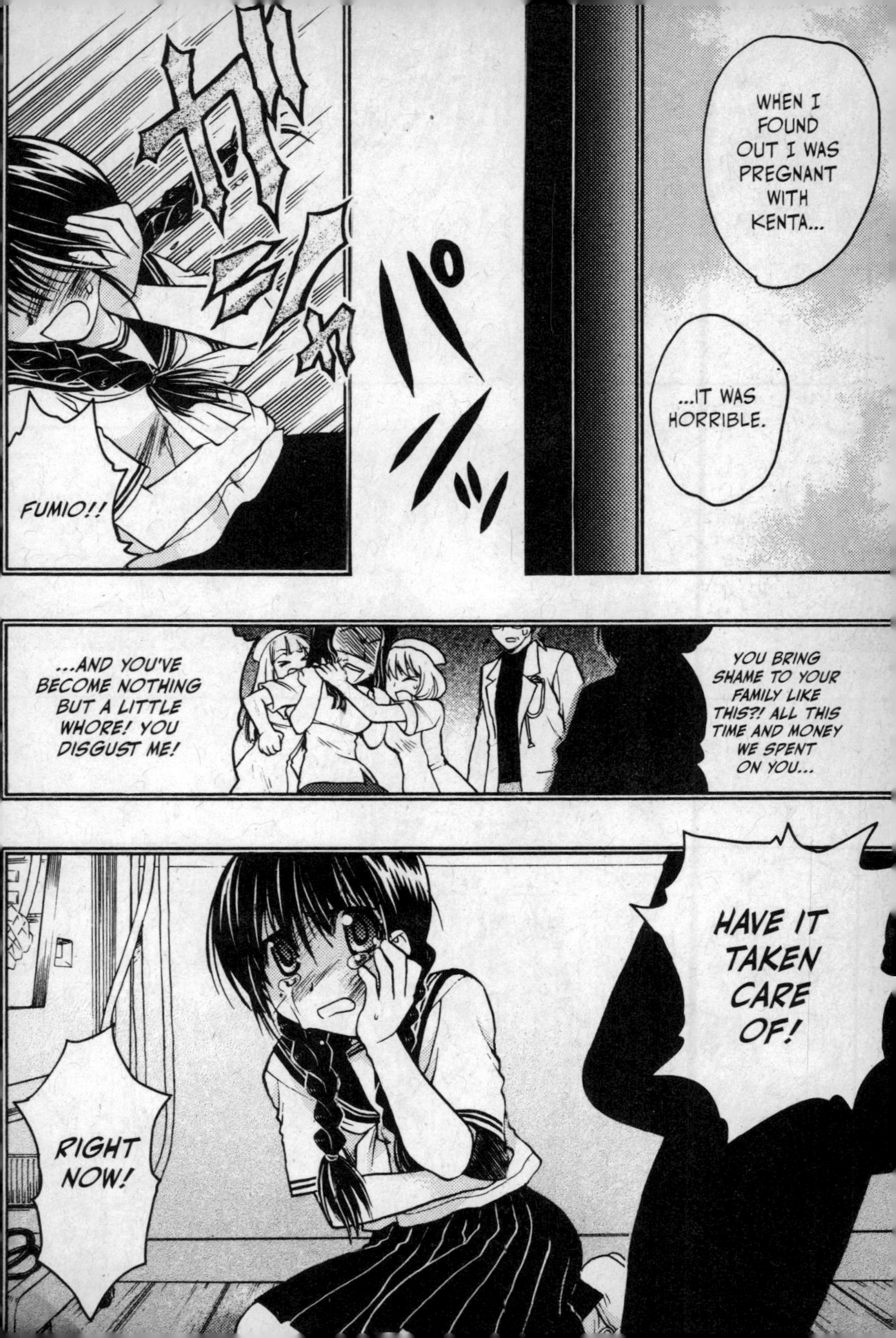
WHEN I FOUND OUT I WAS PREGNANT WITH KENTA...
...IT WAS HORRIBLE.
FUMIO!!
YOU BRING SHAME TO YOUR FAMILY LIKE THIS?! ALL THIS TIME AND MONEY WE SPENT ON YOU...
...AND YOU'VE BECOME NOTHING BUT A LITTLE WHORE! YOU DISGUST ME!
HAVE IT TAKEN CARE OF!
RIGHT NOW!

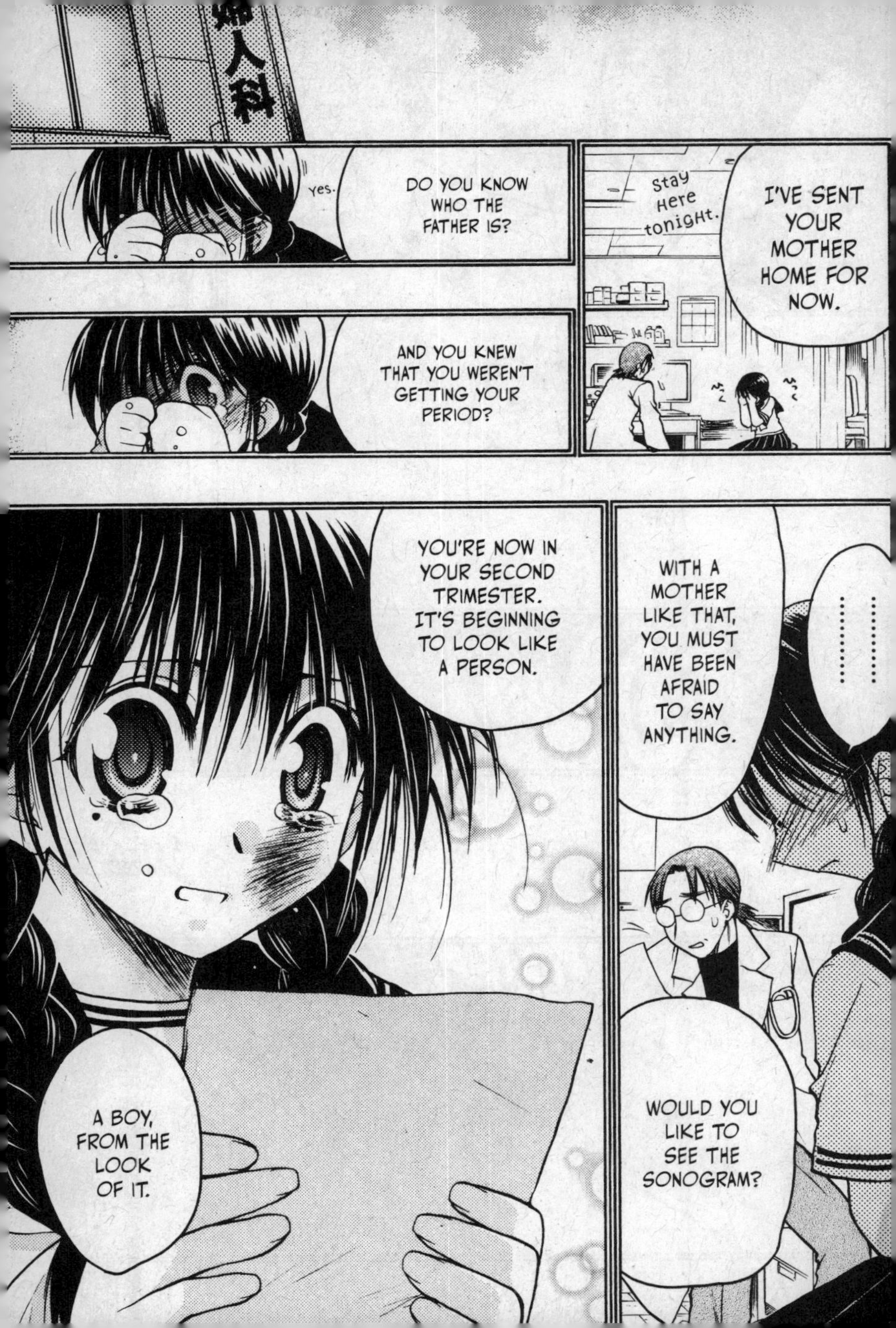
婦人科
I'VE SENT YOUR MOTHER HOME FOR NOW.
Stay Here tonight.
DO YOU KNOW WHO THE FATHER IS?
Yes.
AND YOU KNEW THAT YOU WEREN'T GETTING YOUR PERIOD?
WITH A MOTHER LIKE THAT, YOU MUST HAVE BEEN AFRAID TO SAY ANYTHING.
......
WOULD YOU LIKE TO SEE THE SONOGRAM?
YOU'RE NOW IN YOUR SECOND TRIMESTER. IT'S BEGINNING TO LOOK LIKE A PERSON.
A BOY, FROM THE LOOK OF IT.

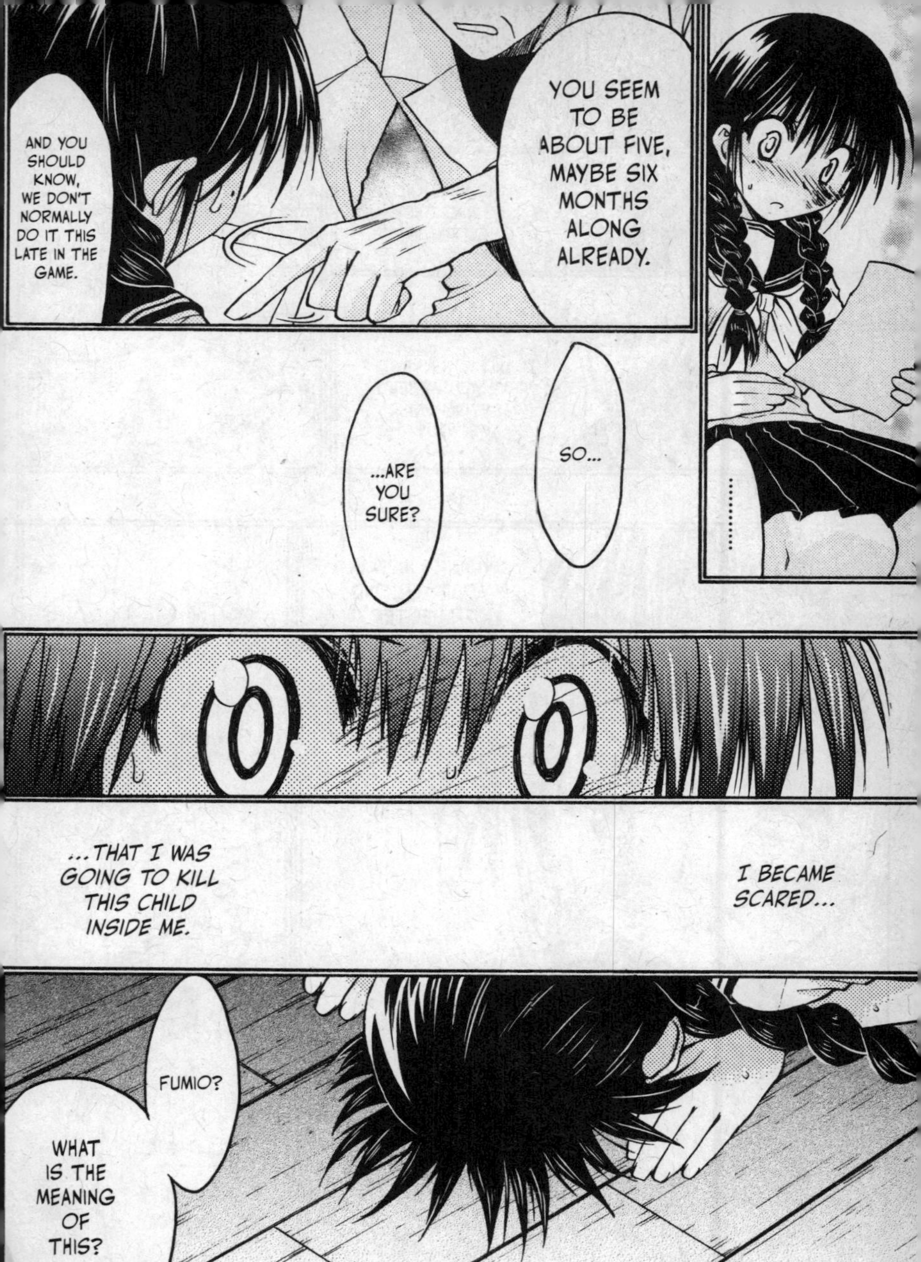
......
YOU SEEM TO BE ABOUT FIVE, MAYBE SIX MONTHS ALONG ALREADY.
AND YOU SHOULD KNOW, WE DON'T NORMALLY DO IT THIS LATE IN THE GAME.
SO...
...ARE YOU SURE?
I BECAME SCARED...
...THAT I WAS GOING TO KILL THIS CHILD INSIDE ME.
FUMIO?
WHAT IS THE MEANING OF THIS?

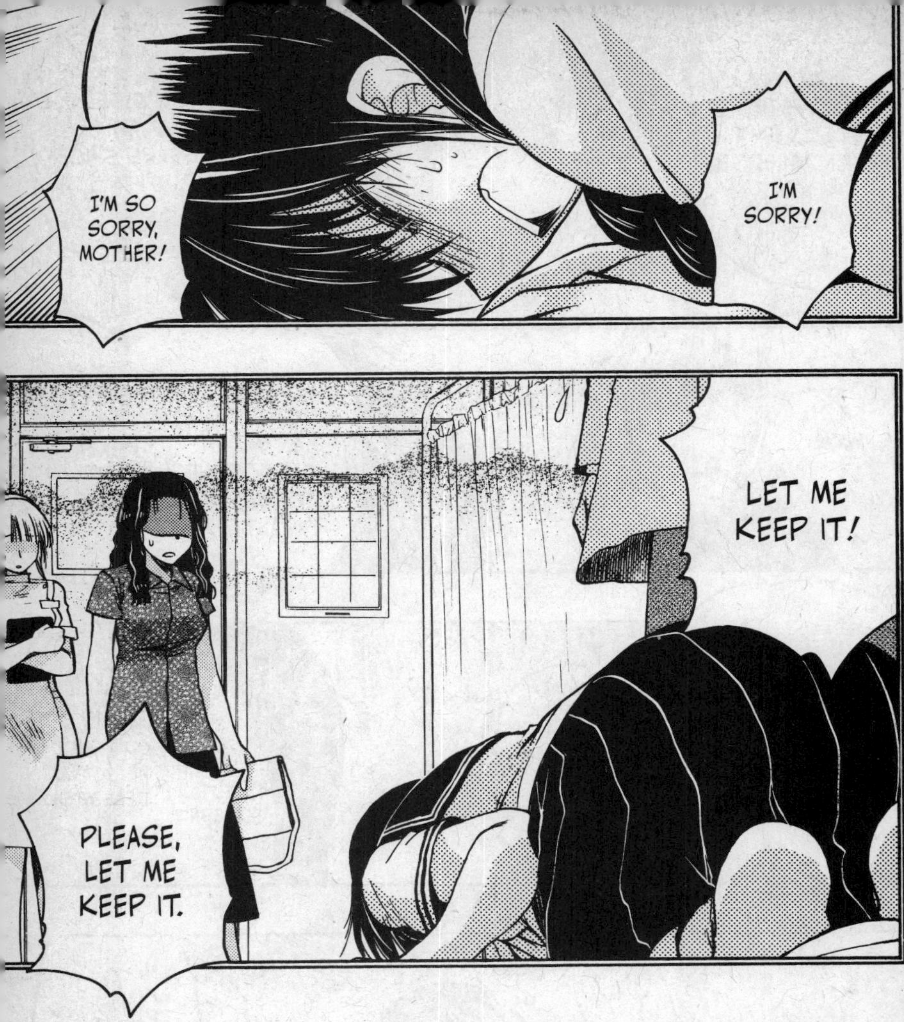
I'M SORRY!
I'M SO SORRY, MOTHER!
LET ME KEEP IT!
PLEASE, LET ME KEEP IT.

THE DAYS AFTER THAT WERE HELL.

MY MOTHER HIT ME AND INSULTED ME EVERY SINGLE DAY.

BUT I GOT THROUGH IT... AND GAVE BIRTH TO KENTA.

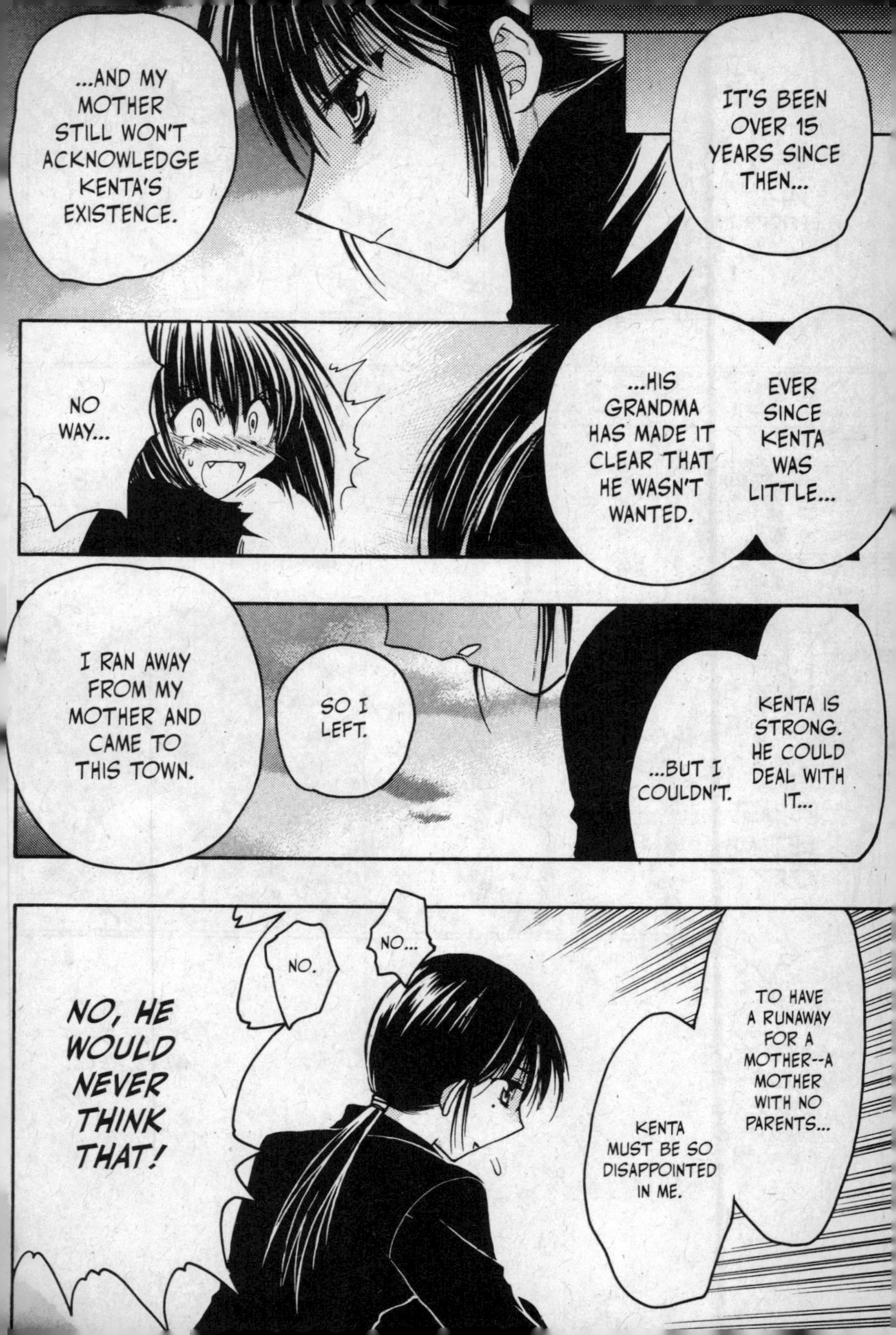
IT'S BEEN OVER 15 YEARS SINCE THEN...
...AND MY MOTHER STILL WON'T ACKNOWLEDGE KENTA'S EXISTENCE.
EVER SINCE KENTA WAS LITTLE...
...HIS GRANDMA HAS MADE IT CLEAR THAT HE WASN'T WANTED.
NO WAY...
KENTA IS STRONG. HE COULD DEAL WITH IT...
...BUT I COULDN'T.
SO I LEFT.
I RAN AWAY FROM MY MOTHER AND CAME TO THIS TOWN.
TO HAVE A RUNAWAY FOR A MOTHER--A MOTHER WITH NO PARENTS...
KENTA MUST BE SO DISAPPOINTED IN ME.
NO...
NO.
NO, HE WOULD NEVER THINK THAT!

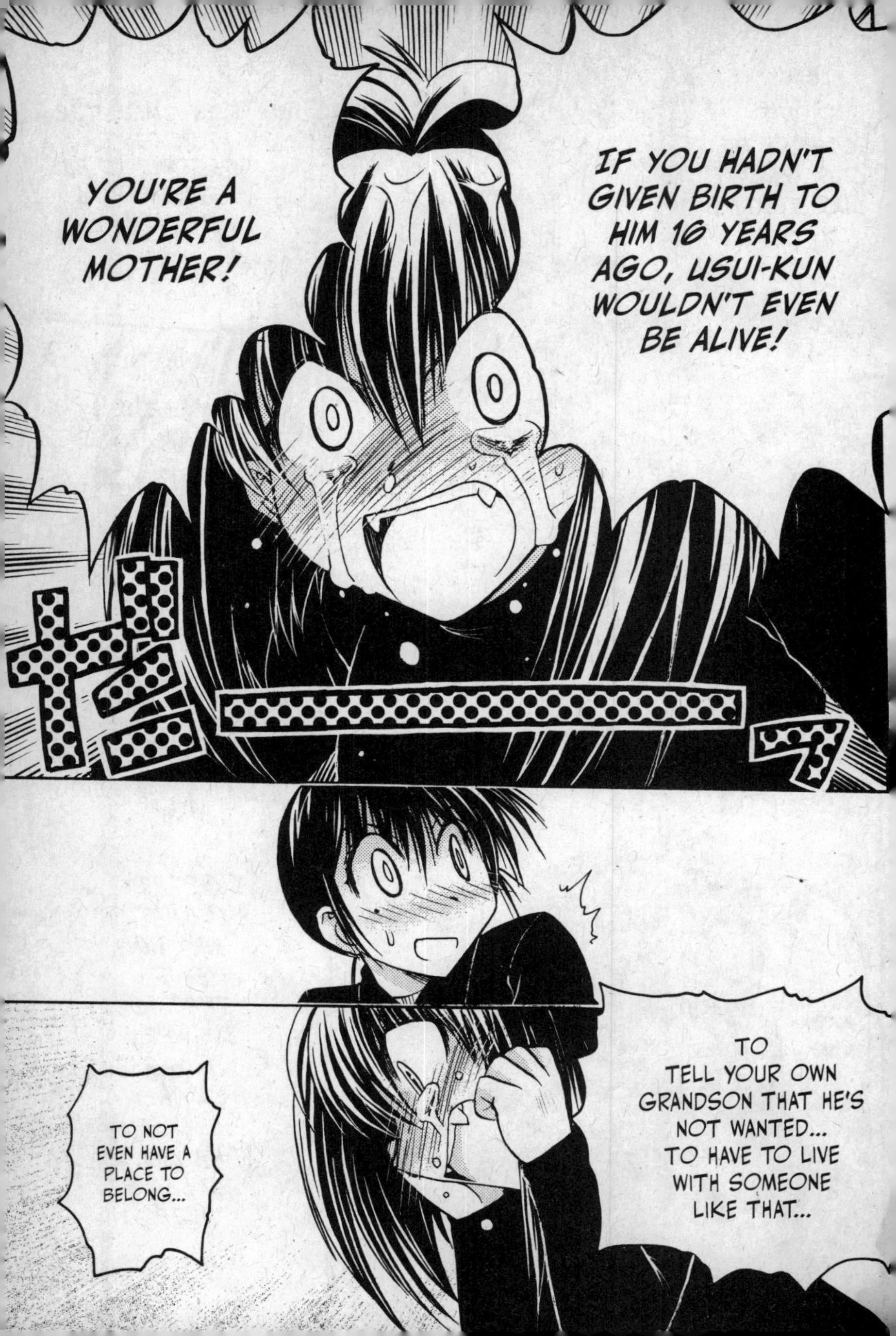
IF YOU HADN'T GIVEN BIRTH TO HIM 16 YEARS AGO, USUI-KUN WOULDN'T EVEN BE ALIVE!
YOU'RE A WONDERFUL MOTHER!
TO TELL YOUR OWN GRANDSON THAT HE'S NOT WANTED... TO HAVE TO LIVE WITH SOMEONE LIKE THAT...
TO NOT EVEN HAVE A PLACE TO BELONG...

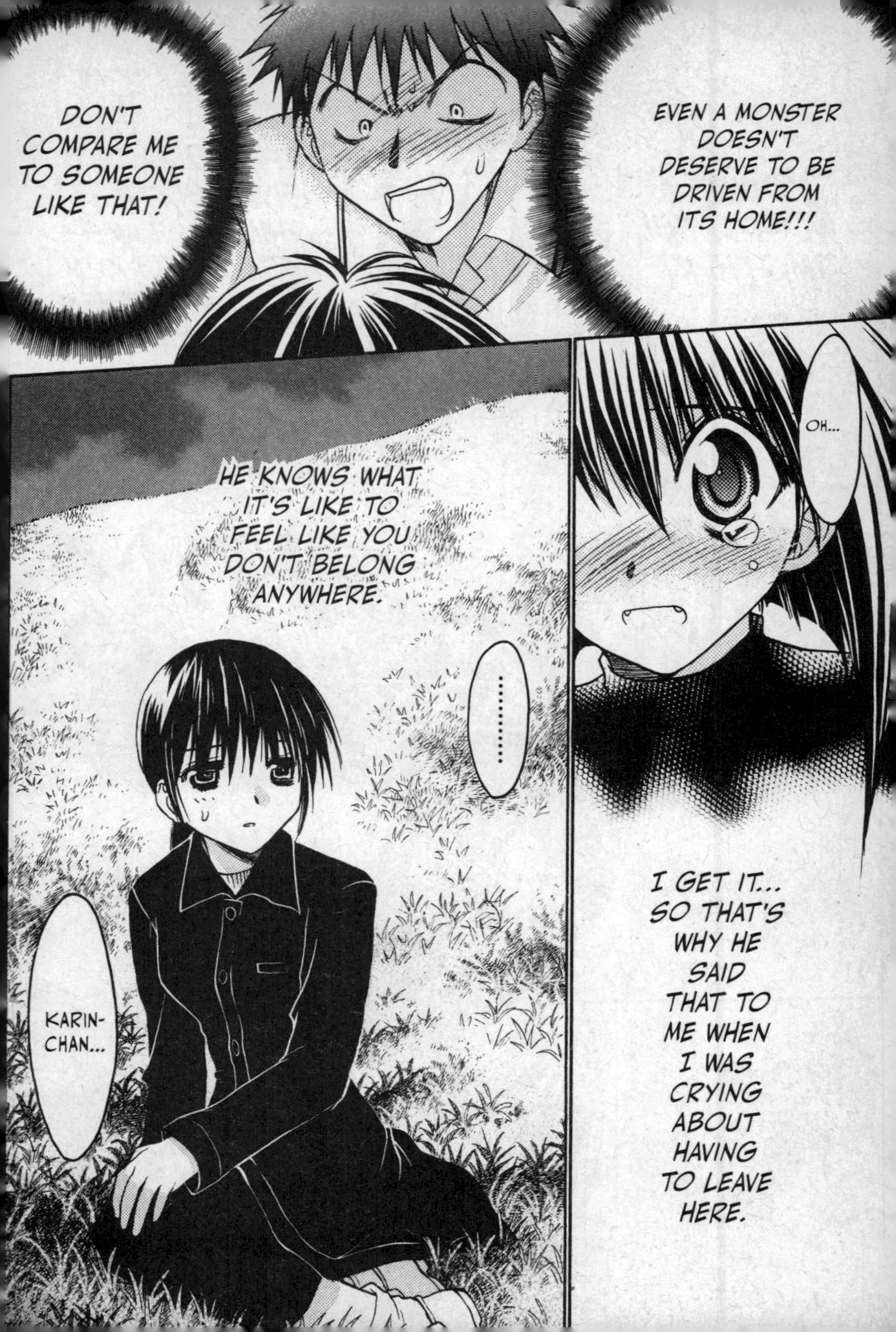

EVEN A MONSTER DOESN'T DESERVE TO BE DRIVEN FROM ITS HOME!!!
DON'T COMPARE ME TO SOMEONE LIKE THAT!
OH...
I GET IT... SO THAT'S WHY HE SAID THAT TO ME WHEN I WAS CRYING ABOUT HAVING TO LEAVE HERE.
HE KNOWS WHAT IT'S LIKE TO FEEL LIKE YOU DON'T BELONG ANYWHERE.
......
KARIN-CHAN...

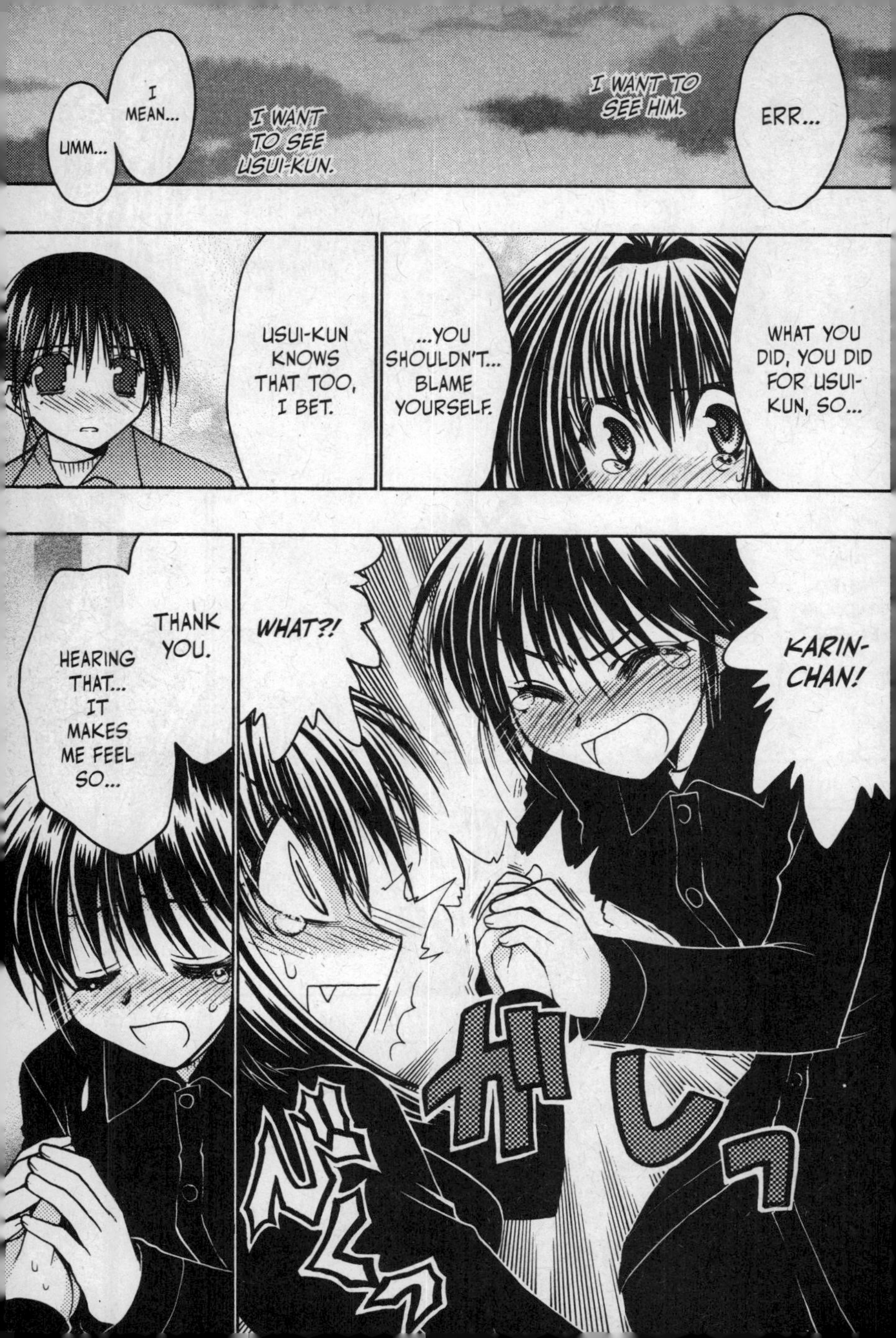
ERR...
I WANT TO SEE HIM.
I WANT TO SEE USUI-KUN.
I MEAN...
UMM...
WHAT YOU DID, YOU DID FOR USUI-KUN, SO...
...YOU SHOULDN'T... BLAME YOURSELF.
USUI-KUN KNOWS THAT TOO, I BET.
KARIN-CHAN!
WHAT?!
THANK YOU.
HEARING THAT... IT MAKES ME FEEL SO...

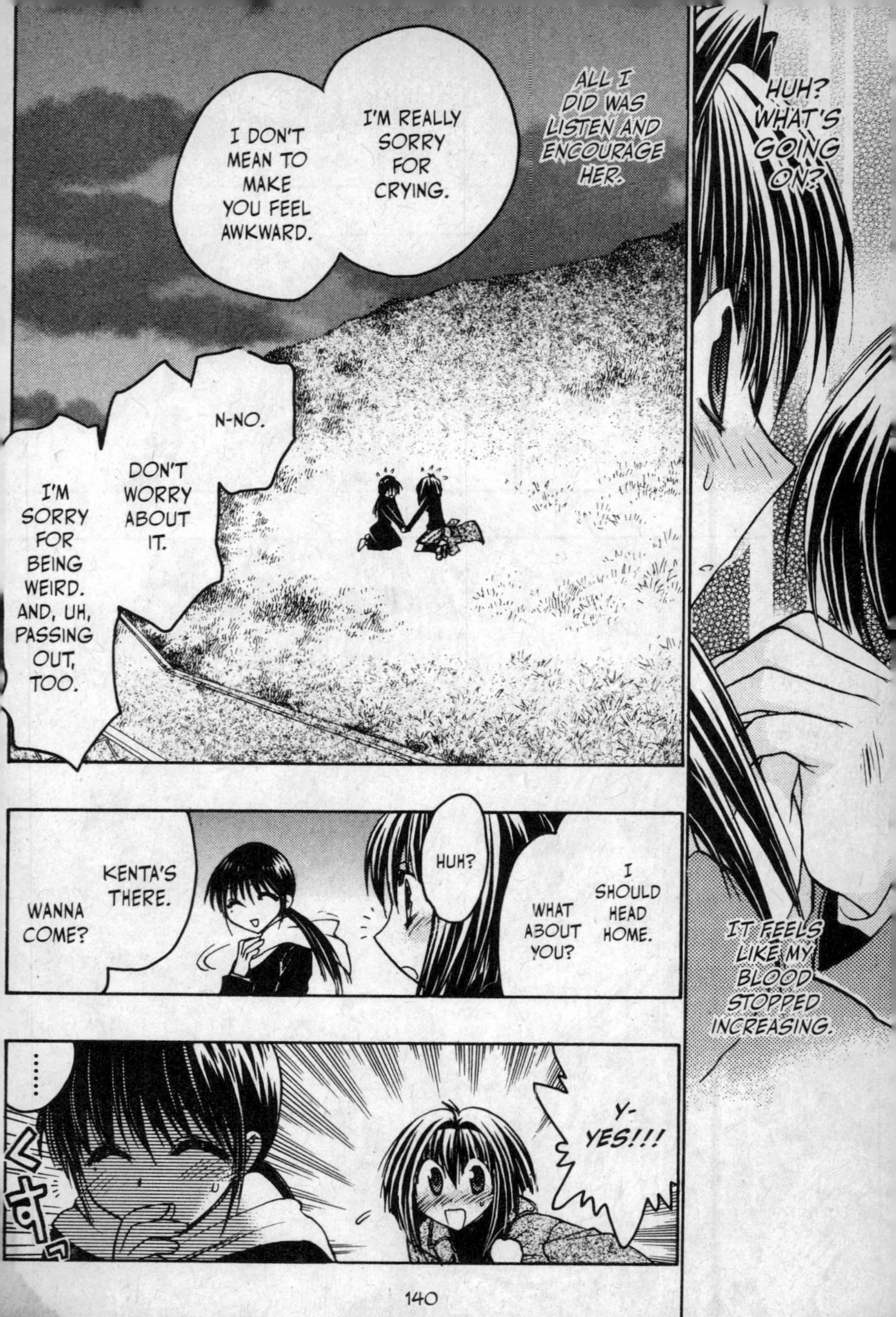
HUH? WHAT'S GOING ON?
IT FEELS LIKE MY BLOOD STOPPED INCREASING.
ALL I DID WAS LISTEN AND ENCOURAGE HER.
I'M REALLY SORRY FOR CRYING.
I DON'T MEAN TO MAKE YOU FEEL AWKWARD.
N-NO.
DON'T WORRY ABOUT IT.
I'M SORRY FOR BEING WEIRD. AND, UH, PASSING OUT, TOO.
I SHOULD HEAD HOME.
WHAT ABOUT YOU?
HUH?
KENTA'S THERE.
WANNA COME?
Y-YES!!!
......
くす

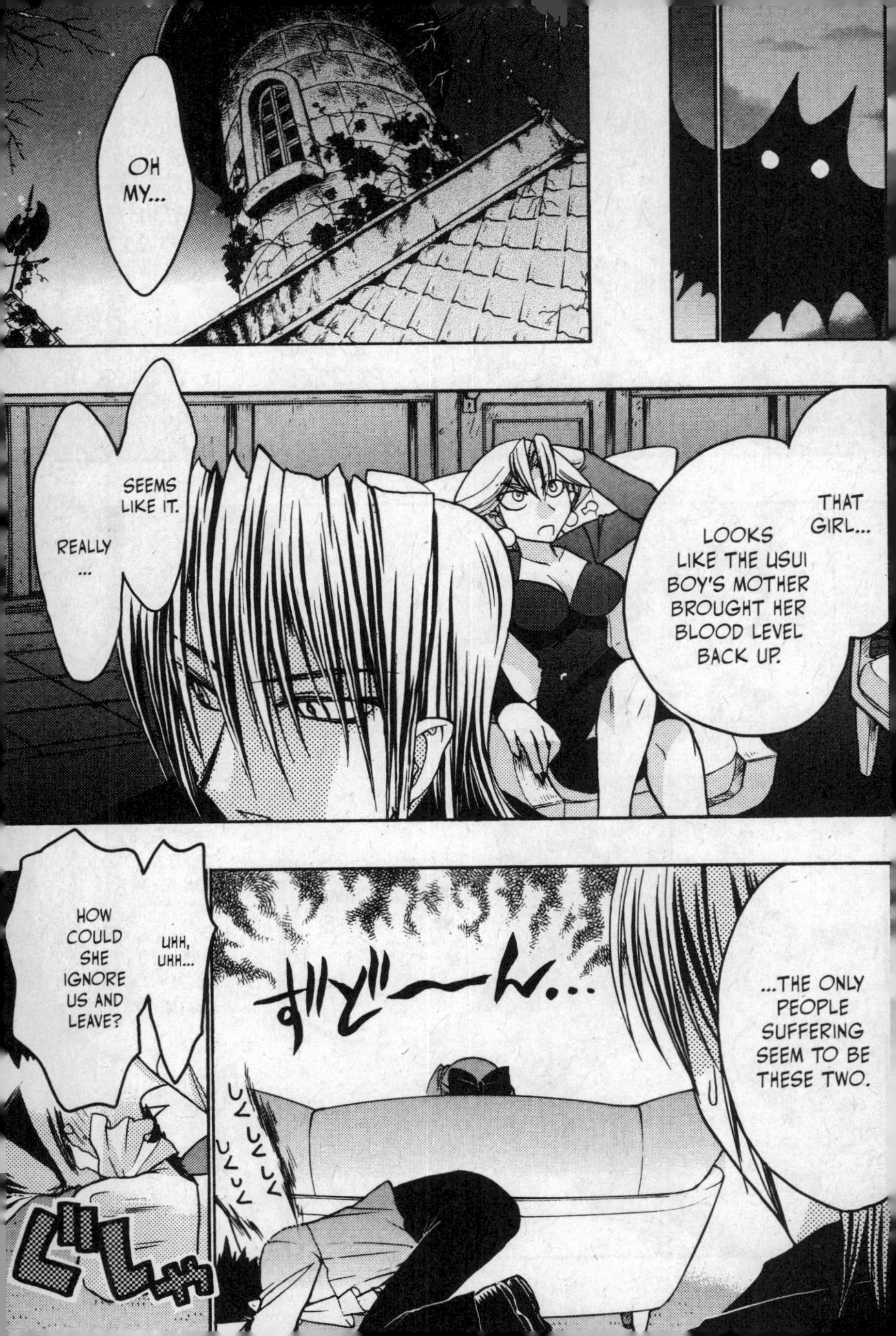
OH MY...
THAT GIRL...
LOOKS LIKE THE USUI BOY'S MOTHER BROUGHT HER BLOOD LEVEL BACK UP.
SEEMS LIKE IT.
REALLY ...
...THE ONLY PEOPLE SUFFERING SEEM TO BE THESE TWO.
ずど〜〜ん...
UHH, UHH...
HOW COULD SHE IGNORE US AND LEAVE?
ぐしゅ

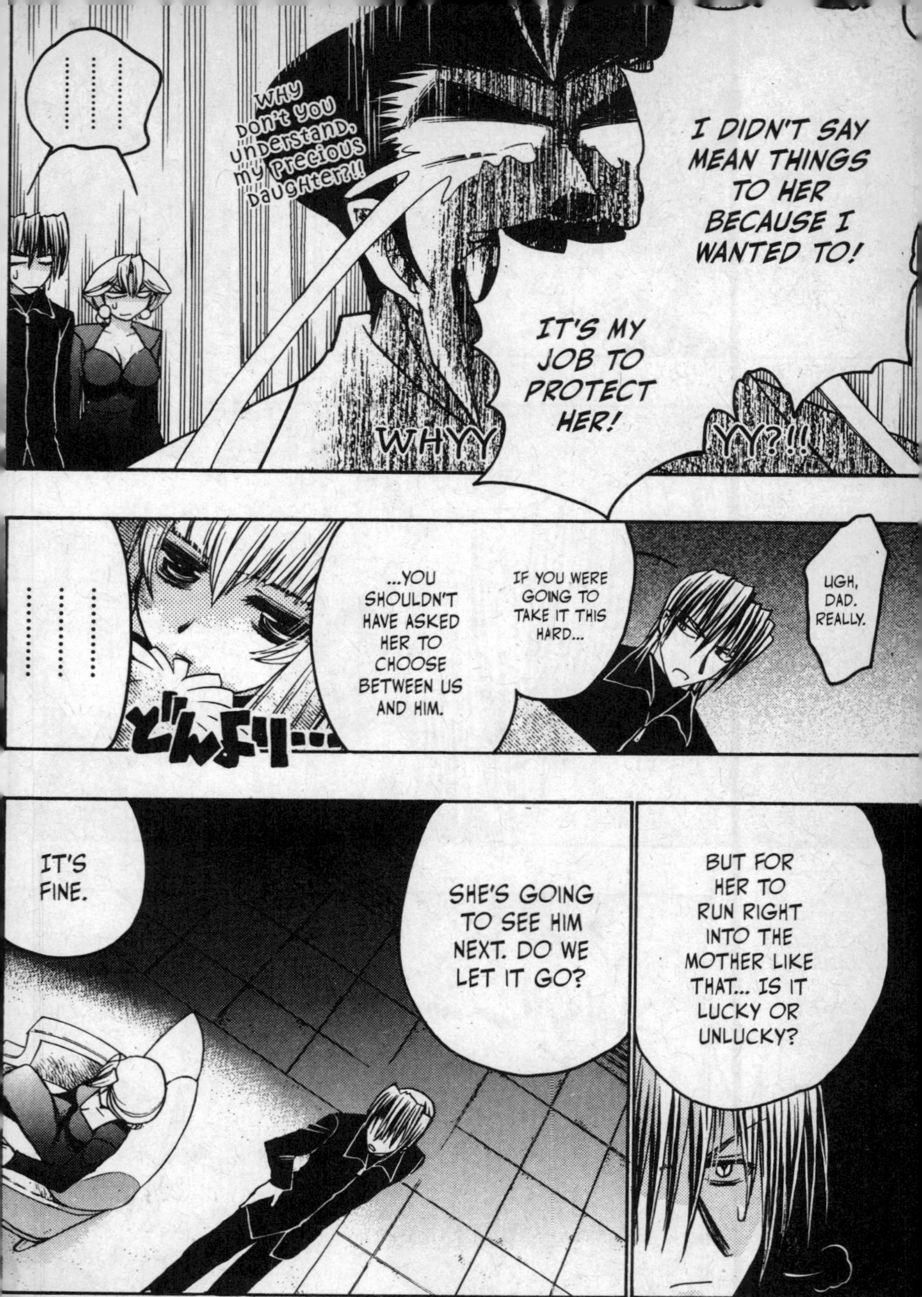
I DIDN'T SAY MEAN THINGS TO HER BECAUSE I WANTED TO!
IT'S MY JOB TO PROTECT HER!
WHYY
YY?!!
WHY DON'T YOU UNDERSTAND, MY PRECIOUS DAUGHTER?!!
......
UGH, DAD. REALLY.
IF YOU WERE GOING TO TAKE IT THIS HARD...
...YOU SHOULDN'T HAVE ASKED HER TO CHOOSE BETWEEN US AND HIM.
......
どんより…
BUT FOR HER TO RUN RIGHT INTO THE MOTHER LIKE THAT... IS IT LUCKY OR UNLUCKY?
SHE'S GOING TO SEE HIM NEXT. DO WE LET IT GO?
IT'S FINE.

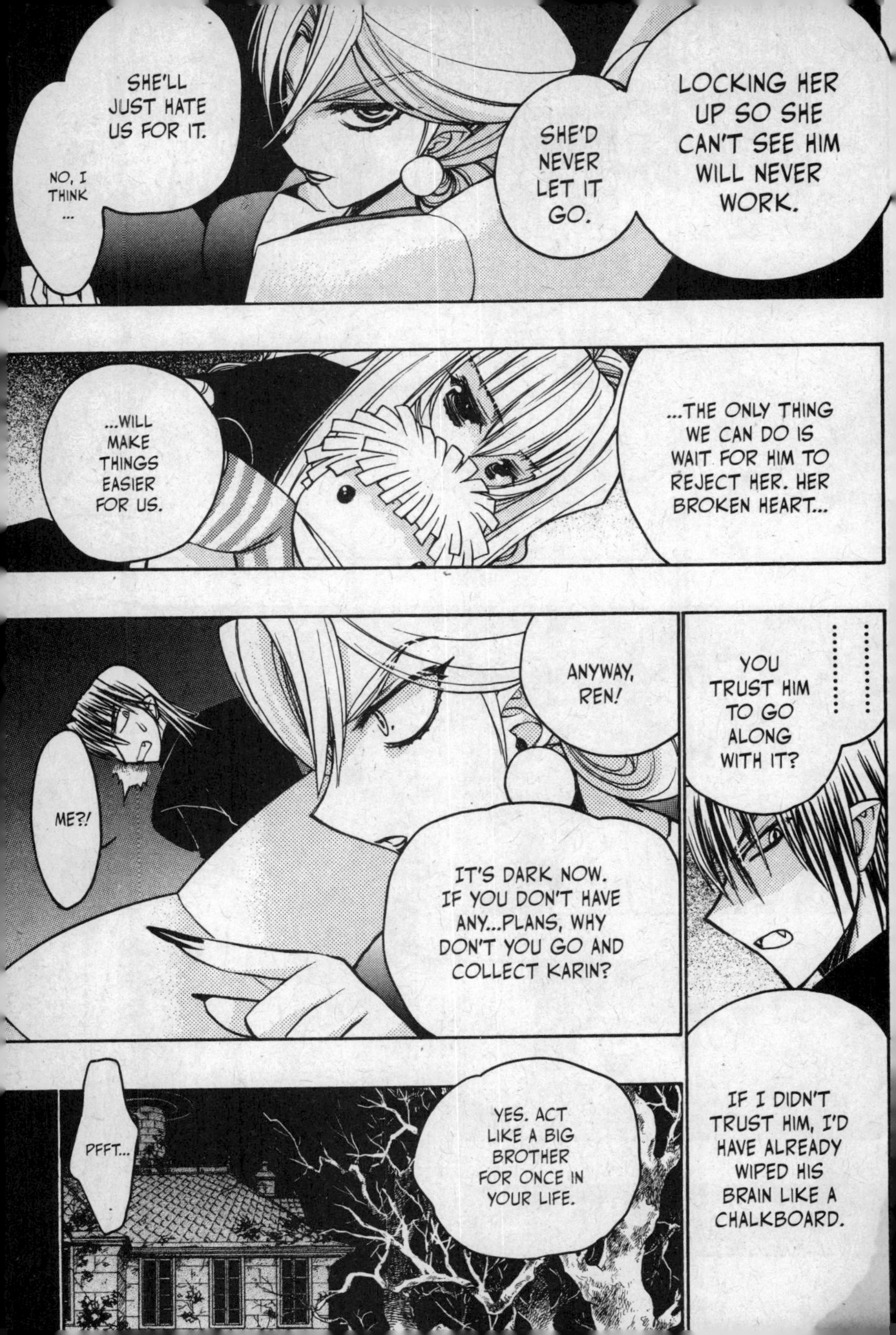
LOCKING HER UP SO SHE CAN'T SEE HIM WILL NEVER WORK.
SHE'D NEVER LET IT GO.
SHE'LL JUST HATE US FOR IT.
NO, I THINK ...
...THE ONLY THING WE CAN DO IS WAIT FOR HIM TO REJECT HER. HER BROKEN HEART...
...WILL MAKE THINGS EASIER FOR US.
....
YOU TRUST HIM TO GO ALONG WITH IT?
IF I DIDN'T TRUST HIM, I'D HAVE ALREADY WIPED HIS BRAIN LIKE A CHALKBOARD.
ANYWAY, REN!
IT'S DARK NOW. IF YOU DON'T HAVE ANY...PLANS, WHY DON'T YOU GO AND COLLECT KARIN?
ME?!
YES. ACT LIKE A BIG BROTHER FOR ONCE IN YOUR LIFE.
PFFT...

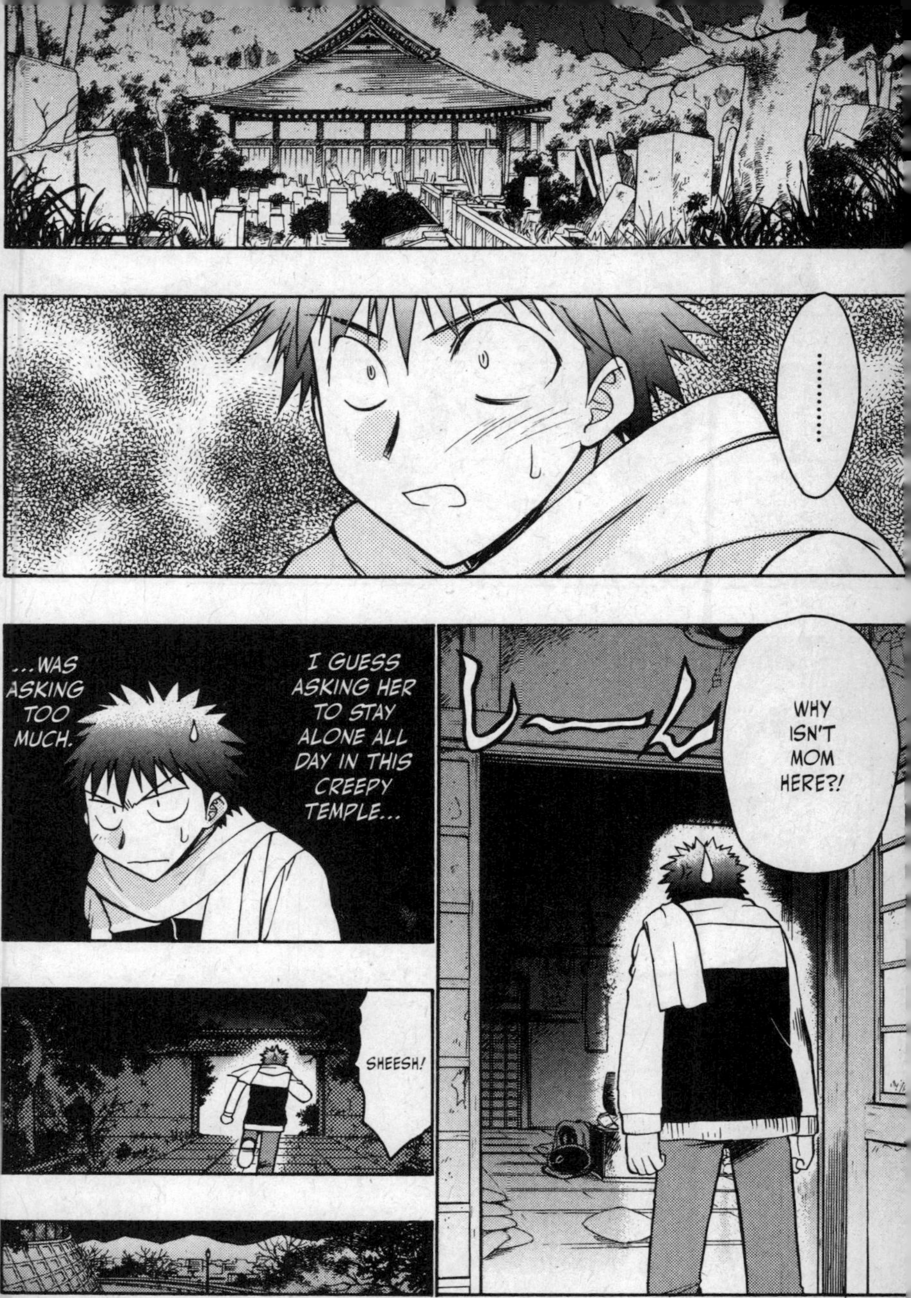
......
しーん
WHY ISN'T MOM HERE?!
I GUESS ASKING HER TO STAY ALONE ALL DAY IN THIS CREEPY TEMPLE...
...WAS ASKING TOO MUCH.
SHEESH!

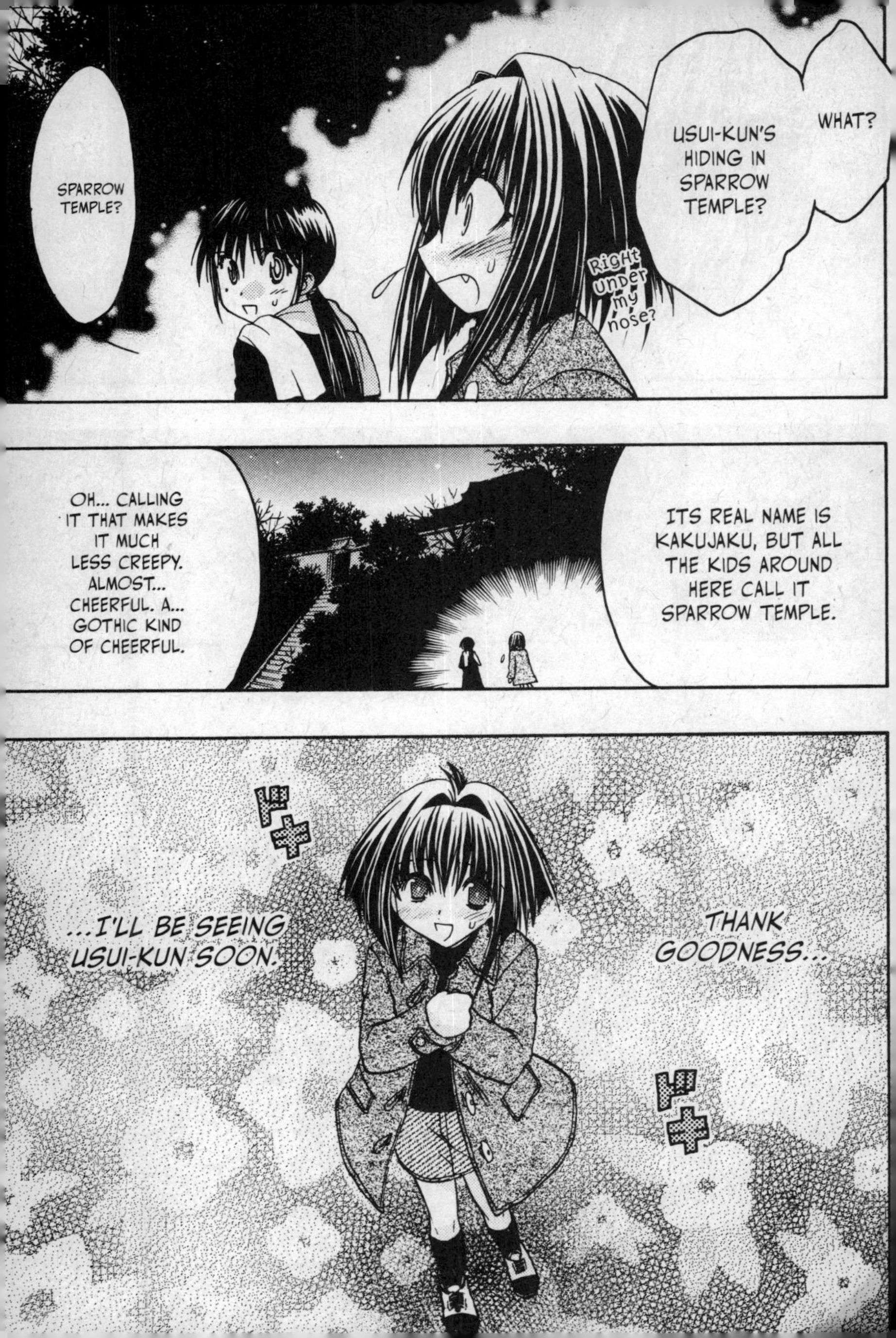
WHAT?
USUI-KUN'S HIDING IN SPARROW TEMPLE?
Right under my nose?
SPARROW TEMPLE?
ITS REAL NAME IS KAKUJAKU, BUT ALL THE KIDS AROUND HERE CALL IT SPARROW TEMPLE.
OH... CALLING IT THAT MAKES IT MUCH LESS CREEPY. ALMOST... CHEERFUL. A... GOTHIC KIND OF CHEERFUL.
THANK GOODNESS...
...I'LL BE SEEING USUI-KUN SOON.

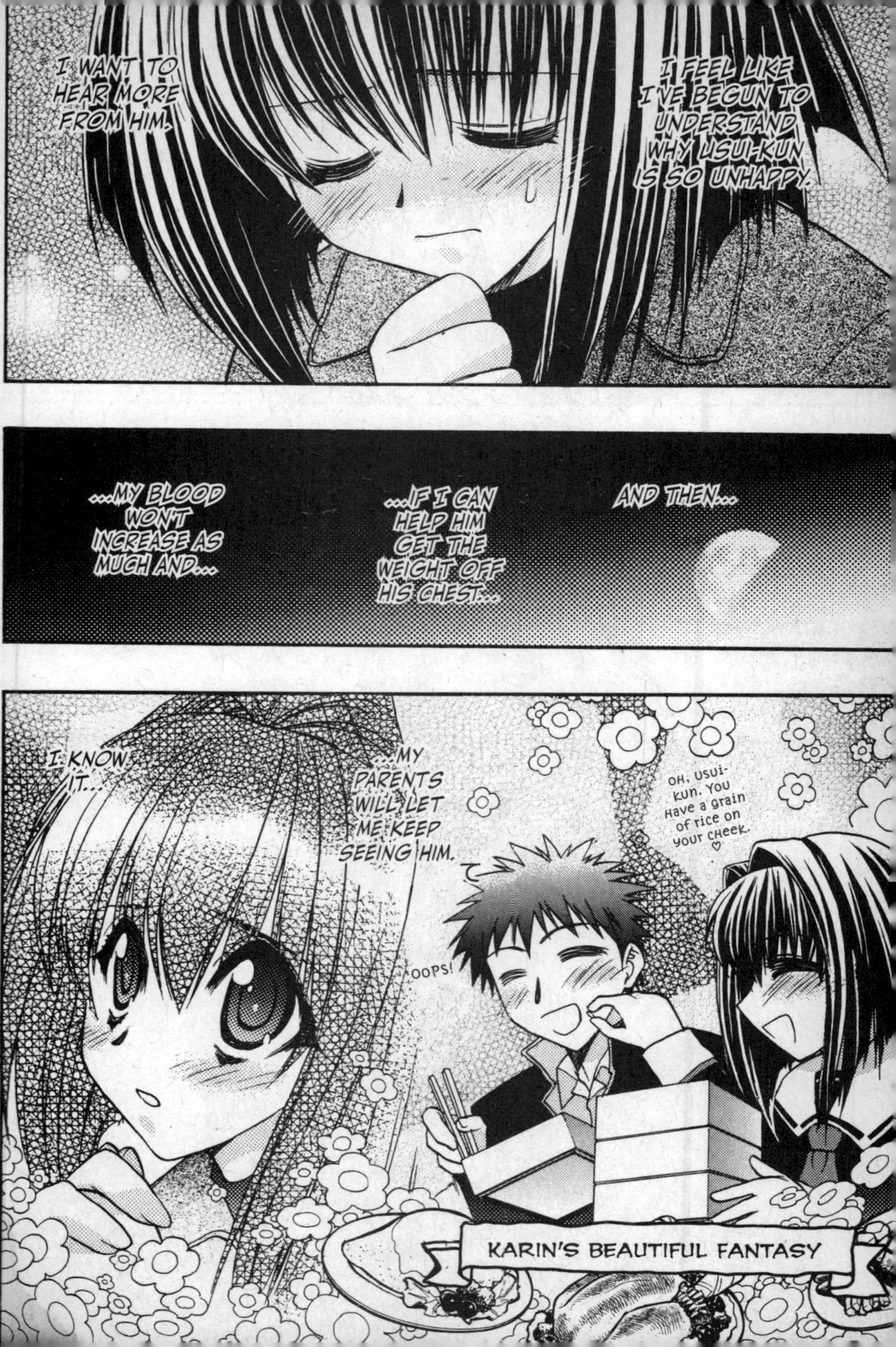
I FEEL LIKE I'VE BEGUN TO UNDERSTAND WHY USUI-KUN IS SO UNHAPPY.
I WANT TO HEAR MORE FROM HIM.
AND THEN...
...IF I CAN HELP HIM GET THE WEIGHT OFF HIS CHEST...
...MY BLOOD WON'T INCREASE AS MUCH AND...
OH, USUI-KUN. You Have a grain of rice on your cheek. ♡
OOPS!
...MY PARENTS WILL LET ME KEEP SEEING HIM.
I KNOW IT...
KARIN'S BEAUTIFUL FANTASY

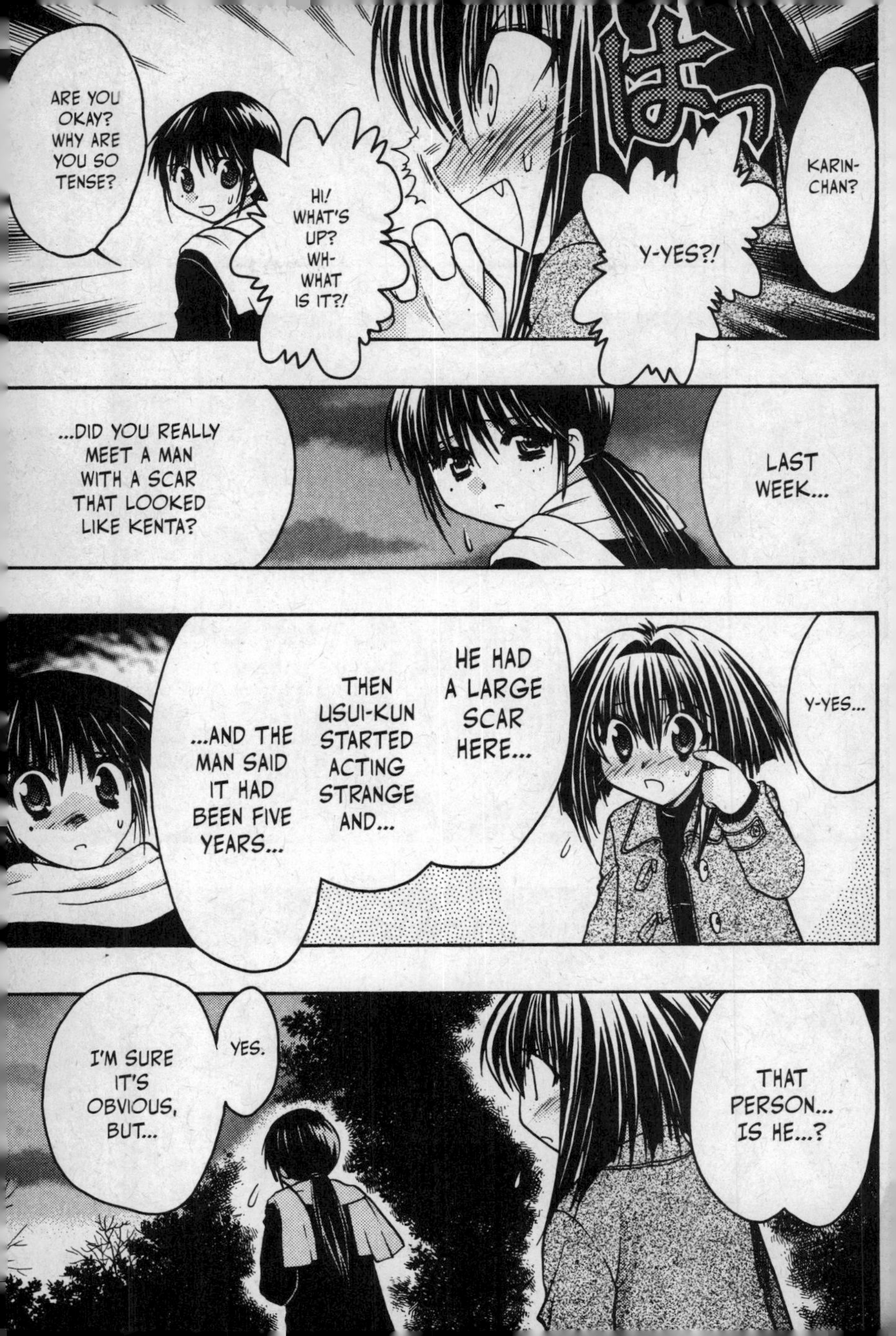
はっ
KARIN-CHAN?
Y-YES?!
HI! WHAT'S UP? WH-WHAT IS IT?!
ARE YOU OKAY? WHY ARE YOU SO TENSE?
LAST WEEK...
...DID YOU REALLY MEET A MAN WITH A SCAR THAT LOOKED LIKE KENTA?
Y-YES...
HE HAD A LARGE SCAR HERE...
THEN USUI-KUN STARTED ACTING STRANGE AND...
...AND THE MAN SAID IT HAD BEEN FIVE YEARS...
THAT PERSON... IS HE...?
YES.
I'M SURE IT'S OBVIOUS, BUT...

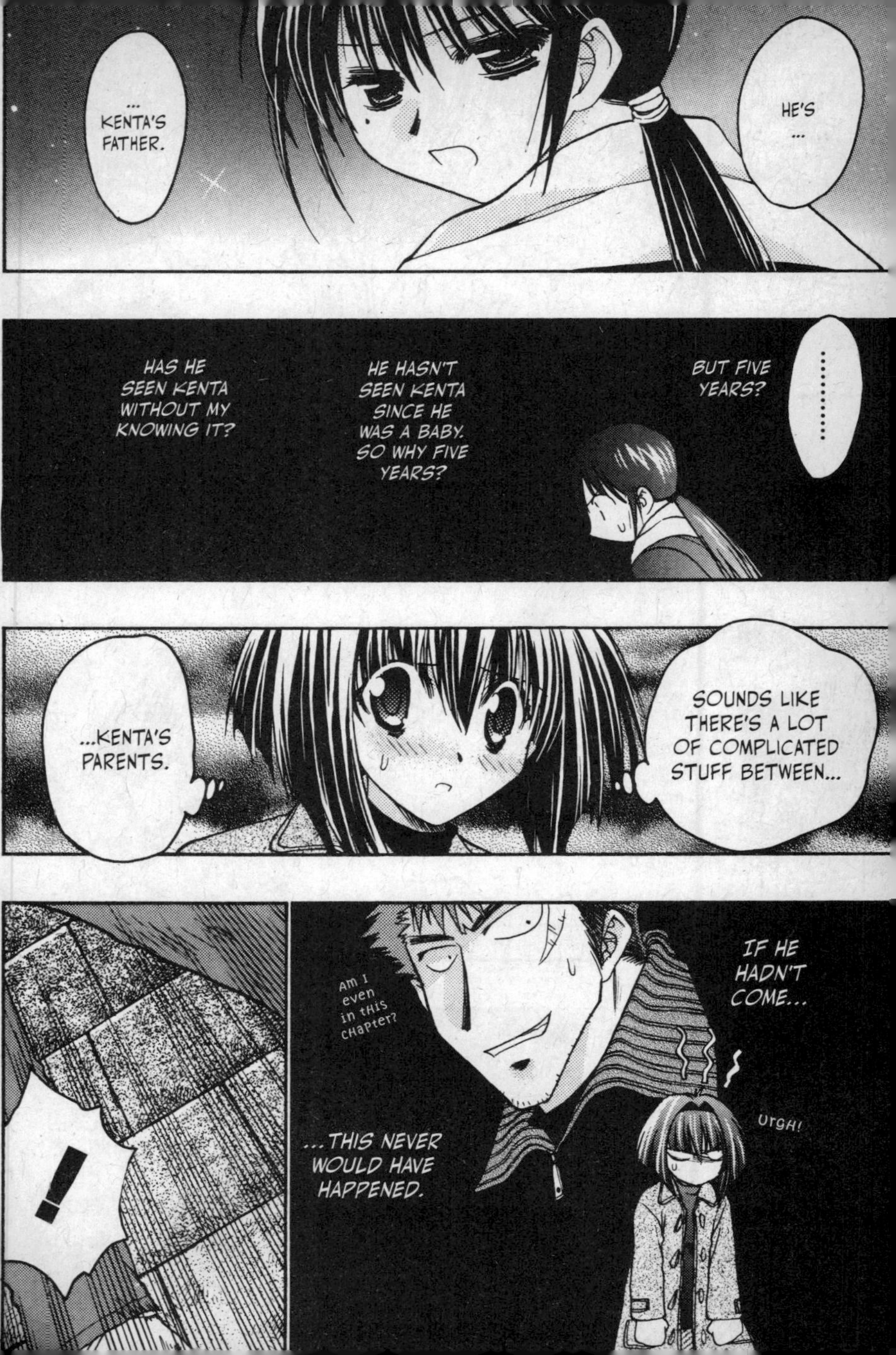
HE'S ...
... KENTA'S FATHER.
......
BUT FIVE YEARS?
HE HASN'T SEEN KENTA SINCE HE WAS A BABY. SO WHY FIVE YEARS?
HAS HE SEEN KENTA WITHOUT MY KNOWING IT?
SOUNDS LIKE THERE'S A LOT OF COMPLICATED STUFF BETWEEN...
...KENTA'S PARENTS.
IF HE HADN'T COME...
Am I even in this chapter?
Urgh!
...THIS NEVER WOULD HAVE HAPPENED.
!

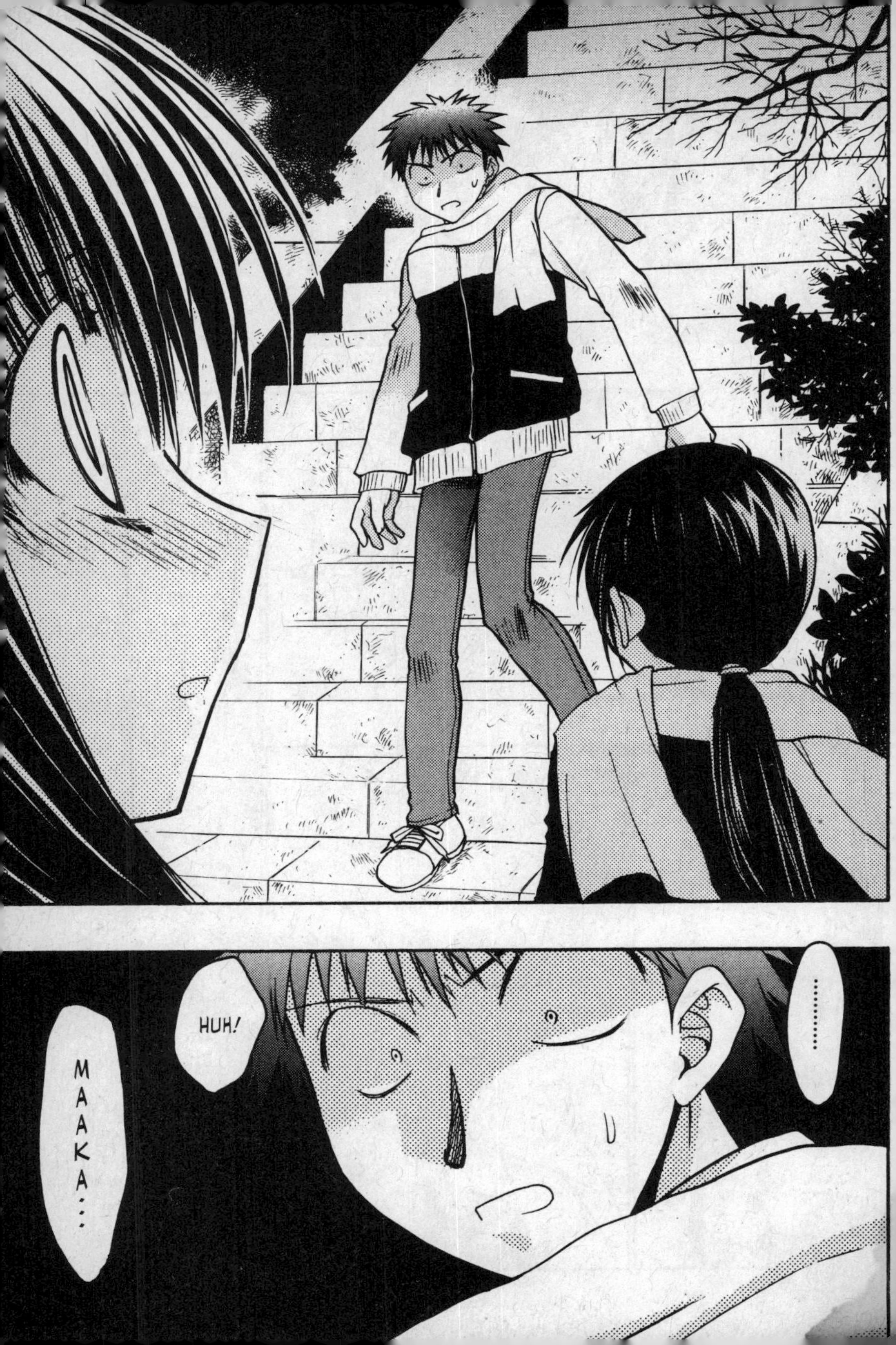
......
HUH!
MAAKA...

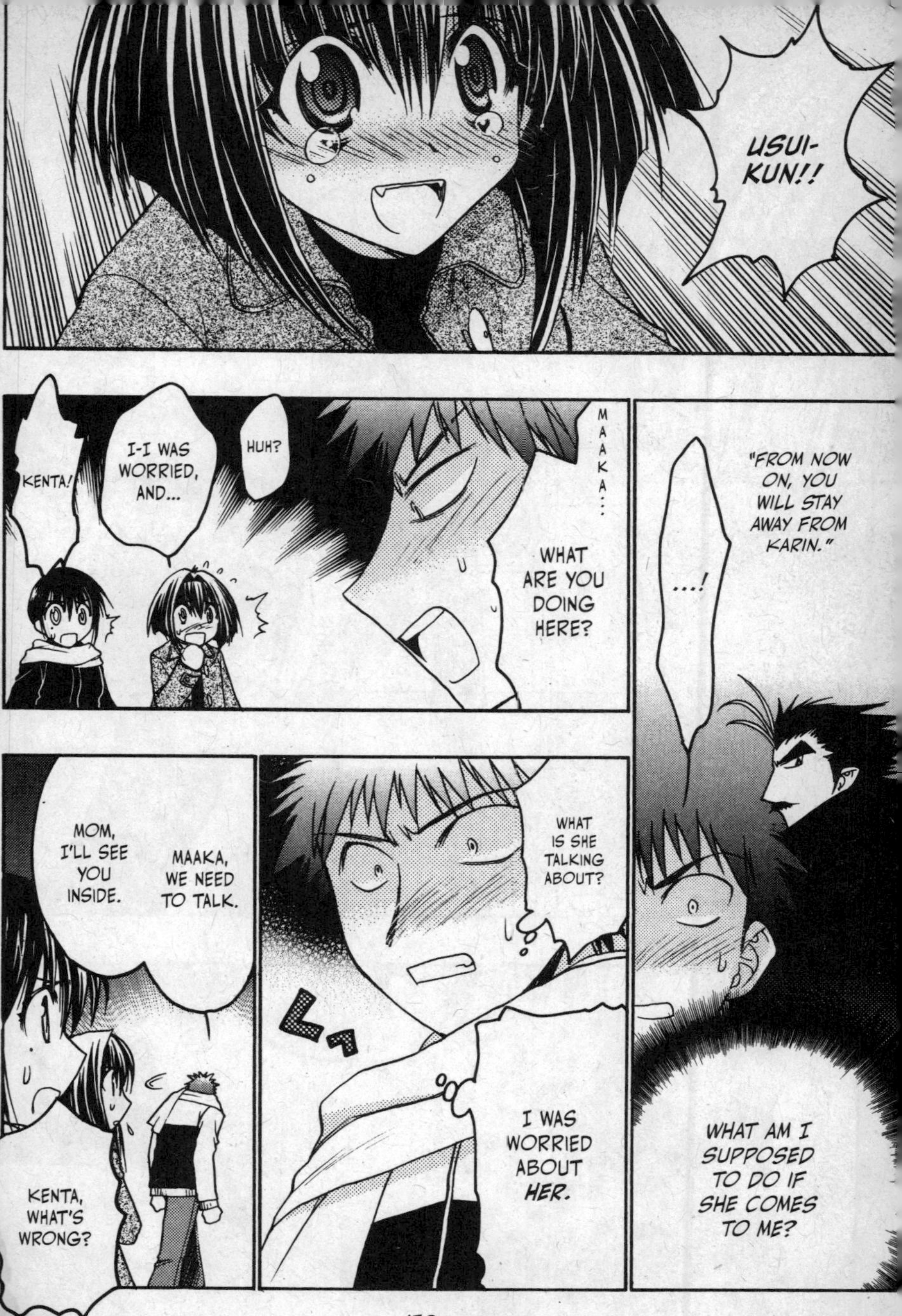
USUI-KUN!!
"FROM NOW ON, YOU WILL STAY AWAY FROM KARIN."
...!
WHAT AM I SUPPOSED TO DO IF SHE COMES TO ME?
MAAKA...
WHAT ARE YOU DOING HERE?
HUH?
I-I WAS WORRIED, AND...
KENTA!
WHAT IS SHE TALKING ABOUT?
I WAS WORRIED ABOUT HER.
MAAKA, WE NEED TO TALK.
MOM, I'LL SEE YOU INSIDE.
KENTA, WHAT'S WRONG?

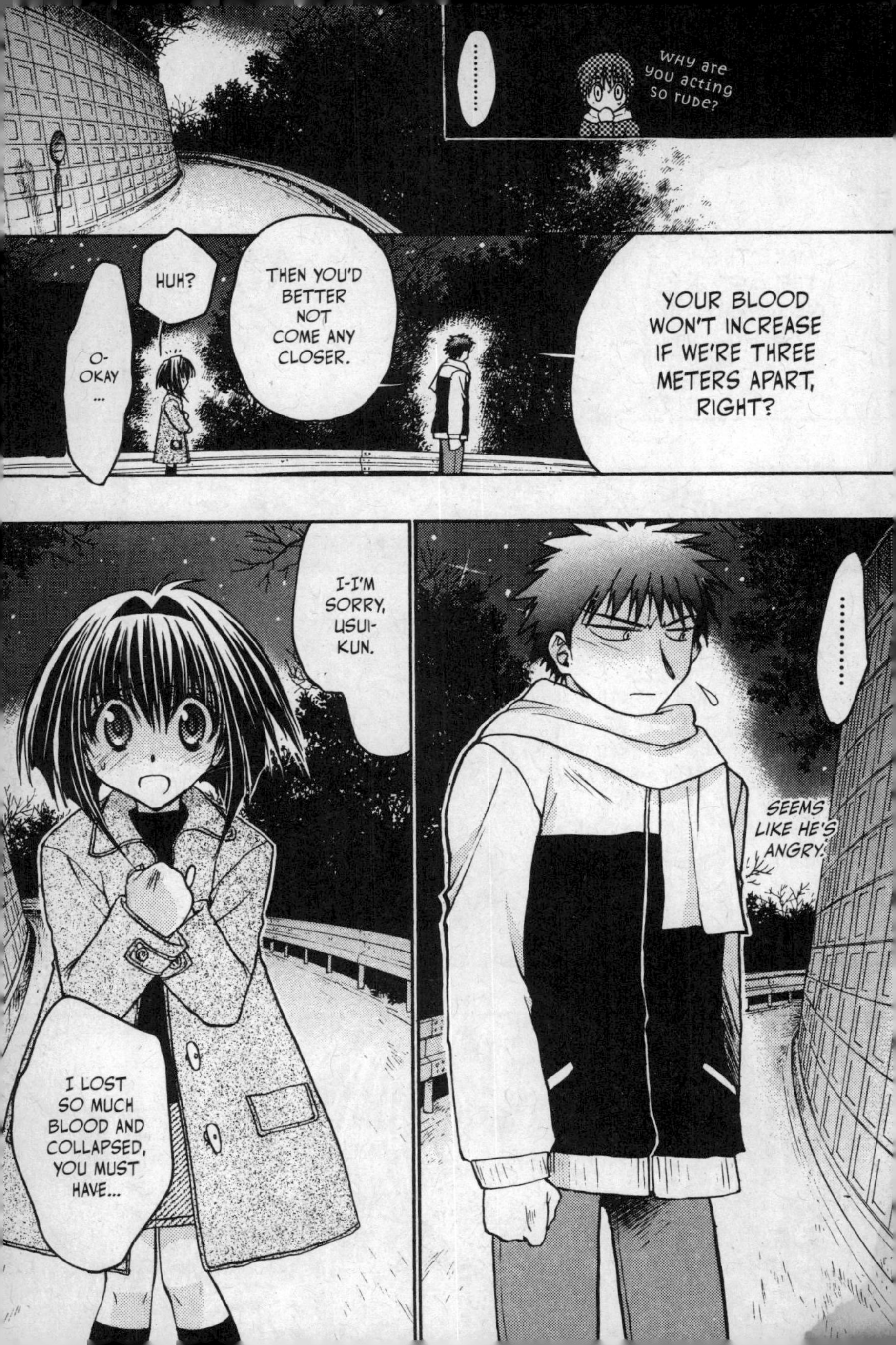
WHY are you acting so rude?
......
YOUR BLOOD WON'T INCREASE IF WE'RE THREE METERS APART, RIGHT?
THEN YOU'D BETTER NOT COME ANY CLOSER.
HUH?
O-OKAY...
......
SEEMS LIKE HE'S ANGRY.
I-I'M SORRY, USUI-KUN.
I LOST SO MUCH BLOOD AND COLLAPSED, YOU MUST HAVE...

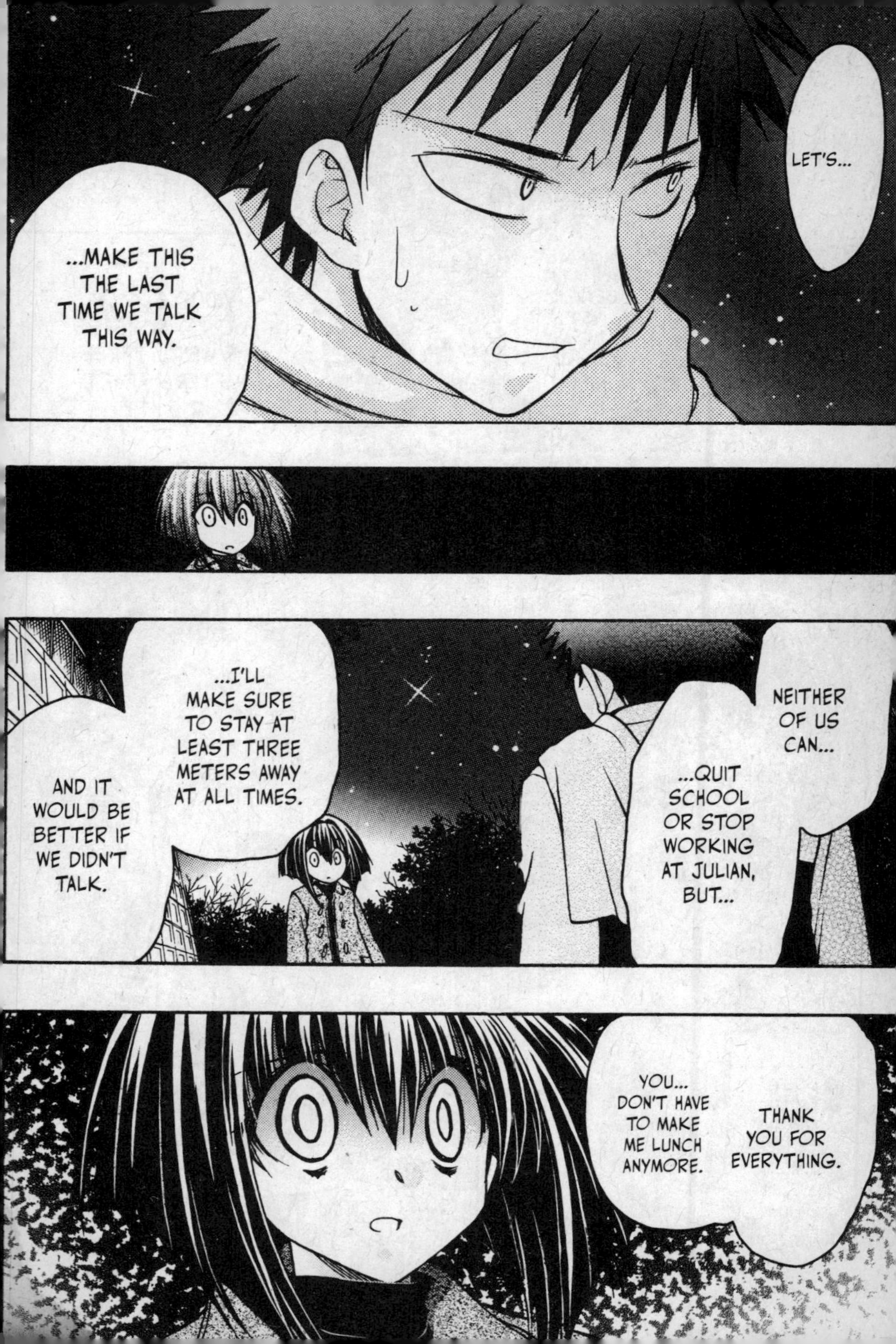
LET'S...
...MAKE THIS THE LAST TIME WE TALK THIS WAY.
NEITHER OF US CAN...
...QUIT SCHOOL OR STOP WORKING AT JULIAN, BUT...
...I'LL MAKE SURE TO STAY AT LEAST THREE METERS AWAY AT ALL TIMES.
AND IT WOULD BE BETTER IF WE DIDN'T TALK.
THANK YOU FOR EVERYTHING.
YOU... DON'T HAVE TO MAKE ME LUNCH ANYMORE.

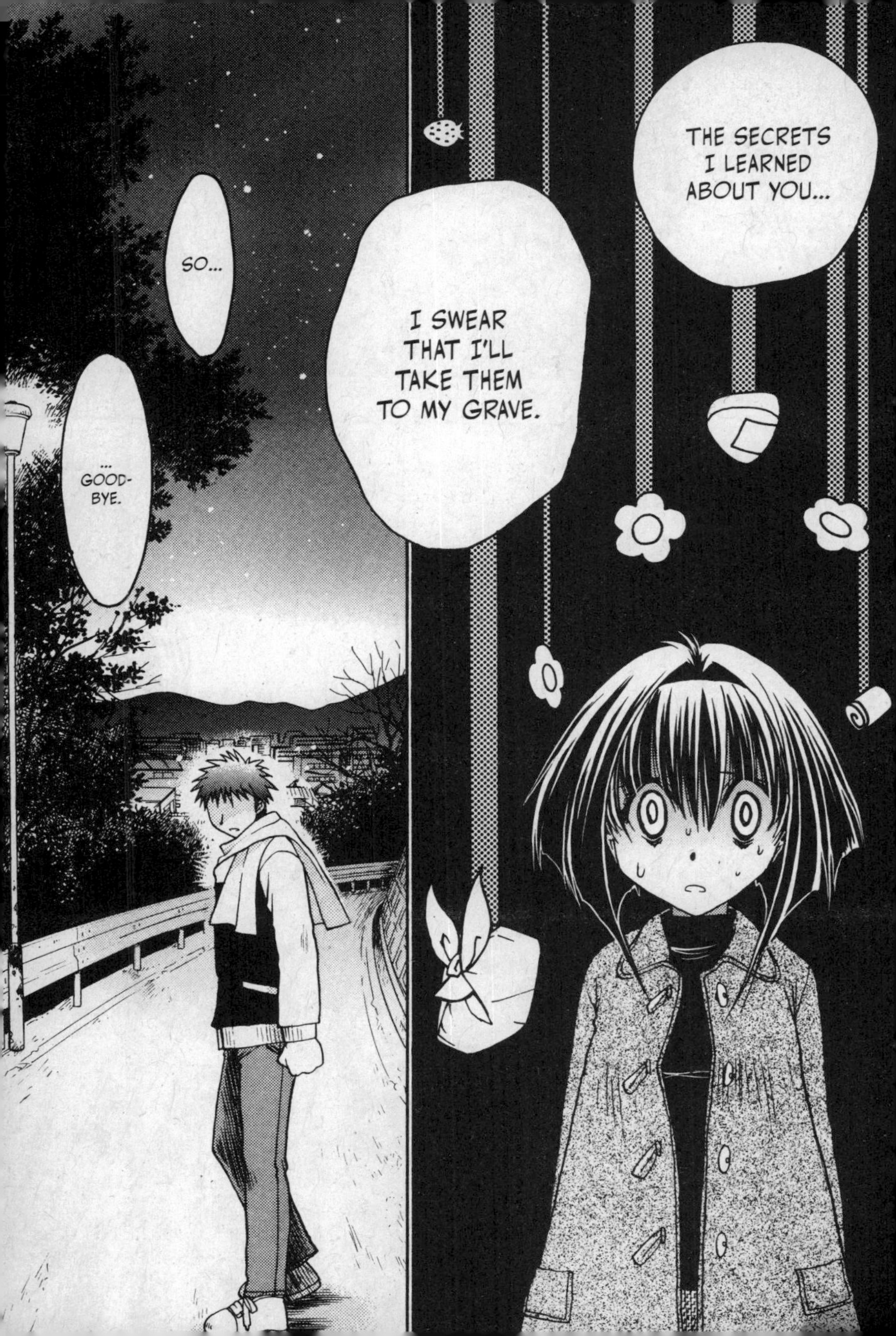
THE SECRETS I LEARNED ABOUT YOU...
I SWEAR THAT I'LL TAKE THEM TO MY GRAVE.
SO...
...GOOD-BYE.

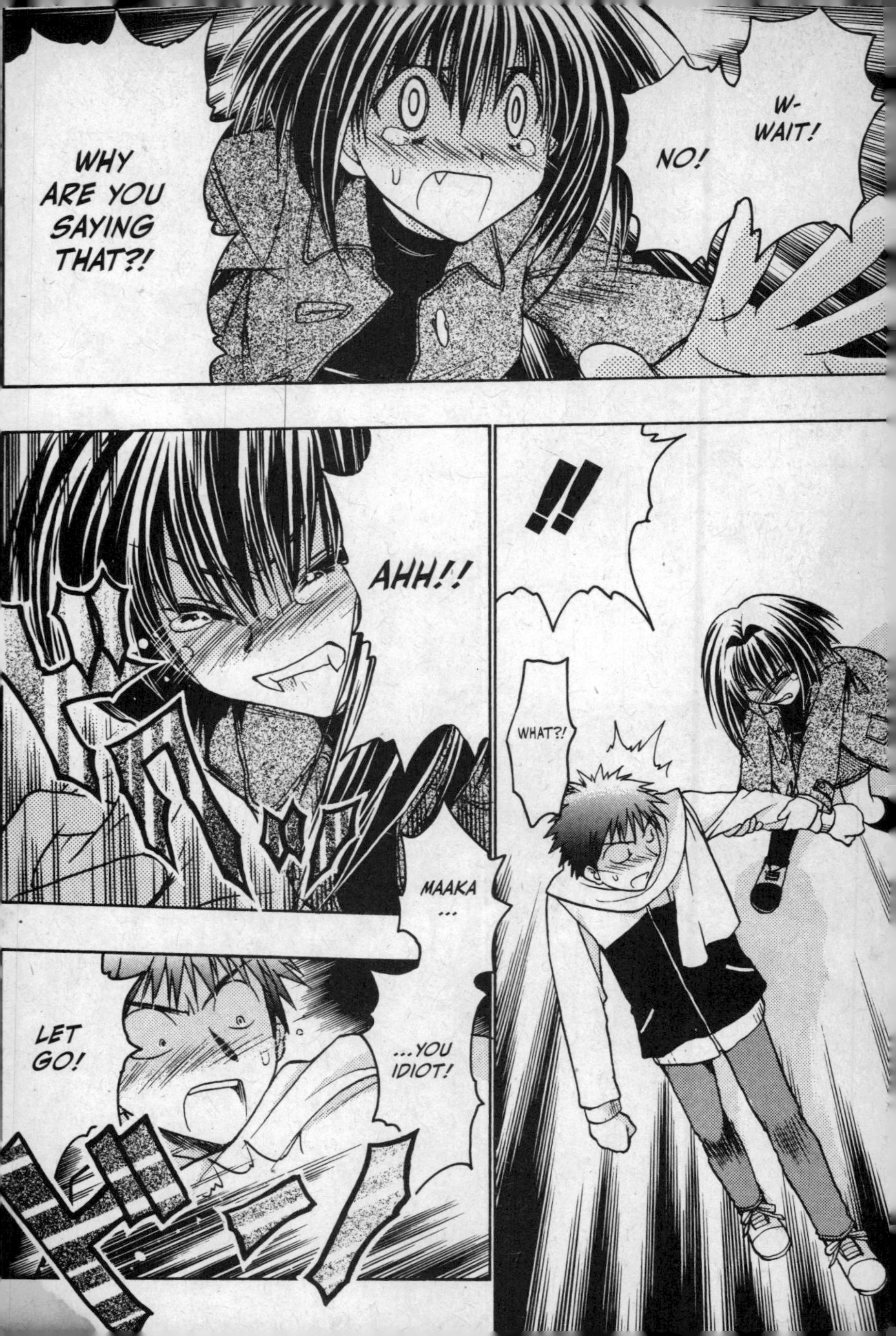
W-
WAIT!
NO!
WHY ARE YOU SAYING THAT?!
!!
WHAT?!
AHH!!
MAAKA ...
...YOU IDIOT!
LET GO!

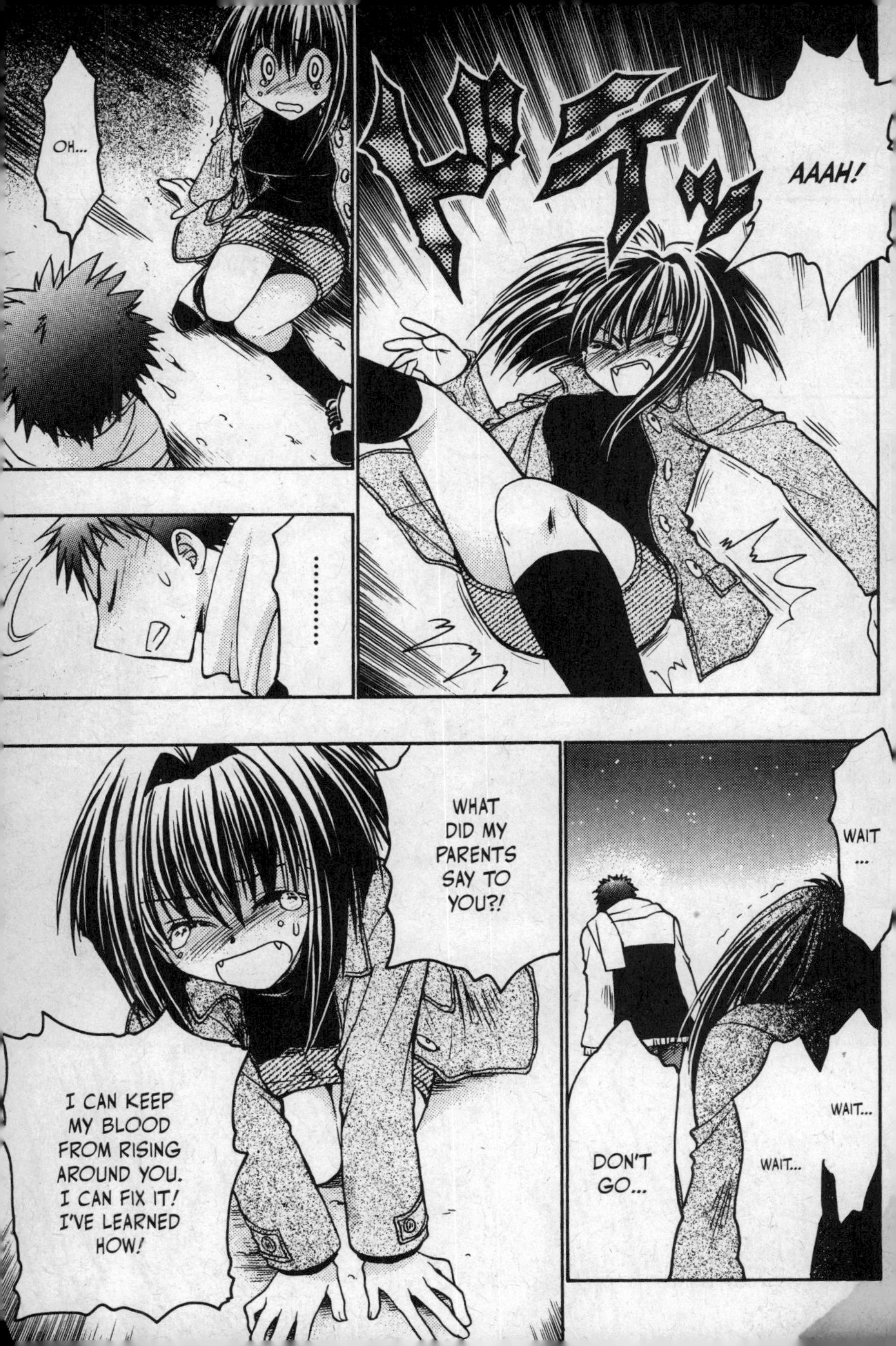
AAAH!
OH...
......
WAIT ...
WAIT...
WAIT...
DON'T GO...
WHAT DID MY PARENTS SAY TO YOU?!
I CAN KEEP MY BLOOD FROM RISING AROUND YOU. I CAN FIX IT! I'VE LEARNED HOW!

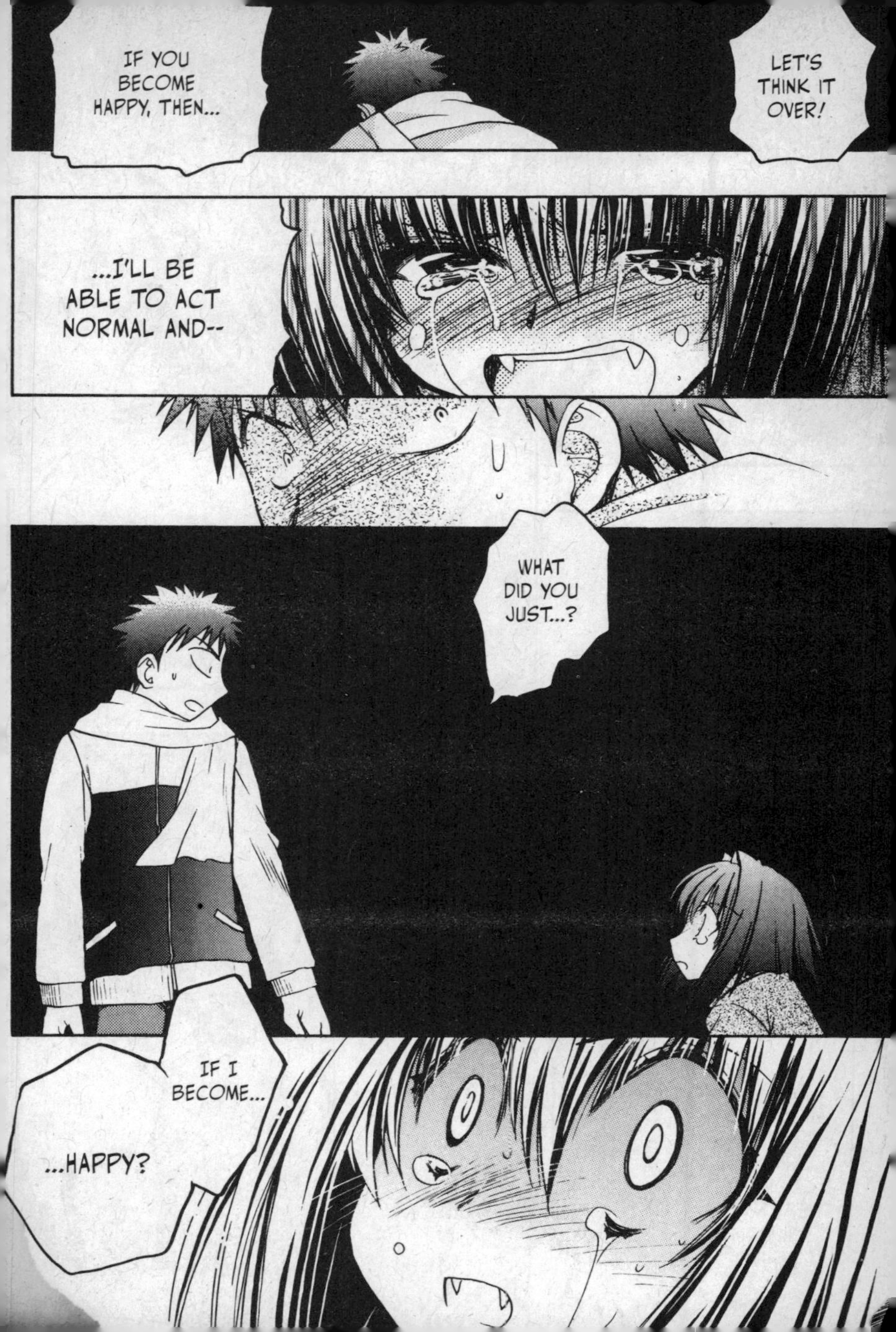
LET'S THINK IT OVER!
IF YOU BECOME HAPPY, THEN...
...I'LL BE ABLE TO ACT NORMAL AND--
WHAT DID YOU JUST...?
IF I BECOME...
...HAPPY?

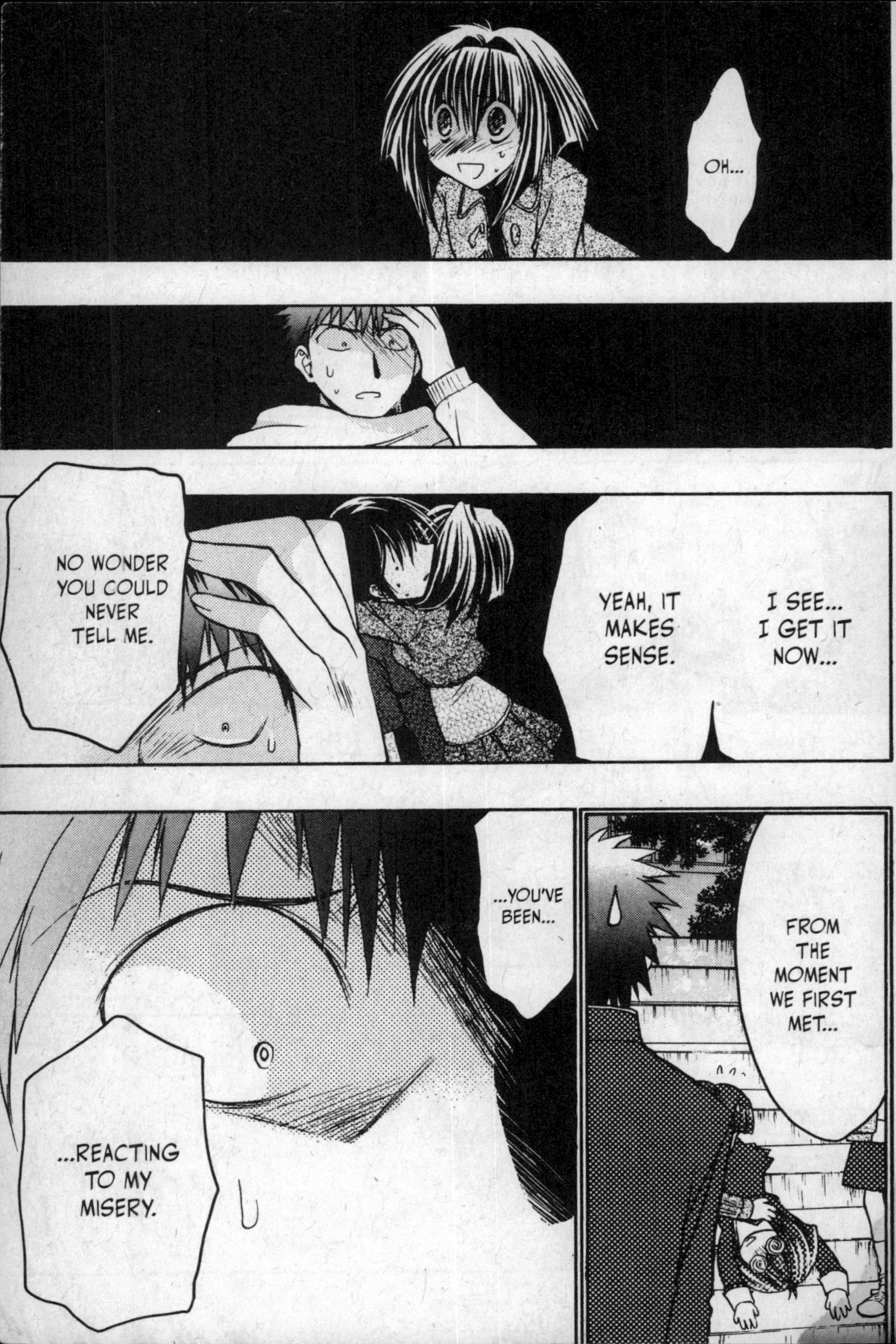
OH...
I SEE... I GET IT NOW...
YEAH, IT MAKES SENSE.
NO WONDER YOU COULD NEVER TELL ME.
FROM THE MOMENT WE FIRST MET...
...YOU'VE BEEN...
...REACTING TO MY MISERY.

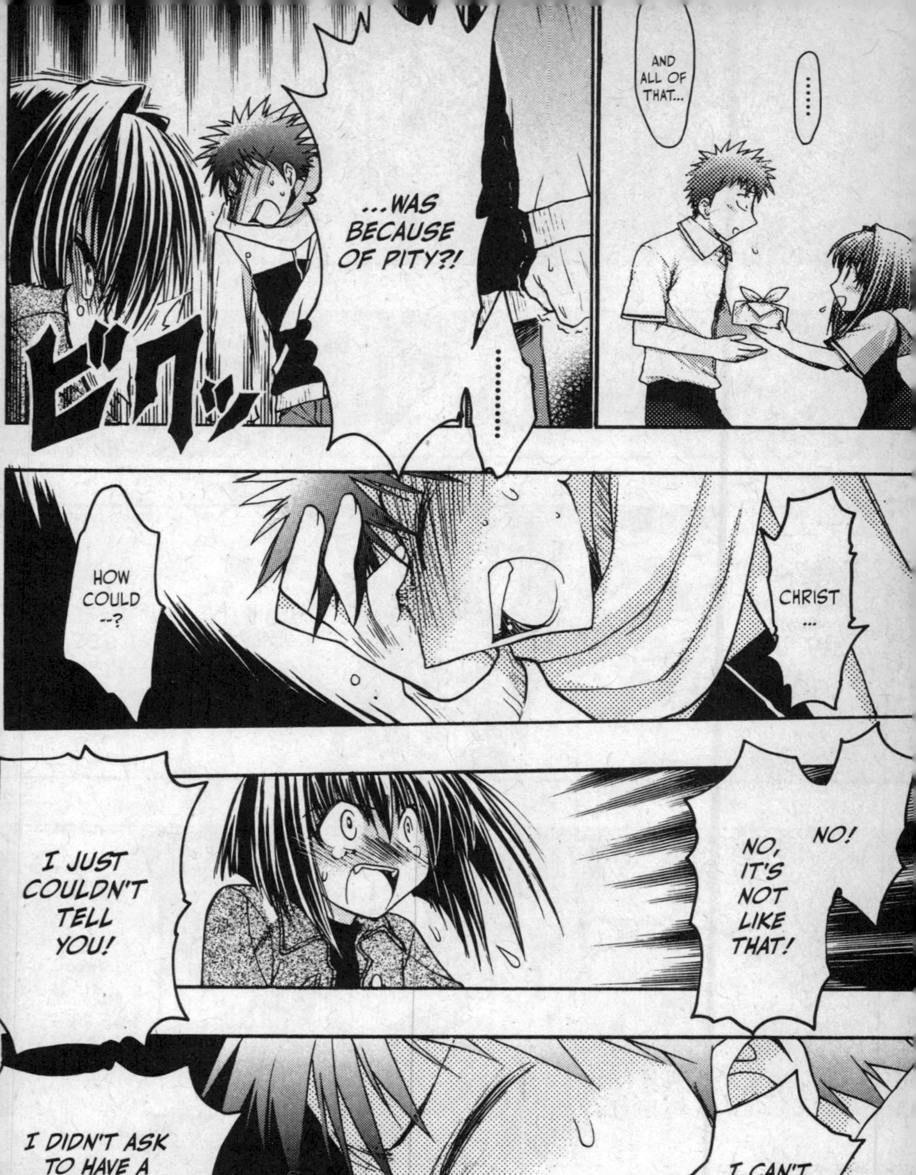

AND ALL OF THAT...
......
...WAS BECAUSE OF PITY?!
....
ビクッ
CHRIST ...
HOW COULD --?
NO!
NO, IT'S NOT LIKE THAT!
I JUST COULDN'T TELL YOU!
I CAN'T HELP IT!!
I DIDN'T ASK TO HAVE A WEIRD BODY THAT JUST... REACTS!

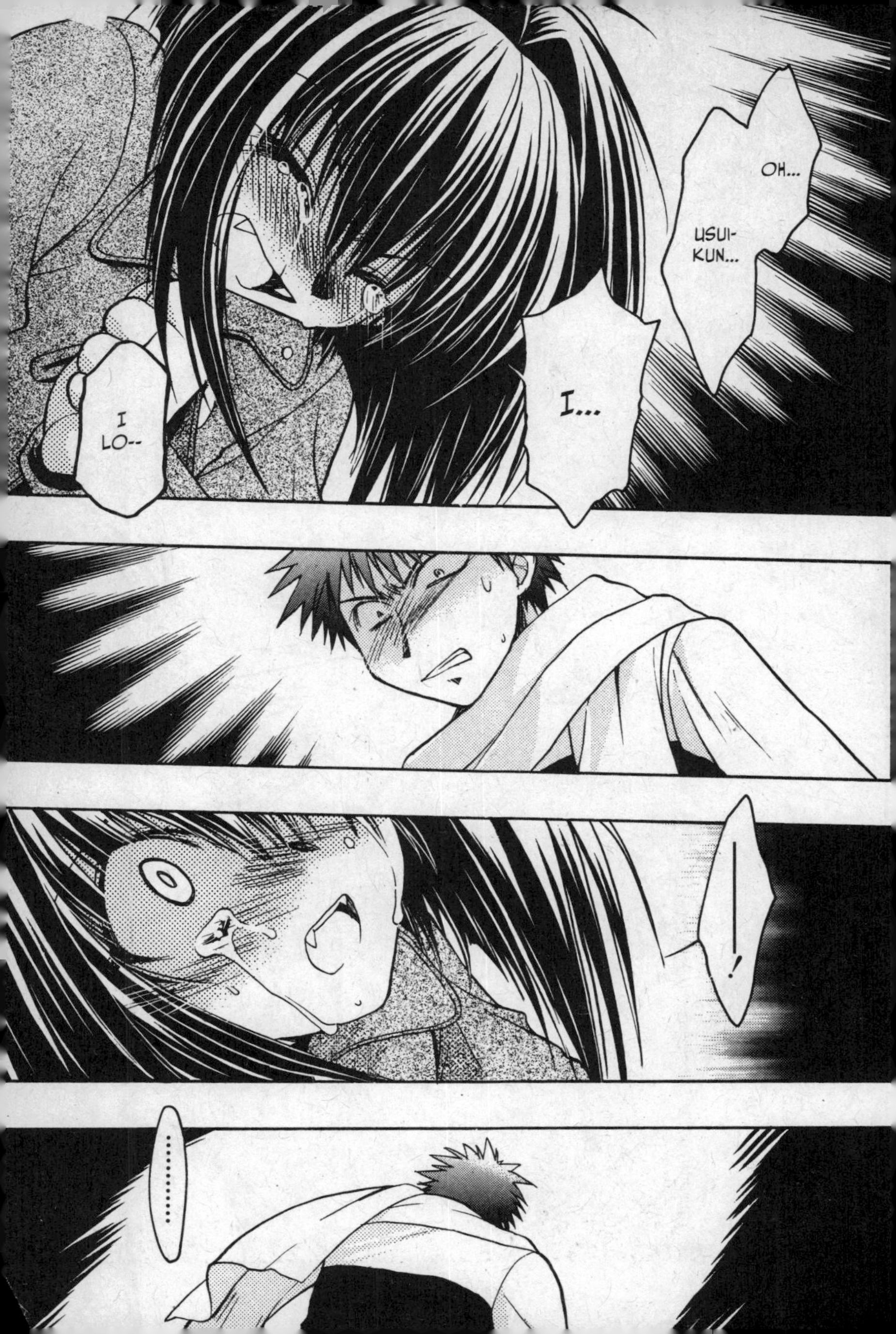

OH... USUI-KUN...
I...
I LO--
!!
......

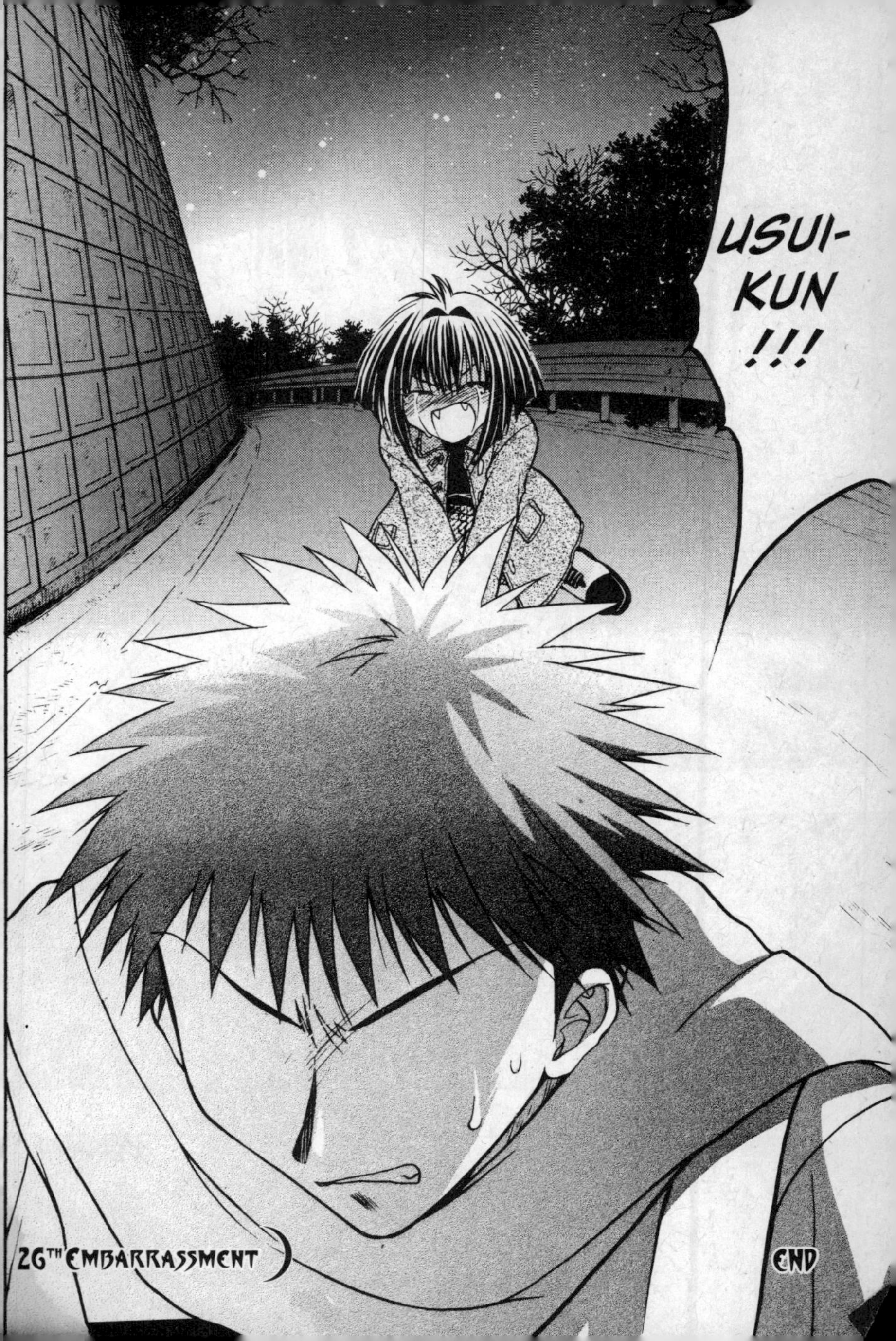
USUI-KUN !!!
26TH EMBARRASSMENT
END

BONUS

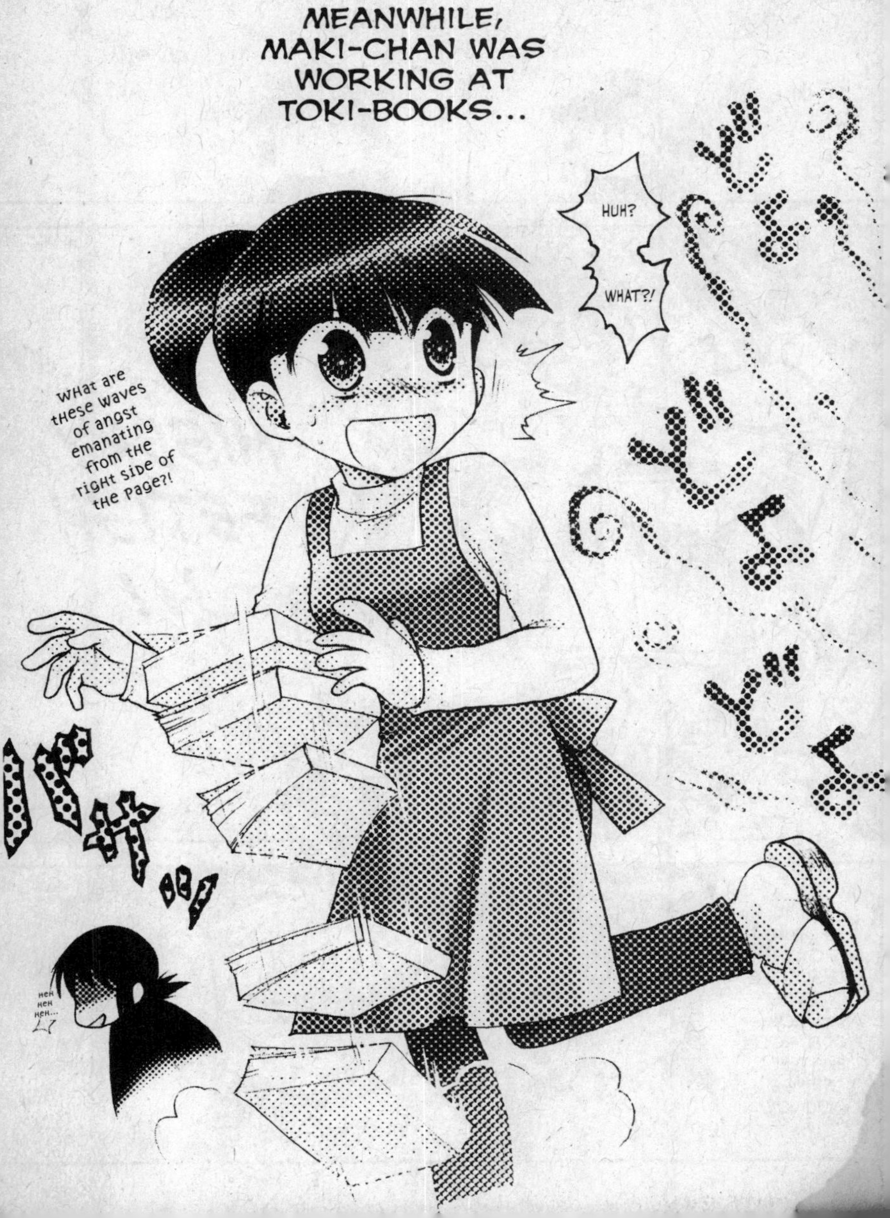
MEANWHILE, MAKI-CHAN WAS WORKING AT TOKI-BOOKS...
HUH?
WHAT?!
WHAT ARE THESE WAVES OF ANGST EMANATING FROM THE RIGHT SIDE OF THE PAGE?!
HEH HEH HEH...

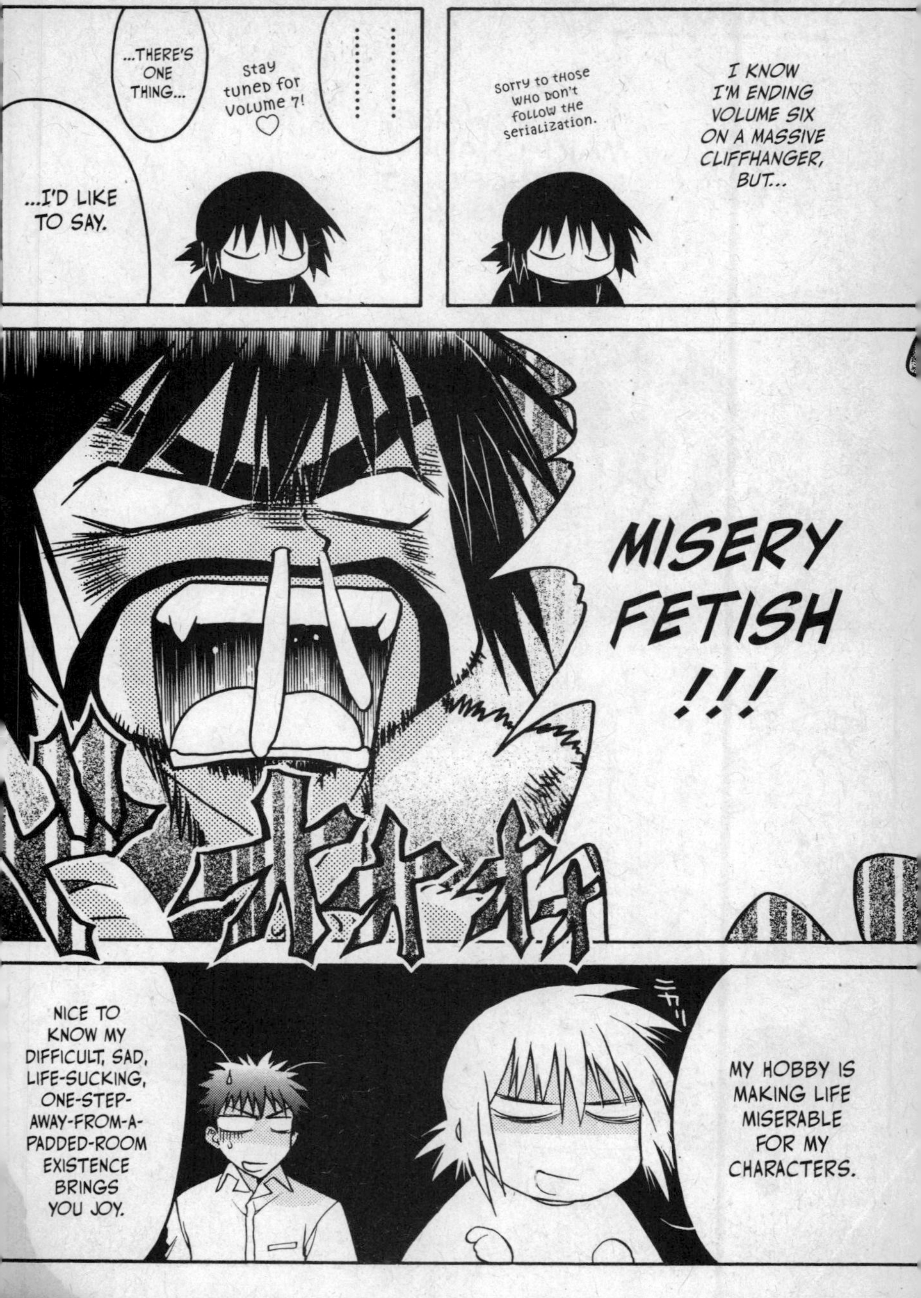
I KNOW I'M ENDING VOLUME SIX ON A MASSIVE CLIFFHANGER, BUT...
Sorry to those who don't follow the serialization.
......
Stay tuned for Volume 7! ♡
...THERE'S ONE THING...
...I'D LIKE TO SAY.
MISERY FETISH !!!
MY HOBBY IS MAKING LIFE MISERABLE FOR MY CHARACTERS.
NICE TO KNOW MY DIFFICULT, SAD, LIFE-SUCKING, ONE-STEP-AWAY-FROM-A-PADDED-ROOM EXISTENCE BRINGS YOU JOY.

THUMBNAILS CHECK

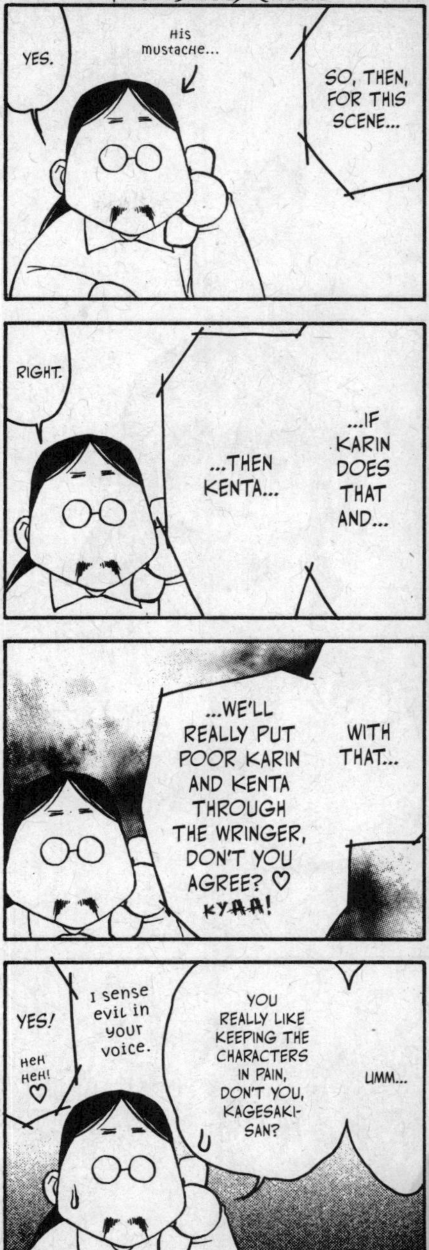
SO, THEN, FOR THIS SCENE...
His mustache...
YES.
...IF KARIN DOES THAT AND...
...THEN KENTA...
RIGHT.
WITH THAT...
...WE'LL REALLY PUT POOR KARIN AND KENTA THROUGH THE WRINGER, DON'T YOU AGREE? ♡
KYAA!
UMM...
YOU REALLY LIKE KEEPING THE CHARACTERS IN PAIN, DON'T YOU, KAGESAKI-SAN?
I sense evil in your voice.
YES!
HeH HeH! ♡

THE TRUTH BEHIND THE 26TH, P.135

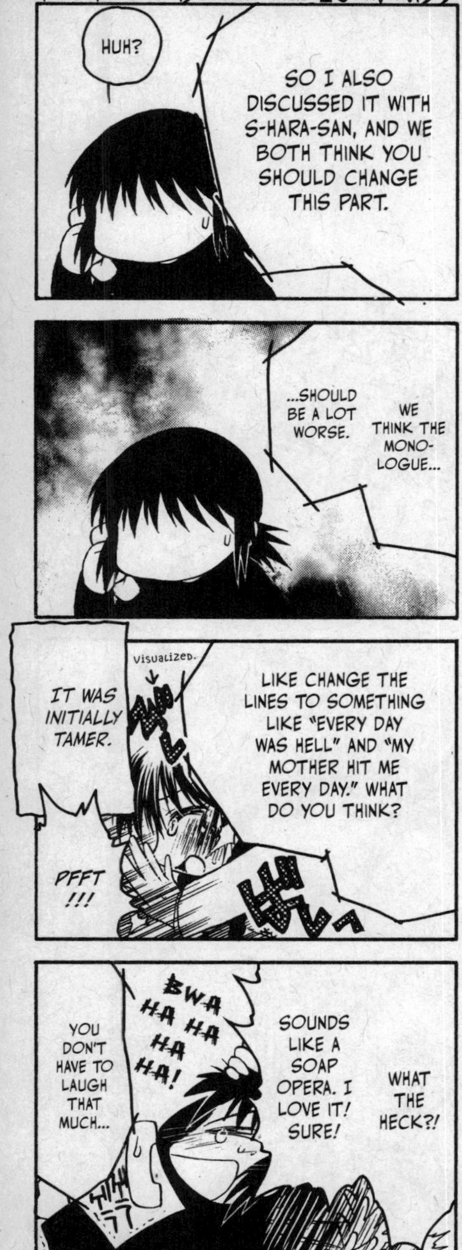
SO I ALSO DISCUSSED IT WITH S-HARA-SAN, AND WE BOTH THINK YOU SHOULD CHANGE THIS PART.
HUH?
WE THINK THE MONOLOGUE...
...SHOULD BE A LOT WORSE.
LIKE CHANGE THE LINES TO SOMETHING LIKE "EVERY DAY WAS HELL" AND "MY MOTHER HIT ME EVERY DAY." WHAT DO YOU THINK?
Visualized.
IT WAS INITIALLY TAMER.
PFFT!!!
WHAT THE HECK?!
SOUNDS LIKE A SOAP OPERA. I LOVE IT! SURE!
BWA HA HA HA HA!
YOU DON'T HAVE TO LAUGH THAT MUCH...

I usually get annoyed with changes, but this one made me smile...

What Karin Could Have Become

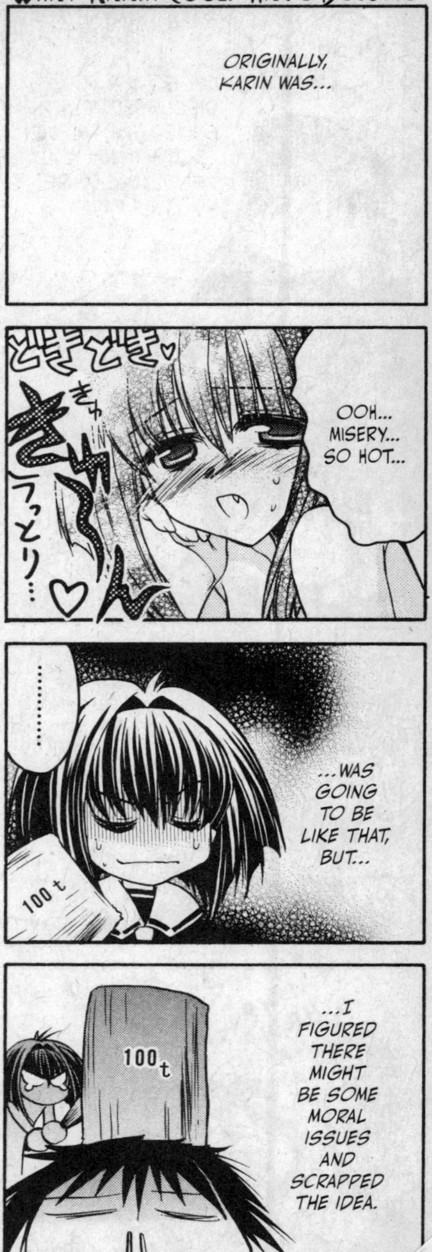
ORIGINALLY, KARIN WAS...
OOH... MISERY... SO HOT...
どきどき♥
きゅ
きゅ～ん
うっとり…♡
...WAS GOING TO BE LIKE THAT, BUT...
....
100t
...I FIGURED THERE MIGHT BE SOME MORAL ISSUES AND SCRAPPED THE IDEA.
100t

Art Misery

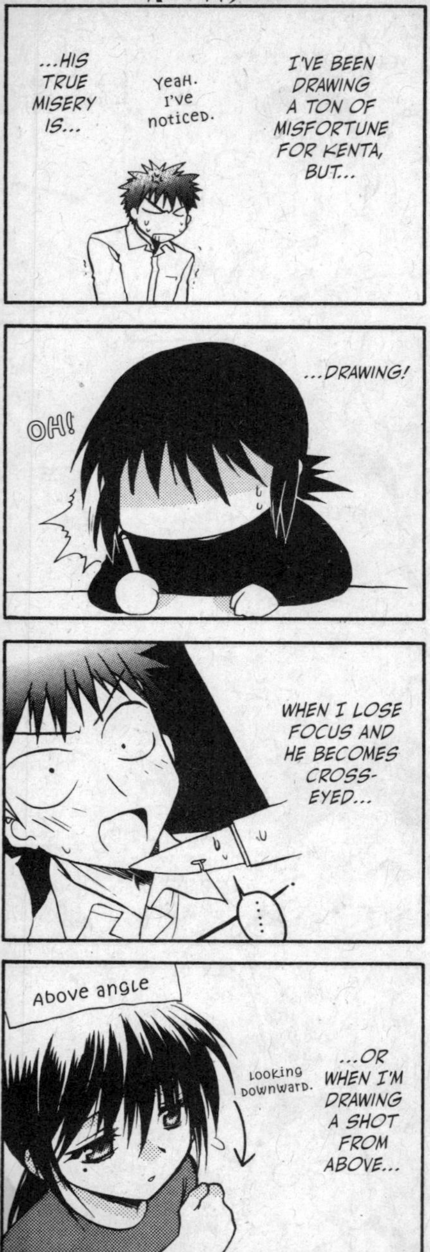
I'VE BEEN DRAWING A TON OF MISFORTUNE FOR KENTA, BUT...
Yeah. I've noticed.
...HIS TRUE MISERY IS...
...DRAWING!
OH!
WHEN I LOSE FOCUS AND HE BECOMES CROSS-EYED...
......
...OR WHEN I'M DRAWING A SHOT FROM ABOVE...
Looking downward.
Above angle

Art Misery, Part 2

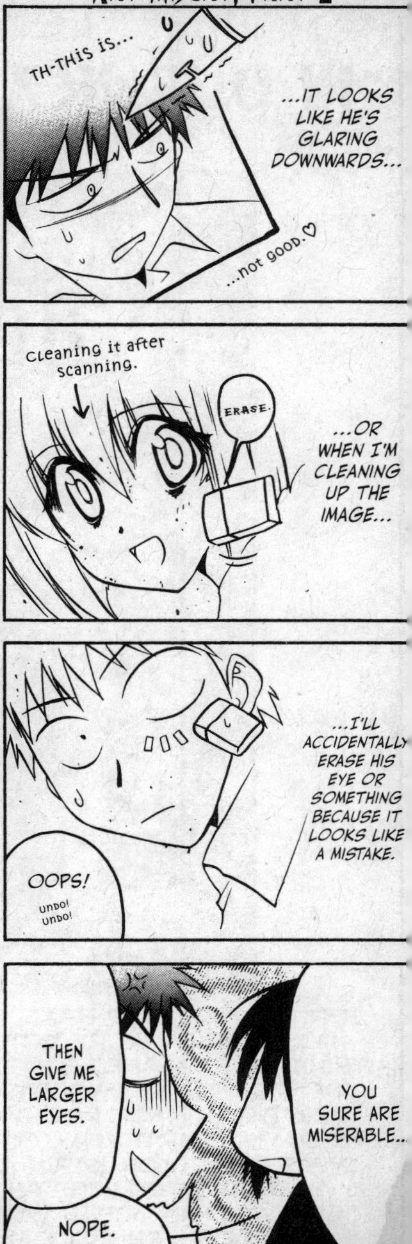
TH-THIS IS...
...IT LOOKS LIKE HE'S GLARING DOWNWARDS...
...not good.♡
...OR WHEN I'M CLEANING UP THE IMAGE...
Cleaning it after scanning.
ERASE.
...I'LL ACCIDENTALLY ERASE HIS EYE OR SOMETHING BECAUSE IT LOOKS LIKE A MISTAKE.
OOPS!
UNDO! UNDO!
YOU SURE ARE MISERABLE...
THEN GIVE ME LARGER EYES.
NOPE. ♡

Dot eyes are easy to draw...

Chinese Astrology

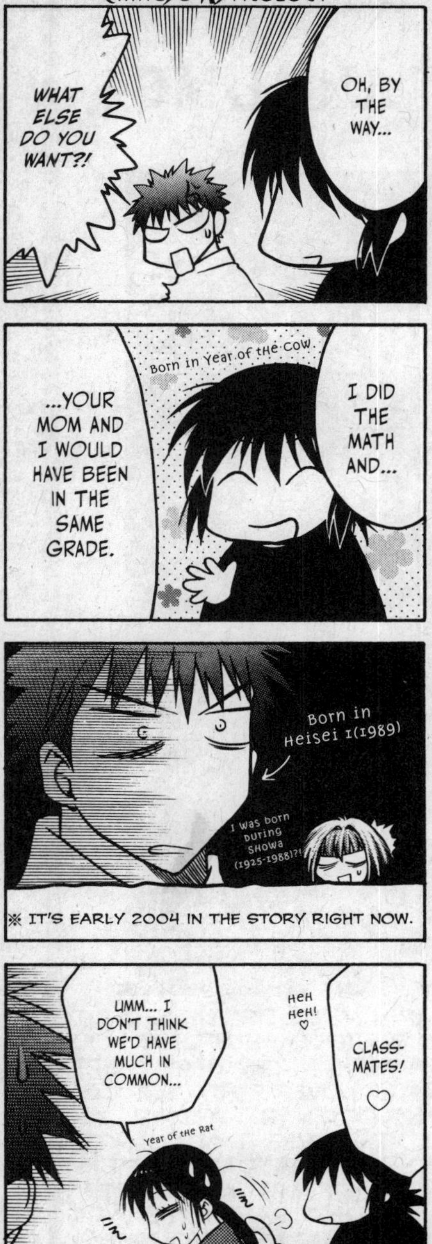
OH, BY THE WAY...
WHAT ELSE DO YOU WANT?!
I DID THE MATH AND...
Born in Year of the Cow.
...YOUR MOM AND I WOULD HAVE BEEN IN THE SAME GRADE.
Born in Heisei 1(1989)
I was born during Showa (1925-1988)?!
※ IT'S EARLY 2004 IN THE STORY RIGHT NOW.
HEH HEH! ♡
CLASS-MATES! ♡
UMM... I DON'T THINK WE'D HAVE MUCH IN COMMON...
Year of the Rat

CONTINUED IN VOLUME 7! I revealed her age on the website...

IN OUR NEXT VOLUME...

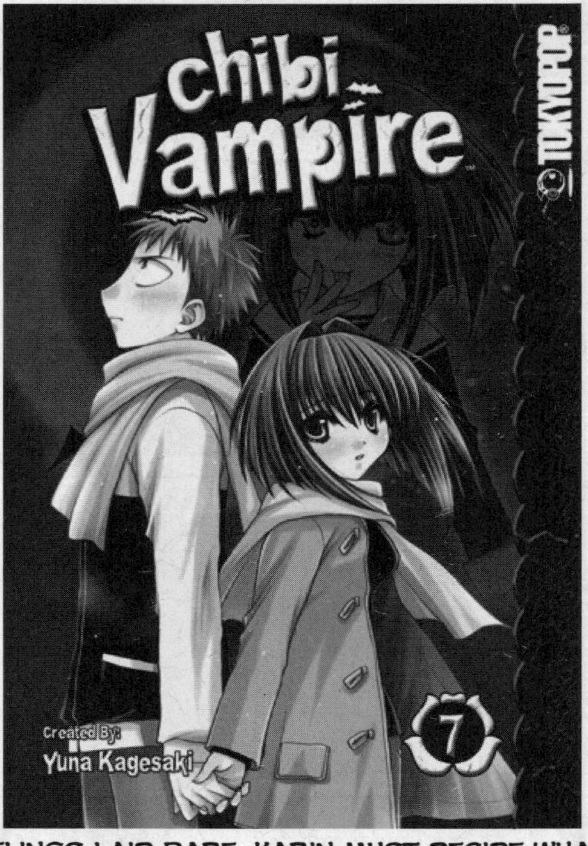

TOKYOPOP
chibi Vampire
Created By:
Yuna Kagesaki
7

HER FEELINGS LAID BARE, KARIN MUST DECIDE WHAT TO DO AFTER BEING REJECTED BY KENTA. BUT LEST YOU THINK WE'RE HEADED FOR TRAGEDY, KNOW THAT THERE'S HOPE FOR THESE TWO WAYWARD LOVERS YET. FOR LOVE IS NOTHING IF NOT ROCKY AND OFTEN IRRATIONAL, AND ONE DAY'S HEARTBREAK COULD FEED RIGHT INTO ANOTHER DAY'S BLISS. FOR KARIN AND KENTA, IT'S ALWAYS BEEN LOVE AT FIRST BITE, AND IT JUST MAY BE THE BITE OF A CERTAIN LITTLE VAMPIRE THAT SAVES THE DAY. DON'T EVEN THINK OF MISSING OUR NEXT VOLUME!

FUMIO'S ETERNAL JOB SEARCH

KENTA! BIG NEWS!
WHAT IS IT, MOM?
CHIBI VAMPIRE IS GOING TO BECOME AN ANIME!
Huh?
Umm...
SO... WHAT ARE YOU DOING?
OH, THIS?
PRACTICING IN CASE THEY'RE HIRING PEOPLE TO PAINT THE ANIME CELLS.

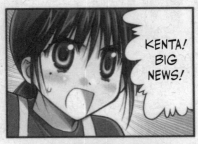

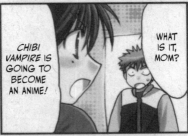

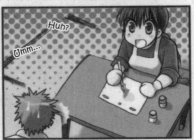

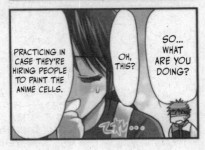

They do that with computers these days...

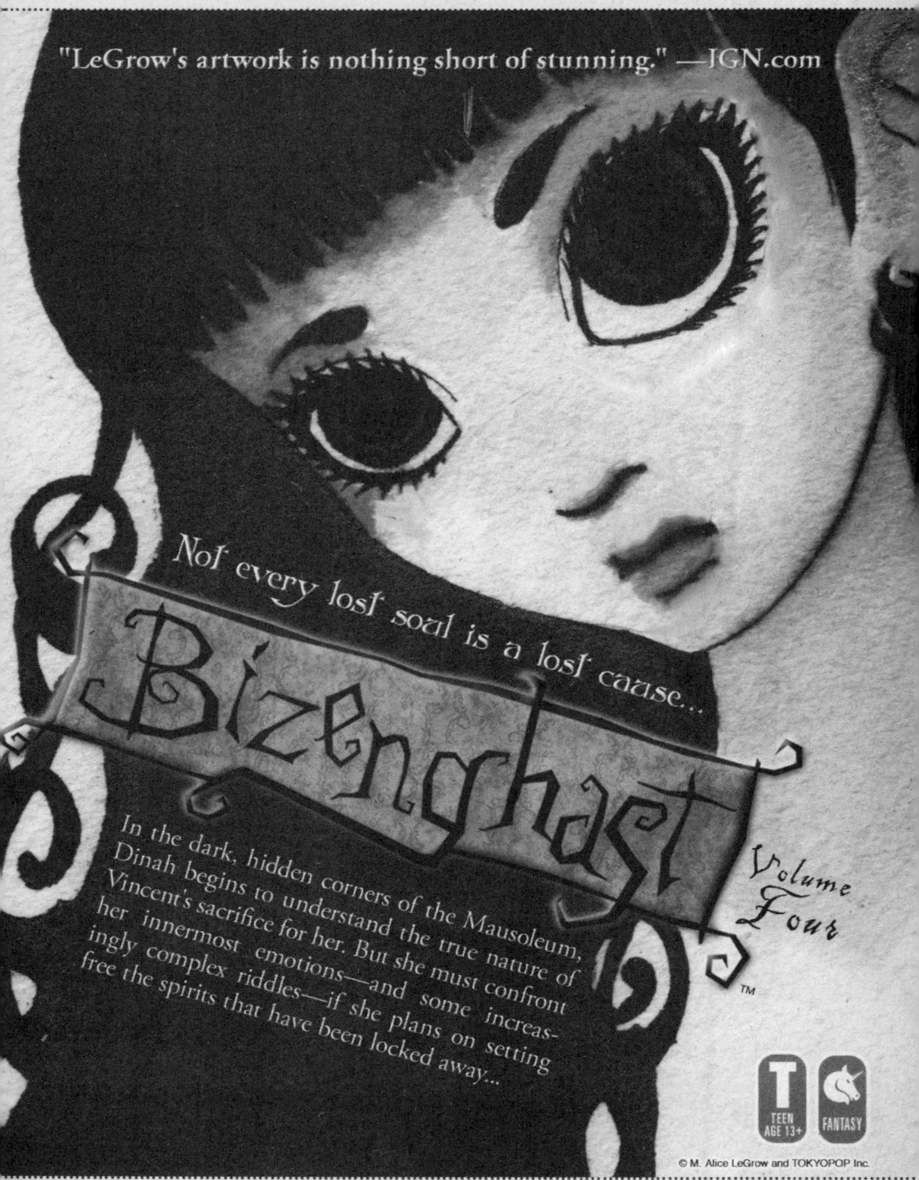
"LeGrow's artwork is nothing short of stunning." —IGN.com
Not every lost soul is a lost cause...
Bizenghast™
Volume Four
In the dark, hidden corners of the Mausoleum, Dinah begins to understand the true nature of Vincent's sacrifice for her. But she must confront her innermost emotions—and some increasingly complex riddles—if she plans on setting free the spirits that have been locked away...
T TEEN AGE 13+
FANTASY
© M. Alice LeGrow and TOKYOPOP Inc.